STEPHEN POLIAKOFF

Playing with Trains
She's Been Away
Century

introduced by the author

Methuen Drama

Contents

A Chronology

of First Performances

Introduction

When *Breaking the Silence* first opened in London in October 1984, a lot of people seemed rather surprised. I had spent much of the previous ten years writing about the urban world, and had become strongly associated with appalling hamburger bars, subterranean discos, early versions of Karaoke, neon and violence. Therefore, a tragi-comic tale set on a train just after the Russian Revolution may have come as a bit of a shock.

On New Year's Eve 1993 my film *Century* opened. A period drama that takes place during the last weeks of the nineteenth century and the first moments of the twentieth, it also appeared to cause some surprise. This was largely due to the fact that the film that had immediately preceded it had been a very modern drama, a love story between a brother and sister, *Close My Eyes*, which is set during a ripe late-eighties summer, and is full of images of the rebuilding of London's docklands.

The tension between the old and the new, my desire to keep on writing about contemporary life, but also an equally strong desire to widen my range and write about the past, is one of the elements that link the plays and screenplays in this volume.

But there is also a second and more powerful link – my increasing interest in writing about science, in how we've ended up with the world we've got.

Breaking the Silence has its origins in what happened to my father's family in Russia immediately after the revolution. My grandfather was, like Nikolai, an inventor, indeed he was one of the first people in the world to record sound on film. He also had his own train when he was made a Telephone Examiner, which he shared with his manservant. He dressed impeccably, making no concessions to post-revolutionary 'political correctness', and yet he was tolerated and in the end flourished under Lenin's regime. He also had to escape from Russia, using subterfuge, like Nikolai, when Stalin came to power in 1924.

What I added to the story was Nikolai's comic obsessiveness, pursuing the invention of the talkies in the middle of the Civil War that followed the Revolution, and the image of the family all having to live together on a train, the women gradually flowering, while the son Sasha grows apart from his father, as he becomes more and more desperate to conform to the outside world.

From the stories and images of my father's childhood, I wanted to carve something fictional and universal, a drama that was much more than just an anecdote. This was easier said than done, for it took me over two years to write the play. I found it very difficult to get the distance from the material that one normally needs in order to lasso a world on stage. And it was only after leaving the play for a while that I managed it.

At the time *Breaking the Silence* opened, the Cold War was still being played out, and the play, among other things, challenged some of the received opinions about the aftermath of the Russian Revolution.

Nearly ten years on, *Breaking the Silence* has now taken on a new meaning. Russia is in turmoil, every bit as dangerous as the chaos depicted at the end of the play, and we are haunted daily by images from Central Europe of dispossession, racism, and enforced exile.

Playing with Trains is obviously connected to *Breaking the Silence* in that it also deals with the world of inventions, and mingles this with the portrayal of a family, although in this case they are being violently torn apart. It is a play about waste, about unrealised potential.

It was written at the height of the so-called Thatcherite economic miracle and yet it shows us a Britain in steep economic decline. In that sense it was ahead of events, as indeed I make an effort to be with most of my work.

I believe that it is one of the roles of the playwright to be consistently a few steps ahead of any current fashion, while simultaneously remaining resolutely unaffected by it. And this belief is reflected in the style of the plays. They were written in the eighties, when a lot of drama was either didactic, or mixed styles and periods in that dreaded phrase, a 'post-modernist' fashion. I remained, clearly, rather untouched by all of this.

Indeed *Breaking the Silence*, *Playing with Trains*, and *Century*, all exhibit a much greater concern with narrative than I showed when I first started. I have become increasingly interested in creating stories that embrace audiences on the primary level of 'what's going to happen next', while simultaneously developing several layers beneath that, using the unexpected movements of narrative to reveal a new way of looking at the particular world I'm writing about.

A good example of what I'm trying to do is the meal scene in the second act of *Playing with Trains*. This nightmare reunion between a father and his two children takes place in the lunch break of a libel action that he is fighting in the High Court. The dramatic climax of the trial, therefore, comes not on the witness stand, but among the soggy peas and over-cooked meat of this terrible lunch, as the world brushes past unconcerned, just outside the door.

The public and private worlds of the play entwine in both a comic and a very emotional way, and because the play suddenly goes into almost real time, the effect is intensified.

Playing with Trains is clearly concerned on one level with why we in Britain have invented so much, but managed to manufacture so little. But on a deeper level, I hope it is about originality versus the desire to be applauded by one's peers, about the loss of possibilities in the modern world.

The love story between father and daughter runs through the public sweep of the play, giving it a visceral, passionate core. I set out to create a sensual epic.

She's Been Away was written for Peggy Ashcroft, and it was the last major role she played before she died.

When she starred in my television film *Caught on a Train*, in which she played an elderly Viennese lady terrorising fellow passenger Michael Kitchen on the Ostend to Vienna express, I had promised Peggy I would write her something else. Initially we talked about a theatre play, but she was worried about whether she still possessed the stamina to do something in the theatre.

The years went by and I still hadn't written her the part. One of the problems was that Peggy said she must have hardly any lines, and because of a hip injury, she didn't want to have to move much at all either. I found these restrictions very hard to overcome, until I had the idea for this film.

In the eighties, the big mental hospitals were being closed down at a rapid rate, hurtling people out into the world, many of whom had been institutionalised for several decades. Clearly there was a powerful film to be made about the hazards of the 'care in the community' programme, as many mentally ill people discovered themselves literally on the streets.

But for better or worse I am not that kind of campaigning agit-prop writer, and I found myself being haunted by another possibility:

The story of a member of an affluent family returning as if from the dead, to wreak havoc on the comfortable upper middle class world, that is ostensibly welcoming her back. A person who has a disquieting effect on everybody she meets, by remaining almost silent, but clearly seeing a great deal.

It was a chance both to stare at the landscapes and attitudes of Britain at the end of the eighties from an unusual angle – something that I'm always searching for in my work – and also to underpin the dark comedy with a sense of real pain and loss.

Peggy Ashcroft had a great triumph in the role of Lillian at the Venice Film Festival in 1989, where she shared the Best Actress award with Geraldine James, who plays Harriet, brilliantly, in the film.

It had been a happy collaboration between Peggy and I, and when you read the screenplay I think you naturally find yourself seeing Peggy's face staring out of the page at you.

Century has a direct link with both *Breaking the Silence* and *Playing with Trains*.

In *Breaking the Silence* we see a very twentieth century idea, the invention of the talkies, emerge out of Nikolai, an extremely nineteenth century character.

In *Playing with Trains* we see a man desperately trying to influence the future by backing good ideas and inventions, and not thinking purely in the short term. His tragedy is that he cannot sustain it for long enough, eventually the desire for short term success proves his undoing.

In *Century* I wanted to actually portray the moment when I think the modern world came into being.

I was influenced by a variety of factors; the obvious attraction as we move towards the millennium of looking at the corresponding moment in the last century, the fact that most British period films tend to portray the past with considerable nostalgia, and the strange coincidence that we end this century with a deep interest in genetic engineering, and the nineteenth ended with a fascination for eugenics, which was to have such a devastating effect on the course of twentieth century thinking.

It has always seemed to me extremely interesting that in the space of a mere handful of years, all the principal inventions of the twentieth century, the car, the telephone, the aeroplane, the movies, the wireless, and electric light, came into being. It was a tremendous surge of change.

Century is set right in the middle of this process, and shows a collection of characters beginning to encounter a world that we recognise, just as it was being born.

It portrays people feeling great optimism about the future, but also coming face to face with darker currents of thought, the sinister turning the pseudo-science of eugenics took.

Eugenics' principle idea was that you could get rid of poverty and mental illness by encouraging desirable 'healthy' people to breed together and to discourage 'the undesirable', in other words the underclass, from breeding so much. The idea soon grew into *preventing* the underclass from breeding at all, sterilising them, and even gassing them.

When one reads pamphlets advocating the gassing of the mentally ill in 1900, what happened later in the century begins to seem part of a process, as opposed to a great black thunderstorm that suddenly blew up out of the hyperinflation of the Weimar Republic.

The contention of *Century* is that all the seeds of what happened later, were discernible in the first moments of the new epoch, in that very first year.

The film moves constantly between light and dark, between the great hopes for the new century, the ability to alleviate pain being high among them, and the considerable sense of dread about the future, the deep fears about racism and persecution.

The film is not about the evils of science, but about the way people can distort science, or create pseudo-science to help justify their prejudices.

I am very interested in writing about science, not as the source of all that has been terrible about our century, as has become fashionable recently, but as a process influenced by the same forces, the same jealousies, the same impulses, as other aspects of our culture. We tend to portray scientists either as saintly boffins, or as monsters who are completely blind to the effects of their work – always as people who are *apart* from the society they belong to.

In *Century* the Professor, Mandry, is clearly a very considerable medical scientist, but he is also a man who does something rather terrible. And yet he remains a consistently sympathetic figure right to the end of the film. In this way I hope he becomes a much more haunting creation, than just a simple representation of the forces of darkness.

The optimism and pessimism that mingle together through *Century* obviously echo, to some extent, the feelings I have about the future.

The tension between most people's natural desire for continuity, and the extraordinary forward burst of technology that is about to hit all our lives, is very strong, very potent. We seem to be utterly helpless before this new onslaught, uncertain whether its effect will be benign or malevolent, unable to influence its progress in any way at all.

For me, as a writer, this is both very troubling, and in a peculiar way, exciting.

And it is this strange tension, hovering somewhere between hope and dread, that will I think dominate most of the work I'm about to do.

Stephen Poliakoff
June 1994

BREAKING THE SILENCE

Author's Note

This play was suggested by what happened to my family in Russia after the Bolshevick Revolution. But it is a work of fiction. I reworked and reshaped events, and invented the relationships and all the characters, *inspired* by the true image of my grandfather, a figure immaculately dressed for the opera, who did for a time have his own train, chugging through Lenin's Russia.

A man of great inventive brilliance, to whose memory I dedicate this play.

Breaking the Silence was first presented by the Royal Shakespeare Company at the Pit in the Barbican Centre, London on 31 October 1984 with the following cast:

NIKOLAI	Daniel Massey
EUGENIA	Gemma Jones
POLYA	Juliet Stevenson
VERKOFF	John Kane
SASHA	Jason Lake
GUARD 1	Richard Garnett
GUARD 2	Campbell Morrison

Directed by Ron Daniels
Designed by Alison Chitty

It transferred to the Mermaid Theatre, London, on 16 May 1985 with the following cast:

NIKOLAI	Alan Howard
EUGENIA	Gemma Jones
POLYA	Jenny Agutter
VERKOFF	John Kane
SASHA	Edward Rawle-Hicks
GUARD 1	Paul Rattee
GUARD 2	Christopher Saul

Directed by Ron Daniels
Designed by Alison Chitty

Time: Russia, 1920

ACT ONE

April, 1920

Scene One

Sound of people struggling with the door, then it opens, throwing a little light inside, and POLYA and SASHA move into the darkened carriage.

The huge imperial-style railway carriage, filling the whole of the stage.

Rich dark wood, a table, chairs set against the walls, at one end a splendid couch elaborately decorated, which had been converted into a bed, at the other end two bunks covered in pale velvet counterpanes, a white stove built into the wall, ornamental woodwork and lamps.

Over the beds and on parts of the floor, there is a coating of dirt, dust, a few bloodstains, some animal droppings, smudging the atmosphere of magnificence in the carriage. The pale bed coverings are especially filthy. The blinds across the windows are also stained yellow and black.

POLYA is in her early thirties dressed in a black maid's dress, with a white bow in her hair. SASHA at the start of the action is in his early teens, but looks young for his age, immaculately dressed in a velvet suit.

For a second POLYA stands in the doorway staring into the darkened carriage then she moves in, pulling up the blinds, to let in light. As she enters the carriage she is carrying two highly polished pigskin suitcases. SASHA is only carrying some rather grubby toy stuffed animal.

POLYA. Stay there Master Alexander (*as she moves into the darkened carriage alone:*) and don't touch, you understand, don't touch anything.

She pulls up the blinds to reveal the state of the carriage.

They certainly haven't bothered to clean it for your father.

SASHA (*in doorway*). What an extraordinary carriage, Polya . . .
What was it used for?

POLYA. Don't come in! I told you, stay there by the door until
I know it's safe for you . . . there might be something here that
can harm you. Something that could give you a disease.

*She moves away from the windows into the carriage, as an
advance guard.*

Whatever this smell is . . . I don't think the original passengers
would have smelled like that.

SASHA (*pointing at floor*). What are those?

POLYA. Animal droppings — they must have used it for
transporting livestock recently. That's why the beds have been
chewed.

SASHA (*moving a little deeper into the carriage*). They can't
really mean this Polya! . . . It needs hosing down before it's
nearly ready for papa. You must have misunderstood. I am
sure they only intend to show it to him . . .

POLYA (*loud, swings round*). Did I say it was safe for you to
come in? No.

SASHA *stops.*

You can stay there now, but don't move. (*She turns back to
her beds.*) Now don't you start causing me trouble, they
haven't allowed me any time to make it fit for the master.
(*She is rolling up the counterpanes.*) The filth that is here . . .
he will never sleep in sheets like this, not under any
circumstances, nobody could make him. I don't know how I
am going to keep my uniform clean.

*With the removal of the stained counterpanes, the carriage is
already looking less filthy.*

SASHA (*as POLYA bustles around*). Everything is such a hurry
now — suddenly the news that Papa has to leave home, having
to pack his things up in a few hours, I am sure we dropped

something on the way here . . . Papa will demand
compensation I expect.

POLYA. If I can get these out of the way before they come, there
must be at least one clean place for the master — thank God I
managed to bring some extra blankets for him.

SASHA. What are these holes? (*He is running his hand along the
side of the carriage.*) Polya everywhere here is covered in
small holes.

POLYA. What do you think they are! Bullet holes of course. (*She
points above the windows.*) There's some marks up there
too . . . it looks as if it was shelled.

SASHA. They must be going to redecorate it. (*Exploring the
carriage.*) What are these red stains here Polya? It's splashed
all over here, over the covers here, it can't be what I think it is
Polya. (*Pause.*) It's not blood is it?

POLYA. Yes, it's blood. The goats they kept, they probably
slaughtered them in here as well.

She looks up to see SASHA *is suddenly very animated,
searching all the corners of the carriage.*

What on earth are you doing? I told you not to touch
anything.

SASHA. I was just seeing if there was any . . . (*He stops and faces
her:*) even the smallest piece of . . . (*Suddenly shouts:*) *food*
had been left anywhere. There's an onion here!

*SASHA picks up a glass jar with one onion at the bottom, he
tries to unscrew the top which is very stiff. He can't get it off.*

I'm so — I'm so hungry Polya.

Suddenly letting his body go limp and falling into her arms.

I'm going to *die.*

POLYA. Your father has the rations, you know that. Stand up.
(*Pulling her body up.*) Come on stand up. (*Firmly:*) Listen
now Alexander Nikolaivitch, don't you *dare* show it when
they come — you're not going to let the Commissar of Labour
see the slightest sign, you understand. You don't want to let

your father down. (*Holding him.*) Come on. You can manage . . . you can get through.

SASHA. I am going to die before the end of the day, I can feel it.

POLYA. Well wait till then at least — (*Turning back to the bed.*) the master will see to everything, *remember* that.

EUGENIA *enters. A fine looking woman about forty. She has a nervous, shy manner. She is dressed in an exquisite and expensive long summer dress.*

EUGENIA. I didn't imagine it would look like this. (*Looking around.*) This is rather sordid isn't it? These beds . . . (*She touches them.*) What a place!

POLYA. Madame, careful where you move. If you want to sit, I think this space is safe.

EUGENIA (*anxious*). I am not sure the master is expecting this . . . have you got all his clothes prepared?

She gets up immediately and moves over.

Is this all there is left? All that remains of his wardrobe. It looks so little suddenly. We had to leave so much . . .

POLYA. We still got all his English shoes.

She pulls them out of a suitcase.

EUGENIA. As far as possible everything must go in its proper place. (*She turns suddenly.*) Do we look all right Polya, not too pale, tell me honestly — we don't seem disgracefully pale do we?

POLYA. No, madame.

EUGENIA (*trying to force the jar open*). It doesn't look as if I'm about to collapse at any moment I hope.

POLYA (*indicating the jar*). It won't open, madame.

EUGENIA (*embarrassed, putting jar down*). I never used to eat onions anyway.

SASHA *is holding his stomach, leaning against the wall of the carriage.*

Sasha! Don't do that.

VERKOFF *comes into the carriage, a powerful burly man in utilitarian clothes, a man in his forties, with a working-class accent. He is full of a sudden, unpredictable energy. Mercurial manner.*

VERKOFF. We are here! (*He turns and looks behind him.*) Where is he? He was right behind me. What are you doing out there Nikolai Semenovitch? (*Loud.*) Get in here! My time is limited.

NIKOLAI *is in the doorway.*

What on earth are you looking so reluctant for? Come on in. Take the plunge.

NIKOLAI *is framed in the doorway. He is an imposing figure in his late forties or early fifties, wearing a truly splendid fur coat, though it is spring, gleaming polished shoes, and a fine English suit. His manner is extremely authoritative and dignified, though there is a very distinctive charm and lightness of touch even when he's being arrogant. Everything about him is redolent of an old world, upper middle-class man. The only thing he is carrying is a medium-sized mahogany box.*

NIKOLAI (*staring into the carriage*). My God . . .

VERKOFF (*moving round, touching everything*). What's the matter — you should feel at home here! Gold-topped taps — what looks like a German commode, right size for one anyway — imperial furniture.

VERKOFF *pulling at the bunks, suddenly jumps onto the lower bunk, scattering dried feathers.*

A little dirty perhaps, but you could sleep through anything in this (*Sharp smile.*) and you may *need* to.

NIKOLAI (*moving into the carriage, calmly*). Is there anywhere in this carriage that it is possible to sit?

EUGENIA (*nervously*). Here . . .

As NIKOLAI sits next to EUGENIA, VERKOFF has resumed roaming the carriage.

VERKOFF (*suddenly pointing at* SASHA). The boy looks terrified, you'll have to teach him not to look at people like that. (*He smiles.*) They could feel unappreciated.

NIKOLAI. He is just a little surprised like all of us.

VERKOFF. So I can see! (*He turns.*) You do understand Nikolai Semenovitch what is happening to you — (*Stopping and staring at him.*) You are now a government employee with all the responsibility that entails. You will take up the position — as of now (*Clicking his fingers.*) of Telephone Surveyor of the Northern Railway.

NIKOLAI (*looking up*). Telephone Surveyor?

VERKOFF. Yes, Surveyor. (*Pulling at pieces of the carriage, touching everything.*) You don't like it? He doesn't like that title, then we can change it . . . (*Sharp smile.*) The only thing that can be changed Nikolai Pesiakoff. Telephone Examiner is acceptable . . . you have just become the first Telephone Examiner of the Northern District.

Silence.

NIKOLAI. I thank you for this unexpected offer, for making the journey specially.

VERKOFF. Which I haven't . . .

NIKOLAI. But of course it is completely out of the question, I will have to refuse.

Pause.

VERKOFF (*loud*). You will have to refuse!

NIKOLAI (*calmly*). I am much too busy I'm afraid.

VERKOFF. Too busy, I don't believe this! You have just been sitting here in the country . . . this is not an *offer* Nikolai Semenovitch, there is no refusal possible. You are MADE Telephone Examiner, it has been decided, once you've been selected and put on board, there is no alternative, no argument — the matter is completely closed.

NIKOLAI (*calmly*). I see. (*Pause.*) I will still have to refuse.

VERKOFF. I don't think we understand each other, Nikolai Semenovitch, I am a busy man and have very little time.

NIKOLAI (*incisive tones*). But I have told you what I need. I made repeated representations to you and your staff, and was made to wait on more than one occasion, sitting on the floor outside your door. I travelled no fewer than six times to your office, I made it absolutely clear what I had to have.

VERKOFF (*slight smile*). Remind me what this was.

NIKOLAI. It was a very modest request, the bare minimum in fact. A room of my own in Moscow, apart from living quarters for my family of course, for the sake of argument say five rooms, a proper staff of my own prepared to work, and sufficient time free of interruption and official interference — to think.

VERKOFF (*incredulous*). To think!

NIKOLAI. Of course. I have some specific ideas of the greatest importance, I thought I gave your advisers all the indications they needed. And I have to admit I fail to see what the problem is, you have my word for it that you will not be wasting your time. What more do you need?

VERKOFF. Nikolai Semonovitch . . .

NIKOLAI (*carrying straight on*). Furthermore, you gave us absolutely no warning that this was about to happen, you suddenly inform us that you will be taking over our whole house.

VERKOFF (*ebullient*). Warning! You don't get any warning, you know about it when it happens to you.

NIKOLAI (*amazed tones*). And why me? How was I chosen? I'm afraid I am not the right person to watch telephone poles being erected.

EUGENIA (*nervous*). My husband means that he . . .

NIKOLAI (*calmly*). In the chaos of a new filing system it is obvious there must have been a mistake, stumbling on me to be Telephone Surveyor is not a rational act, do I look a likely candidate? It is not a disgrace to admit there has been an error and have it rectified — immediately.

VERKOFF (*mercurial smile*). There is no possibility of an error I assure, *I* made the decision personally — you were after all supposedly head of your family's engineering firm were you not? How many times you were ever there is another question of course.

NIKOLAI. We did not concern ourselves with telephone poles.

VERKOFF. Don't try to test my patience — it can have dramatic results.

He points at the women and SASHA.

You three will pack up *all* your belongings (*Slight smile.*) in that sizeable house of yours, which I'm told the Army needs, and be ready to move immediately he returns.

EUGENIA (*very nervous*). Move where, comrade?

VERKOFF. You will all live in here, of course.

NIKOLAI (*momentary pause*). That is clearly impossible. In no circumstances can I allow my wife to live inside here.

VERKOFF (*loud, very animated*). Listen to him! My God, there have been people dying all along the line, whole households starving, wiped out, and he complains about being here.

VERKOFF's *bulky shape moving about the carriage, his hand jabbing out.*

I have many urgent calls to make before the light goes . . . Now, this is where thing get serious. There are certain things you have to know and do, so you better be listening. (*He suddenly swings round and shouts.*) Are you comrade?

NIKOLAI *looks up in surprise.*

Because these matter.

NIKOLAI *is impassive.*

EUGENIA. Of course . . . we do realise . . .

VERKOFF (*staring at them*). Guns. (*He pauses.*) There must be no guns of any sort kept here. You are civilians — as you know, new laws have been passed — any civilian found with firearms or explosives will be executed. (*Sudden sharp smile.*) If you have any, this is not a time to be shy, give them to me and no action will be taken.

NIKOLAI. That is the law? I had no idea.

VERKOFF. Are you going to give them to me? I urge you to take this seriously comrade, otherwise the consequences for you and your family could be disastrous.

Silence.

NIKOLAI. Quite. Thank you for your warning. There is no need to labour the point. What is next?

VERKOFF. You are required to keep ledgers, official records that must be up to date. The exact times and places, and the progress you find. I am giving you ten thousand roubles.

He throws the money, which is in a bag, on the floor of the carriage at NIKOLAI's *feet.*

This will be used for railway business only, the bonus scheme we have in operation for rewarding good work, all the usual things.

NIKOLAI. What is usual for a Telephone Examiner?

VERKOFF. You will take this first trip, which will be a gruelling one, and then you will wait in a siding for further instructions.

NIKOLAI. In a *siding*? That can't be necessary . . .

VERKOFF (*ignoring this*). If you ever wish to summon a locomotive in an emergency, you will walk the eighteen miles down the line and use the railway telephone to the depot. (*He points suddenly at* EUGENIA.) What's your name?

EUGENIA (*nervously glancing about her*). My name . . . you mean me? It's Eugenia Michailovna.

VERKOFF (*staring straight at her*). You think he's been listening, Eugenia Michailovna? You ought to make him. People have been turned off trains before now, in the North, and made to walk the thousand miles home. (*Lightly.*) I wonder how he'd manage.

NIKOLAI *is sitting impassively in his fur coat.* VERKOFF

suddenly turns towards POLYA.

And *you*, what's your name? What is your position here?

POLYA. I am the second chamber maid, comrade — I mean I *was* in Moscow, there was me and Anya . . . (*Suddenly nervous.*) and Liuba who cooked. (*She looks away, embarrassed.*) I . . . I was going to be married to the porter of an apartment block near us in Moscow but we lost touch . . . with all the moving round the country. (*She stops.*) I'm sorry, my name's Polya.

VERKOFF. And you're going to *stay* with this lot?

POLYA. Yes comrade, I have nowhere else to go. (*Looking down at the floor.*) At the moment anyway.

VERKOFF (*moves swiftly across the carriage to* NIKOLAI). Your pass and badge of office. Wear that at all times.

NIKOLAI (*as it is pinned on his fur coat*). My dear fellow, I assure you this is a major blunder, I urge you to reconsider while there's still time.

VERKOFF (*turning at the door of the carriage*). I almost forgot the most important thing — what about food?

SASHA (*from the heart*). Food!

VERKOFF (*mercurial smile at* SASHA). Yes, do you remember what it was like. (*To the adults:*) Have you got enough, do you need some?

Agonised look from SASHA, EUGENIA *looks at* NIKOLAI *and then away. They wait for* NIKOLAI. *Silence.*

NIKOLAI. No that will not be necessary.

VERKOFF. You're sure? You wouldn't be stupid enough to be too proud to ask — I'd have no patience with that.

He watches their faces as he mentions each piece of food.

I can supply some eggs, meat, fresh cheese, smoked fish, fresh bread. (*He smiles.*) That would mean soft doughy bread, baked today, like these rolls.

He produces large rolls out of his deep pockets. EUGENIA *and* SASHA *turn away trying not to look at them.* VERKOFF *holds out the bread.*

Everybody looks away do they?

SASHA (*desperately*). Maybe we . . .

VERKOFF (*sharp moving*). So you have managed to farm all your own food, unlike nearly everybody else in this area. I'm delighted to hear it.

He leaves the bread lying conspicuously. Pointing at EUGENIA.

You look magnificent madame. (*He stops in the doorway.*) You are now working for me Nikolai Semenovitch — the Northern Railway and me. I don't know when we'll be seeing each other again but we certainly will be — (*With feeling:*) I hope you're not going to let me down.

VERKOFF *exits. As soon as he's gone,* SASHA *bolts over and gets the bread he left behind.* EUGENIA *also makes a move, less violent but almost as eager.*

NIKOLAI. Don't disgrace yourself Sasha — charging after food like a starving dog.

EUGENIA (*taking the bread*). Shall I? I'll divide it up.

NIKOLAI (*waving his portion away*). We do not need food from him. We are certainly not going to accept food like beggars.

The women and SASHA *are feasting on the bread.*

I will leave you with all the rations we have, including my own. And I will bring food home. I will provide all the food we need and more.

SASHA *licks every crumb that is left.*

POLYA. Make it last . . . not so quick Sasha, make it last as long as you can.

EUGENIA (*smiling*). One's body can't cope with the shock at all. (*She leans against the wall.*)

NIKOLAI (*calmly*). It appears we have been selected to spend time in these surroundings — something I didn't anticipate. So on my return we will divide it up. Eugenia . . . this will be your room. (*He indicates the area in the middle of the carriage.*) The child will be over there. (*Pointing to the bunks.*) Polya's quarters will be down there, (*Pointing to the area near the bunks.*) and the rest will be for my use, study, bedroom and morning room combined. (*He indicates the rest of the carriage.*) We will keep to these. We may be able to arrange partitions when I return . . .

The noise of a locomotive approaching in the distance — calling down the line.

POLYA (*frantic*). His clothes and bed are not ready. I haven't had a chance to make it even passable for you Barin. You will be away so long, and there hasn't nearly been time to unpack.

Both women flit about the carriage like terrified bats, with the sound of the locomotive getting louder.

POLYA (*laying out his clothes*). The only pair of pyjamas that are left . . .

NIKOLAI. There is no need to panic, they will wait for us.

EUGENIA (*stopping, staring at him*). Nikolai, I think . . . please don't be angry with me . . . I think you will need me to come with you. Who will put out your clothes, with no manservant, and Liuba gone as well, nobody to do your laundry, find things for you to wear each day?

POLYA. It's not a job for you, Madame.

EUGENIA. Let me come Nikolai, I won't be in the way, I won't touch anything. You know I won't bother you. You will never notice me, but you *need* someone . . . can I come? Please, (*Suddenly loud.*) please let me come. I can make it all easier for you. (*Loud.*) Let me . . .

NIKOLAI. That will not be possible my dear.

POLYA. You can't go on your own, Barin, I must come . . .

EUGENIA. Make him see sense.

NIKOLAI. Polya you must stay with Madame. She must have the very best that is possible in the circumstances. (*To* EUGENIA:) Do nothing without Polya's help my dear.

The locomotive really loud and close, the sound of it braking and coming to a halt.

I will take the boy — if he thinks he can manage the journey, I will take Sasha.

SASHA (*excited*). Me Papa? You want to take me?

The sound of the locomotive hissing to a halt.

EUGENIA. Is that sensible Nikolai? Neither of you are used to being on your own, he can't organise everything for you, Sasha can't deal with everything.

SASHA. I can, I will.

NIKOLAI. I am going to take the boy.

EUGENIA (*urgent*). We must get more clothes for him, he'll need them for the cold.

POLYA (*urgent*). It'll take at least two hours to get to the house and back, and I don't know how much is washed, how much is clean.

EUGENIA (*moving*). Quickly, Polya, we'll have to go and get them.

EUGENIA *looking back.* POLYA *goes.*

NIKOLAI. Don't worry, we will not leave before you come back.

EUGENIA (*in doorway*). You won't . . . you won't take any risks Kolia, you know it could be dangerous, please try to be more careful than usual.

NIKOLAI. Don't worry. They will know who I am.

EUGENIA *goes. Silence.*
NIKOLAI *staring across at* SASHA.

We will be alone together you and I.

SASHA. Yes, Papa.

NIKOLAI. Certain things have to be understood — the terms on which we accompany each other. (*He pauses.*) Sashenka, can you pass me that box, yes that one there, give it to me.

SASHA *gives him the mahogany box he came in with.*

I have something vital to occupy me — something of the highest importance. If certain actions are taken — by me — it will be because of that. At the moment nothing more can be discussed.

He takes a pistol out of the mahogany box, it gleams in the light.

Do you understand me?

SASHA. Yes, Papa.

NIKOLAI (*with gun*). There will be no problem, nobody will dare touch us.

Blackout.

Scene Two

The noise of the train immediately filling the blackout, moving through the night, changing into the wail of the locomotive, then into screaming brakes, the sound of their progress violently stuttering to a halt, then silence.

The night carriage. The blinds are down. The lights glowing. SASHA's arms are wrapped around himself; he is now wearing a miniature version of his father's magnificent coat, and he is pulling it tightly round him. NIKOLAI is sitting bolt upright and still.

SASHA. Papa — we've stopped. (*Moving to the window.*) I think we've arrived somewhere again.

NIKOLAI. We will not have heard of it whatever it's called.

Pause.

SASHA. It's very cold anyway! God my hands, I can hardly move them. (*Moving away from the window.*) I'm going to eat my rations for today, Papa.

NIKOLAI. It is up to you when you eat.

NIKOLAI *remains absolutely still. Silence.*

SASHA (*picking up a small brown morsel*). Except the taste of dried millet is beginning to be . . . rather revolting . . .

NIKOLAI. I have told you — use your imagination. What is it

there for? Transform the food.

SASHA. Will you do it for me again?

SASHA *begins to eat as* NIKOLAI *proceeds.*

NIKOLAI. Imagine the delicate flesh, fish . . . fresh baked with a
touch of sorrel the way Liuba used to cook it for us, pink,
with a little butter, and flaking . . . (*Suddenly stopping, sharp.*)
How long is it since we left in this — how many days now?

SASHA. I am not sure, we have stood still so often with just
blackness out there, they don't even have stars here! I've got
lost, I think.

NIKOLAI (*calmly*). You promised me you were keeping count
Sasha — what month is it, we must know that, is it still May?

SASHA. I think it's May, or June, May . . .

NIKOLAI. Put it up on the wall, say it is now Day 21, notch it
up on the wall. We start serious counting from now on, you
must not lose count again, time has become important.

Sudden violent knocking on the door.

Make yourself respectable.

SASHA *is pushing his hair straight, and at the same time
picking crumbs of food off his coat.*

SASHA. Is there anything here people shouldn't find papa, that
we should move before . . .

The door crashes open and two pale faced GUARDS *in
military uniform burst into the carriage with startling ferocity.*
GUARD 1 *is tall, thin, and in his late twenties,* GUARD 2 *is
burly, about ten years older, unshaven, hands stained with
nicotine. Both* GUARDS *are armed.*

GUARD 1. Right!

He stops for a second in surprise at seeing NIKOLAI
*resplendent in his coat, sitting on the magnificence of the
carriage.*

All right — could you stand up please. (*Sharp.*) Come on stand
up.

GUARD 2 (*fast*). State your destination — arrival date, departure date, and nature of your business.

GUARD 1. We need to see your travel permit and your identification card, where are they?

GUARD 2. We're going to look at your luggage as well, so lay it out along here . . .

NIKOLAI. My dear comrades, none of that need concern us.

NIKOLAI *has remained seated*, SASHA *has stood*.

GUARD 1. What do you mean that doesn't concern us — everything that comes down this line concerns us.

GUARD 2. Where are you going for a start?

NIKOLAI (*simply*). I have no idea.

GUARD 1. Do you know where you are now?

NIKOLAI. I have even less idea of that — a remote settlement where it seems people have the sense not to live. (*He smiles.*) I assume you didn't choose to be here. (*He looks straight at both of them.*) Gentlemen, through some appalling error — for which I have yet to find the culprit — I am your new Telephone Examiner.

Silence.

GUARD 1 (*momentarily astonished*). You mean you . . . you work for the Northern Railway?

NIKOLAI. For the moment, yes. Why else do you think I would be here? (*He points to* SASHA.) That over there is my son who is accompanying me on this mission. (*Smiles.*) We are not going to waste our time in not believing each other, I would hardly invent such a story — there is no obvious advantage for me in having to wander up and down the line . . . unless I officially *had* to.

Slight pause.

GUARD 1. No, we believe you.

GUARD 2 (*smiles*). If you say that's who you are — we believe you.

GUARD 1. Forgive us comrade, we have been here so long, and we haven't seen anyone for several months, not since the men working on the line left.

GUARD 2 (*sharp smile*). All we see is the occasional freight train, we wait by the line praying for lights to appear, howling for a train! And when one comes all we get are people staring down from the locomotive as they rumble past . . .

GUARD 1. But comrades we don't have much news here about telephones to give you — the poles haven't even arrived yet.

NIKOLAI (*calmly*). I expected as much.

GUARD 2. Where are you from comrade — which depot are you from?

NIKOLAI. I'm afraid I have never been inside a depot. We are from Moscow, though we have been in the country for . . .

GUARD 2 (*cutting him off*). Moscow! — you're from Moscow. (*To* GUARD 1:) He's from *Moscow*, at last we've got someone.

Both GUARDS *exploding with excitement, questions tumbling out, cutting each other's sentences.*

GUARD 1 (*loud*). How are things there?

GUARD 2. There's so much you'll have to tell us . . .

GUARD 1. What is happening? What is the latest news, are things easier, are more goods getting through to the shops?

GUARD 2. Will we recognise the place? Are all the streets renamed? Is the new station built? They were just starting it, it was going to be enormous!

GUARD 1. Is there still fighting in the East — are things quieter now?

GUARD 2 (*earthy smile*). What sort of moving pictures are playing in Moscow — have you any of the latest jokes, we need a few!

GUARD 1. We've had to sense what's been happening, imagine it all, from this distance.

GUARD 2. We've missed so much already! We caught somebody's eye at the wrong moment.

GUARD 1. We must have looked dumb enough!

GUARD 2. Tell us what the good news is, start with that and . . .

NIKOLAI (*cutting them off and holding up his hand*). Gentlemen. Quiet. (*Pause.*) I have no news I'm afraid.

GUARD 2. None? At all . . .

NIKOLAI. None. (*Facing them, calmly.*) But we can do a transaction. We have little time to do it . . . we have a drunken driver who decides to take off suddenly and with little warning . . . so listen carefully because this is a matter of the utmost urgency. (*He pauses for this to sink in.*) I need the following — which I am sure you will be able to provide. I need some foreign newspapers — any foreign newspaper. Any scrap of especially English or American journals you have, any stray piece that may have come into your possession off the trains from the northern ports.

GUARD 2 (*taking it in*). Foreign newspapers . . . foreign news.

NIKOLAI. Second, I need some metal goods, any spare objects made out of metal of a transportable size, any metal appliances generally, everything you have.

GUARD 2. Metal appliances?

NIKOLAI (*suddenly to* SASHA). Have I left anything out? (*Sharper.*) Come on, have I?

SASHA. Me, Papa?! . . . *No.*

NIKOLAI (*calm smile*). I am willing to pay for this of course, that goes without saying — I will pay one thousand roubles if what you supply is satisfactory.

GUARD 1 (*bewildered*). One thousand roubles! As I understand it — all you want is some rubbish.

GUARD 2 (*grins*). We only have a limited amount of that round here — it's a very small station, take one step through the door and you've seen all there is to see.

GUARD 1. We get a few odd things off passing trains, and there's some of the debris from the two large estates that were about fifty miles from here and were burnt by bandits, we've got a little of that.

GUARD 2. It's all charred that stuff, you know it's burnt — (*Grins, eager to help.*) You want some of that comrade? We can arrange it . . .

NIKOLAI (*suddenly standing up*). I think I will have to examine it for myself. (*To* GUARD 2:) Show me the way.

NIKOLAI *exits with* GUARD 2.

SASHA (*loud*). Papa!

SASHA *is alone with the tall* GUARD.

GUARD 1 (*looking at* SASHA). This is a magnificent carriage, comrade.

SASHA. It needs cleaning.

The GUARD *is moving around the carriage fascinated, looking at everything.*

You should have seen our apartment in Moscow, we had nine or ten rooms like this, with grand pianos in three of them . . . my father has very high standards, he has the best of everything, usually.

GUARD 1 (*discovering with relish books in the carriage*). Books! Quite new! — I've had to read the same three books here over and over again. (*Flicking the pages of the official book, intrigued smile.*) There is nothing in the ledger — none of the stops you have made have been recorded.

SASHA (*thinking quickly*). That was deliberate on my father's part — if we'd been captured by bandits there would have been no record.

GUARD 1 (*looking at* NIKOLAI's *clothes*). That is an extraordinary coat your father is wearing. (*Friendly smile.*) He's a very exotic visitor for us, something special. (*Turning to* SASHA's *coat.*) All these clothes are foreign aren't they? (*Holding* SASHA's *coat.*) The smell of women, I can detect that even after weeks; English clothes are they?

GUARD 1 *moves on, looking near the box with the gun in it.*

SASHA (*watching closely*). My father likes English things — even the pigs on our estate had English names, before they all died

— Victoria, Hubert, Neville, and Lancelot, and Westminster.

GUARD 1 (*picking up the box of guns*). What are these?

SASHA (*before the GUARD can open it*). I think you may be exceeding your authority, my father said none of this must be touched. It's all *Railway* business.

GUARD 1. I just want a look, I won't do any harm.

SASHA (*really sharp*). Do you know who my father is — he's one of the most important men in Russia.

GUARD 1 (*taken aback*). He is?

SASHA (*loud*). Yes, you're not being visited by any old Telephone Examiner — by a run-of-the-mill official just dropping in out of the night, he's one of the most significant people you're ever likely to meet.

GUARD 1. Why?

SASHA. Why? What do you mean why? (*Suddenly unable to answer.*) Because . . . he is a man of importance.

NIKOLAI *enters, followed by* GUARD 2, *wheeling a baby carriage, an ornate low baby carriage with faded roses painted on the side and full of charred remains from the great estate.*

GUARD 2 (*smiling at SASHA who is staring in surprise*). You won't be able to fit in this easily will you!

NIKOLAI (*indicating a corner*). Leave it there . . . Sasha, pass me the money.

SASHA *carries across the bag of money.*

Gentlemen, looking at this — (NIKOLAI *indicates the baby carriage.*) it is clear we will have to do better. (*Holding out the money.*) I am going to give you the one thousand roubles, some of which is for this, some of which is in advance for what you are still going to find for me — before we leave.

GUARD 1. You want some more?

NIKOLAI. And in return, if I have the opportunity — I will use my new office to put in a word for you. Gentlemen, I will recommend you be moved to a better and more important

posting. Include your personal details in the next consignment
you bring for me.

GUARD 2 (*really loud*). We'll be back! (*Rushing to the door.*)
Don't you go till we're back. We'll certainly be back with
more.

Both GUARD 1 *and* 2 *exit with urgency.*

NIKOLAI (*indicating the baby carriage immediately.*) Are there
any newspapers in there — have a look.

As SASHA *searches through the charred remains.*

We travel over a thousand miles — to find two young men
going insane with loneliness! Feeling they're missing
everything. The taller one is a pleasant boy, reminded me of
one of the servants who left us for the war. Where are they
now? I can't even remember what some of them looked like.
The one with the rolling walk, what was his name? (*Suddenly
back to* SASHA:) Have you found some Sasha? Bring me what
you've got . . .

SASHA *is moving over, handing him fragments.*

I've had no foreign news for so long — and this is the best they
could do, like bringing water to a man dying of thirst but only
a few drops at a time . . . (*Staring at tattered pieces of
newspaper.*) Where is this form? England, that's good . . .
that's very good.

SASHA *also has a piece.*

Look through your piece Sasha and tell me what you find.

SASHA. What am I looking for Papa?

NIKOLAI. This does not look like a useful part of the paper —
garden parties and the obituary page. Dead diplomats. Find the
date — it is vital we find the date. (*Without a pause.*) Have you
found it?

SASHA. It's in English, Papa!

NIKOLAI. All that education he was given, how many
governesses were there — I lost count — and he can't even read
the date in English.

SASHA (*struggling*). November 12, 1919.

NIKOLAI. My God! That's seven months ago. (*Incisive.*) That's the nearest we can get, and we don't even know *that*, because we've lost the current date as well. We will have to go through all this, Sasha, column by column, inch by inch. (*Tossing news scraps away.*) This paper smells of cats. We will have to continue this by daylight. Pass me that box, where's it gone? You know the one I mean, the one with the weapons inside it.

SASHA *is gingerly carrying the box for him.*

I just have to check to see if they are fully loaded.

SASHA. But you know they are. (*As the lid is raised:*) What are those other things in there?

NIKOLAI. Diamonds. Just a very few. All that is left — all that we were able to save from Moscow.

SASHA *moves to the stove, very nervous in case somebody comes in. The noise of the* GUARDS *as they search outside continues throughout the scene, with occasional banging against the back wall.*

SASHA. I will try to make the tea for you . . . I am getting better. I am still practising it.

He *goes about it as if preparing for a major operation.*

NIKOLAI (*glancing in* SASHA's *direction*). I will tell you an interesting fact — I have never felt a kettle. Certainly not when it has been boiling. I have never actually handled one. (*He smiles.*) I don't think I should start now.

SASHA (*looking at the guns*). They could come back at any moment Papa. (*Lowering his voice.*) Do you think they really turn people off trains like we were warned, making them walk into whatever's waiting for us out there.

NIKOLAI. It's more than possible. But why should anybody try to do that to us? Don't worry . . .

SASHA *turns back to the tea. Suddenly* NIKOLAI *lets out a really loud cry, an extraordinary and alarming wail of frustration.*

What the hell do I do?

SASHA *turns, truly startled.*

How do I manage it now? . . . prevent it escaping . . .

SASHA (*very worried*). What is it Papa? Are you unwell?

NIKOLAI (*voice dropping to a rapid murmur*). Being incarcerated alive . . . caged up like an animal . . . it's not possible now.

SASHA. What is it? What's the matter? (*Suddenly moving closer.*) What were you looking for in the paper? Tell me Papa.

NIKOLAI *is murmuring.*

What's happening? Tell me, please.

Silence.

NIKOLAI (*voice suddenly calm and authoritative again*). What have I always told you matters most, what is it our duty to do?

SASHA. To . . . to achieve, Papa?

NIKOLAI. Have you any idea what work I do?

Slight pause.

SASHA. No.

NIKOLAI. When I went into that large office, what do you suppose I was thinking about?

SASHA. Business?

NIKOLAI. Business — don't show your ignorance child, you make us sound like merchants.

NIKOLAI *is clutching the catch on the gun,* SASHA *watching, tense.*

Since there appears to be no one here, other than ourselves, who could be listening? (*He looks straight at* SASHA.) Nobody has ever been told what you are about to hear.

SASHA. No, Papa.

NIKOLAI *moves in the half-darkened carriage.*

NIKOLAI. If you were to think your father had found a way of making the moving pictures talk — of recording sound on film and then so enlarging the volume so the picture talks . . . If you were to think I had found a way of doing this . . . (*Slight pause.*) Almost, nearly . . . you would be right.

SASHA (*very quiet*). You've done that! Nearly done that!

NIKOLAI. *Nearly,* yes. In Moscow, I'd found a way of printing sound directly onto film, but I can't unlock the answer to the final stage, how to *enlarge* the sound. The problem is frustratingly simple and the equipment required is reasonably rudimentary. If I can do that . . .

Noise of GUARDS *outside.*

Why do you look so alarmed? You're old enough not to be terrified of ideas. If I succeed Sasha, of course I will be the first person in the world to do it.

SASHA (*hushed*). The first one . . . of all?

NIKOLAI. Which will have a considerable effect on all our lives. Not merely fame, recognition on an international scale, but it will give me the power to acquire the resources and staff I need.

SASHA. That was why you were looking in the paper.

NIKOLAI. Yes, to see if on their theatre pages there is a comment on such and such a film performer's voice.

SASHA. Do you think they could have done it already? Before you?

NIKOLAI. No. I am fairly certain I am three or four years ahead of the rest of the world. Naturally I have no evidence for that, such a proposition is by its very nature unprovable, until I, or somebody else, achieves it. But I *sense* I am ahead. But we must not dwell on that. If I think all the time about being overtaken — we will go insane.

Silence.

SASHA. I have never been to the moving pictures.

NIKOLAI. Neither have I.

SASHA (*surprised*). *You* haven't Papa?

NIKOLAI. No, never. Not in public.

SASHA (*suddenly, seeing his father still holding the gun*). Papa, if they find you with your guns now, it may not help you.

NIKOLAI. They won't ever come in here without knocking.

Noise of GUARDS' *voices from outside.*

It is interesting, Sasha, don't you think, how time and time again the same idea happens in totally separate places at the same time — in completely different parts of the globe. They come out of the ether together. Simultaneous progress . . . But on this I have a real start.

SASHA. Yes, Papa . . .

NIKOLAI (*smiles. Suddenly really loud*). BUT, MY GOD, THE ODDS, SASHA — the odds against us are enormous. I am at least one thousand miles from Moscow, shut up in this wooden box — alone with a child. And on my return, the *women* have to live inside here, have to share this space with us . . . (*Pause.*) . . . a situation so bizarre I can hardly believe I have allowed it to happen to me.

SASHA. I will help, I can do things.

Noise of the GUARDS.

NIKOLAI. I didn't know such vastness, such space out there and being alone, could be so disturbing, left without our staff, servants, without any support.

SASHA (*very quiet*). It frightens me too, Papa.

NIKOLAI. You must never admit to being frightened, Sasha. (*Tone lightening, picking up the money*.) At least there is one unexpected advantage — I have been given plenty of money.

SASHA. For railway business . . . isn't it?

NIKOLAI (*suddenly looking at him sharply.*) Have you taken in what I have just said Sasha?

SASHA. Of course, Papa.

NIKOLAI. Look at me — look at me straight in the eye. You must learn to look people directly in the eye, anything else makes you seem dishonest.

SASHA. Yes.

NIKOLAI. It is stating the obvious Sasha — but this is a night of grave importance between us, more than any other.

SASHA. I know, Papa.

NIKOLAI (*firmly*). What are you afraid of now?

SASHA (*trying not to sound scared*). I am not anymore . . . I won't be.

NIKOLAI (*calmly*). Stand up and face me, and give me your word you will never repeat to anyone what you have heard tonight. (*Pause.*) The work must never be discussed in front of the women, or anyone, you understand.

Pause.

SASHA. I give you my word.

NIKOLAI. Good. (*Calmly touches his coat.*) You must be careful to keep up your appearance, Sashenka, especially when meeting ordinary soldiers like tonight . . .

They look at each other .

You may go back to your room now.

SASHA (*moving across the width of the carriage*). It is a kind of race isn't it, Papa, what we're in?

NIKOLAI. In a way.

SASHA. And you'll come first?

NIKOLAI. There can only be one result. (*Louder:*) Let neither of us be in any doubt what is at stake from this moment on. It will need such energy Sasha.

Suddenly lifting the gun — pointing at the ceiling.

My God what are we doing still here! If they are not coming back, we are being kept waiting for no useful purpose. (*Very loud:*) Come on you drunken bastard we've got to be underway now. Get this thing moving!

He lifts the gun, about to pull the trigger.

SASHA (*screaming*). Papa! Remember!

NIKOLAI (*turning*). Remember what! They won't dare to bother us. But maybe we don't want holes in the roof — not till we get back to the South.

The door is thrown open, light pouring in. NIKOLAI makes no attempt to conceal the gun. GUARD 1 moves into the doorway of the carriage and throws a large black bag of extra junk inside. It clanks as it hits the floor.

GUARD 1 (*friendly smile*). We found everything we could, comrade! Every scrap there is. You'll soon be off now. Our names and personal histories are in there too, comrade, don't lose them! *We will meet again.* (*Smiles.*) When the new phone exchange is opened, we'll make the first calls! Goodbye, comrade, we won't forget you.

NIKOLAI. Thank you my friend. I will not forget your promotion. If you get your release you'll be more fortunate than I.

As the door is closing.

And comrade, tell our driver he is not to stop, don't let us stop at all now, till we hit the sea!

Blackout.

Scene Three

A hot sticky late summer afternoon in the carriage, the two women, EUGENIA and POLYA, are alone.

EUGENIA *is dressed in a full-length white dress, long sleeves, lavishly dressed as if to entertain friends for an evening meal, but her clothes are now stained and streaked with dirt from months of being in the carriage. She is sweating profusely, constantly wiping her face. POLYA, dressed in a black uniform but with bare legs, is kneeling on the carriage floor; between deep intakes of breath she is half singing, half talking down a speaking tube, the sort that could have come from a large house. It snakes out of the carriage door, which is just open enough to let it through. There is a partition around NIKOLAI's area.*

POLYA *continues to half sing, half gabble into the tube*.

POLYA (*loud*). Can you hear this . . .? (*Then very quiet*.) Is this loud enough? . . . Seventy-seven, seventy-eight, seventy-nine, seventy-ten . . . You see, after a day of this I can't even count any more . . . my brain is throbbing. (*Loud*:) Can you hear it throbbing? (*Leaning her head forward*:) Should be ear-splitting? Can you hear me at all!

EUGENIA. He will stop soon, I'm sure he must finish with you any moment, it's not physically possible to go on much longer.

POLYA (*into the tube*). That's true of me, is it true of him? Maybe the Master needs a drink . . . (*Into the tube*:) He is beginning to feel thirsty now . . . getting a little cramped in that hut . . . he's just thinking how welcome a cool, slow drink would be . . . (*She continues to sing the song she began with very hoarsely*.) I used to sing this while doing the stairs in Moscow, the Master likes it. I don't think I ever want to hear it again after today.

She continues breathing into the speaking apparatus a smattering of song, and a nursery rhyme; her neck is soaked in sweat.

EUGENIA. If only he'd let me help you, he's always found the idea of me working extremely unpleasant. (*Nervous smile*.) He told me once he found the thought repulsive. (*Lightly*:) and I seem to be forbidden more than ever before to touch any of his work, even to glance at it. (*Looking at* POLYA *kneeling on the floor*.) Sometimes, Polya, I have an intense desire to go through everything of his.

POLYA (*into the tube*). Can the Master hear any of this . . .?

EUGENIA (*gently*). And now when he's divided up the carriage like the dacha, pinning us to this side (*She smiles*.) he's tried to shrink the house. (*She turns*.) You know I've never slept in public before, till these past months, not with somebody in the room other than Nikolai.

POLYA (*looking up*). Yes you squeezed yourself to the wall that first night didn't you, Madame . . . trying to hide in the luggage rack. (*Back to the tube.*) Thirsty . . . getting thirsty!

EUGENIA. Our neighbours, and my friends, would never believe
this, that I ended up in this carriage . . .

POLYA (*finishing a verse of the song*). I wonder what I am doing
all this for? (*Slight smile.*) After a time it does cross your
mind, after fifty days, you do begin to get just a little curious.
(*Into the tube:*) What's the answer? Are you still there?

EUGENIA. At least you don't have to dress like I do — in this
heat. (*Holding herself.*) Do you know what it feels like shut up
in this?

POLYA (*looking up*). I would go mad, Madame, if I had to wear
that all the time.

EUGENIA. There are good reasons for it. (*She moves.*) As you
know the Master always wants me to have the best, the best of
everything. He needs to live like that, regardless of where he is.
I shouldn't be saying this to you, Polya, but maybe because of
us being Jewish, we were among the first Jewish families to be
allowed to live in the capital. The Master, of course, has never
considered himself inferior to anyone . . . so he always looked
more part of Moscow society even than the oldest families,
aristocratic in everything he chooses . . . everything he does.
So I *have* to wear all this, it's what he wants of me. (*Looking
at* POLYA, *she stops.*) I really oughtn't to say such things to
you.

POLYA (*looking straight at her*). I know, Eugenia
Michailovna . . . it's all right. (*Loud into the tube:*) I am sure
the Master is no longer there. (*Calling down:*) Are you? He's
walked off and left me singing to an empty railway line.
(*Loud.*) So he won't notice, if I quite . . . suddenly . . .
just . . . (*Very loud.*) stop.

POLYA *gets up and moves away.*

EUGENIA. Is that wise, Polya?

POLYA. We'll see if there is any reaction.

She is by the window.

I can't see him anywhere.

EUGENIA. I wonder if I dare take these off? (*Self-mocking smile, indicating her stockings.*) Do you think I should take the risk? If he notices you know how violently angry he can get. (EUGENIA *hesitates.*)

POLYA. Go on, he's too busy to notice.

EUGENIA *is pulling off her shoes and stockings.*

EUGENIA. I suppose, Polya, this must seem foolish to you, a grown woman making such a business of taking her shoes and stockings off, making it seem an important event, but for me it is. (*Smile.*) Bare legs in the sun. (*She stretches her legs out.*) My God that feels so good! (*She fans her dress.*) Sweat trickling out, fresh air! Polya, why has it taken me this long? (*She moves to the window.*)

POLYA. See he *hasn't* come.

Silence.

EUGENIA (*by the window*). Sssh. (*Pause.*) You realise we have no idea what is going on out there. None. We can only stand here, and wait for what is coming. I often think something is about to come out of the silence at us, suddenly appear down the line.

POLYA. Remember those corpses in the ditch by the dacha — all squashed up at one end with those hundreds of butterflies fluttering on top of them, murdered by bandits. I'll never forget those faces, their mouths open, one of the heads was sliced in half.

EUGENIA. I don't just mean the bandits and if they attack . . . (*She turns.*) So many things may have changed *without us knowing*, Polya. (*Pause.*) Our street in Moscow will be completely different — it could have been torn down, they may be using it as barracks, soldiers sleeping in our bedrooms, or the apartment may have been swallowed up by Government offices, (*Slight smile.*) the Transport Department, my old room full of bus routes, and filing cabinets in the bathroom . . . And the language will be changing, how you address people in the street, if I met somebody I used to know, have coffee with, this will sound stupid, but I start wondering what would

I do, what would I call her? . . . What should I say? (*Pause.*)
We are so ignorant, Polya. (*She turns.*) I am. It terrifies me
sometimes. (*Suddenly breathing into the speaking tube:*)
Vastly ignorant. (*She looks up. Pause.*) The Master will never
discuss his work with us and nor should we expect it.

POLYA. No?

EUGENIA. But Polya have you any idea why we have heard
nothing from the authorities?

Pause.

POLYA. Madame — I think there is something you ought to see.

She moves towards NIKOLAI's private space.

EUGENIA (*hesitating*). What — we have to go in there?

POLYA (*turning to face her*). I found these — I didn't know
whether to show you.

POLYA *is pushing her hand down the side of NIKOLAI's bed,
bringing out handfuls of large pristine white official letters
with the Government seal on them.*

EUGENIA. They're not all official letters are they — and none of
them opened? He must have opened some of them?

POLYA. Not one.

*She is producing letters from every crack and corner, from
behind lamps, from under the bunks, from behind the stove.*

EUGENIA. The Master never forgets anything — he didn't open
these *deliberately*.

POLYA (*scrambling on the top bunk, and near the roof*). There
are plenty more, even under his sheets! These are the worst I
think. (*She comes down with more.*) Telegrams . . .

EUGENIA. Because I'm not allowed to collect the mail, Polya — I
had no idea these had come.

POLYA *hands her the red-bound envelopes.* EUGENIA *stares
down at them.*

What do you think they all say — what do you think they
want?

POLYA. We could open them, Madame.

EUGENIA. Open his letters! If he found out . . .

Silence. Suddenly pushing them into POLYA's *hand, nervous smile.*

You open them. No, you can't read can you Polya?

POLYA. Not quite.

EUGENIA. Give them back. I'm not that much of a coward! I'll do my own dirty work.

POLYA *crosses herself as* EUGENIA *opens the telegrams and reads them out.*

URGENT. MUST HAVE *NEWS*, DETAILS TELEPHONE EXAMINER IMMEDIATELY. WHAT PROGRESS?

POLYA *tears open another and gives it to* EUGENIA.

WHY NO NEWS? REPORT STATE OF WORK WITHOUT DELAY. MOST URGENT. REPLY ESSENTIAL. (*Looking at* POLYA.) I think we get the idea. (*Staring at the other envelopes.*) I hope they don't get even worse.

POLYA. They better go back.

She starts hastily pushing letters back into cracks.

EUGENIA. God knows what else there is we don't know about.

POLYA. Well, Madame — if you really want to see.

She looks at EUGENIA *as she pushes the letters back.*

EUGENIA (*quiet*). You better show me everything, Polya.

POLYA. There's this, the official ledger the Master has to keep. (*Indicating the huge bulky volume.*) There is not a word in it, it's completely bare.

EUGENIA (*opening the huge ledger*). Not one entry? About the long trip he made with Sasha. (*Staring.*) All these blank pages!

POLYA. And this is the most serious.

EUGENIA. Why?

POLYA (*indicating the bags of money from the drawer*). He's spent some of the money, he's spent over half I think.

EUGENIA. And there is no record of it? (*She moves in agitation.*)
He must have spent it on all those things he brought back for
his work — and the food he bribed off people to feed us with.
I wondered how on earth he'd got it. I didn't dare ask.
(*Sharper:*) I didn't want to know.

POLYA. None of it is railway business — whichever way you look
at it.

EUGENIA (*facing her*). No, Polya. If he's misappropriated
government funds that could be disastrous — if it was
discovered, even the Master could be . . . (*She stops.*) even
he . . .

Pause.

POLYA. The Master could get shot, yes.

EUGENIA (*sharper*). It's almost certain. (*She turns.*) You mustn't
mention any of this, Polya, that we've seen . . .

*A noise at the door; they bolt across the carriage back to their
places, as the door opens and SASHA enters.*

EUGENIA (*shouts*). It's you, Sasha — you shouldn't give us
shocks like that. (*Really loud:*) What do you think you're
doing? Why didn't you knock? Don't you ever do that again!

POLYA (*by the window looking out*). Where's the Master? He's
not right outside anymore . . .

SASHA (*standing still*). I haven't seen him. I've been walking
down the line by myself.

EUGENIA. Sasha — I have to ask you something serious, are you
listening carefully?

SASHA (*watching closely from the wall*). What is it?

EUGENIA. Tell me what your father is doing? (*Pause.*) When you
went off with him on that long journey for all those months —
what did he tell you?

Pause.

SASHA. He didn't tell me anything.

POLYA. I don't think that's true. (*Looking straight at him.*)
You're lying, Sasha.

EUGENIA. We're here in the middle of the country and your father is doing all this work with Polya. Why?

SASHA *is watching them.*

POLYA. Did he talk to you about his work? Yes or no?

SASHA (*quiet*). I think he did.

EUGENIA. Sasha — I realise we're not meant to know, normally I wouldn't ask. But you have to tell me, it could prove very dangerous to all of us if you keep it to yourself.

SASHA. He told me everything he was doing.

POLYA. He did?

SASHA (*slowly*). But I was so scared while he was telling me, I was so frightened — I don't remember what he said . . . only that it's important. I can't even remember where we went.

EUGENIA. Sasha — is that true?

POLYA. I don't believe it.

SASHA. Yes! I realised hours afterwards I couldn't remember what secret he told me.

EUGENIA. You can't even remember a part of it?

SASHA. Nothing.

EUGENIA (*suddenly moving*). One thing is certain, sooner or later somebody is going to follow these up, they are going to seek us out, to find what has happened. They'll burst in here one day, and that will probably be the end of all this.

POLYA. And us as well — probably.

EUGENIA. Yes. (*Looking at them.*) And we can't escape anywhere, obviously — they will come after us. So . . . (*She moves, picks up a letter.*) we've got to reply to these, (*Pause.*) write letters on his behalf and put something in here, Polya. (*She indicates the official ledger.*) Somehow we've got to discover Railway details, make up false records, fill up this with what he's discovered on his trip, so it appears he's made an effort.

POLYA. Give them something to read! (*She moves.*) How are we going to do it?

EUGENIA. I don't know — have to try to remember the
geography my governess taught me, my schooling, towns and
small places in the northern district, all the bits that were
always the most boring. (*She moves.*) Maybe we'll find a map
among his private papers we can use.

POLYA. I'll go through them.

EUGENIA. We have to lie, Polya — lies that won't be too specific,
too obvious, about the things we found — (*She corrects
herself.*) — that the Master found, 'in such and such a place
some progress was noticed, the workers conscientious'. Maybe
they will take so long to check with the northern depot —
communications can't be good at the moment — that when
they find out, it won't matter so much by then. (*Looking at
the ledger.*) We're living on explosive leaving this blank.

POLYA. Do you know anything about the Northern Railway,
Madame — I don't.

EUGENIA. No, or telephones. But we'll have to use our
imagination — (*Self-mocking smile.*) — if I have any. We invent
if necessary.

*Lifting the pen from the desk towards the virgin white pages,
she writes.*

'Day one, departed.' (*As she writes:*) The Master must not
know anything about this of course, he would tear it all out
at once. We're just helping him because he's so very busy.

POLYA. Who are we more afraid of, Madame, him or them?

EUGENIA (*sharper*). Polya — you shouldn't talk like that.
(*Looking down.*) What do you think the penalties are for
doing this — they may be worse than for not doing anything
at all.

NIKOLAI *is standing in the doorway; EUGENIA starts, closes
the ledger and moves across the carriage, holding it behind her.*

There you are — I was wondering where you were.

NIKOLAI *is not even looking at her.*

NIKOLAI. I thought you must have stopped, Polya. What
happened to you?

He stares down at POLYA *who is dripping with sweat, her hair matted back.*

POLYA (*looking at him, then away*). I had to have a rest, Barin — so I am taking one . . .

NIKOLAI. So it appears. (*Pause.*) Did we agree it was time to stop?

POLYA (*quiet*). No, Barin.

EUGENIA. Nikolai, I want to ask you — have you had any messages from Moscow, any letters or telegrams from the authorities?

NIKOLAI. From Moscow? Not of any significance. (*He turns back to* POLYA.) Polya, time is important to us, interruptions will prove very damaging. We are involved in a race against time.

POLYA (*very quiet*). But I needed to have a break.

NIKOLAI. Of course. I don't want you to be over-worked, Polya. If it has been a strain, then, certainly you must take a pause; we will start again in one and a half minutes.

POLYA (*suddenly*). When I am ready Nikolai Semenovitch, we will go on, not before.

Startled pause.

EUGENIA (*worried by her boldness*). Polya . . .

POLYA (*facing him*). I am so hot, I am filthy. Look at me.

NIKOLAI (*very firm, all his authority*). I need you to do it Polya. (*Watching her defiant face.*) You can have all my rations for the rest of the week, in return for more work tonight.

POLYA. I don't think you should try to bribe me, either. And you must not interfere with the ration allocation, Barin — it will put the accounts in an even worse mess and we'll go back to starving.

Silence. She faces him.

NIKOLAI. She disobeys me — and she threatens me. (*Lightly.*) And I cannot dismiss her — because there is no obvious replacement waiting outside. (*Sharper.*) We will resume in less than a minute.

POLYA. Nikolai Semenovitch, when I go on — it will be because I want to and because Sasha says it's important, what you're doing, though he hasn't been able to tell us what it is.

NIKOLAI. What I do *is* important, naturally. I wouldn't ask people to waste their time.

POLYA (*nervously, but staring straight at him*). Are you going to tell me what it is, Barin?

NIKOLAI. Your break for a rest is now over.

POLYA. I believe it *is* something important. But I would like to know what . . . what I am doing this for, Barin.

NIKOLAI (*ignoring this*). We must go on now. (*Sharp.*) Polya, I have to have your help — I can't do without it.

POLYA *stares at him.*

POLYA. I know that. If I do it — it will be in my own time, (*With great dignity she kneels before the tube.*) which may be now, for a strictly *limited* time. (*Sharp:*) You better go back to where you should be, Barin — or you'll be losing the time you've got me for.

She begins to sing, on her knees, into the tube, a loud, piercing, powerful song.

Blackout.

Scene Four

SASHA *is alone in the carriage, a distant sound of guns, the outside world encroaching. There is grumbling gunfire, for the moment in the distance, sniping and occasionally the much larger sound of a field gun going off, shells falling — the noise is sporadic. SASHA is sitting at the far end of the carriage, holding one of the pistols and pointing it straight at the door. There is a sudden, much louder sound of calls and shouts right outside the door, excited cries. SASHA stands holding the gun out in front of him, pointing at the door.*

SASHA. Who is that? (*Pulling back the catch on the gun.*) Who is out there? I warn you — I am *armed*.

EUGENIA and POLYA burst through door, hair untidy. Distant gunfire behind them in the night.

EUGENIA. What are you doing pointing that thing at us Sasha . . . ?

SASHA. I didn't know who was out there. (*Very real apprehension.*) You never know what could come in from out there — especially on a night like this.

EUGENIA and POLYA are licking meat fat off their hands, having been cooking outside. There is a new earthiness and directness in their manner to each other.

EUGENIA. Do you think we burnt it? (*Glancing back through the door.*) It looks like we may have burnt it!

POLYA. I'd completely forgotten the taste of meat — there're some things you could almost commit murder for, aren't there! (*Licking fingers.*) If only the comrade from Moscow had brought more of it.

EUGENIA. Took so long to pluck them — I had to restrain myself from just tearing the birds apart — (*A last lick.*) — little sputters of blood going everywhere — my cooking is so rudimentary Polya.

POLYA. They won't notice.

EUGENIA (*suddenly*). What are we doing? We're not ready! We have to prepare the table, they could be back any moment.

SASHA. Papa's not going to make us all sit down to eat, is he? He can't hold a dinner party during a battle.

EUGENIA. Of course — something small like that is certainly not going to stop him. If I could think of any possible way of preventing him I would do it, it's not exactly what we want the Commissar of Labour to see.

POLYA and EUGENIA run around the carriage and produce a beautiful white table cloth from the drawers under the bunks,

*silver candle sticks and cutlery, fine quality china. During the
following exchanges the table is prepared to its full splendour
and the candles lit, the gunfire in the distance beginning to roll
towards them.*

EUGENIA (*hearing the field gun*). Remember those nights in the
apartment the first days of the Revolution, Polya, hearing the
noise, just like this.

POLYA. The night everyone ran for shelter from the guns to the
hotel across the street, during dinner.

EUGENIA. You were carrying all the luggage we could snatch in
the time, weren't you? I piled you with so much silver you
could hardly move. (*Imitates* POLYA's *tottering figure.*) You
lurched down the stairs like this.

POLYA. Yes, silver was dropping behind me all the way down
the street — if I tried to pick it up, I just dropped more . . .

EUGENIA. And the passage of the hotel filled with all those men
keeping their hats on all night, walking up and down standing
guard on us, everyone of them dressed like the Master.

POLYA. Yes, but not quite as well.

EUGENIA. Hundreds and hundreds of them squashed into the
corridor, I came out in the night and there was just this sea of
bobbing black hats.

POLYA (*laying the silver round the table*). And the cavalry
officer, remember him, Madame, what was he called? The one
that sheltered in our room the next afternoon for a rest. I had
to tie his tie for him when he woke, he'd never tied it for
himself — he crawled out of the hotel during the shelling.

EUGENIA. And the Master demanding where room service was.

The gunfire becomes a little louder.

SASHA. Is it nearer?

EUGENIA. God, I've forgotten half of it already — those
extraordinary faces staring at me . . .

POLYA (*moving around the carriage lighting all the candles*).
Perfect strangers kept on giving me orders, pushing messages

into my hand, and saying, 'Just run along the passage for me
to such and such a room.'

EUGENIA. If I'd known what it meant — I would have
remembered it more. I knew things wouldn't be the same
again, but I just had a sense of total irritation all the time
constantly being kept awake, the firing, like somebody kicking
you in the ankles all the time, so you're in a terrible nervy
temper — feelings hardly matching the size of the occasion and
how near we were. (*Sharp.*) How inadequate one's immediate
responses often are, mine anyway. (*She moves. Loud:*) Was
that them? Are we ready?

POLYA. Sasha put that gun away . . . No, hide it properly, not
there, that's the most obvious place.

SASHA *had put it under his pillow. He now puts it behind the
stove.*

EUGENIA. Polya, we have to do everything in our power, and I
mean everything, to make sure the Commissar of Labour
doesn't interrogate the Master. Steer him away from anything
about railway business. And we can't let him mention his
work.

POLYA. Yes. (*Kicking the tube into a corner.*) If he sees
anything, we say it's part of the heating system.

Pause.

EUGENIA. You know if we got the food in here now, and we
were able to move this carriage on our own, we could ride off
with all this for ourselves, slide off down the line away from
danger . . .

VERKOFF *enters with* NIKOLAI. VERKOFF *is flushed from
watching the gun battle. As* NIKOLAI *takes off his coat, we see
he is formally dressed for dinner.*

NIKOLAI. They are waiting to feed us.

VERKOFF. We should be safe in here. (*To* EUGENIA:) I hope
I'm right, you look concerned. What a night! We got quite
close to the action didn't we Nikolai Semenovitch, caught
glimpses of them through the trees!

NIKOLAI (*calmly*). I saw nothing, the smoke got in my eyes.

SASHA. Who are they fighting?

VERKOFF. They are flushing out some white bandits. Some renegade soldiers, and a collection of bandits have teamed up, a really seedy bunch! But they've got themselves three old guns somehow, and are roaming the forest. (*Gunfire. He smiles.*) Shouldn't be many of them left by morning.

NIKOLAI (*staring down at the table*). There are no table napkins, Polya — for some reason they have been forgotten.

POLYA *rushes for them as* NIKOLAI *pours wine.*

This is the best bottle I have left, it may be a little thin.

VERKOFF (*looking around*). What have you done to this place? Railway life seems to be suiting you comrade!

NIKOLAI. Despite the monstrous administrative error — a little progress has been possible.

VERKOFF. What monstrous error is that?

EUGENIA. Polya! You better bring the food at once — (*Sharp:*) — as quickly as you can.

POLYA *exits with a silver tray.*

NIKOLAI (*charming smile*). What you have singularly failed to rectify. Do not be fooled by the appearance of luxury — you have left us in a corner where even the peasants do not live . . . When it rains you can hear the rats squealing and scuffling underneath; some of them poke their heads through to peer at me. (*Slight smile.*) And they are free and I am caged.

The sound of guns, all the time slightly nearer.

VERKOFF. Don't worry — they won't be able to shoot straight. (*Looking at* NIKOLAI's *table.*) If they could see what was going on inside a Government train!

POLYA *comes in with the food — small roasted pieces of some bird, scattered across a large silver platter. The amount of meat is tiny on the huge tray.*

EUGENIA (*nervous*). Here's the food, Comrade.

VERKOFF. And we're going to be eating it off English silver?

NIKOLAI. Of course, it's English.

VERKOFF. Only the best naturally!

NIKOLAI (*charming smile*). I have never been rich enough to afford to buy anything but the best.

POLYA *is dividing the meat up, the smell of freshly roasted game filling the stage.*

(*Unabashed:*) In England you find quality everywhere. An immensely civilized, comfortable place — arriving there is like sliding into a warm bath (*He stares at* VERKOFF.) which nobody is suddenly going to try to empty. People never argue there, the clothes are beautifully made, the service superb.

The food is now ready in front of them.

VERKOFF (*staring at him, suddenly very loud*). Nikolai Semenovitch you are the biggest snob I have *ever* met and I have met a few. (*Pointing at him.*) It's shameless! And it gets *worse* with him!

EUGENIA (*hastily*). My husband finds it difficult to break old habits.

VERKOFF. The way you dress! Even here where nobody at all can see you — a Jew that behaves like a Grand Duke, who had to be the best-dressed man in Moscow. Someone that can serve a meal like this on his family silver in the middle of a forest, during a battle!

NIKOLAI. If the mind is to function it has to be looked after. It's as simple as that.

VERKOFF (*sharp smile*). You know you could antagonise certain people behaving like this, it has been known! (*Looking straight at him.*) It's as well you've been employed on railway business isn't it?

EUGENIA *looks at* POLYA. VERKOFF *points at* NIKOLAI's *feet. Really loud.*

I shouldn't think there's another pair of shoes left like that in the whole of Russia!

NIKOLAI. Comrade — I thought you had a revolution so you

would be able to dress like me — not I like you.

They look at VERKOFF. *Silence, followed by a sudden loud laugh.*

VERKOFF. Did you hear him? (*Pause.*) People have been shot for saying less.

The sound of shelling, growing gradually closer all the time.

NIKOLAI. I don't necessarily disapprove of everything that has happened (*Indicating himself.*) though of course a mistake like this should have been avoided. Despite that — the astronomical incompetence that was allowed before, that was freely tolerated, it amazes me now.

VERKOFF (*sharp*). He admits that much.

NIKOLAI (*incisive*). Before it happened there was an unhelpful nervousness too — a general unease, people hurrying faster between the front door and their carriage, myself included.

VERKOFF. He had to run into his house!

NIKOLAI. Yes, a listlessness when in public places (*Slight smile.*) . . . Waiters became unpredictable. (*Pause.*) There was a constant sensation of something pressing, pressing down on one like a weight on the walls — needless to say I was completely unaware of it until everything 'erupted' . . . then quite suddenly I realised it had been there all the time.

SASHA (*suddenly really loud, famished*). Papa — *please* can we start, aren't we going to eat now! We've been *waiting* to eat this — I can't wait any more, please let us begin.

Silence.

NIKOLAI. Sasha. (*His manner is truly formidable, dangerous.*) What is the meaning of this? Have you forgotten there are guests present? (*Pause.*) Remove yourself to your room and eat there . . . and take a knife and fork, I will not have you not eating properly, you are not to eat with your bare hands.

NIKOLAI *turns back to the table.*

Let us begin.

Everybody falls on their food violently except for NIKOLAI.

There is no hurry, the food will not run away.

The gunfire is getting nearer.

VERKOFF. We want to eat before we die! (*Tearing at the meat furiously.*) My family were all butchers you know.

EUGENIA *looks nervous.*

But they all hated meat. (*Looking up.*) If I'd known you were hungry I would have brought some more . . .

EUGENIA *tries to resist eating with her fingers.* POLYA *sitting separate, pulling meat up to her mouth. A sound comes out of her, a crying noise. She curls her body to the wall.*

EUGENIA. What is it, Polya — are you all right?

POLYA. Oh yes — it's just slightly good. (*She makes a deep famished cry again.*) Just a little nice, you know.

The gunfire is now very close. VERKOFF *looks at* NIKOLAI *presiding over the table.*

VERKOFF (*with relish*). Look at him now! I would love to see the shock people have as you go about your railway business — that I would pay to see. (*Loud.*) I would queue to see it!

EUGENIA (*nervous*). Have some more wine, Comrade, here . . .

VERKOFF (*loud, moving around, his fingers stabbing out*). They have started sending our special trains from Moscow with performing groups on them, young people, actors, musicians, spreading across the country, explaining, informing, communicating — the idea of *them* passing *you* at some remote station, it is wonderful. Rolling back the door of the carriage and finding this apparition — this figure looking as if he's stepped out of the last century, if not before, dressed for going to the opera, waving his stick at them and shouting, go away, don't interrupt me, I am too busy, my work is vital!

NIKOLAI. Why should it be extraordinary?

VERKOFF. I love the idea! (*Sharp look.*) What rich times these are, eh, Nikolai Semenovitch!

NIKOLAI (*calmly*). It is only children and government officials that can't hold two totally separate — seemingly opposing —

ideas in their head at the same time.

A shell breaks closer to the carriage as the battle rolls towards them. EUGENIA and SASHA instinctively duck.

NIKOLAI (*calmly*). I am engaged in a struggle where the outcome can never be totally guaranteed — but it is a reasonable prediction to make that this carriage will become as famous as the one they signed the German surrender in, and we are by coincidence also in a forest.

The noise of sniper fire is suddenly closer as well.

(*Glancing at* VERKOFF:) If I do what I am capable of — this, my appointment, will be the highlight of your career.

VERKOFF (*broad smile*). As Telephone Examiner!

NIKOLAI (*lightly*). You will be erecting plaques on this wall in years to come and showing your grandchildren. People will be coming here to inspect where it was all done (*Charming smile.*) though for the convenience of the public they may wish to move the carriage nearer to civilisation.

The loud whistle of a shell seemingly descending directly above them hangs in the air for a second, as the battle reaches them.

VERKOFF. Careful! They're getting really close. Take cover!

POLYA, SASHA *and* EUGENIA *move over to the bunks,* VERKOFF *crouches; only* NIKOLAI *remains sitting absolutely erect as the shell explodes directly behind the carriage, a bright white flash behind the window. The walls of the carriage shake violently. The wine falls over, spreading a huge red satin over the tablecloth and dripping down the side.*

NIKOLAI *still sits absolutely erect.*

NIKOLAI (*calmly, seriously*). I can assure you my friend — the modern world is grinding around in this carriage, forcing its way out, coming into existence right here, but any disturbance now does not help.

The loud whine of a second shell descending.

I'd appreciate them being reduced to a minimum.

The shell explodes behind the carriage.

Having to operate surrounded by one's family . . . women and children, is a problem.

Silence. A pause in the bombardment. POLYA *and* EUGENIA *look up from the bunk.*

VERKOFF (*up again, moving sharply around the carriage*). It has stopped for the moment. I must get my inspection over before it starts again.

EUGENIA. What inspection is that Comrade — I thought you'd seen everything you'd come to see.

VERKOFF. The official records of course. Where has our money been going?

EUGENIA (*sharp*). Money?

VERKOFF (*to* NIKOLAI). Until recently we were not getting any replies from you to any of our messages.

NIKOLAI. I was not aware I had replied at all.

VERKOFF (*rifling through the papers on the desk*). How were they all? I haven't seen them for months. How is Varyov, the one with half a moustache, and the little squat ugly one, who always has his flies open, what's his name? At the depot? How have you been getting on with him?

NIKOLAI. I will not conceal facts, I cannot lie to you, I have never been to the depot.

POLYA (*moving across the carriage with the huge volume*). Here is the ledger — all the records we have, comrade, are *here*.

NIKOLAI. I can save you wasting your time.

EUGENIA. Nikolai, you must move from there, the wine's dripping. Why don't you come here?

POLYA *crosses herself as* VERKOFF *flicks the pages of the ledger.*

VERKOFF (*flicking, reading*). 'Progress considerable' . . . 'work satisfactory' . . . 'tolerable progress' . . . This is such an extensive record. (*Strides.*) Places I had forgotten existed. (*He turns a page.*) Places I've never heard of — you have been conscientious Comrade! I must keep this.

EUGENIA (*sharp*). Keep it? Why comrade?

VERKOFF (*sharp smile*). To study, to read at nights. (*Slamming the ledger shut.*)

NIKOLAI. You must show me, you must let me see this, there's been a mistake, I wouldn't wish you to leave here with a false impression.

The gunfire is further off again now, to the side of the carriage.

VERKOFF. I must go — I must leave while I can still get out.

EUGENIA. Yes, Comrade.

VERKOFF (*suddenly really loud, volatile smile, full of relish*). You're an impossible man, Nikolai Semenovitch — what an absurd creation we have here. What an infuriating bastard.

He is moving around, his powerful body seeming to fill the carriage.

And he flaunts it!

He suddenly physically lifts NIKOLAI up off the ground in a single movement and holds him like an enormous doll.

He revels in it. (*Holding him.*) He's got 'made at the Ritz' stamped on his arse. He has! I can feel the crest right here.

NIKOLAI (*calm, great authority*). Put me down, Comrade.

VERKOFF (*carrying straight on*). Hang you up on this peg as an exhibit in your own carriage — an item for future generations to wonder at.

He puts NIKOLAI down and points.

This is the man I made Telephone Examiner, see! I did! (*Moving — very loud.*) I will tell you this my friend, I will never forget you — I will *not* forget you.

NIKOLAI. Somebody else said that to me recently.

VERKOFF. Has that penetrated that thin skull — gone all the way down?

Suddenly his tone changes, as he produces an envelope from his pocket. Serious.

You have new orders now. Their contents will not surprise you, I think. Read them and goodbye.

NIKOLAI (*seeing* VERKOFF *at the door*). I must accompany you, then.

VERKOFF (*to* EUGENIA). He wants to escort me off his 'estate'!

Gunfire in the distance.

Come on then before it's too late.

He goes.

EUGENIA (*loud*). Kolia!

NIKOLAI *turns in the doorway.*

You will be careful, don't say any more — just let him go. Leave him.

Silence.

NIKOLAI. Am I to understand you are giving me instructions . . .?

EUGENIA. No, I'm just warning you. I mean . . . (*Looking down.*)

NIKOLAI. There are obviously things going on here — things you have done, Eugenia, that I do not know about. (*Pause. He looks at her.*) We will discuss them when I return. (*He goes.*)

POLYA (*turns, stares across at* EUGENIA). Eugenia Michailovna. (*Slight pause.*) We did it!

EUGENIA. I don't know . . . I couldn't tell . . .

POLYA (*very excited*). We did, we did!

She physically catches hold of EUGENIA, *squeezing her arm.*

We've *survived* the visit, haven't we . . . we made it work, we've managed it.

EUGENIA. Yes . . .

POLYA. God, every time he looked round, though, the Comrade Commissar, my heart started going like this — I'd rather have been out there where the guns are going off. (*She looks at* EUGENIA.) We did all right, didn't we?

EUGENIA. I hope so . . . (*Suddenly urgent:*) Polya, you'd better go after the Master, I think; we can't take the chance, keep by his side, don't let him explain anything.

POLYA. I'll catch them. (*Running across the carriage to grab her shawl.*) I'll talk non-stop, gabble all the way to the Comrade's car. Nobody else will get a word in . . .

POLYA *goes. EUGENIA and SASHA are alone — the huge red wine stain dripping off the tablecloth, the charred chewed bones of the bird spread across the tablecloth.*

EUGENIA (*urgent*). Have we managed it, Sasha?

SASHA. Mama?

EUGENIA (*moving across the carriage*). The orders? (*Sharp.*) Where are the new orders?

She tears open the envelope.

We're being moved at once to Moscow.

She stares at the paper.

In this carriage. They're sending a locomotive to take us across country at night, next week.

SASHA. What does that mean? Is it bad news? (*Watching her.*) What are they going to do with us?

EUGENIA. That's all it says. (*Very quiet.*) We are going to be met at Moscow. (*She moves across the carriage.*)

SASHA (*worried*). By whom, mama?

EUGENIA (*moving, thinking*). We could have all died on several occasions over these past months because of your father — left to his own devices that might have happened . . . Have we helped him or not? *Did I do the right thing?* (*Surprised at herself.*) Without even asking him! I wish I knew more. Will he ever let me help him again if I have the chance?

SASHA. What do you think will happen in Moscow?

EUGENIA. There is no telling. (*Louder, very strong.*) We mustn't lose the protection of being here Sasha — we must fight to keep it, the protection of his job, I am *not* going back to starving, chewing nuts crawling on one's knees licking the ground.

The sound of gunfire suddenly louder again.

If we lose this, if we're thrown off here, we don't all survive. It's as simple as that. (*She turns sharper.*) What are all those things he talked about . . . grinding around in this carriage . . . modern . . . going to be the highlight of people's lives. What did he mean?

SASHA. I don't know mama.

EUGENIA (*suddenly*). I am going to find out what he's doing. Private space or no private space — I have to know.

She pulls the partition down around his part of the carriage.

Why haven't I done this before. (*Pulling out his drawers.*) What am I hunting for? Will he have written it down. Will it suddenly be here, staring at me. (*She pulls open the cases.*) Tell me — do you feel different, Sasha?

SASHA. What do you mean mama?

EUGENIA. What do you think different means?

EUGENIA is emptying NIKOLAI's drawers and pulling open all his hidden places, her mood excited.

(*Going through his papers. Lightly.*) You know Sasha, my whole adult life, every waking moment seems to have belonged to your papa . . . his world, his determination, the power of his moods.

Another piece of furniture is upturned.

So where is it? What *is* his work Sasha, where's the answer?

SASHA (*watching her from a distance*). I *told* you, I don't know, mama.

EUGENIA (*excited as a flare goes up outside the window*). Oh if only he'd let me do something, your father, — let me do more, *let me.*

She is framed in the light of the flare, sensual energy.

What is happening to us Sasha? What is happening to me?

She turns powerfully towards SASHA.

You don't like me talking like this . . . do you?

SASHA. No, mama, it's alright.

SASHA watches her closely.

EUGENIA. It's because you have never heard it before. Not used to it.

She moves towards him.

You look older, Sasha . . . (*Touching his face.*) Is that hair, a beard, there's a man growing here.

She returns to NIKOLAI's belongings that she has strewn across the stage, she pulls out of the last pigskin case, a camera, bulky film camera, smothered in dust.

Just an old camera! That can't be it. He hasn't used it since we arrived in here. It's covered in dust. (*She blows dust off the camera.*)

SASHA (*staring down at the camera, pushes it with his foot*). Is it possible, do you think, for somebody to have new ideas; somebody who never goes out, never talks about it to anyone. (*Watching her.*) Is that possible? Somebody who can't boil a kettle.

EUGENIA. Who can't boil a kettle?

SASHA. Nobody . . . no-one.

The noise of a shell whistling and screaming down towards them, exploding behind the carriage.

That was very close. They're coming back!

EUGENIA snuffs out some of the candles and pulls SASHA towards her, in the middle of the carriage. Her mood is strangely excited.

EUGENIA. You should remember tonight, Sasha — write it down, we've constantly been on the edge of great events, do you realise, just outside, in Moscow and here on the edge of a battle, so near we've been able to smell them. (*Facing him.*) You will remember it for me? You will?

SASHA. Yes, mama.

EUGENIA. Better than you have been? We both will.

SASHA (*staring at her as the shells begin to fall*). I had a dream about papa earlier today — they tore off his clothes and tied him to a gate in a field and shot him in the head. Do you think we're going to be alright — or are they going to try to kill us (*Staring at her*.).

Pause.

EUGENIA. Do your dreams often come true?

SASHA (*pause*). Yes.

EUGENIA. Let it not be for a while, then. (*Slight smile.*) Not quite yet. (*Touching him.*) You never know we may be lucky.

Fade.

ACT TWO

January, 1924

Scene One

The carriage. Cold, snow outside, the sound of the rail shunting yards. A military band can be heard rehearsing in the distance, stopping and starting, sudden, dissonant, edgy noise; silence, then rapid brassy playing, sometimes ceremonial, sometimes mournful, little spiky bursts sporadically heard through the scene as the musicians rehearse. We do not hear the main tune of the piece they are playing in its entirety.

The carriage is full of steam, clothes hanging up to dry, towels, sheets and other clothes including underwear drying on the bunks, and hanging from the ceiling. There is a much more informal look to the grandness of the carriage, piles of apples, carrots, and potatoes, and other food stored, kitchen utensils hanging up.

POLYA is pouring hot water from a large white china jug. EUGENIA, dressed only in her petticoat, kneeling by an enamel bath, is having her neck washed, steam pouring from the jug as hot water slops into the bath. SASHA, dressed in plain clothes and looking older, is pacing the carriage learning something from a book.

EUGENIA (*mock terror*). Stop it, Polya, stop! It's too hot you're going to boil me alive . . . don't — (*Screams as if scalded.*) Don't! See, I'm going scarlet.

POLYA (*standing over bath*). Don't you dare move till I've finished.

EUGENIA (*shrieking in half-mock pain as water falls onto her arms*). Polya, it hurts, you've never known such pain! For goodness' sake stop . . .

POLYA (*smiles*). You're not going to move till I tell you to.

EUGENIA. I'm going to be late, you realise, terribly late, and I can't be today. (*Getting up, laughing.*) You're going to let me go. (EUGENIA *gets up.*)

POLYA. What's so special about today?

EUGENIA *shivers furiously, her bare shoulders shaking. During the following exchanges, she dresses at a furious rate, pulling on heavy socks and shoes, a plain black skirt, a brown sweater and at the end a long great coat — she is totally transformed.*

SASHA (*pacing up and down the carriage trying desperately to memorise facts*). The Moscow drainage system is now the envy of the world . . . the weight of refuse now being dealt with has increased by six times in as many years. (*He looks at his notes.*) No, four times, . . . cutting through the old foundations of the city . . . the new drainage boasts three million, is it three millions . . .?

Jarring notes of the music outside.

POLYA (*shouts out of the window*). Play in tune, can't you! (*Turning.*) If we have to have a band just out there — why can't they play something a bit better? (*Looking at* EUGENIA.) Why are you rushing so much?

EUGENIA. We start making the new Railway Timetables today — and we have to notify all the regions of the new ticket price, it's going to be a rush to make the deadline.

POLYA (*sharp smile*). Sounds as if it can wait five minutes to me.

EUGENIA. It's an office full of men. I'm the *only* woman there still — so I have to be on time. (*She smiles as she dresses.*) The whole of that building smells of men.

POLYA. Bring some of them back here sometime!

EUGENIA (*fast, smiling*). I'm getting a little less afraid of them. They keep on wanting to know where I come from, really curious about us having the tiny apartment but also being allowed to keep this. (*Indicates the carriage.*) They want all my personal history. I give them a little bit at a time.

POLYA. At the mail sorting office we've got a miserable collection of males at the moment. People just 'passing through' . . . (*She smiles.*) Means a lot of wandering hands! (*Suddenly shrieks with laughter.*) But *nobody* discovered about my reading, you were right, how basic it was, (*Loud:*) deeply basic at the start. Me peering at letters, hopefully throwing them in the right holes, letters going off in all directions. If people had bad handwriting they didn't stand a chance with me!

EUGENIA (*teasing smile*). To think some letters travelling *two thousand* miles and then having to end up with you, Polya!

POLYA. Now I'm really efficient — there isn't enough post to keep me quiet. (*Sombre noise outside the window.*) Shut up!

SASHA (*testing himself*). At the deepest point in the drainage system — how deep is it?

POLYA. Sasha, what on earth are you doing?

SASHA. It's another school dissertation, you could either write about a member of your family — or an aspect of Moscow.

EUGENIA (*incredulous*). And you chose the drains?

SASHA. I deliberately picked an unpopular subject so I was bound to do well — I mean nobody knows anything about the city drainage system and what's found in it, I'm certain none of the teachers do.

EUGENIA (*slight smile*). And what about your family, does nobody know about them?

SASHA (*hesitates for a split second*). No . . .

EUGENIA (*moving very fast, putting her scarf on*). I'll probably kill myself, won't I, going from being that hot into that cold; it's really snowing, but I *will* not be late. Where's my identity card? (*Moving.*) I haven't seen Nikolai for days, it seems . . . (*By the door as she pulls it open.*) Come on! Head down and charge.

She goes out into the cold.

POLYA (*calling after her, as she pushes the door shut*). Don't run in the snow, you'll fall on your arse. (*Loud, smile.*) You will anyway.

POLYA *closes the door, as the band plays a burst of music.*

What an unearthly noise! Why do you think they're rehearsing that sort of music? . . .

SASHA (*by the window, jumping up*). I can't see them. Just out of sight, as usual! There've been a lot of comings and goings . . . soldiers arriving by train last night, cars moving across the shunting yard.

POLYA. Yes, I heard officials from all over the country had been arriving since early this morning. I think something has happened.

POLYA *looks across the width of the carriage at him.*

Now — for you, Sasha. Do you need a wash? Very definitely I should think.

SASHA (*in a strangely adult manner*). Do I?

POLYA. Ages since I washed you. (*Something stops her.*) I don't think I even ought to try now.

SASHA (*pulling his top off, washing himself*). No — I don't think so.

POLYA (*sharp smile*). You used to call for me with that noise, used to bray for me, remember? 'Pol-ya' — that's how it went.

SASHA (*lightly*). You were always slow in answering, too.

POLYA (*doing the call*). 'Pol-yaa make my bed' . . . 'wash me' or in the middle of the night 'I'm afraid, come to me quick, I'm frightened of the demon with three heads.'

SASHA. What demons? I was stupidly over-sensitive. (*Looking at her, slight smile.*) When you came to me, bent over the bed, you had that particular smell — I've always been meaning to tell you.

POLYA (*loud*). What smell?

SASHA. The cheese smell of course — all those days you did it, and it stayed with you.

POLYA (*loud*). Did what?

SASHA (*teasingly*). When you carried cheese — before we found you and brought you to Moscow. You coming to the house from the village wearing that long black dress, so long it scraped the ground, carrying those horrible curd cheeses; that smell was always there.

POLYA (*angry, loud*). You're not trying to tell me, Sasha, it's still there!

SASHA. Maybe.

POLYA (*moving towards him*). You rude little bastard. Come here.

SASHA. You haven't got a hope of catching me anymore.

They circle each other.

POLYA. You know what *you* looked like then, in your little velvet suit and floppy golden curls — a puppet child.

SASHA. I know I looked hideous! Was appallingly spoilt, (*Sharp smile straight at her.*) a very good example of what used to go on.

He moves past her, dodging her, getting to the other end of the carriage.

You know Polya, I still can't dress the way I want to.

POLYA (*mocking*). That's very serious.

SASHA. It is! I manage to hide the expensive gloves and scarf he makes me wear (*Moving*) and when he's not looking I wear this coat (*Indicates a grey coat.*) and then I look exactly the same as everybody else, almost *normal*. (*Very loud.*) Except for those shoes Polya — these terrible English shoes!

POLYA. What's the matter with them?

SASHA. What do you think, it's like they're on fire, they stand out a mile, everyone points at them.

He starts kicking the walls, smashing his feet against the corners, rubbing furiously.

I try to beat them down, I scuff them all the time, on the way to school every day.

POLYA (*laughs*). But they won't change!

SASHA. They're indestructible, they're so bloody strong, nothing I do makes any difference.

He sits, his legs splayed out, mauling the shoes, POLYA *laughs.*

When I have to go for a walk with Father — I keep well behind him.

Suddenly he's imitating his father in the middle of the carriage. POLYA *continues to laugh.*

He looks so ridiculous, strolling along, in that great coat, with a cane, in the shunting yards, among all this rolling stock here, freight being unloaded, and there he is saying good morning to everyone with a wave, like he's greeting farm labourers on his estate.

POLYA (*watching him*). What does it matter? If he thinks like that, I expect they enjoy it.

Pause.

SASHA (*slight smile, suddenly*). I tell people at school, I tell everyone he's an engine driver.

POLYA (*surprised*). You don't do that Sasha! You wouldn't.

SASHA. I do. (*Suddenly serious.*) Do you realise, Polya, he has never done a proper day's work in his life, not one, he's never even contemplated it!

POLYA. Of course he works — he has *his* work.

SASHA. What work? You don't mean *this*, I take it?

POLYA (*defiant*). Yes.

SASHA. The idea we have believed this for so long, haven't admitted what's happening, it's extraordinary — not even questioning it, just whispering about it when at last he's left that corner and gone out.

POLYA. *I* have never whispered about it.

SASHA. If I think of all the days since I was small, of creeping round the place in case I disturbed him . . . (*Loud:*) The truth is, and we've got to face it, Polya — (*Pointing at* NIKOLAI's *corner.*) this is all useless, utterly useless — he's just a self-deluding old man.

POLYA (*shocked*). Sasha . . . (*Then sharply.*) He's not that old for a start!

SASHA (*incisively*). He contributes nothing, he receives money from the state for another purpose entirely, he has official duties which he ignores completely (*Loud:*) absolutely totally . . . That's the part I can't forgive; he takes the money which isn't his and then plays with his little pieces in a corner.

POLYA. Just plays, does he!

SASHA. He can't even fit these scraps together.

POLYA (*watching* SASHA's *sharp, piercing stare*). I had no idea you were growing into such a nasty young . . .

SASHA. No, no, listen. (*Very incisive, trying to persuade her.*) Examine the facts Polya, please, for the first time in your life, this is very important. (*Moving, a commanding tone.*) It is not just that we have never seen him consult a single technical journal, or even use a single technical term when he's talking . . .

POLYA (*sharp*). So?

SASHA. We are being asked to believe that someone obsessed by eating off the right silver plate, using the right silver fish fork, is doing something of significance, is involved in technological progress!

POLYA (*defiant*). Yes!

SASHA (*continuing straight on*). It is a ludicrous proposition, obviously preposterous — it doesn't stand up to a moment's analysis. I mean he can't even boil a kettle. (*Loud.*) He can't even boil a bloody kettle, Polya.

POLYA. Nor could you till recently. (*Watching him.*)

SASHA. He told me what he was doing.

POLYA. He did?

SASHA. At the time you asked me I still remembered — but now I've long forgotten. He is a dilettante, Polya, a perfect instance of somebody refusing to change, placing his own needs above everybody else's — his individualism destroys others. I am *ashamed*, Polya, to be seen with him, to be associated with him in any way.

POLYA (*moving across*). You've got to stop this Sasha — you will stop it or I'll make you.

SASHA. Deny it if you can . . . you know you can't.

POLYA. Look at you. (*Catching hold of him, catching hold of his legs.*) Burrowing away to try to be as ordinary as possible.

SASHA (*incisive*). And what's more you still can't tear yourself away, can you — you can't bring yourself to leave despite having a room of your own now. (*Loud.*) You still come back for more — and he goes on exploiting you just the same.

POLYA (*loud, close*). Don't you start patronising me — give me lectures about what I should be doing. (*Very loud.*) It's my affair, don't you dare tell me what to do — if you ever talk to me like that again . . .

POLYA *seizes the fur coat* SASHA *does not wear anymore. The band plays outside.*

SASHA. I am just explaining the situation to you, Polya.

POLYA (*pinning him to the wall*). What a crude little animal you're turning out to be — afraid to stand out in a crowd are we?

She starts forcing him into the fur coat.

We'll see to that!

SASHA *tries to resist. They grapple by the window,* POLYA *winning. She gets the coat half on him, forcing his arms above his head.*

NIKOLAI *enters.* POLYA *has* SASHA *pinned against the wall.*

NIKOLAI *stands poised in the doorway in his fur coat, fur hat, and stick. He removes his hat, staring past them into the carriage.*

NIKOLAI. Is the place ready for me again? The washing is still out. (*He moves into the carriage.*) Bring me my tea, Polya, my tea and notes, my gloves need to dry . . .

NIKOLAI hands POLYA his wet gloves, puts his stick on the table, and sits in the chair that is always reserved for him. SASHA leans against the wall watching POLYA run around.

I have news. I have sent off through the emergency railway messenger service for a special delivery of my work — it is an unexpected bonus of this job, which is proving more and more useful . . .

SASHA and POLYA exchange looks. NIKOLAI smiles. Waving a paper.

I hear the special delivery should be arriving at any moment. (*He turns.*) Where is the tea?

POLYA (*sharp*). All right.

SASHA (*watching*). I have to write a dissertation, Papa, I was going to write about this city — but now I think I might write about an aspect of my family. (*Pause.*)

POLYA (*looking up, sharply, pause*). You wouldn't dare?

She suddenly moves over and starts bustling him out of the doors in his reluctant fur coat.

SASHA (*startled*). What are you doing?

POLYA. Sasha was just leaving, wasn't he? He's started to wear his old clothes again hasn't he?

She pushes a startled SASHA out of the door, calling after him.

Try taking that off — and you'll freeze to death before you get to school!

She pushes the door shut. The band is still rehearsing outside.

NIKOLAI. He is working hard, he is doing well at school.

POLYA. Who told you that?

NIKOLAI. He did of course. He wouldn't lie to me. (*Pause.*)

POLYA. He's very eager to fit in. (*Quiet.*) He'd do almost anything for that.

NIKOLAI (*suddenly*). Eugenia! I saw her just now, hurrying along the bridge. I must tell her how well she looks, years younger, at least ten. (*Lightly.*) You must remind me to tell her, Polya — but she has no need to work.

POLYA. She wants to.

NIKOLAI. She insists on doing a job! It is so utterly unnecessary — Polya, why are you so slow today?

POLYA (*boiling kettle, making tea, loud*). Slow — I'm not being slow!

NIKOLAI (*lightly*). You know at the moment there is only one mechanism that I do not fully understand — (*He smiles.*) that is the one that releases ideas, causes them to take shape. (*Charming smile.*) It is becoming almost embarrassing how many ideas I have at the moment, I am being bombarded by them. Why now specially? (*Loud:*) Come on tea!

POLYA. Stop it. (*Loud:*) You don't yell for it anymore, remember you wait for it now.

NIKOLAI. It seems I have little choice. Nevertheless hurry! I have a lot to do. (*Slight pause.*) I have just completed my first task, Polya. (*Calmly.*) I have made moving pictures talk. I have solved the problem of amplification.

POLYA (*swinging round*). I thought so . . . I knew it! I guessed it was something like that, when we found the camera under here. (*Banging the drawer.*)

NIKOLAI. I am having some lenses made — the express order for the northern railway.

POLYA (*excited*). Lenses! . . . Are they ready?

NIKOLAI (*smiling, calmly*). I have told them I need the equipment urgently to record the erection of more telephone poles for posterity. Even so, they've been extremely difficult to obtain. When the lenses arrive I will be able to make some film and record the sound at the same time, it will be complete. (*Pause.*) And I am the first — I hope!

POLYA. You will have done it, Nikolai! (*Correcting herself:*) Nikolai Semenovitch. You will have done it!

NIKOLAI (*calmly*). The world has been working on two approaches, racing together, sound on phonograph records matched to keep pace with the image, and sound printed directly on film — I have achieved the second, which is undoubtedly the best and where the future lies.

POLYA (*moving excitedly*). So, when are they coming? The emergency delivery. When can we start?

NIKOLAI. Very soon. (*Calmly, simply:*) The effect naturally will be quite devastating. For better or worse it will revolutionise popular entertainment.

POLYA. Yes!

NIKOLAI. More importantly, it will alter communications — people will be able to talk to a huge audience out of the cinema screen, in a country of this size! Even quite complex ideas and information can now be spread across the continent. (*Pause, he smiles.*) I don't want to spend my time making grandiose claims, Polya — nothing could be more tiresome, nor more vulgar; but as you know, I *never* exaggerate.

POLYA. Once or twice, it has been known.

NIKOLAI. Absolutely wrong — it has never been known.

POLYA (*full of energy*). Where's it going to happen?

NIKOLAI. Here of course — you will all be photographed in this carriage. (*Lightly.*) The fact that the first sound film in the world will be recorded in the railway shunting yards outside Moscow . . . is not my fault.

POLYA (*loud*). You mean *us* on the screen — *me*! (*Suddenly, tone changing.*) I am not singing any of those appalling songs you made me sing — I don't sing well enough for that for a start. If I really have to sing — it's going to be a song of my choice. (*She moves.*) I might read a passage from a book.

(*Self-mocking smile.*) Whatever shows me off to my best advantage.

NIKOLAI. It will be a considerable shock to the outside world, that this is coming not out of California, or Paris, or even London, but out of here — coming out of the supposed darkness of this country.

POLYA (*moving backwards and forwards, excited, spirited smile*). Will our name be on it? Will mine? In the programme . . . "Polya, former domestic servant, second chambermaid, now a sorting clerk in the postal service, *recites.*" Me, flickering across the screen, thirty feet high!

She mimics flickering, jagged, movement across the screen. We suddenly see her as she would look on the screen.

All over the world. *My* voice squeaking out.

NIKOLAI. You may well become the best remembered postal clerk in Russia. A celebrity, someone people will want to meet. (*He smiles.*) I am confident nobody will realise it is a railway carriage — they will all assume it is a suite at the Hermitage if photographed correctly, so a semblance of dignity will be preserved, despite the farcical conditions in which history is being made.

POLYA *turns to face him.*

POLYA. It is exciting Nikolai Semenovitch!

NIKOLAI. Yes. Important as it is, and easily graspable for the general public though it is, it is comparatively trivial compared to what is to follow. (*He begins to move.*) There is much to do, I have made considerable progress on two other ideas, I need you for many more hours . . . to redraw my diagrams, you're much neater than I am, to prepare future model work (*He paces.*) — there is a limit I can use railway labour.

POLYA (*stops, her tone changes, firm*). No! I told you I can only fit you in after work, and I can't always go on as late as you want. (*Looking straight at him.*) I often won't be able to.

Pause. NIKOLAI *looks at her.*

NIKOLAI. You realise technological progress is being held up,

Polya, because you have to sort the grubby letters in the postal depot . . . major advances, may be halted just . . .

POLYA. I have explained to you many times why, and you still . . .

NIKOLAI (*cutting her off*). My God, Polya! — how can you be so wilful and stupid.

POLYA. Quite easily, I'm not going to work for you when I don't want to, only when I choose. (*Suddenly loud:*) Do you ever wonder why I stay, why I come back, time after time? No, you haven't, have you! Probably never crossed your mind.

Loud interrupted burst of band rehearsal outside, with sudden drumming, which ends as suddenly as it started.

(*Loudly, continuing as the band plays.*) And how I've never doubted your work. Never! Though I've been kept in almost total ignorance the whole time.

NIKOLAI. Why on earth should you have ever doubted it?

POLYA. Why!

NIKOLAI (*pacing too, they are both excited*). I can't believe we're wasting time with this! . . . I can't negotiate with you, Polya, there's too much to think about. (*He suddenly stops; his tone changes.*) I will continue your reading lessons, I will complete your studies, make sure you can read fluently.

POLYA (*furious, fiery*). I've been able to read for ages! Books this thick! You mean you haven't noticed that? (*Loud:*) No wonder you haven't mentioned it! (*Loud, moving:*) I could become a professor at a university and you still wouldn't see any difference.

NIKOLAI. I never thought you'd become so temperamental, Polya — so ridiculously pleased with yourself for some reason — and at such an inappropriate time!

POLYA. Me! I *am* — I'm being temperamental? (*She stops, loud:*) Why shouldn't I be anyway!

NIKOLAI *suddenly stops in the middle of the stage.*

NIKOLAI. I will do it without you! This time I will! Why should

I wait, for heaven's sake? (*Pause.*) I can't do it without you. There're certain things I cannot do. A few. (*Pause.*) How do you want me to ask you?

POLYA (*looking at him*). We'll do it together. (*Sharp:*) All right. But on my terms — (*Slight smile.*) — you're not paying me after all.

NIKOLAI. If I could explain to you what there is at stake — it is far more than talking film.

POLYA. Why don't you try telling me? Take the risk, I might even surprise you . . .

NIKOLAI. It is too technical for you.

He moves the width of the carriage; a solitary bell has started clanging in the distance.

(*Sharp, as he moves:*) I'm working on ways of advancing the use of wireless, making it far more accessible, ideas that have major implications for industry, and also, a by-product of the same idea, help the deaf . . .

Suddenly the band who have been making the noise outside the carriage break into the full, uninterrupted tune of the piece they have been rehearsing. It is a loud, stirring, but mournful funeral march. Behind the noise we can now hear many more bells clanging out.

Both NIKOLAI and POLYA turn towards the windows; a moment's silence as they are surprised by the noise. They are still.

My God what a noise. What's that for? Why can't they do that somewhere else?

POLYA (*by the window, loud*). They seem to have got it right at last. (*Calling out:*) About bloody time! (*She turns.*) It's a funeral march. Who do you think can have died?

Pause. The band plays the march. NIKOLAI draws the blinds down on the windows of the carriage as the bells rasp out.

NIKOLAI (*turning towards her*). Polya — we must to work now.

Blackout.

Scene Two

The music of the band and the rasping, tumultuous bells break into the noise of other trains moving round the carriage, clanking close; the sound of major movements, loud noises, then silence.

SASHA, *now back in his grey coat, enters the darkened carriage. In the middle of the carriage, standing where the bath was, is a large unopened packing case.*

SASHA *approaches it; he is unaware there is a figure sitting in the dark at the end of the carriage.*

SASHA (*starts, lets out a cry*). Comrade — I didn't see you, I didn't know we were expecting you.

VERKOFF *remains seated in the dark.*

VERKOFF. You weren't. (*Staring across.*) I must see your father at once, it is exceptionally urgent.

SASHA. My father's not here, as you can see.

VERKOFF. Where is he?

SASHA. I don't know, Comrade.

VERKOFF (*loud*). You have to know.

He gets up. His clothes are splashed with mud.

What happened to my letter? It must have arrived. (*Loud.*) It *has* arrived hasn't it?

SASHA. I am sure it has Comrade . . . my father tends to get a little behind with his correspondence — because he often throws letters away, but he will get better I assure you.

VERKOFF (*shouts*). You're not telling me he hasn't read it. (*Straight at him.*) Has he read it or not?

SASHA. I don't know, Comrade.

VERKOFF. You better find out.

A pale, blank stare from SASHA.

Who's been here?

SASHA. How do you mean?

VERKOFF. Has anybody visited here in the past weeks — been

poking around, looking at things, asking you questions?

SASHA. I don't think so, Comrade.

VERKOFF (*sharp*). Don't look away like that — look at me, come on tell me, what did they say? What did they want?

SASHA (*startled by his intensity*). Nothing . . . there was nobody here, Comrade.

VERKOFF. Don't you lie to me. (*Half mock-threatening, half-real:*) It can have terrifying consequences, do you understand me? (*Pause, slight smile.*) You *should* be afraid of me now.

SASHA. You know I'd tell you at once — if there was anything to tell.

VERKOFF. We shall see. (*He turns towards the packing case.*) What is this?

SASHA. That? (*Thinking quickly.*) Railway business, some supplies my father was just checking on. He's been waiting for them since just before the night Comrade Lenin died.

VERKOFF (*pushing the case*). Don't be ridiculous, this is not railway supplies. (*Loud:*) What did I just tell you?

He looks around for something to open it with, then picks up one of NIKOLAI's sticks and prises the top off.

SASHA. He talks more and more railway business, Comrade . . .

VERKOFF (*getting the top off, looking down inside, picking one of the lenses up gingerly*). So this is what he's been up to! (*Looking at the clutter of NIKOLAI's work things.*) I knew I was right about him — sometimes I wondered, I admit. But I knew I was right!

SASHA. Just a hobby, just a game of his.

VERKOFF. Shut up, be *quiet*. Stand over there where I can see you. Go on. (*Looking down at work things.*) I should have moved him earlier! (*Suddenly pointing, loud.*) Don't forget it was me who put you here. (*Loud:*) Never forget that!

SASHA. Yes, Comrade — I know.

VERKOFF (*moving, looking at everything*). When I first saw you all, together, that first day in the country, standing in here, like relics from some Imperial Ball but looking pale and bloody terrified. Afraid to touch the sides in case you caught something.

SASHA (*hesitates, unsure of* VERKOFF's *tone*): . . . Yes, Comrade.

VERKOFF (*moving, loud*). I won't meet someone like your father again — the Jew so obsessed with his personal appearance, wrapping himself in the finest of everything, incapable of any form of political discussion, and then (*Looking down into the packing case.*) look at this! (*Loud.*) I *knew* I was correct about him!

SASHA (*suddenly*). I don't think you are correct about him, Comrade. My father is getting better. I know he's been neglectful, deviant, sometimes he's made me almost die of shame, but he will do his job, it takes a long time with him — to change him, to teach him.

VERKOFF (*loud*). You're going to teach him are you! (*Pause, he turns.*) You realise what I've done?

SASHA. Yes.

VERKOFF. What do you mean 'yes'? You don't have to give a blind sycophantic yelp to everything I say.

SASHA (*pauses*). Yes, Comrade.

VERKOFF (*suddenly exuberantly, lightly*). What I've done is incredibly important.

SASHA. I know.

VERKOFF. My job — the job I am doing — people could look at in years to come and see what looks like simple bureaucratic organisation, railways, telephone exchanges, drains, it might seem tedious, routine, mere clockwork — in truth the work was *fantastic*. You know why?

SASHA. Why, Comrade?

VERKOFF. Because I used my imagination — in a thousand different opportunities, small things, and major ones, I made some surprising decisions — every case was different, every case on its merits. (*He smiles.*) It was an inspired burst of planning.

SASHA. Yes I know — I've been forced to miss so much, having been away in the country so long, I'm only just catching up.

VERKOFF (*wry smile*). And who is going to remember an obscure official, tell me — one of the ministers of labour, of public works.

SASHA. They will, Comrade.

VERKOFF (*lightly*). People will always remember the obvious figures, naturally — everyone else gets bludgeoned onto the sidelines. Forgotten! (*Slight smile.*) But that is not the way things actually happen at the time. They will never realise what I did! That the department is spectacularly successful. Does it matter? It matters like hell to me at the moment. (*Pause. Suddenly sharp.*) And I can assure you I intend to keep it as long as possible. I'm certainly not done yet!

Pause. SASHA stares at him.

What a blank look that is. (*Pause.*) Your ignorance frightens me, boy. (*Suddenly, tone changing.*) Why am I here anyway? This is just one small part of my department, one tiny corner, why am I wasting my time with a child?

SASHA. Yes, Comrade.

VERKOFF *stares at the pale face of the teenage boy.*

VERKOFF. You're as bad as them do you know that — you have to be told what you ought to think, have to be absolutely sure what the correct thing to say is before you dare open your mouth.

SASHA *stares at him.*

The physical effort required to talk to people who only deal in certainties, you have no idea! It's so bloody tiring! (*Pulling him closer.*) Come here — so who was it that came here, come on, tell me, I know somebody was.

SASHA. No. They haven't, I promise you.

VERKOFF (*slight smile*). Just checking, I'm not at all sure I believe you. (*Pause, staring at the boy.*) The furniture has suddenly been changed in my office.

SASHA. Has it, Comrade — is it an improvement?

VERKOFF (*shrewd look*). We shall see . . . now listen to me carefully, so there is no possibility of error, I'm instructing you to leave the country — and this instruction has to be obeyed in the next few days!

SASHA (*stunned*). Leave the country? What do you mean in the next few days?

VERKOFF. That's what you have to do.

He scrawls a one-line note on a scrap of paper.

SASHA. Has papa been that negligent? I told you he will get better — he will do his duties . . .

VERKOFF (*lightly*). I will put it very simply so it can be intelligible even to you — it is a small matter of life and death.

SASHA. Life and death?

VERKOFF. For all of you.

SASHA. All of us?

VERKOFF. Those are my orders to you. And find that letter! (*He moves.*) If you ever get to the border that letter might make it a great deal easier for you to leave. (*Pause.*) Or it might not.

SASHA (*worried*). That isn't very clear, Comrade, if I may say so . . .

VERKOFF. I must go! I have so many people to see. (*Suddenly looking down at his clothes, at the door.*) Good God, I'm covered in mud, I never noticed, why didn't you tell me? Didn't you see? (*Sharp smile.*) Because it's a form of uniform you never noticed! (*As he goes:*) You know what you have to do, you have to try and leave.

He goes.

SASHA (*moving over to the door, calling after him*). But he won't go — he won't go until he's finished his work, Comrade. (*Pause, anger rising.*) Don't you understand, he won't leave until he's finished his crazy work — he's under the impression he's doing something important. (*Loud shouts, close by the door.*) What am *I* meant to do — he won't listen to me. He can't be made to stop don't you realise? He won't stop his 'work' don't you see! (*Turning back into the carriage.*) How can I do anything? . . .

He breaks off, staring at the box in the middle of the carriage. He lifts off the top prised open by VERKOFF, *and lets it drop onto the floor.*

I think whatever these are . . .

He dips his hands in and lifts up a glass lens wrapped in straw, so the glass catches the light, flashes out brightly.

Whatever they happen to be — they will have to go.

He drops the lens back onto the others in the box, making a clanking noise.

Can I do it? (*Staring into the box.*) It has to be good enough to *stop* him.

He picks up a hammer and a long knife from among the equipment lying in his father's corner; he moves back to the box; he lifts one of the lenses again and runs the top of the knife down it, scratching its surface. Then he knocks the lens with a clean, sharp hit from the hammer. It splits in two.

Very pale, he stands with the hammer and a long metal bar taken from the side, staring down into the box. He chooses to do it with the hammer. Suddenly he swings it again and again into the box. The hammer goes up above his head, coming down with startling ferocity with each blow.

Must destroy it so he can't start up again — no *chance* of him trying to start again. It mustn't mean we have to stay even longer. (*Loud:*) Has to go!

A ferocious burst of destruction as he pummels the contents of the box.

SASHA *hears the sound of them approaching,* POLYA's *voice and laughter.*

(*Looking around him very fast.*) Better do something else . . .

SASHA *runs round the length of the carriage upturning furniture, turning drawers out, tearing sheets down the middle with the long knife, slashing some of the chairs, the beds. Just before* POLYA *enters he begins to try to scratch some graffiti — a slogan on the ornamental panelling — but drops the knife and kicks it under the bunk, as* POLYA *reaches the door. He leans against the wall very still, looking pale.* POLYA *enters, stares at the destruction.*

POLYA (*shocked, quiet*). Sasha — what on earth has happened?

SASHA *stares from the far end of the carriage.*

SASHA. There's been an attack — some people got in . . . and they've done this —

POLYA *moves slowly into the carriage.*

POLYA. Who were they? (*Pause.*) I mean they've torn the place apart, Sasha.

SASHA. I've just come back . . . I just found it, now.

POLYA (*suddenly looking at him, moving close to him*). Are you all right — not hurt, Sasha, love? (*Touching him.*) They didn't do anything to you, didn't attack you . . .

SASHA (*as she touches his face*). I just missed them . . .

POLYA. No, nothing . . .

She withdraws, disappointed at herself for showing such warm feelings towards him.

You were very lucky.

She looks across the carriage.

Who would have wanted to attack here?

SASHA. He may have enemies, he's a target now . . . (*Suddenly:*) The Commissar of Labour came — just now — he saw it, he couldn't stay, he left this note, Polya.

POLYA (*looks down at the shattered glass and equipment in the box*). Oh my God not here, too.

She picks up a broken lens.

SASHA. No point doing that — it won't work. You can't do anything.

POLYA (*looking very pale, suddenly moving*). Your father — what will he do? He's just coming, he's waited months for these. It's so *important*. He could kill people for this. (*Quiet:*) So could I. (*Sharp:*) Why did they come just now, how did they *know* this was here? (*Moving.*) What can we do to lessen . . .

NIKOLAI *enters with* EUGENIA. *He immediately stops in the door, stock still.*

NIKOLAI. What have you two been doing?

EUGENIA (*staring around her*). Oh no, Sasha. (*Sharp:*) Who's done this?

POLYA. Nikolai Semenovitch prepare yourself . . . There's been an attack as you can see, and . . . (*She stops.*)

SASHA (*quiet*). There's also a note from the Commissar of Labour telling us to leave.

He holds it out and EUGENIA *takes it.*

Silence.

NIKOLAI (*standing in the doorway pointing at the packing case with his stick, calmly*). Are they all broken?

POLYA. Yes, they're broken.

NIKOLAI (*calmly*). Not just the lenses. All of it?

POLYA. All of it.

Pause.

NIKOLAI (*voice very precise, deadly calm*). I don't think that will prove too much of a problem.

Slight pause.

All of them smashed, all broken — it doesn't present too much of a problem, no . . .

Pause, voice rising, suddenly dangerous.

It just means I will not be able to finish my work.

He is very still, but the rage is beginning to pass through his body.

Those who did this have to be found — they will have to be dealt with in the only way that is fitting . . .

Pause. They all stare at him.

They will have to be hunted down wherever they have chosen to hide themselves and be destroyed.

EUGENIA (*moving, not daring to go too close to him*). Nikolai . . . I know . . . what's happened is a terrible shock, (*Holding* VERKOFF's *note.*) but there's also this.

NIKOLAI (*cutting her off, suddenly the shout comes out*). My God, why do people do such things — have this desire to smash and tear up anything they don't understand — this compulsion to stamp all over it. I hope they realise I am capable of just as much and *more*. I can be as violent as they are and more effective. They will be found. They will be made to face what they have done, they've tried to extinguish — four years' work — waste all the effort that has been going on in here. Kill it.

POLYA. Maybe we can . . . (*Looking at the broken pieces.*)

NIKOLAI. I can assure you — they will not succeed. I will not let them succeed.

Pause.

EUGENIA. My love, I'm not sure we can afford to ignore this note from the Commissar of Labour, instructing us to leave the country; he says he sent us a letter . . .

NIKOLAI *takes the note, but continues to pace. Pause.*

NIKOLAI. I will do it still. That is both a promise and a warning and nothing can stop that now.

Pause. A quick glance at the note.

And there is no question of me fleeing this country. (*At the door.*) Whoever did this didn't realise one thing, I can still manage to do it.

He goes. Both women move back and forth across the carriage automatically, picking up the shattered pieces, trying to patch the torn interior of the carriage together.

EUGENIA. Nikolai . . . (*Staring at the mess.*) I knew something from the outside would come bursting in here one day, all the different things moving round us in this shunting yard. I'm almost surprised it's nothing worse.

POLYA (*staring at the broken equipment*). It's bad enough. But he will find a way. Whoever tried to stop him, won't.

SASHA *stares from the wall.*

EUGENIA (*loud, suddenly*). Polya — this could just be a taste of what is to come — do we try to stay or do we leave?

POLYA. I don't know.

EUGENIA. Even if we get to the border we might have to stay there for weeks and if anything went *wrong* there . . . (*Her voice falls off.*) No second chances. (*Turns, determined.*) We have to find that letter from the Minister of Labour before there are any official changes, we have to use it . . . perhaps we could use a health reason. (*She is moving up and down.*) If we decide to leave — I heard people were doing that — (*Pause.*) we could say something like mine or Sasha's health is unlikely to stand up to another winter . . .

POLYA (*smiles*). It's only spring now.

EUGENIA (*moving*). I know!

POLYA. It might work . . .

EUGENIA. Nikolai would never agree of course.

POLYA. I could use your travel permits, travel with you, some of the way to the border, and then move down south, get away from the trouble here, find a new job!

EUGENIA (*looking up*). You might be better off leaving at once — the danger may be getting contagious, being with us.

Slight pause.

POLYA. Not yet.

EUGENIA. I don't know, Polya, I would never forgive myself if something happened to you because of us.

POLYA (*turning*). It will be fine . . .

EUGENIA. Maybe Nikolai, to finish his work, can get supplies from abroad. I know so little about it.

POLYA. You've got to *tell* him, Eugenia, whatever you decide . . . it's your future too.

EUGENIA (*turning, unsure*). It may not matter — our extraordinary luck will probably hold.

SASHA (*watching them*). Polya should stay with us as long as possible.

POLYA. You want that now, do you? (*Pause.*) What for? Protection?

SASHA. Advice . . . We'll need your advice.

POLYA (*advancing towards him*). Really? The problem is I don't like you very much at the moment, Sasha. Remember?

SASHA. That doesn't matter now.

POLYA (*staring at him, then touching his hair*). Speak for yourself.

Blackout.

Scene Three

The carriage at the border — the sound of movement, of trains passing very close, loud braking noises, the wrenching of metal, the feeling of large important movements of people, of machines, in the night. Voices calling sporadically in the distance, phones ringing and stopping and ringing again, a sense of contained chaos. The noise punctuated by bouts of silence.

The sounds continue to erupt again from time to time, close to them, brushing right up to them, near the window.

SASHA, EUGENIA, POLYA and NIKOLAI all together in the carriage. It is night, the packing cases have been pushed back into a corner — the pigskin luggage is splayed all over the carriage half open, but most of their possessions are still around the carriage. EUGENIA is moving around with their clothes, POLYA lifts the blind of one of the windows to stare out, a passing light stabs through at them and is gone. Their mood is tense but excited, NIKOLAI sits calmly in the middle of them all.

POLYA pulls the blind right up.

EUGENIA. What can you see, Polya?

POLYA. Just an old woman holding a fluffy dog out of another train window so it can pee.

SASHA (*by the other window*). Just blackness here; there's that ringing all the time — I can't see from where. (*Jumping up by the window, climbing up.*) I can just see the corner of something, a shape. (*Excited smile.*) As usual it's just out of sight — another hundred yards and we'd have a much better view!

Incessant ringing in the distance.

POLYA. It's one of the telephones ringing in the Guard posts by the other platforms — nobody ever seems to answer it.

EUGENIA. We've got here anyway — I never thought we'd do it, reach the border. (*She turns.*) We probably shouldn't have given our passes to those young soldiers — we should have kept them with us, not given them too long a look.

POLYA. They were friendly enough.

NIKOLAI (*lightly*). They will be no problem, they have seen I am with you. They are just clearing a path so they can move us across the border. The next train that has been approved to go through — we will be joined up to that one.

POLYA (*sharp smile*). You've always hated to queue anyway! (*She moves.*) There're so many trains here, going back in all directions, I'm spoiled for choice, which one I take to the south.

EUGENIA (*quietly*). I keep thinking you ought to have got off earlier, Polya . . .

NIKOLAI. We will be allowed to stay in this until they turn it round across the border. (*Indicates the carriage.*) The last we'll see of this won't be until we're in Poland, (*Quiet:*) where we will drink the champagne, (*Indicates the champagne.*) one of the few bottles left. (*Pause.*) When I return in a few weeks I will of course reclaim the carriage.

EUGENIA (*moving*). You will remember, Nikolai, you're not going to talk about your work to them — or even much about your job for the government. The less we say the better — we're not going to tell the *whole* truth.

NIKOLAI (*calm*). I remember, yes.

EUGENIA. And we still haven't found that letter from the Minister of Labour.

POLYA (*sharp, by the window, the noise close to them*). Did you see they were letting no one stay on the platform — people sitting and sleeping on the bank along the line for about three miles.

EUGENIA. And they seemed to have dropped their belongings everywhere, all over the rails, a lot of people do it on purpose I think — getting rid of valuables they think they better not risk.

POLYA (*climbing up by the window, straining to see*). Yes, you can just see back there, on that huge pile of coal by the line. It's shining with all the things they've thrown out of the windows, people's silver . . .

EUGENIA. Thank God we got rid of ours, and the firearms, too.

NIKOLAI *is sitting calmly in the middle.*

POLYA (*to* SASHA). Are you going to do well — do what you have to do?

SASHA. I think so.

EUGENIA (*nervous smile*). Does he look pale enough, do you think?

POLYA. His cheeks are blooming, of course — (*To* SASHA:) Try to make you look ill and you seem to get healthier by the minute, never seen you look so well! Come on, let's hear you cough, harder, *cough.*

SASHA. I am coughing!

NIKOLAI (*quiet*). That won't be necessary.

POLYA (*touching* SASHA). I haven't liked you for many months you know, not until the last few days.

SASHA. Polya — there's something I did, I'll have to tell you one day.

The door opens, GUARD 1 *and* GUARD 2 *enter.*

They are dressed in heavy coats, new uniforms, very bulky in the confined space. They look totally different, almost unrecognisable, older, more haggard. The small, stocky GUARD 2 *much less exuberant, much more deferential to the younger* GUARD 1, *who is more efficient, confident, authoritative. They show no sign of recognising* NIKOLAI, *their manner brisk from having had to process so many people.*

GUARD 1 (*looking at his clipboard, then at the passengers grouped at one end of the carriage*). These your papers here ... Nikolai Pesiakoff ...

NIKOLAI. Yes ...

For the first time his manner is unsure, not certain how to dissemble.

As you can see they are clear, everything is self-explanatory, there is no problem.

GUARD 1 (*looking down at the papers*). Destination London, via

Berlin . . . that certainly is clear enough. Three travel permits.

EUGENIA (*sharp*). Yes!

GUARD 1 (*looks up at* POLYA). What are you doing here?

POLYA. I'm not staying with them. I'm just a friend, I am here to change trains.

NIKOLAI (*suddenly looking straight at the* GUARDS). What are your names?

GUARD 1. Our names? That need not concern you. (*Looking at him.*) Allow us to ask the questions.

NIKOLAI. I am almost certain, I don't think I'm wrong, we have met before. At another station, much smaller than this one, somewhere along that vast bleak stretch of the northern railway, which at one time I had to move up and down.

GUARD 1 (*calmly*). I can assure you we have never met before. (*Moving with the papers.*) Now what are your reasons for wishing to travel outside the country, comrade?

EUGENIA. The reasons are on our papers. It's all set down, we told the other guards.

GUARD 1 (*calmly*). I know what your papers say — but I want to hear your version. (*Staring at them.*) It's our normal procedure.

NIKOLAI. You want me to tell you? (*Pause.*) The reasons we are leaving, I mean we're travelling . . . I am escorting my family out of the country because . . . (*He stops.*) we have obtained permission because . . . (*He falters, finding it difficult to lie.*) because my son's health is . . . because when, if the winter is, when the winter . . . (*He stops.*)

EUGENIA. My husband has had a long journey, please remember.

NIKOLAI. Because my son must . . .

SASHA. Papa, I will tell them.

NIKOLAI. No! (*Pause.*) I am not going to go on with this, it is an unbelievable excuse, I am not going to lie to you, I have not had enough practice for one thing and do it poorly, and it insults your intelligence.

He looks straight at the GUARDS.

I am Nikolai Pesiakoff. I am taking my family across the border and then I will be returning almost immediately — in time we will all return I assure you. I am appointed the Telephone Examiner of the northern district by Commissar of Labour Alexei Verkoff — this carriage has been made available for my use.

Pause. They are all watching him.

More importantly I have some vital work to complete which should prove of some use. (*Pause.*) I will be ordering some new components and equipment from abroad and returning, so you see you have merely to rubber stamp our permits. It is all a formality. Moreover, I am certain you must remember this now, I recommended you two for promotion when we stumbled across each other, in exchange for some help you gave me in finding some equipment for my work. (*He smiles.*) It happens to be one of the few official letters I ever wrote. You will remember this all now taking place I am sure, in the northern district — (*He smiles straight at them.*) so although it appears to be a coincidence that we find each other, it is in fact only a partial one.

Silence. The GUARDS *are watching him.*

GUARD 1. I have been very patient . . .

GUARD 2. You are trying to tell us you were the Telephone Surveyor of the Northern Railway.

NIKOLAI. Of course.

GUARD 2 (*loud*). That is not true.

GUARD 1 (*moving around the carriage, looking at everything, manner methodical, but sharp*). It is certainly not true. I did indeed meet him. I can't remember it all, it was some time ago and a great deal has happened since then, but one thing I know for certain, he could have been nothing like you.

GUARD 2. I remember him a bit, he arrived out of the night, and he was nothing like you, (*Sharp, party manner.*) a very conscientious official. *Punctillious.*

NIKOLAI (*calmly*). That person was I — it seems odd that it is
you who look different not me, but I recognise you. (*Lightly.*)
I recommended you for a position of increased responsibility.
It appears to have worked almost too well.

GUARD 2 (*loud*). You're not him, all right? No influence was
used in getting us where we are, either, I can tell you.

He begins a search of the carriage.

EUGENIA (*sharp*). What's he doing?

NIKOLAI. Who do you think I am then? How else could I
possibly be in this — (*Indicating the carriage.*) — and got it
joined to a train coming to the border?

GUARD 1 (*very incisive; suddenly we see how overworked and
tense he is*). My God — don't waste my time, we have people
arriving here in all sorts of ways, all forms of transport, having
bribed, cajoled, sometimes killed, to get here — even just to get
themselves a compartment to themselves. (*As* GUARD 2
searches.) And we have to deal with them all. People being
arrogant or worse, obsequious, people trying to squeeze
through holes that haven't been plugged, before it's too late.
Pushing, refusing to wait, shouting out and complaining all
night, grabbing hold of your arm, poking you in the face with
their sticks.

GUARD 2. Last night somebody shouted at me — what I thought
was a frail old man — he screamed, 'I don't expect you've ever
seen a golf club before, you ignorant fool.' He then lifted it
above his head and smashed it through the air at me.

He demonstrates, then turning to EUGENIA, *hands her some
letters he's uncovered.*

Are these yours?

EUGENIA (*grabbing them*). Yes.

GUARD 1 (*looking at* NIKOLAI). And the lies we have to deal
with too, some very clumsy, so obvious, but some very
elaborate, people producing whole new histories for
themselves, whole new lives they say they've led, views they've
never held, reasons why they *have* to travel.

GUARD 2. Some of them don't pretend at all but *demand* to be let out at *once*.

GUARD 1 (*quiet, strong*). So many of them desperate to leave the land of their birth — the country is disgorging people at the moment, the waste that didn't leave before is finally leaving now. Some of it can be allowed to drain out, many others have to stay because of what they've done. (*He moves.*) We have lists, and we can't afford to make mistakes.

A phone rings in the background.

That telephone never ever stops ringing with news, instructions. Of all the teams working here, we are the team being held responsible.

GUARD 2. I have never worked so hard in my entire life!

NIKOLAI (*calm*). You will remember me.

GUARD 2 *suddenly moves across the carriage, having found a package in a silk bag.*

GUARD 2. Look at this! (*Handing it to* GUARD 1.)

GUARD 1 (*holds the silk bag*). Can you explain these, comrade?

NIKOLAI (*calmly*). They are diamonds.

EUGENIA (*surprised by this find, but immediately recovering*). We were *allowed* to take some diamonds out, family possessions, we . . .

GUARD 1. Nobody is allowed to take such things as diamonds out of the country. (*Staring at them.*) Why weren't they on your form? Among your papers?

EUGENIA (*sharp*). There's so much to write down, somehow they got left out.

GUARD 1. You left out diamonds?

POLYA. They would have been better hidden if we'd intended to hide them, wouldn't they?

NIKOLAI (*calmly*). They were not hidden in any way, I would never allow that.

GUARD 1 (*staring at them*). None of you must now leave this carriage, for any reason. You will remain here. (*Pause.*) If you are right and you sought permission, which was granted, this will be the first time this has happened. If you're wrong — the consequences could be grave. (*Moving to exit.*) We will have to make a telephone call. We will see.

GUARD 1 *and* GUARD 2 *exit*.

EUGENIA (*loud*). Why did you keep those, Nikolai — why on earth did you bring the diamonds with us? (*She looks at him.*) I thought we had got rid of everything.

NIKOLAI. I wanted you to have security abroad when I had to leave you, some source of income. (*Pause.*) Perhaps you should have been wearing them — we should have been even more straightfoward.

EUGENIA. Whatever the reason, that wasn't wise, Nikolai . . . it could be very serious.

NIKOLAI. Don't worry — at the worst they will attempt to confiscate them — but I will get them back.

EUGENIA *starts looking through the unopened letters the* GUARD *found.*

He couldn't remember me, the guard. He was not lying, I don't blame him, he is quite busy. He was thinking how I must have looked in retrospect — slightly nervous of the truth, so he simply altered it. He'll remember.

EUGENIA (*looking up sharply*). This is *the* letter Nikolai, the one that was thrown away so effectively, the Minister of Labour's letter.

POLYA. It's found.

NIKOLAI. What does he say? Is it of any use to us?

EUGENIA (*staring down first page of letter, eager*). He says . . . he says . . . my God!

POLYA. What?

EUGENIA (*reads*). 'When you first came into my office with all those ideas — this ludicrous even grotesque figure, I had to restrain my clerks from tearing you to pieces — but your *ideas*, your papers you submitted? I didn't understand them — but they were extraordinary'.

SASHA (*surprised*). Extraordinary?

EUGENIA (*carrying straight on*). 'Despite the fact that they were written on note paper from the Ritz Hotel in Paris!

NIKOLAI *is impassive*.

'You certainly didn't look a likely inventor of anything — could such modern notions which would actually work be churning around in such a person?'

Pause.

'The answer was *yes* . . . maybe, perhaps. The trouble was if I gave you space to work in Moscow people would literally probably strangle you inside a week.'

NIKOLAI. Proceed.

EUGENIA (*excited*). I can't believe this. (*She reads*.) 'I had an inspiration! One of the many I had at the time — I WILL MAKE HIM TELEPHONE EXAMINER BEFORE THERE IS ANY REAL NEED FOR ONE.'

POLYA. What! (*Reading over her shoulder*.) 'I will give him a place of his own, a Government appointment that will protect him, access to labour and funds if he chooses to use them.'

EUGENIA. 'I knew you wouldn't do a stroke of Railway work — as it is I received some delightful lies from your wife.' (EUGENIA *breaks off*.) He might have told me, mightn't he! (*She returns to letter*.) 'Some of which are on my wall staring at me now.'

POLYA. Yes, yes, why didn't he let *us* know?

SASHA *suddenly grabs the second page of letter and starts to read from the top of the page*.

SASHA. 'I knew if you succeeded, Nikolai, you would break every door down in Moscow to show people — if you failed, if you were a fraud, I could just write it off as Railway expense.' (*Reading fast, agitated, realising his own grave mistake*.) 'And Nikolai, I knew if I told you the *truth* you wouldn't stand it for a moment and would be camping on a doorstep, refusing to go, telling my staff they weren't dressed properly, that they were all ignorant peasants! *So, you got put in the carriage — and it is just beginning, I hope, to bear some sort of fruit'.* (*To himself.*) Oh! 'I have to break off in a hurry, I have other urgent letters to write.'

NIKOLAI (*loud.*) Give me that letter!

SASHA (*moving away*). Oh my god, what have I done . . .? Polya, you don't know what I've done. I've been so stupid, didn't see anything. I have done something terrible, truly terrible.

POLYA (*concerned*). What's the matter with you?

NIKOLAI (*commanding*). Sasha, quiet . . . (*Silence. He takes the letter. Calmly:*) The idiot — why didn't he explain this to me, he treated me like a child. I failed to understand the use of 'ludicrous' and 'grotesque' . . . and he seems almost as vain as I am. (*Pause.*) Nevertheless he could have done worse — it is true he could have done much worse.

EUGENIA (*with feeling*). Yes.

NIKOLAI. There was a mind at work there, an intelligence. (*Slight smile.*) He enjoyed my contradictions. (*Lightly.*) It might even be a document of historical interest — all the more reason to complete the task.

POLYA (*tense smile*). And you can still do it with *me*, which is important, still got the chance. (*Moving, febrile, by the window.*) Find some new equipment round here and as the first talking film, you can have me singing at the border. Wailing out of a window!

NIKOLAI. Yes.

The sound of movement outside.

POLYA. You can use some of the people outside, the people queuing, and the guards, you can have them all telling their stories, record the faces and shouts from the border . . .

NIKOLAI (*slight smile*). Finding the equipment here, Polya, is slightly unlikely, but this — (*Holding the Minister of Labour's letter.*) — this is a splendid find, we have no problem now. We just give them the letter — it shows who I am — it is a proof of everything.

EUGENIA. I don't think that would be wise. (*She takes the letter.*)

NIKOLAI. Why, how can it not be?

EUGENIA. We don't know where he is now — what has happened to him. Until we know that, I'm not sure anyone should read it. (*Glancing down at the letter.*) He's written this in such a hurry, so urgently, it's stained all over with ink, and sweat.

The door opens suddenly. GUARD 2 enters.

NIKOLAI. You have brought our papers now I hope.

GUARD 2 (*pointing straight at POLYA*). Right, she has to leave, come on get your things and *out.*

POLYA. Me? (*Startled pause.*) Why now?

GUARD 2. You don't get to ask questions, you do as you're told. You've got to leave, so you get up, take a few things, and you get out of here!

POLYA. I will leave how I like, in my own time.

GUARD 2 (*shouts*). Don't play around with me — I haven't slept for three nights, you realise, and it's getting worse all the time, it never ever stops —

Phones and noise in the background.

So don't you try arguing. (EUGENIA *lifts her head.*) The rest of you keep quiet!

POLYA (*moving deliberately over to SASHA*). Sasha, despite everything — (*Gives him a kiss, slightly formal.*) — I think I might even miss you.

Then turning, instinctively reverting to her former role for a second, checking clothes.

You know where all your winter clothes are — in which suitcase, where the thick socks are?

SASHA (*moving after her*). Polya, you're not still angry with me? (*Loud.*) You're not to be. I wanted so much to belong, that's all — wanted to be part of things, what was happening . . .

POLYA (*looking at him again*). Yes, I know.

SASHA (*quiet*). . . . and all the time it seems I was nearer to it than I thought, Papa's work . . .

GUARD 2. I told you to get a move on . . .

SASHA. One day I'll tell you what I did . . . when things are easier I'll . . .

POLYA (*staring at him*). When that happens, I'll want to hear it.

SASHA. I destroyed something, Polya.

POLYA (*touching him*). Worry about things in the past later, you've got to be strong now, Sasha.

GUARD 2 (*suddenly turning to* NIKOLAI). Right, now you, take that coat off and give it to me.

Pause.

NIKOLAI. For any particular reason?

GUARD 2. Just do as I say — everything will be much simplier if you do that.

NIKOLAI (*calmly, taking the great coat off*). Do I get a receipt?

EUGENIA. What are you doing? What's happening?

GUARD 2 (*to* NIKOLAI). Now the jacket, and the shirt, go on give them to me. (*To* EUGENIA:) Your husband is shortly going to be removed from this carriage, he will be charged tonight, and taken away from here for sentence.

POLYA (*loud*). Why?

EUGENIA. Where's the trial? Where's he going?

GUARD 2 (*cutting her off*). You and the child are forbidden to stay, you continue out of the country tonight. (*Sharp.*) You understand? (*To* NIKOLAI:) Now take your shoes. (*Pointing at his polished feet.*) Fine shoes there, take them off, and your socks, off! (*As* NIKOLAI *hesitates*:) I don't want to hurt anybody, but there's an allocated time for each person, so just do it.

NIKOLAI. I have no intention of running away.

NIKOLAI *obeys their instructions. Without his magnificent coat, gloves, hat, the jacket of his suit, his shirt, he is left in his vest and trousers, barefoot, looking frail and vulnerable, suddenly older, whiter; but he is sitting very straight, in the middle of the carriage.*

POLYA (*watching* NIKOLAI *undress*). You don't have to do that to him.

GUARD 2 (*looking at* POLYA *and her papers*). Why on earth did you bother staying with this lot anyway? (*Glancing at them.*) Cleaning up after them, running around . . . why?

POLYA (*facing him*). So *you're* allowed to ask questions and I'm not.

EUGENIA (*warning*). Polya . . .

GUARD 2 (*sharp*). Why?

POLYA. I did it for my own reasons, because *I* wanted to. Because I was doing something important here with him — yes, with *him*.

Indicating NIKOLAI, GUARD 2 *looks disbelieving.*

One way and another a lot of me had gone into it, it was my work as well as his. (*With feeling:*) And I really *did* want to see it through more than *you* can imagine. And we've just reached a point as it happens when . . .

A phone rings in the distance, but louder.

GUARD 2. There's that phone! Come on, get ready now! (*Holds the rolls of fur that is the coat, and looking at him*). That's more like it.

NIKOLAI (*calmly to the women*). It is all right, this is only very temporary.

GUARD 2. Everything out of the pockets, empty the pockets.

He shouts through the window at the ringing phone.

Stop that ringing for God's sake, answer the bloody thing.

POLYA (*loud, powerful*). He'll die the death of cold — I haven't spent all this time with him — to see him wiped out by pneumonia. (*She turns.*) What harm has he done, what harm could he possibly do?

EUGENIA (*warning*). Polya . . .

GUARD 2. We're finding out a lot more about him now — information is still coming through from Moscow. (*To* POLYA:) Now have you got what you want — otherwise you will leave with nothing. (*He looks around the carriage.*)

POLYA (*loud*). And stop ferreting around — there is nothing else to find.

NIKOLAI. Polya . . . there is no need for that.

POLYA (*facing him*). I've known each of these people for years — it is not possible to say goodbye in a few seconds and I won't . . .

GUARD 2 (*briskly, not unpleasantly*). You get extremely used to seeing people do it, all ages, all kinds of relationships, it's much simpler this way I can assure you.

POLYA (*to* NIKOLAI). They will realise they are making a mistake.

NIKOLAI. Naturally, I will be returning ready to resume very soon Polya. (*To the* GUARD:) Some heating here would now be appreciated.

GUARD 2. No chance, this is no longer a hotel. (*Really tense.*) Don't give me any more trouble, all right?

POLYA *goes up to* EUGENIA.

POLYA. Eugenia . . .

EUGENIA (*touching her*). I don't know how I will live without seeing you.

POLYA. You'll manage — you know where everything is.

EUGENIA. I didn't mean that. (*Worried.*) You know I didn't mean about domestic things, Polya, I . . .

GUARD 2 (*breaking in, pulling* POLYA *by her arm*). Come on, that's enough.

POLYA (*back to* EUGENIA). Of course I . . . (*Fighting the*

GUARD.) Stop it, stop that.

The GUARD *grabs at her, short sharp grabs at her. She fights him off, till he's really got her. Suddenly she's dragged out of the carriage very forcibly and is gone.*

EUGENIA. She's left and I didn't make myself clear what I meant. (*She moves. Loud.*) She's gone and she thought I was talking about domestic work.

POLYA *appears framed in one of the windows, staring back at them, looking startled, pale, as there is the sound of the door being fastened from the outside. Then she is forcibly moved away, suddenly, looking very frightened, telephones ringing in the distance.*

NIKOLAI. Polya . . .

EUGENIA. Why are they being so rough with her? They'll let her get her train, won't they?

NIKOLAI. Yes, they will.

EUGENIA (*to* NIKOLAI). What are they going to do, how will they treat *you*?

NIKOLAI. Sasha, don't look so frightened.

SASHA (*very quiet*). No, Papa . . .

NIKOLAI. There will be no further problems — they seem to be being terrified by messages down the telephone, but they won't seriously attempt to detain me. (*Pause.*) My feet are cold, that's all. (*Sitting in his vest, carrying on as if nothing had happened.*) It may be difficult, though, for me to return here to Russia — for some time.

Pause.

(*Acidly:*) What a destination! What a fate. To end up in England!

EUGENIA. I thought that's what you always wished for, above all.

NIKOLAI (*astonished*). Always wished for! (*Pause.*) The idea horrifies me. (*Self-mocking smile.*) When I went there I had an utterly miserable time, grey and utterly sodden. (*He looks round the carriage.*) They're terribly slow the English, you have to explain everything so many times, they think in such a literal way. It is all so rigid there, they treat their servants appallingly. (*Incisive:*) There is no energy of ideas, they instinctively distrust nearly all ideas on sight, and they like you to apologise for having thought of them. They thought I was mad and exceedingly arrogant, they backed away from me when I came into the room, always looked at their feet. They have a terror of everything foreign. (*Lightly:*) They will not believe in me, this 'grotesque' did not and will not go down well. (*Slight smile.*) Also, and even more important, the coffee is disgusting, undrinkable.

EUGENIA. You never told me — you never told me that's what happened.

The sound of movement around them.

NIKOLAI. No, and we haven't got the money to reach America. (*Slight smile.*) Might be worse of course. (*Tone changing:*) It is interesting isn't it, being on the edge of the country. Nothing I have ever read or been told in my life has prepared me for this shock, the sheer physical sensation when one is faced with leaving one's native land permanently — like you are being pulled away from a magnetic field and that everything will then stop. It will have been severed. (*Calm.*) An illogical fear maybe but my God it's strong. As far as I'm aware mere fame has never been what drove me on in my work. I wanted to do it here. Leaving suddenly feels distinctly unnatural and dangerous.

EUGENIA. I know, I can feel it. I'm not sure that's all that's going to happen, Nikolai. (*She puts a blanket around him.*)

NIKOLAI. If they were going to shoot me — they would have probably done it already. But it's such a remote possibility. Don't worry about it my dear.

EUGENIA (*suddenly sharp*). Nikolai, we both know what they're going to do. (*Loud.*) Let's not pretend, all right. (*Pause. She looks across at him. Loud:*) Why didn't you tell me ever?

NIKOLAI. Tell you what?

EUGENIA. Tell me what you were doing — what your work was. I heard it from Polya — all these ideas. (*Looking at him.*) Didn't I have a right to know?

NIKOLAI. I did not discuss such things with you . . . you knew that.

EUGENIA (*her head going back, quiet*). Yes, I knew that.

They're sitting wide apart in the carriage, SASHA *crouching in the corner, the phones ringing in the distance.*

I don't know how long we've got — when they're going to come back, maybe in the middle. (*Tracing a pattern on the wall with her finger, not looking at him.*) I have no idea if I can go through with this . . . but if I don't say it now I'm never going to be able to say it. (*Tension is in her voice. She is trying to keep control.*)

NIKOLAI. Eugenia, what is it?

EUGENIA (*with real force suddenly*). I want you to realise what it was like, Nikolai, before, our lives together. Before we came here. (*Forcing herself to say it.*) What it meant for me . . . how . . . how (*Forcing herself.*) how I had to support and not ask, (*Not looking at him.*) give to you but never touch, serve (*Quieter.*) but never . . .

NIKOLAI (*cutting her off*). I don't know you should say these things now — the boy is here, Sasha is here.

EUGENIA. I have to, Kolia — I have to tell you. (*Quiet with feeling.*) But it isn't easy. (*Not looking at him.*) Your work — this enormous weight in the air always, a world I was forbidden to enter . . . but for some reason I always believed in it, I don't doubt it for a moment, I know it's real.

But my God, when you left me in the country how I hated those summers, those horrible summers, endless languid days and how I *hated* you sometimes. (*A momentary look at him.*) Yes.

NIKOLAI (*looking up*). Hated me? Eugenia . . .

EUGENIA (*with feeling*). I could hardly think for myself. Waiting for you . . . all the time waiting for you to *see* me, to discuss with me, *anything*, to *acknowledge* me.

If I ever have to live through that again with me festering underneath, (*Matter of fact.*) beginning to scream and cry inside . . . (*Holding herself.*) I felt there was so much in here . . . trapped in here . . . it was like burrowing out of a grave.

Nikolai, forgive me. (*Pause.*) But . . . (*She stops.*)

NIKOLAI. Go on, proceed. Say what you have to say.

EUGENIA (*who has looked up, is staring at him*). This is the most difficult conversation of my life — if I look at you I can't go on.

Trying to keep control — after waivering, her voice incisive again.

But if I don't try to do it I won't be able to cope afterwards at all.

She turns away, leaning against the side, forcing herself to go on.

It's just the daring it took to break with all I'd thought before — and do the few things I did, forging documents, making up train times, tiny little acts which led to my getting that job, . . . absurd as it may seem now they were terribly important at the time, the release I felt doing that, it was extraordinarily strong — what welled up because of that . . .

She looks up again.

What I am trying to tell you is, though you seem to have been completely oblivious of it over these last months. (*Pause.*) But it changed my life, Nikolai, I want you to understand that, (*Pause.*) because otherwise . . . if you go away now . . . I feel there're things we never said . . . and then . . .

She stops.

Oh, Nikolai, say something, help me —

Silence.

NIKOLAI (*detached tone*). It is very interesting I think . . .

EUGENIA. What is — is that all you can say? (*Sharp:*) At this time . . .

NIKOLAI (*continuing, not looking at her*). Large events, great events even, have happened just outside, and we've seen most of them — or heard most of them to be more accurate. Meanwhile in here, locked up in this, squashed into this matchbox.

EUGENIA. Rather a large matchbox, Nikolai.

NIKOLAI (*continuing, detached tone*). And yet the energy generated in here, felt at times, if you will allow the slight exaggeration, felt it could flatten city walls. It seems to me, Eugenia, in this messy clump of all of us, all of us tangled up together, a way was found of releasing our separate energies. (*Pause.*) Unlocking things.

EUGENIA (*not looking at him, sharp*). That's how you'd put it is it?

NIKOLAI (*slowly*). And I know some of that (*Staring at her.*) . . . a lot of that is because of you.

Silence, EUGENIA *looks up.*

EUGENIA. Yes it is. (*She looks at him.*) And Polya . . .

NIKOLAI (*staring at her*). Just because I find certain things difficult to say doesn't mean they aren't true. (*Slight pause.*) I've been meaning to say many things to you.

EUGENIA. Yes.

NIKOLAI (*slight smile*). And you know before this I never could think on trains — I never had an idea on one in my life.

EUGENIA (*looking at him, but not yet moving to him*). Kolia, is there anything we can do when they come?

NIKOLAI. No — (*Detached tone:*) it is interesting when I think usually, I nearly always have some sense of the future; you can see distant shapes, people you are about to meet, ideas you are about to have. For some weeks there's been nothing there, just a rather dark cold void.

SASHA. I know, Papa.

The light has imperceptibly changed, the place oppressive.

EUGENIA. Yes — it suddenly seems to be growing smaller in here.

NIKOLAI. It appears to be shrinking because we're locked in.

EUGENIA. It's claustrophobic for the first time. Suddenly it's rather horrible.

SASHA (*moving over to his father*). Papa, I'm sorry, I am, I am so sorry, Papa.

NIKOLAI (*detached tone*). Yes, but there's no need for that. You know I never thought waiting for one's possible execution one's mind would be so clear. It's a pleasant surprise. It's *interesting* to find that . . .

EUGENIA (*suddenly moving over to him, touching him*). Kolia, don't say that any more, stop that. Look at me. You don't have to talk like that. (*Touching him.*) I can't believe I may have to say goodbye to you. (*Looking at him.*) I'm deliberately refusing to try.

The door bangs open. GUARDS 1 and 2 enter.

NIKOLAI (*calmly*). So here you are, you left rather suddenly. I didn't know whether you were coming back.

GUARD 1. Nikolai Pesiakoff, you are under arrest — you have to come with us now. You may bring no personal belongings.

GUARD 2. Don't cause us trouble, you've had time to say goodbye by now.

NIKOLAI. What is the charge?

GUARD 1. You know perfectly well — apart from trying to remove valuables unlawfully from this country, you have lied about being a government official; both are capital offences.

GUARD 2. The Minister of Labour you referred to, they'd never heard of him when we telephoned. We told them to look again, they think he's been arrested.

GUARD 1 (*pulling and tearing apart what remains of NIKOLAI's equipment*). These ridiculous scraps shouldn't be here.

The two GUARDS *hurl the pieces out of the carriage. They move, bulky dangerous presences around the carriage, bludgeoning the place apart, getting rid of things.*

(*To* NIKOLAI). Right, stand up — time to move.

EUGENIA (*staring up*). You going to try to take him just like that are you? No shoes.

GUARD 2. That's how we have to do it.

EUGENIA (*suddenly*). How dare you treat somebody like that — how dare you touch him.

GUARD 1. Don't try to get yourself arrested as well — it is not something I want to have to do.

EUGENIA. And how dare you not believe me. (*Staring at them.*) Didn't you hear him tell you what he did — he worked for the Northern Railway.

SASHA. He did!

GUARD 1. He could never have.

EUGENIA (*cutting him off*). We wouldn't make up such a mad lie.

GUARD 1. Many do.

EUGENIA. How do you *know* he's not? I'll prove it to you. (*Sharp, keeping her eyes on them.*) Do you know who the station master is for instance at Vologda, come on who is he? Tell me. Sergei Goncharov — (*Before they can stop her:*) — or do you know for instance what is now different about the night train from Omsk to Moscow, have either of you any idea?

GUARD 1 (*watching her, intrigued*). No.

EUGENIA. Of course you don't — it is the first time a through Express has ever been run on that line, it's being run for an experimental period of three months.

GUARD 1 (*intrigued smile*). An uncommon sight — a woman spouting railway statistics from the heart!

EUGENIA. Don't you patronise me, Comrade — (*Staring at him.*)

When is the delivery expected of the new locomotives, the ones built entirely in this country? October 31st.

GUARD 2 (*disbelieving*). Really?

EUGENIA. How many suburban lines are about to open in Moscow. Four, with a total of forty-two stations, the original plan was for fifty, go and check that one, go on, you will find it is totally accurate. And while we're about it, when is the new phone exchange having its official opening, the one that will serve a third of the city? Only a very few people know the official date, do you think you could find anybody at this border that knows that — it is September 14th. (*Watching them.*) Tell me how could we possibly know these things — unless *he* was the telephone examiner of the Northern District. (*Loud:*) What other conceivable explanation is there, just let me hear you suggest another?

Startled pause.

(*Very forceful:*) You have no legal right to arrest this man and if what I tell you is true, which it is, you could be making a grave mistake, Comrade, for which you will be responsible. Don't you try to touch him again — I warn you, don't you maltreat him again in any way. (*Loud:*) Go on, let go of him, and let us be on our way at once.

EUGENIA *faces them, the phone ringing in the background.*

GUARD 1 (*staring at her*). Madame . . .

GUARD 2 (*tense*). We've got another load to deal with in three minutes, it's coming in now.

GUARD 1 (*staring at her*). I am making this decision for the wrong reasons and I will regret it, because none of the evidence adds up, these scraps of metals — (*Flings the last one through the door.*) the look of the place. But for one moment, a moment that will no doubt seem absurd tomorrow, (*Staring at* EUGENIA.) you have convinced me, Comrade, that he did indeed do that job. I have no idea why — look at the man! (*Pointing at* NIKOLAI *sitting in the middle of the carriage.*) But you have. There still remains the diamonds. We will say we found them on another train. I will make no record of this incident. Nor of your departure, none will exist anywhere.

They both move.

I don't advise you *ever* to try to come back.

They both leave. Silence.

NIKOLAI (*calmly*). You truly can be said, without exaggeration, to be the Telephone Examiner of the Northern District.

EUGENIA (*leaning her head against the side*). Not for long, not in a few minutes . . .

An ear-splitting screech, the sound of a locomotive backs up towards them, a piercing sound of movement and violent braking that touches the pit of the stomach.

EUGENIA. Oh God. (*Turning her head.*) I really don't want to go — how much you realise it now, when you can't turn back. (*Very quiet.*) I wish something would happen to stop us going.

NIKOLAI. Yes. I will have lost the race too, Eugenia, to be the first in my work, I have no money or resources now.

EUGENIA. You did it, though. I know you did. We know we existed.

The crunch of a locomotive up close, the sounds are very violent, wrenching.

NIKOLAI (*slight smile*). Yes, I can see myself bleating out in an omnibus in the middle of London, a hunched figure on the back seat, pointing at a queue outside a talking motion picture house and saying I was the first to do that! — and we started from much further behind.

SASHA (*moving*). I will write it up here, Papa, I will leave it on the wall, a record, there must be a record, the date . . . and what happened here.

The carriage begins to shake.

EUGENIA (*quiet*). I wonder what this is going to be used for, what's going to be put in here.

NIKOLAI (*his tone loud and angry*). BUT WHAT WE COULD HAVE DONE EUGENIA IF WE'D STAYED . . .

EUGENIA (*lying down as the carriage shakes, slowly curling up, trying to control the emotions*). I know — I know that.

NIKOLAI (*really loud*). There was a great deal more to be done. (*Pause. The loud, tearing noise of the train as it moves.*) And God knows what's on the track. What already has been disposed of — we're crunching over, passing over it as we move.

Loud, violent noise.

EUGENIA (*looking around the carriage*). People going to be herded in here by the hundred.

SASHA (*trying to write with a knife on the woodwork*). I can't make it write . . . (*Loud:*) Oh god, I can't make it write.

NIKOLAI (*quietly*). I'm just beginning to experience that tearing at the insides, Eugenia, that feeling cutting through one . . . of helplessness. It's much colder suddenly, Eugenia.

EUGENIA (*curled up, letting out a cry of anger*). I don't want to leave.

NIKOLAI. No, my love.

The lights fade fast so they disappear into darkness as the carriage lights go out; the loud noise of movement continues.

My God, it's cold. This is the worse part, can you still see me, can you? (*Louder:*) Can you?

EUGENIA. Just. (EUGENIA *curls up as the carriage shakes.*) Just . . . I don't want to go, Nikolai. I . . . (*Loud:*) I don't . . . I don't want to leave.

PLAYING WITH TRAINS

Playing With Trains was premièred by the Royal Shakespeare Company, London on 29 November 1989 with the following cast:

BILL GALPIN	Michael Pennington
ROXANNA GALPIN	Lesley Sharp
DANNY GALPIN	Simon Russell Beale
GANT	Ralph Fiennes
FRANCES	Lesley Dunlop
MICK	Mark Lewis Jones
QC	William Chubb
JUDGE }	Robert Demeger
VERNON BOYCE	

Directed by Ron Daniels
Designed by Kit Surrey
Lighting by Geraint Pughe

The action begins in the summer of 1967

ACT ONE

Scene One

ROXANNA *standing in a spot, front stage left. She is dressed in school uniform. At the beginning of the action she is 18 years old. She is pulling hard at her school tie, loosening it round her neck. She has a light Midlands accent.*

ROXANNA. July 15th – could be a very important date, a date in my progress, I suppose, in our fortunes.

It's bloody hot, anyway, and I still have to wear this for a few more days, for the last time. I have started a countdown till the end of term, hour by hour.

But the great news today *is*, or possibly very grim news – depends how you look at it. And I'm not at all sure how I'm looking at it, because today is the day when I realised we are about to be hit – by money. A great deal of money. It could come pouring through the door at any moment. Or it could not.

It depends on him of course.

Lights up behind ROXANNA, *and she turns. The set is comprised of russet-coloured walls, which remain throughout the action.*

Across the stage is a great pile of packing, half a lifetime of belongings, old suitcases, large boxes crammed tight, old armchairs, some of which have split, tables on top of each other, carpets rolled up, some rugs unrolled, cricket bats, pictures, chairs with their legs sticking in the air, some sixties lamps and several gramophones are prominent. Clothes too, lots of shoes and boots, children's toys and books.

Most of this is closely piled together in a large heap, packed tight enough for someone to walk on. But there are smaller outcrops, spread around, including smaller battered suitcases.

Hot summer light.

ROXANNA *picks something off the floor, an old toy, and throws it on the pile as* DANNY *enters. He is two years younger than* ROXANNA, *in grey trousers, pale shirt, carrying a bicycle with a twisted, mangled, front wheel. He has an enthusiastic, open manner, and the same light Midlands accent, difficult to place exactly.*

DANNY (*with mangled bicycle*). What about this? At last I've found something we don't have to take. We can leave this behind surely?

ROXANNA. No, we can't. We're taking everything. You never know when we may need that.

DANNY. Really? What on earth are you expecting to happen!

ROXANNA (*smiles*). And I may just be able to fix it.

DANNY. OK here – (ROXANNA *takes bicycle,* DANNY *staring towards pile.*) who would have thought all this junk could have come out of our house?

ROXANNA, *having glanced at it, tosses bicycle onto pile. She moves confidently. Despite her age, she has great natural authority.*

ROXANNA. We have no idea how long this is going to last, Danny, anyway.

DANNY. If it begins at all that is.

ROXANNA. What do you mean?

DANNY. He just turned down the deal.

ROXANNA. I don't believe it, again! – he can't do that.

DANNY. He can. He's asking for more.

ROXANNA (*startled*). For more! We're moving house, he's bought another house already, he has to say yes.

DANNY. He's asking for so much now! Because each time he says no, they want him more, to buy him out even more, there's no limit it seems to what he can ask for.

ROXANNA. Of course there is. He's in danger of over-doing it. (*Sharp.*) And he's got to get a guarantee on jobs as well.

DANNY. I think it's brilliant. (*Moving suitcases.*) If we could find the phone that's buried somewhere under all this, maybe we could listen in.

ROXANNA. Go on! (*Anarchic smile.*) Find the phone, I want to interrupt negotiations, tell him to take it.

FRANCES *enters, in her early twenties, working-class girl, intelligent eyes, unafraid. She's carrying two bulky portable gramophones, piled on each other.*

ROXANNA. And who's that?

FRANCES. Your father's new assistant, Frances.

DANNY (*giving a welcoming smile*). So he's got an extra secretary now too.

FRANCES. Acquired a new assistant, that's right. (DANNY *offering to take gramophones.*) I can manage.

ROXANNA (*glancing towards where the phone might be*). This better bloody work, hadn't it! (*Moving forward, warm smile.*) Hello, we can't shake hands, obviously. What are you doing with those?

FRANCES. I just arrived for my interview. (*She heaves gramophones onto pile.*) After twenty seconds he said, 'You've got the job'.

ROXANNA. He took as long as that, did he?

FRANCES. Then he said, 'Take these, they're packing everything up in there'.

ROXANNA. Yes – he's right. We have to take the gramophones.

DANNY (*lifting lids of gramophones*). That's what all this is about.

FRANCES. About these gramophones here?

DANNY. Yes, the automatic turntable, his firm created it when they were a very small concern, they developed the idea, he found the money somehow and it totally altered the manufacture of the gramophone.

ROXANNA (*very authoritative*). The automatic record changer existed before of course Danny, but they totally revolutionised the design . . .

DANNY. And so now they're miles ahead of the field because . . . Roxanna's much better at all that than me – at technical things.

ROXANNA. The design change enabled it to be made much cheaper, mass produced much more easily. I'll do a drawing later, show you what they did. So he makes gramophones, lots and lots of them.

DANNY. And, all being well, he's about to be bought out – for a very large sum.

FRANCES. I joined at the right time it seems.

ROXANNA (*excited smile*). Maybe. And if he does the right thing (*Warm.*) otherwise this will be the shortest job you've ever had. (*Moving.*) Jesus, the smell from this pile.

DANNY (*embarrassed*). Roxy . . . I can't smell anything.

ROXANNA *climbing onto part of pile, walking along the top of it, looking down at them.*

ROXANNA (*to* FRANCES). *You* can smell it, can't you?

FRANCES (*smiles*). Oh yes, very clearly.

ROXANNA (*on heap, moving along plateau at top*). Starting at this end, the deep aroma of really bad times, when money was always disappearing, the smell of those foul chairs, ingrained with all those meals of baked beans and burnt toast.

DANNY. Yes, when we had to sell the car . . . when things got pretty bad.

ROXANNA (*moving further along pile, standing on the objects*). And then things temporarily looked better, moving upmarket here, around these formica tables, nice cluster of anglepoise lamps here, and then a bad wobble . . . (*Kicking an object with her foot.*) followed by a plunge down, into dark times, round these stained carpets and overgloves with holes, when Mum left (*To* FRANCES.) when she'd had *enough* and cleared out.

DANNY. Cleared out so effectively, we never see her, she's in the US and gone. (*He smiles.*) We didn't even get an invitation to the re-marriage.

ROXANNA (*lightly, reaching another section of piles*). And then here, when he was so busy there were no new saucepans, no new clothes for us, everything has its handle missing, and you have to wade through the hundreds of letters he sent to the local press here, an obscure electrical engineer bombarding them with ideas about every possible products – from the suburbs of Nottingham!

Shower of papers falls to ground.

And then here, he produces something people seem to want, and so we hit the new coffee table, and the oriental rugs, and his collection of unread 'Book of the Month' and here I am at last standing on good times, if he doesn't fuck everything up now.

BILL *enters.* ROXANNA *is still on top of the pile of books and belongings and is staring down at him.*

BILL *is casually dressed, a sense of contained energy about him. He's in his early forties, with a startling informal quality in his manner, in the way he addresses his children. His voice can be surprisingly quiet but then change almost in mid-sentence, becoming extremely animated. He has a light Nottinghamshire accent.*

ROXANNA (*staring down at* BILL). Did you hear that?

BILL. Yes.

ROXANNA. So have you?

DANNY. What's happening Dad?

BILL. Why's everybody in such a hurry? Now – don't either of you shout, but I've turned them down.

ROXANNA. Down! You've turned them down. Again . . . !

DANNY. I knew you'd take them all the way, as far as you can.

ROXANNA. If you wait too long they won't need to buy you out, they'll have developed a new kind of gramophone themselves.

BILL (*looks up at her*). Oh I should have you consulted you, should I?

ROXANNA. Of course. (*To* FRANCES.) Though he hates to admit it – he sometimes does.

BILL. Come down from there, come on. (*Lifting* ROXANNA *down, holding onto her.*) I bet my children have been as rude as usual and haven't introduced themselves – have you?

FRANCES. Half introductions – they started and never finished.

BILL. This is my daughter, Roxanna – her mother gave her that strange name, I didn't – and Roxanna is the trouble round here (*He smiles.*) though she has her uses, which include constantly provoking me. You will notice she even has to wear her school uniform in a perverse way – little anarchic flourish.

Looks across.

And that's Danny . . .

DANNY (*nervous smile*). Yes. This is me.

Slight pause.

BILL. And Danny is quite sensible – usually.

ROXANNA (*tone warm, combative, totally as an equal*). Have you seen, Dad, on the pile here – all sorts of things we were forbidden as kids have bobbed up to the surface, for all to see.

BILL (*lightly*). What do you mean – you weren't forbidden anything as kids!

ROXANNA. You didn't know about them though, did you?

DANNY. Like Roxanna's comics and shocking red tights, and packets of fags, and her weird diaries with yellow covers.

ROXANNA (*indicates pile*). Not to mention Danny's schoolboy porn splashing everywhere.

BILL (*grins*). What makes you think I didn't know about them anyway?

ROXANNA (*straight back*). Because I hid them too well. And if you had known – you would undoubtedly have stolen some of the fags. But you will also notice how my beautiful technical drawings and diagrams are on display. Pride of place, in fact.

BILL. Yes, not bad.

ROXANNA (*mocking*). High praise! (*Right up to him.*) Dad if you blow this deal now . . .

BILL (*straight back*). *If* I blow it – what. (*Combative smile.*) Little girl.

ROXANNA *moves.*

You're not usually this cautious.

ROXANNA (*swings round*). I'm not unpacking all this for a start! Do you realise how long this took – this is staying just as it is.

BILL. Yes, I see you've mashed this so tight together. (*Trying to pull chair free of the pile.*) squeezed it so close, it's not going to be easy to take down. (*Looks at her.*) Trying to make sure there's no turning back, are you?

ROXANNA. Of course there's no turning back now.

BILL (*slight grin*). Isn't there!

ROXANNA (*loudly but lightly*). I thought we were really getting out of this place at last. Out of this bloody town. You've bought a new house, you haven't sold this one, you need the money.

BILL. A small detail – the deal has to be good enough. (*To* ROXANNA *as if in reply.*) And have a guarantee about jobs! But it has to be a really improbable amount, otherwise it isn't worth taking, because I won't be able to do what I have in mind. (*To* FRANCES, *suddenly.*) What do you think?

FRANCES (*looking straight at him*). I agree.

BILL. You should say what you mean around here you know.

FRANCES. I gathered that. I haven't the slightest idea what you have in mind, but I like the sound of it. I agree with you.

BILL (*smiles*). You see, I have support here . . .

DANNY (*to* ROXANNA). You know how much he'll be worth – if he brings this off. I'm guessing, but it will be in seven figures.

BILL (*sharp*). Danny, stop it, that fact on its own is absolutely of no interest.

ROXANNA (*to* BILL). So why are you trying to push the price up so far then Dad?

BILL. You'll see.

ROXANNA (*sharp*). Who needs a lot of money! And (*Lightly.*) I'm not sure all this money will be good for you anyway. You'll probably go to seed, become flabby and destructive and boring, (*Provocative.*) go into steep decline.

BILL. You don't trust me. (*To* FRANCES.) They don't trust me.

DANNY. Of course we do.

ROXANNA (*straight at him, sharp smile*). Do we? Apart from everything else, I just don't want to have to put up with your cooking any more – every third day when it's your turn.

Phone rings, faint ring from under belongings.

BILL. If we can find the phone – which you've managed to bury – maybe we can do a deal.

ROXANNA (*urgent*). Don't play around any more Dad. Go and do it. (*As* BILL *unhurriedly moves debris to look for phone.*) Quick – take it on the other phone – go on!

Blackout.

Scene Two

ROXANNA *front stage, taking her school blazer off, and putting on a brightly coloured well-fitting sweater. Then she brushes her hair back, sharp, more mature, the schoolgirl image falling off with each stroke.*

ROXANNA (*tone excited, but wary*). May 17th. Guess what. (*The sweater going on.*) Unbelievable isn't it, but true. We are moving *again*. Yes. Another violent disruption because of a second new discovery. I've hardly had time to visit all the rooms in this house – in fact I've still to find at least two of the bathrooms. And all this because of a development in the the single reflex lens, pioneered in Japan in 1905.

As she speaks the second large pile comes onto the set. She watches it being added to the heap of belongings of the first scene. This time it consists of luxurious junk, late sixties junk, two trolleys of it piled high, packed ready to move. There is a half unrolled snow white carpet too.

1905. Yes! A dramatic advance in camera design so far ahead of its time that nobody had done anything about it, even in Japan. And Dad, with a reasonably brilliant stroke, spotted this small English firm trying to redevelop the idea and going bust in the process and he poured and poured money at them, helped them modify it, and then desperately looked around for a British company to come in with him to mass produce the cameras. But there have been no takers naturally. (*She smiles.*) They ran in the opposite direction as soon as they saw him coming.

So he's had to join up with the . . . Japanese. Yes, having seized an idea they themselves had missed, (*Lightly.*) it looks like making Dad another fortune of course and this time quite a big one . . . the gramophone tycoon has struck again. (*Slight pause.*) He seems to have backed the right idea.

Lights up on set. BILL packing, caged energy. He has taken his jacket off, in same shirt and trousers, but striking, new, fashionable shoes.

ROXANNA. So this is what you had in mind, was it?

BILL *moving by the pile.*

BILL. What do you mean?

ROXANNA. What you're going to do with yourself from now on, moving house every year, throwing them away like paper cups, had this one, so . . . (*Makes a chucking movement over her shoulder.*)

BILL. This has been a disaster hasn't it – this mansion, being behind an electric fence, a total disaster!

ROXANNA. It might have helped if we had ever unpacked.

BILL. It doesn't suit us living like this.

ROXANNA. I am not sure it suits anybody (*Pulling at a chair tightly packed in pile.*) – chairs tend to be quite useful you know.

BILL. No – in this style (*Energised.*) I have the swimming pool here totally retiled –

ROXANNA. To impress the young girls you have lazing around here.

BILL. – and it is immediately over-run with frogs. They even seem to have a special species here, the Chertsey frog, hops around from the pools of the surrounding pop stars.

ROXANNA. Slightly stoned and over-weight.

BILL. I give a couple of enormous garden parties, like you are meant to, and it pours with rain, a deluge for each one! And all the time we are here the burglar alarm is ringing – going off in the middle of the night, police cars roaring down the drive.

ROXANNA. Yes, my only memories of this house will be endless white rooms and burglar alarms going off. (*Slight smile.*) We've been strangers in somebody else's place.

BILL. I have never understood how people can shut themselves away in large houses, cage themselves up, ridiculous way to live, who needs it . . .

ROXANNA. Now he realises!

BILL (*sharp smile*). My puritan daughter – I had to see for myself . . . didn't I?

ROXANNA (*straight back*). Did you? (*Touching him.*) Don't do it again.

BILL. No.

ROXANNA. Still trying to get into a gentlemen's club are you?

BILL. Oh yes, very definitely.

ROXANNA (*warm*). Haven't they all turned you down yet!

BILL. No, no, I'm waiting to hear back from the Saville Club any day.

ROXANNA (*warm*). I'm going to have to do something about your taste you know.

BILL (*smiling at her*). You reckon so.

FRANCES *entering with some garish ornamental belongings.*

ROXANNA (*staring at these*). Definitely! (*Warm.*) And did I
actually see you with a *book* last week? With a hardcover even!
Reading some literature for once.

BILL (*back at her*). It's possible . . .

FRANCES (*confident, excited*). The trucks are coming soon, I hope
you haven't left anything, should be doing your last round of
checking. I'm taking no blame for what's left behind, I warn
you!

BILL (*smiles at* FRANCES, *moves among luggage*). She gets ruder
by the day . . .

MICK *enters, carrying more belongings, a gangling boy of about
22.*

ROXANNA. Who's that?

BILL. Oh that's Mick.

MICK *grunts.*

BILL. I'm backing some of his ideas. Interesting engineering
modifications, some fine drawings, one or two possibly
remarkable inventions.

ROXANNA. Oh really! So why's he having to help us move
house?

BILL. He offered to.

MICK (*surly*). He asked me to.

ROXANNA. An offer you couldn't refuse. Obviously. (*Turning to*
BILL.) Having inventors to do your packing now, are we!
(*Lightly to* MICK.) I should get away from here as soon as
possible, that's my advice, run like mad. Get away from him!

MICK. Why?

ROXANNA (*lightly*). Because he's probably only playing at this,
acquiring some new distractions.

FRANCES (*indicating* MICK). I don't know what his inventions
are like, but he's a bloody good removal man. Can lift
anything. (*To* MICK.) Come on, one last search of the house.

MICK *and* FRANCES *exit.*

BILL (*indicating* MICK *as he goes*). No, this is serious Roxanna. You will see.

ROXANNA. Will I? When?

DANNY *running on with more, new garish belongings.*

DANNY. These nearly got left behind.

ROXANNA (*quiet, eyeing these belongings*). We don't have to take everything do we . . .

DANNY. I love moving. (*With paper to* BILL.) You know what else I found, the map of millionaires I made. My research, millionaires in five European countries where their homes are – I've marked the spot – how much they're worth, and where you come in the list, in the league table I've made of the wealthy.

BILL. Not now Danny, not now, OK.

ROXANNA. I don't think he's in the mood for that somehow.

DANNY. You are moving up the table fast, although there's a long way to go of course. I'll show it to you later.

BILL *is pulling chair out of tightly packed pile, having to yank it with real force.*

BILL. I want to talk to you both. (*Moving with chair.*) It has not pleased me, the business about the camera – having to lose the idea back to Japan.

ROXANNA. You tried all you could.

BILL (*clicking his fingers*). Something else has just gone too you know, which nobody here seems to have noticed at all – a breakthrough with magnetic tape, audio and video recording.

ROXANNA (*immediately*). Being able to squeeze tracks tightly together on the same tape? Be able to really shrink in size, won't they?

BILL (*sharp*). That's right, Roxanna. It'll probably be extraordinarily successful. (*Suddenly powerful.*) But it's not going to keep on happening – not if I can help it. (*Loud.*) Something has to be done . . . (*Glance at* ROXANNA.) You know Roxanna your Cambridge entrance result, the more I think about it, the better it seems.

ROXANNA (*lightly*). Yes, you crammed me well didn't you?

BILL (*anarchic smile, stabbing finger*). It was nearly what I expected.

ROXANNA (*warm*). Good – then I can take a rest then, can't I!

BILL (*looks round*). And Danny . . .

> DANNY looks at him.

. . . we're still seeing how things are turning out. (*Ruffling DANNY's hair.*) But they seem to be going quite well too . . .

DANNY. Yes, Dad . . .

> BILL looks at both of them.

BILL. Roxanna's going to study engineering I hope. Danny it looks like being physics.

DANNY. Yes, I think so Dad.

BILL (*moving along belongings on pile*). Christ, there's a lot here now isn't there. (*He turns.*) Now you two, I just want to find this out. Do you want – money? (*Anarchic smile.*) I don't particularly want to give it to you, but do you want to be set up with an income? (*Looks at them.*) Some money now?

DANNY. No, no, totally not. We're going to do it ourselves.

ROXANNA. I wouldn't take a penny.

BILL. Come on there's no need to overdo it! Jesus . . . it sounds like you've been rehearsing between you. Say what you feel, not what you think I want to hear, I'm talking real money you understand, not pocket money, real money. (*Sharp.*) Say now . . . do you want it?

ROXANNA (*strong*). We don't want it Dad. Absolutely not.

BILL. Good. That's what I knew you'd say.

> *Blackout.*

Scene Three

*In the blackout, music bursting down, the theme tune of a television
programme, a voice booms out,* Ladies and Gentlemen, live from
Shepherds Bush, 'In the Hot Seat' *(Theme tune rises and dips.)* and
to face the probing questions of Vernon Boyce tonight is – dynamic
entrepreneur and flamboyant businessman, the gramophone tycoon,
Bill Galpin.

*Swivel chair in the middle of the stage in spot, by itself.
Everything else is in darkness. Vernon Boyce fires his questions outside
the lighted ring, seated in silhouette.*

BILL *walks on and sits on chair, alone in spotlight. He is wearing
a new grey jacket, same trousers and shoes.*

BOYCE. Mr Galpin, welcome. What does money mean to you?

BILL *(his voice throughout a mixture of the quiet tentative, and then
loud and direct).* Money . . . ? Money itself, money means
nothing to me of course. OK, nothing may be a bit simple . . .
not much. It's what you do –

BOYCE *(cutting him off).* Many people watching may not believe
that.

BILL *(briskly).* No, no it's true. I like having enough of course, I
didn't always . . . have, but when you've made some money
through luck or circumstance or whatever, it really doesn't
take any special talent or intelligence to make more of it – it
really doesn't, it's –

BOYCE. Are you a vain person?

BILL. So you're going to shoot straight from the hip right from
the start.

BOYCE. They're all going to be straight from the hip questions,
you've obviously not watched the programme.

BILL. Oh yes *(He smiles.)* I've watched your show, it's attempting
to be a popular, cruder version – isn't it – of an earlier more
famous show, when the interviewer also lurked . . . in the
darkness.

BOYCE. Thank you, I'm reassured to hear you're a regular viewer.
To return to the question – would you be surprised if people

called you a vain person?

BILL (*moving in chair*). I've never thought about it, till this moment, maybe not. (*Sharp smile.*) I'm no saint certainly . . . I think I am capable of certain things, yes, which given a chance I want to talk ab-

BOYCE. Please don't move the chair, the hot seat.

The chair has slid back slightly, out of the spotlight.

If you do move it like that, you just disappear, vanish suddenly into total darkness.

BILL *moving chair back. Edge of spotlight, half lit, during the following exchange he moves again, into full central brightness.*

BILL. Disappear? Into blackness. I'll try to keep still then. (*He smiles.*) Depends on the questions.

BOYCE. So how *would* you describe yourself – as a tycoon? A flamboyant tycoon who . . .

BILL. I keep on hearing that expression, no. As a businessman, entrepreneur, and I hope, unfashionable as this is, a patron. I am not an inventor myself, though I can make suggestions sometimes about ideas, modifications, but I want to discover and back –

BOYCE (*cutting him off*). But you live a very flamboyant lifestyle don't you, in large houses, being photographed with pop stars, holding great parties that –

BILL. My parties tend not to be successes. Disasters in fact.

BOYCE. But since you've burst on the business scene, you've had a fabulously successful few years.

BILL. Fabulous no, good yes.

BOYCE (*loud*). Is it important to you how much you are worth?

BILL. You want me to tell you in public, how much I am worth?

BOYCE. I want to know how important to you that is.

BILL. Money . . . money again. You don't want to accept what I tell you do you – you want to go on asking these voyeuristic questions about how –

BOYCE. You think they're voyeuristic? . . . Are you guilty about having made so much?

BILL. Certainly not.

BOYCE. But you are an extremely rich man?

BILL. A rich man.

BOYCE. An enormously rich man.

BILL. A rich man.

BOYCE. And you're an ambitious man too, after the years of obscurity, there is a feverish, almost anarchic energy, as if you are making up for lost time?

BILL. I want to try . . .

BOYCE. And in the way you've spoken out on several issues. You're a man in a hurry –

BILL. I'm not in such a hurry that I don't have time to finish the answer to your questions, something I'm finding extremely . . .

BOYCE. And you haven't exactly hidden from the attention you've received have you? Like coming on this show for instance –

BILL. No, because I intend – and I'm going to get this out whether you like it or not – I intend to back certain things that interest me, to sponsor bright young engineers and scientists. There is an extraordinary inventiveness in this country, and I wish to publicise that and ask are we encouraging it enough?

BOYCE. And make money out of it at the same time, obviously.

BILL (smiles). It's important not to go broke naturally.

BOYCE. So you're appealing to people to share your enthusiasms, you are a person of sudden enthusiasms are you not?

BILL. No, no, constant enthusiasms.

BOYCE. You were very quick to correct that, why is that so important to you?

BILL. I've always had intense enthusiasms since I was a boy. For better or worse I'm not inclined towards the arts, but to machines of all kinds, and also bridges, buildings, viaducts, and pipes.

BOYCE. Pipes! Are you serious?

BILL. Oh yes. Good drainage works are very exciting. (*Sharp smile.*) Don't you find? Among the most exciting things, can have a peculiar, unique kind of beauty. I trained as a civil engineer . . .

BOYCE. Despite the blaze of publicity which you've encouraged – why are you so private about your background, your family?

BILL. Am I? I don't think I am. My father ran an ironmonger store and before you jump in and ask (*Smiles.*) yes, it could be that is where my love affair with metal objects began! And my children . . .

BOYCE. Ah, yes, you have two children, don't you?

BILL. I'm quite proud of them, my son and daughter, Danny and Roxanna. My son's finishing his education, my daughter Roxanna is . . . (*Slight pause.*) a very talented engineer. More girls should do it of course – in fact she shows every sign of being, possibly, brilliant at engineering.

BOYCE. So there'll be two of you! Two of you to watch, will there?

BILL. You make it sound like a threat! (*Sharp smile.*) Maybe there will – she can be both more sensible and more fearless than me at times, (*Looks around.*) very possibly there will be two of us, yes . . .

BOYCE. Now, you would accept, Mr Galpin, that when you've made the amounts of money you have, that brings with it a considerable degree of power?

BILL (*moving in chair, both chair and him sliding out of spot*). Depends what sort of power you are talking about.

BOYCE. You've disappeared into utter darkness again Mr Galpin. (*Sharp.*) Literally removed yourself . . . Could you move the hot seat back, because you are totally invisible at the moment.

BILL *leans forward. Just his actual face visible, rest in darkness.*

BOYCE (*moving back into light, totally illuminated, incisive*). All I've said is – we're putting up buildings at the moment all around us, this extraordinary expansion of high rise buildings, which are based on a faulty engineering principle, calculated only to work in ideal conditions on totally flat ground. The whole basis of system building, which is what is being used because it's cheap, is that every part will fit absolutely perfectly into every other part, all right for an intricate machine like a watch but impossible in a building, which means the blocks going up now will begin to leak and crack, almost from birth!

BOYCE. This is getting very technical – please can we . . .

BILL. It's not technical – a child of three can understand it! It's important people don't glaze over when they hear such things, (*Moving in light.*) I can see you are glazing over. The viewers can't but I can tell you he's totally glazed all right.

BOYCE. I'm glazing over, because this is too specialised for a show like this. I want to return . . .

BILL (*cutting him off*). These buildings are unsound. It's going to be a massive billion pound failure over the next 20 years.

BOYCE. Mr Galpin this is not the Open University, no doubt you can arrange to appear on that as well, but we are here.

BILL (*cutting him off*). I don't know if there is going to be a record of this programme, whether the tape will be preserved, but I saw *now*, people will be dismantling some of these new buildings, blowing them up within a very few years.

BOYCE. I realise you are here to propagate your views Mr Galpin, but they are irrelevant to what concerns –

BILL. Irrelevant – how?

BOYCE. I don't want to come to blows about this, but we must resume the normal personal questions which is the point of . . .

BILL. I thought you wanted a fight! I was promised tough questions, but I had tougher questions than this in an interview I did for a school magazine last week.

BOYCE. You like using aggression do you?

BILL. Depends on whom. On you. Yes, at this precise moment, most certainly.

BOYCE. Let's take a look at these qualifications of yours shall we?

BILL. Why not. Absolutely! (*Ebullient.*) And let's take a look at you too – let's break down these artificial barriers, let's pull you into the light.

BILL *slides his chair and then gets up in pursuit of* VERNON BOYCE.

BILL. So come on, let's see what's lurking here shall we.

BOYCE (*loud, urgent*). And that concludes tonight's show. Thank you and good night. Are we rolling? Music?

BILL. No, don't be bashful, let's shatter this gimmick shall we.

Pulling balding man into spot, both in spot for a second as music rolling.

Let the viewers take a look at your 'qualifications'. That's right . . .

Blackout as music rolls.

Scene Four

ROXANNA *leaning against the proscenium smoking, behind her sounds as if from a busy street, mixed with music as if from a busker. She's got heavy make-up on, her clothes late sixties, but not stereotyped, showing an unconventional taste.*

ROXANNA. October 13th – something odd happened today. Quite by chance, having not seen him for many weeks I met him in the street, in the middle of the West End, Dad – who by now hardly goes anywhere on foot.

It was like he'd willed the accidental meeting to happen, demanded that there I would be, right in his path, at that very moment.

He was wearing these startling clothes, in fact I saw his coat first, and then his strangely coloured shoes, of course, before I looked up and saw who was wearing them. As usual his efforts to be fashionable were just slightly off, slightly wrong, but the effect is typical of him, rather crude but also something more interesting, a sort of mixture of bludgeon and elegance.

And he was bearing down on me, bristling with energy, with the boy genius trotting at his heels.

BILL *enters dressed in a cashmere coat, unbuttoned, with its fine scarlet lining showing, and his gun-metal grey shoes. The effect is striking.* MICK *following him, in jeans and an anorak, and holding papers under his arm.*

ROXANNA. I thought I recognised that walk.

BILL. Roxanna – I might not have recognised you. (*Up close.*) What's all this? Smudges all over your face. (*Slight smile.*) You haven't been home for a while.

ROXANNA (*lightly*). If you go around looking like that – it's not surprising, how can I be seen with you?

BILL (*sharp smile*). What's wrong with the coat?

ROXANNA. I don't know what I'm going to do about your choice of clothes. (*Touches his collar.*) I was going to write any day now – I've been really busy.

BILL. Busy at what, what've you been up to?

ROXANNA. This and that. I'm hanging out with some interesting people. (*Lightly.*) You wouldn't like them. (*Tone changes.*) I thought you'd be angry with me still, after all those letters, after I quit the engineering course. Just for a year of course, quit university.

BILL. No. (*He smiles.*) Not worth the effort. OK – you need time to look around. I'll give it to you.

ROXANNA. Will you?

BILL. You want me to try to stop you – is that it? I'm not going to do that. (*Shrewd look.*) You'll come back when it's right.

ROXANNA. Yes, I know.

MICK (*very impatient*). We're going to be late you realise.

BILL. Yes – that means we must be. He never says anything usually, so obviously we're very late!

ROXANNA (*glancing at the boy, then back at* BILL). All these projects, I've lost count of them! And they're beginning to get written up in the papers as well –

BILL. You're reading about them then? Good.

ROXANNA (*close to him*). Can't help it, can I – you keep on sending me the cuttings. You should stop appearing on television so often you know, you're being over-exposed, but *if* you do any more, you have this extraordinary two-tone delivery you realise, you mumble and then right in the middle of the sentence you bark out the rest, there's no need for that.

BILL (*slight smile*). Any other lessons you want to give me?

MICK. Come on for chrissake – we mustn't be this late.

BILL. Yes – he's right. We're about to go and rip away some cobwebs, get his ideas away from some of the idiots who've been sitting on them. (*He smiles.*) A meeting I hope they're dreading. (*Moves, then suddenly turning back to her.*) Why don't you come and see? (*Quiet, inviting.*) Come on . . .

ROXANNA. I'd like to but – (*Slight pause.*) No, I can't Dad – not now. Another time . . .

Lights up on table and two chairs front stage left. GANT, *a slight blond man, in his early thirties, standing waiting.*

ROXANNA *watches them approach the table before she exits.* GANT *has a long pale expressive face, flapping hands, he is full of a sudden, surprising intensity.*

GANT. It's terrific, absolutely terrific, to see you here in person, to welcome you. Best thing that's happened to me all week.

BILL. That's the kind of greeting we were not expecting.

MICK. In the circumstances it's the least he can do.

BILL. Maybe we should come in again – see if it gets even better the second time.

GANT. I mean it.

BILL. Nevertheless this will be the only conversation we ever have (*Looks at him.*) unless we can work something out now.

GANT. Exactly. I feel the same.

BILL. This boy is gifted (*Dangerous smile.*) is he not? A little difficult, but genuinely very gifted. He looks at machines and structures with an original eye, sometimes startlingly original. *So where the hell are his designs?*

MICK (*loud*). What have you done with them?

BILL (*sharp, moving*). He comes out of nowhere – a tiny engineering firm in the Midlands, with spectacular ideas! You take options on his designs, an especially long option on one of the best, the quiet diesel engine.

MICK. Which has the potential for selling all over the world . . .

BILL. And you've been sitting on that idea for two-and-a-half years – doing absolutely nothing.

GANT *standing still, facing them.*

GANT. It's an appalling situation I know. It's indefensible.

BILL. And so now you are going to try to defend it.

GANT. Absolutely not. I have just taken over the department and what do I find? I was expecting it to be bad, even very bad, but what I've been greeted by is literally indescribable.

MICK (*out of corner of his mouth*). I can describe it.

GANT. I don't think it's possible for me to exaggerate the incompetence I have found here.

MICK. At least he's realised that much.

GANT (*with surprising intensity, back at him*). Of course I've realised it. (*Moving, animated.*) Would outsiders ever believe what goes on here? The main government agency for research and development – you know we now have actual first refusal on discoveries and inventions pioneered in our universities, yes, all the time we have so many different people coming to us – and what have we done? What do we do?

BILL. You do fuck all. That's what you do.

GANT (*unblinking*). Fuck all. Precisely. (*Straight back at him.*) There are no fucking decisions taken if it can possibly be helped.

BILL (*watching him*). And no risks are ever taken.

GANT (*loud, animated*). No risks at all. That's right! Not even small ones. It's like they are forbidden by edict. And things take so long here.

BILL. People publish their discoveries rather than try to market them.

GANT (*loud*). That's absolutely right!

BILL (*forceful, testing for his reaction*). . . . Because at least they get some recognition that way, who can blame the bastards? And a whole range of inventions escape abroad to be gleefully picked up by others, who can't believe their luck. It's –

GANT. It's unforgiveable. And it has to be stopped. (*Straight at BILL.*) Doesn't it! You know we were founded to prevent them escaping and yet they are going all the time. (*Tone changes.*) The things we have lost, some genuinely great ideas. When I think of them . . . (*With feeling.*) the sheer *waste*. (*Suddenly really animated.*) And can you believe the patent system we've still got!

BILL (*warming to this*). The worst in the world, without doubt. It's one of my favourite topics.

GANT (*to MICK*). It can take six years for you to get the patent for your ideas – at least – six years! By which time somebody abroad of course has done it already.

MICK. But we're talking about this organisation – and this organisation is no better.

GANT (*sharp*). No you're wrong. (*Straight at them both.*) We're worse in fact. Considerably worse. We have *one man* to judge all the private inventions that come flowing in here, to decide if we proceed with them or not, how can he be an expert in so many subjects? I have no idea – (*He smiles.*) nor does he. (*Pointing at MICK.*) You know this boy was incredibly lucky to get past him, less than one in a thousand do.

BILL. And look what good it's done him.

MICK. None – worse than none!

GANT. So far. Remember I'm here now. (*Loud sharp.*) Please
remember that.

BILL (*sceptical*). So you're going to really change things are you?
Looking round here, this miserable set up, it certainly doesn't
look like the nerve centre of research and development.

GANT (*with feeling*). I know, I know. I've been thinking about it a
lot recently, it hits you very quickly. Outside the streets are
alive are they not, the new music, the new clothes (*Sharp
smile.*) like you're wearing, the city is vibrant, the country is
vibrant out there, but up here, in these rooms high up here
we . . .

BILL. You should be part of all that. What's happening out there.

GANT (*really animated*). That's it. Exactly. We should, this should
be one of the most significant places, because we're not
ephemeral, we're about the future, ideas that will last – but
instead we are a complete shambles and nobody outside
realises it! Inventions landing here and drying up, dying in
fact. They are. Because there isn't anybody here who will take
the chance. Till now. I have to be able to change that.
(*Looking at him.*) *We* have to.

Slight pause.

MICK. He's bullshitting – this is just to stop us making trouble.
He knows this is what we want to hear.

BILL (*dangerous smile*). That's more than possible.

GANT. If it wasn't such a pleasant autumn evening, I would resent
that. (*Loud, with surprising passion.*) Do I sound like a normal
civil servant, does this seem like the usual crap you get from
them? Am I what you expected? (*Looks at both of them.*) I have
just taken over this place, and I'm still young (*Self-mocking
smile.*) rumour has it, and if I survive in this job, *if*, it will
soon be unrecognisable round here. I will make it happen Mr
Galpin. (*Pointing at the boy.*) And his ideas which I happen to

know are good, one of them is breathtaking in fact, are going to be a top priority.

BILL. They better be.

GANT. Yes, we need somebody to help develop them with us, your interest is just what I want. (*Looking at* BILL.) There are such possibilities now. I can tell you, I've been watching what you've been saying and doing on the media, trying to galvanise support for innovation, reaching out, I really admire that. You are attempting to become a significant patron for new ideas, that's a wonderful notion, don't for godsake stop, you've only just begun!

BILL. Absolutely, I've only just begun, you don't have to tell me that.

GANT. We need people like you, I need people like you, out there, working on the outside, giving a lead. (*With intensity.*) Please, please, whatever you do, whatever happens, don't *stop*.

Blackout.

Burst of sixties pop music mixed with electronic bleeps and other noises.

Scene Five

Spot on ROXANNA *in virginal white wedding dress, standing in spot front stage – as the lights on the main set come on gradually behind her.*

ROXANNA. August 17th – I think it's my wedding morning.

Sometimes you do things that seem truly crazy – to a lot of people anyway . . . including yourself.

DANNY *and* FRANCES *on main set,* FRANCES *draping flower decorations over the great packed heaps.* DANNY *is setting up a row of three machines along base, cylindrical but slightly stocky tubes.* ROXANNA's *shoes and belt, lying on floor.*

ROXANNA *turns, throws her veil back.*

I feel extremely sick.

FRANCES. Natural on your wedding day – you've got to throw up at least once.

ROXANNA (*pulling at dress*). It's like being coated all over in icing sugar – how did I end up doing this?

DANNY. Because you know it's the only way he'd let you get married.

ROXANNA. Oh really, (*Pointing at heaps.*) like this you mean! He's doing it in yet another new house, but he hasn't bothered to unpack!

DANNY. Of course he hasn't – because he'll be moving again, in another few months.

FRANCES (*by heaps*). At least he's taken the plastic wrappings off some of this in your honour!

DANNY. He can't settle anywhere – he's constantly on the move.

ROXANNA (*up to cylindrical machines*). And what are these? I still haven't found out what they are.

DANNY. I think they are some new sort of heat pump.

ROXANNA. Heat pump!

DANNY. Filtering air from outside, or converting or – I don't know, you'll understand it better than me.

ROXANNA. They're all over the place. (*Touching pumps.*) This is truly eerie isn't it – sharing my wedding reception with heat pumps. Pride of place going to the miniature kidney machines, yes have you seen, prototypes of dwarf kidney machines on display right next to the wedding breakfast – they are practically sitting in the bowls of chicken mayonnaise. (*She looks around.*) It's wonderfully vulgar . . .

FRANCES. Of course, you don't expect him to miss a chance like this, to display his likeliest projects, have his wares on show. (*Slight smile.*) And he thought it would be an original touch.

DANNY. Even the musicians are having to play on new lightweight instruments, Roxy, the innovation players, a sort of perspex music, (*Sharp smile.*) only kidding.

ROXANNA (*by heat pumps*). I dread to think what I'm going to get as a wedding present.

DANNY. He has an extraordinary eye for projects at the moment doesn't he – of course a lot of them may not show a return for some time. (*Nervous smile.*) I have to tell him about my new job . . .

ROXANNA. He won't want to hear what *I've* got to tell him . . .

DANNY. He won't approve about this job, he never does, I don't mind, I'll exaggerate the salary if he asks. If only I didn't get so tongue tied when I talk to him, I splutter like an idiot, or suddenly become really leaden, just say the most stunningly obvious things all the time! He shouldn't have that effect on me still.

ROXANNA. Why are we talking about him? I'm the one meant to be getting married and it's getting really close. (*Then immediately turns to* FRANCES.) Who's he bringing today – which of his many girls?

FRANCES. Could be any of the current six – or all six at once of course. He's been Hoovering them up at the moment, girls, just recently.

ROXANNA (*lightly*). Dad only needs a little casual sexual refreshment, a quick snack, it probably only lasts a few minutes with him, and then he's off again alone, working for another six months.

BILL *enters*.

ROXANNA (*without a break*). Did you hear that?

BILL (*straight back at her*). All of it, yes.

DANNY. Hi Dad – you look great.

BILL *in elegant summer suit*.

BILL. Thank you, Danny.

DANNY. And this is all terrific – nobody has ever had a wedding like this, I shouldn't think!

BILL. Clearly. (*Looks across.*) It suits you Roxanna, the dress.

ROXANNA. No it doesn't – I feel ridiculous.

BILL. I was joking, I never thought I'd see you looking like that.

ROXANNA. Neither did I. I suppose I did it to please you. (*Self-mocking smile.*) Extraordinary as it may seem.

ROXANNA *puts a belt on – a red snake round her on top of the otherwise totally white dress.*

BILL. That's much better – that's more like you, isn't it.

DANNY. I have a new job Dad – the one I wanted, at a good firm, Johnson Fulbright, isn't that great news.

BILL (*ruffling* DANNY's *hair*). Well done Danny.

DANNY (*nervous, loud*). It is good isn't it! Better than I thought, they do the accounts for many leading firms, I knew you'd be pleased, half pleased, aren't you?

BILL. It's good Danny. It's fine.

ROXANNA. Don't be so grudging.

DANNY. He's not being, he's not!

FRANCES (*finishing, arranging heat pumps*). So I've done the heat pumps, and the kidney machines, (*Animated.*) that just leaves the super twist liquid crystal display – simple. (*She moves off, abrasive smile.*) OK. I'll expect something for this, extra champagne at least. (*She exits.*)

DANNY (*following her, loud*). I'll help you – this is going to be a wedding that nobody is ever going to forget, I'm sure . . . (*He exits.*)

ROXANNA (*tightening her red snake belt*). So why am I having such a weird wedding reception, Dad?

BILL (*light*). I suppose I thought it would amuse you. Extraordinary as it may seem.

ROXANNA. A wedding full of prototypes! So are all the guests going to be oddly shaped boffins?

BILL. I knew you'd hate a conventional wedding.

ROXANNA (*suspicious*). Is that the real reason?

BILL. Of course. (*Sharp smile.*) You're always saying how old-fashioned I am – in everything but my work – I'm sure people will think this deeply trendy.

ROXANNA (*wary smile*). Oh yeah? Christ knows what Charlie will make of it.

BILL *looks blank for a second.*

Charlie, you know, the man I'm about to marry, my husband . . .

BILL. Oh him! He'll understand. (*He moves.*) I want to tell you about some of the things here – I'm beginning to shift from ideas that . . .

ROXANNA. Dad no. I knew that's why you were doing this! (*Staring straight at him.*) I think you should move several feet from anything breakable right now, go on, because I've got to tell you something. (*Looks at him, then away.*) I'm going to art college. I'm giving up everything else. I'm not doing what you want.

Momentary silence, she stares at him nervously.

Yes, I know, I'm being very predictable aren't I, thinking I can paint, going around smelling of dope, barefoot in the street, slogans on the wall, it's very ordinary I know. (*Loud.*) But I'm doing what I want.

Slight pause. She smiles.

Go on scream at me, tear up the floorboards. (*Defiant smile.*) Whatever you try, I can handle it.

Momentary pause.

BILL. You'll never be any good.

ROXANNA (*combative smile*). That's nice and subtle for an opener! You don't know that at all, you know I've always been good at drawing.

BILL. Not that kind.

ROXANNA. You've never seen anything else I've done.

Slight pause.

BILL (*briskly, watching her*). Right!

ROXANNA (*circling*). Is that it! Is that all I am going to get? I'm
looking for a real fight, come on Dad, aren't I going to get it?

BILL. It's your wedding Roxanna. (*Watching.*) You've chosen the
day very cleverly, to tell me. We can't fight on your wedding.

ROXANNA. Can't we. It's today or nothing.

An alarm goes off, loud and bleating.

Jesus, what the fuck is that?

BILL (*smiles*). Oh just a new form of burglar alarm I'm thinking of
backing, that's the prototype, the guests will constantly set it
off this afternoon as they come in.

ROXANNA (*warm, straight back*). At least it'll drown the speeches
then – including yours for once.

BILL. I'll show you how it works in a minute. (*Moving towards
her.*) These are exciting times you know Roxanna.

ROXANNA (*straight back*). Oh I know that! It's my wedding.

BILL. – and all that knowledge you've got has to be kept ticking
over.

ROXANNA. It's childhood knowledge that – it's going . . .

BILL. You'll find you can't get rid of it.

ROXANNA. Can't I? – I've managed to forget the makes of all the
cars you taught me, on those walks as a kid.

BILL. I'll give you a test and we'll see.

ROXANNA (*watching him, moving slightly as he gets close*). You
know when we got to the park on those walks, because I was
always so excited being with you, I used to imagine the pond,
instead of having boring old ducks in it, was full of a dynamic
subterranean filter system, with superbly engineered new
pipes, twisting around, doing wonderful things. (*Right up to
him.*) So we're declaring an armistice are we, you and me?

BILL. Maybe . . . yes.

ROXANNA (*lightly*). Do I trust you? (*Wary.*) I expected you to
attack harder. Your tie needs retying. (*She begins to do it.*)
Otherwise you don't look bad at all, almost elegant. (*As she ties*

tie.) I'm more than a little worried about what *you're* doing you know.

BILL (*surprised*). What *I'm* doing?

ROXANNA (*lightly*). Yes, some of it could be good, although I wish you were a little more socially aware, to put it mildly, gave something to charity for a start.

BILL. I do!

ROXANNA. Not enough. (*Stronger.*) And you have to be careful you're not backing too many things, spreading yourself over too many areas.

BILL (*surprised*). First you tell me I'm going to seed, now you say I'm doing too much.

ROXANNA (*forcefully*). And you don't delegate.

BILL (*really loud*). You're *always* telling me to do that – you used to yell from your cot 'delegate, delegate, for chrissake delegate some more!'.

ROXANNA. You don't know how to, that's your problem. And you're bombarding people too much at the moment, you're always popping up somewhere with your ideas.

BILL (*amused smile*). I'll tone some of it down then.

ROXANNA. Yes, I don't want you making too many enemies – a few is good of course.

BILL. So – my little girl . . . always giving advice.

ROXANNA (*animated, energised*). That's right – your 'little girl'. Got any normal parental advice for her on her wedding day, about sex maybe. 'Get enough of it, make sure he satisfies you.' (*Sharp smile.*) Actually he's above average in that department, good, solid performer. (*Looks at him.*) I don't see why *I* should give all the sound advice around here . . .

BILL. Since you ask, since you want to know.

ROXANNA (*loud, immediately moving away*). That was really stupid of me wasn't it – no don't say what you're about to, OK, don't you try to –

BILL (*cutting her off*). Would I tell my only daughter not to get married 50 minutes before her wedding?

ROXANNA. Yes you would – no doubt about it at all.

BILL. Then I will. You shouldn't do this Roxanna – I can't put it any other way. He's not right for you.

ROXANNA (*furious*). Jesus!

BILL. And you don't really want him either.

ROXANNA. I wondered when your real assault would come, you think he's influencing me away from what I should be doing – is that it – you're completely *wrong*.

BILL. No – I think you want to be part of what I'm doing, this is not like trying to force one's kid to do something they don't want, quite the opposite.

ROXANNA *looking at him*.

For some reason at the moment you won't let yourself – but this guy is not going to make you happy Roxanna, I promise you.

ROXANNA. Oh yes he will, everything is always so screamingly obvious to you isn't it, you feel you can just beam in on my personal life for a few minutes, and know all about it.

BILL. I think about you quite a lot, more often than you will ever guess. (*Calmly.*) And to make you even more furious Roxanna (*Looks at her.*) – I'm usually right aren't I?

ROXANNA (*shouting*). No, not always, no . . . no.

BILL (*softly*). Don't do it Roxanna.

ROXANNA. I'm warning you, stop it for chrissake, just stop it. (*Strong, dangerous.*) You hear.

Pause.

BILL (*quiet*). OK . . . OK.

Music in distance.

ROXANNA. That wasn't funny you know.

BILL. I was only testing.

ROXANNA. No you weren't, that's rubbish, total shit, that's not worthy of you, you were deadly serious and you know it. And you're not going to be able to resist another push, are you? (*Looks at him.*)

BILL (*lightly*). Come here – come on.

ROXANNA. Why?

BILL. I've been taking dancing lessons – I want to try a few steps.

ROXANNA. How typical – the constant 'self-improvement' classes you insist on doing. Hoping to go to society balls are you?

BILL. Maybe.

ROXANNA. You still want that, don't you, to belong to all that! Thrilled at last to be accepted by, which club was it? The Saville?

BILL. The RAC. The Saville turned me down.

ROXANNA (*moving closer*). I bet you took lessons in two sorts of dancing as well, ballroom and tap probably, wasn't it?

BILL. Yes. Totally correct. So we'll dance? Just dance. OK . . . I'll try out my waltz . . . Can even talk about your painting.

They dance.

(*Sharp smile.*) You know I thought you were bright enough to see that things arty are not more glamorous . . . than, say, heat pumps!

ROXANNA (*slight smile, straight back*). I'm quite bright enough – to see that.

BILL (*as he dances*). As I've got hold of you, I'll just tell you a few of the things I'm investing in, a few of the projects I'm backing, and maybe you'll give me your opinion, just for old times' sake, Roxanna?

ROXANNA. I knew it. (*Slight smile.*) There's no way, Dad, I'm coming back, you do realise that. Absolutely no way.

Blackout.

Wedding music continues, fades into the buzz of electric typewriters.

Scene Six

The table and two chairs front stage, GANT waiting, new leaflets and brochures piled high on table, sharp pencils and a large stapler.

GANT standing stock still waiting for them.

BILL and MICK move towards him. BILL is wearing same suit as wedding, but with new cashmere coat over it and with another brilliantly coloured lining. MICK is more soberly dressed than in previous scene with GANT.

GANT. Gentlemen – welcome. How terrific to see you . . . I've been expecting you.

MICK. I bet you have.

BILL. Just wait a moment Mick. (*Restraining hand on boy.*) Let's see if we can do this in a civilised way . . . (*Dangerous.*) as far as is possible.

> BILL *sits authoritatively, his coat spread out, smoking.*

(*Dangerous smile.*) Something's been happening, something which very rarely happens to me – you haven't been returning my calls . . .

GANT. I haven't been returning your telephone calls! That can't be so. Of course I'd return them – I would be quite mad not to answer calls from somebody like you. (*Making a note.*) There must have been a failure of communication around here. I'll look into it straight away.

BILL (*icily*). You haven't been answering my letters.

GANT. Letters! Ah letters are different – they may have gone to one of my colleagues, they deal with the mail – I'll investigate this personally.

MICK. What shit is this?

BILL. Patience, patience. (*Staring at GANT.*) Do you know how long it is since we three first met?

GANT. A little while – I've been hoping you'd be in touch.

MICK. But he has been in touch!

BILL. Thirty-four months – just roll that around for a moment and feel its length, how does it seem? Is that long enough?

GANT (*calmly*). Thirty-four months, really? Time evaporates doesn't it, vanishes – must be even truer for someone as busy as you are.

BILL. And you know what the funny thing is?

GANT (*surprised*). What's the funny thing?

BILL. You look so well on it – (*To* MICK.) He's positively blossoming isn't he!

MICK (*loud*). He's definitely blossoming yes – while he does fuck all.

BILL (*restraining hand*). Gently, gently. Can you tell me very simply, very directly, what's going on here?

GANT. I can tell you precisely. We've been very busy having to process everything that comes in here, thousands of unsolicited ideas. (*He smiles.*) Mostly in brown paper parcels you'll be interested to hear, in fact for a time you couldn't move round here without stepping on a brown paper parcel. We've been restructuring and now the department is transformed, as you can see. Look at these leaflets you'll . . .

BILL (*straight at him*). You've got this boy's designs and inventions and you are effectively destroying them by doing nothing for year after year, that is criminal – it's not even as if they'd cost that much! There can be no defence for such behaviour.

GANT. No, no, we are not doing nothing. That is totally unfounded. We are waiting, and waiting hard, any day we expect . . .

MICK. Waiting for what for chrissake!

GANT (*to* BILL). Waiting for certain people we have approached about his ideas, people who might develop them with us, to respond. And we're going to hear very soon, all being well.

MICK (*incredulous*). I don't believe this! I just can't.

BILL. Not so loud. (*Staring at* GANT.) Correct me if I'm wrong – but I was under the strange impression that you already had an entrepreneur who was rather eager to commit money to this boy's ideas! A great deal of money, to develop them, either in partnership with you, or to take them off you entirely, for *ever*.

MICK (*loud*). If only you could.

GANT (*to* BILL). And you'll be next, I assure you! You are the very next one on our list. Yes! Without doubt, if these others don't come through, I'm sure . . .

BILL (*moving by small table*). You have turned this place into a mad house you realise.

GANT. Our ways may seem a little strange at the moment, but there is method here, and I'm personally still totally committed to putting an end to the waste of the past, we must take more risks, the situation is crying out for it. (*He smiles.*) You know I'm flattered that a tycoon of such passion and energy and somebody who is investing in a whole range of other ideas, should be spending so much time, is so obsessed with this one.

BILL (*moving*). Obsessed. Did you say obsessed?

GANT. Please don't feel I think you are over-concentrating on it, no, let me say at once, I think you have a very good nose for finding winning ideas.

MICK (*loud, imploring*). Just give me my designs back – OK – just give them back. I'll do anything to get them back!

GANT. No, no we can't do that. We can't return them. I can see true possibilities in them, as you know. They're *major* ideas.

MICK (*shouts*). Jesus! . . .

BILL (*to* MICK *as he moves round desk, bearing down dangerously on* GANT). Don't get angry, that's a mistake, don't raise your voice at him.

GANT. Absolutely. We are after the same thing totally. You are stirring things up and so am I. Every day we take a step nearer making it happen here, backing good projects. I *assure* you I am not just saying this for your benefit. Things are changing at last. I think we'll surprise each other, I do.

BILL (*catching hold of him*). I have that feeling too, I have that feeling really rather strongly, right at this moment.

GANT. I think now I may have a call coming through, I have to take . . .

BILL (*rage controlled, but frightening*). I can see us coming back year after year, and you flapping around this office, waving your hands, shouting 'everything is changing, it really is', becoming a kind of nemesis for us, getting more and more passionate with each fucking visit.

MICK (*alarmed*). Bill, careful –

GANT (*loud*). I have an urgent call about to come through, I can hear it, will you kindly just . . .

BILL *has got him by the tie.*

BILL (*indicating MICK*). He thinks you were always full of shit – but I think for a moment you really meant it. (*Pulling tie.*) You did – and then you got to the brink and decided doing nothing was much easier, for some reason. (*Loud.*) You won't act will you, and that's going to go on and on and on.

BILL *staples him to desk, jabbing down on tie.*

I am not going to let that happen, my friend.

Blackout.

Scene Seven

Applause dying away, as if at the end of a public speech, rustling, buzz of conversation, a slide screen being lowered with spotlight on it, a single microphone on stand in middle of the stage. Frontstage DANNY and ROXANNA, extreme left, on edge of stage.

DANNY smart suit and tie, small hamper at his feet. ROXANNA dressed in black, her voice different, new languid tone. They are passing a bottle of wine between them. ROXANNA's face is like chalk.

ROXANNA. Is he on soon? I don't like this suspense . . .

DANNY. I think any moment – still writing his speech somewhere under the stage probably.

He stares around, holding the bottle, taking a gulp.

It's a weird sight – the whole of the Albert Hall filled with company directors.

ROXANNA (*taking the bottle off him*). I think I'll need several bottles to get through this.

DANNY. You've missed the hamper lunch. (*He smiles.*) Every captain of industry has one each, a hamper to himself, to tuck into.

ROXANNA. Maybe they'll be so full, they'll sleep through his speech, heaving stomachs all round.

Looking at microphone.

Is it going to be embarrassing Danny? He's not going to strut about all over the place is he? – I don't want it to be embarrassing.

DANNY. I don't know, I'm not sure how he'll play it . . . Just so long as he doesn't pitch it to the TV audience. It's not the done thing . . . the people here wouldn't approve.

ROXANNA (*another swig of the bottle*). I never realised that a hall entirely full of managing directors would have such an amazingly pungent smell.

DANNY (*sharp smile*). Cigars lighting up, although all smoking's banned! (*Staring up the side of the proscenium.*) Ash falling on our faces . . . You know I want to be among them, one of them, more than anything else, Roxanna, I admit it. (*Broad smile.*) It's simple, it's all I want . . .

Lights dimming on them, spot brightening middle of stage.

ROXANNA (*with bottle*). What's happening? Is this it?

DANNY. I hope Dad isn't tempted to attack them in any way, it may not go down too well – he's a lot more successful than most of them.

ROXANNA (*as light fading on them*). Where are you? I'm going to hold onto you, in case this is going to be really bumpy.

BILL *enters in spot, in his pale suit, and defiant red and white shoes.*

Danny those shoes – what on earth is he doing in those shoes?

BILL *taps microphone.*

BILL. Afternoon.

Behind him on screen plump face of Victorian gentleman appears.

I want you to take a look at this face, this undistinguished flabby face, usually these are the people that escape for ever, the ones that say *no*. This man is a good friend of mine – Sir William Preece. Who? Precisely, his name hasn't been heard in public for eighty years. (*Barking it out.*) Preece, head of the British Post Office. (*Anarchic smile.*) It could become a new expression 'to Preece', 'preecing' . . .

Slide changes, another view of same gentleman.

In 1873, he turned down Thomas Edison's development of electric light, declaring that it was a 'completely idiotic idea' – in 1876 he turned down the telephone saying it might be all very well for the Americans, but the British had plenty of small boys who could run messages for them . . . Not bad going was it, in the space of three years turning down two of the most important inventions of the nineteenth century and still having time to be chairman of his club's wine committee. (*Staring up at the fat face.*) I have his picture above my desk, and I'll be handing out copies for you at the end – because my contention is we are all Sir William Preeces now, all of us *here*. Maybe he was the beginning of the end, the end of the age of risk.

Slide changes, another view of Sir William Preece's smug face, which continues to stare down during speech.

I am going to use a very filthy word now – a word that shocks and is generally considered obscene, I am an engineer! Yes, an engineer. They will bleep that out of the telecast, it is already erased, otherwise people will be phoning in to complain.

Moving in spot.

Why has that become such an unfashionable, discredited

occupation? (*Glancing around, sharp smile.*) Just look at your reactions, the revulsion up there – we have to promote the idea of the engineer as superstar – to capture the minds of the young (*Close, soft, in microphone.*) . . . and why my friends are we so *afraid*, all of us, businessmen and financiers sitting here on this sleepy Friday, afraid of innovation, of backing it . . . terrified of failure.

Takes microphone off stand, moving, spot following him.

We believe we're progressing don't we, to a hot technological future, but this is an illusion of course because only a tiny fragment of the progress and inventions that are created are *allowed* to happen.

FRANCES *coming on with large basket, moving a little nervously into spot.*

Because for a start we often suppress them don't we? Large corporations for miscalculated business reasons buy up patents and kill the ideas. Simple ideas that could make a difference to all our lives. We all know the example of the ever-lasting light bulb developed some years ago – and suppressed but, by an extraordinary coincidence, I have some here.

FRANCES *with large basket of snowy white light bulbs.*

(*Sharp smile.*) How did I get hold of them you'll be asking? Aren't they beautiful – first time, they've been seen in public for many years, we'll be handing them out at the exit later, (*He smiles.*) to a lucky few. Thank you, Frances.

FRANCES *moves off with bowl of light bulbs, as she passes BILL, he plucks one out of the basket.*

(*Looks out, direct, as if they were all personally responsible.*) But far more important than the suppression we go in for – is what we've allowed to escape. We allowed the jet engine to get away of course didn't we, the whole commercial development of penicillin, the computer naturally, even an early form of lego, the most successful toy in history – because *we* just wouldn't back them when they asked us. (*He clicks his fingers.*) Ideas are escaping right this moment as we sit here – and of course because we hate them.

He glances out sharply.

Yes we do don't we, we entrepreneurs. I'm guilty of this, I freely admit it. We hate the individual inventor, the loner, who comes arrogantly along with an idea out of nowhere. Ask any patent agent and he will tell you there is an officially recognised jealousy factor that inventors must be aware of, the manufacturer deeply resenting profits accruing to an individual who dared to come from outside the firm. Some people not in industry find this hard to believe but we know it's true. (*Smiles.*) We know we can be jealous bastards.

FRANCES *coming back on, joins him in spot, carrying two rifles.*

I can see people ducking, don't worry, I am not going to shoot the worst offenders today.

BILL *taking the rifles, one in each hand, holding them, his arms high.*

Let's take the story of two guns, a very vivid and savage example of the jealousy factor at work all the way from the war in Vietnam, you see how far it stretches.

BILL *standing with two guns.*

The M14 and the AR15 – (*Sharp.*) this doesn't get too technical so don't worry! The M14, (*Waving one gun.*) the gravel belly is inefficient and unsuited to jungle warfare. Along comes an outside inventor, that detested animal, with this. (*Waving other gun.*) The AR15, fully automatic, easily loadable. Despite huge pressure, the American Army of course won't take it – but when eventually they are forced to, what do they do?

He tosses one gun at FRANCES, *moves with the other round stage.*

So as not to lose face – the jealousy factor – they have to 'develop' and 'militarise' it, which means (*Pulling back catch on gun.*) it now jams most of the time when it worked perfectly before, and it has such a big kick (*Moving with gun.*) that if I took a shot at – Sir William Preece for instance . . . (*Lifts gun.*) it will probably split my head open. Do I have any volunteers?

Swings round with gun.

The brutal truth is, the Vietnamese didn't even bother to take these off dead bodies. (*He smiles.*) Usually the J. factor only kills ideas not people. Thank you Frances.

FRANCES *leaves. He has retained one gun. He moves back, close to microphone.*

(*Direct, incisive.*) People are *not* getting the technology they deserve I'm sure you agree, (*Sharp smile.*) we're not giving it to them, are we? Someone said to me, just last week, all the fun is in computers now, because cars and planes and most machines are a static product. Well computers are beautiful of course and vital and I have put money into them. *But* the motor car has basically not changed in 40 years and pollutes like hell! And of course people are not getting the buildings they deserve either – a particular obsession of mine as you may know, but you'll be spared that right now (*Spins round.*) except I just want to ask how many here have put up a decent corporate building recently? (*Moves across stage.*) Come on anybody? I see no hands, one at the back – we'll all be along later to have a look.

Pause, he stands staring at them.

So . . . you're asking what the hell is he doing about it? If anything!

He makes a signal into the wings.

Can we have them now please . . . (*He looks back at them.*) I'm attempting in a relatively small way to back individuals and groups with original ideas who have a real excitement about the future and I hope a lot of you will join with me this afternoon.

FRANCES *and* MICK *come on from either side of stage, wheeling on scale models about the size of a child's pedal car, of a road-rail vehicle, a stocky craft with a dynamic and startling pointed nose. They arrange the vehicles around* BILL.

One never knows where knowledge will strike from does one – where ideas will be born. And here is an example.

Moving the boy into the spotlight.

This is Mick, a mechanical engineer and inventor of brilliance, possibly genius, who has designed this rather magical craft, his very latest idea. Like nothing you've ever seen before. (*Sharp smile.*) These are scale models of course, next time I'm here I'll bring the real thing! This is a road-rail vehicle, that can run on roads and very rough roads at that, and then move straight onto rails and then back again, effortlessly, retracting one pair of wheels like retracting claws.

In the Third World, over large portions of the globe this will have a vital use, revolutionise transport, for it can go up mountains and down sheer valleys, no longer will land have to be flattened, forests cut down, hugely expensive tunnels built. It combines the adaptability of the landrover with the power and grace of a train.

Moving with craft, wheeling it along stage.

Feast your eyes on this craft, it is a simple and world beating idea, and I am going to build it. Who will join me today on this great adventure? (*Brisk.*) Thank you.

Blackout.

Scene Eight

Music behind her, ROXANNA is standing in spot front stage in her dark clothes winding a dark scarf around her neck, her head half turned away, as if from the light. Her voice has a new, languid, slightly stoned, drawl. Half-way through speech she watches the boy, MICK, lifting the models of the road-rail craft and putting them on a pile in the half light.

ROXANNA. September 8th. Heavy days . . . and nights . . . curtain drawn, hot little room, claustrophobic, dark, shutting out everything, even on the brightest mornings. (*She turns.*) Certainly tasting things I've never tasted before . . . having to struggle through a sea of mess on the floor to get to anything – including my husband. Dirty sticky sheets, old joints floating in the coffee cups – and me curled up . . . in this tight little black ball . . .

ROXANNA *turns as lights up on main set, moving in the dark coat, shoulders hunched, face pale. The models being thrown on the pile, suitcases being shut, sheets being folded, exuberant sense of movement, of imminent departure, clothes and old possessions being collected up.* FRANCES *strapping boxes and slapping labels on the suitcases.* DANNY *moving things,* MICK *sitting on top of the great pile.*

DANNY (*staring at* ROXANNA's *white face*). What's happened to you?

ROXANNA. A rough night, that's all.

FRANCES. Looks like one of several to me.

ROXANNA. One of several hundred more like – life's so busy you see. (*Touching the packed objects.*) So he's off again – never can keep still can he!

MICK *on top of pile, walking along, collecting various items he wants.*

MICK. Yes – we're off! It's incredible isn't it? – He's really going to build this, (*Holding model.*) a prototype and then a whole network over hundreds of miles, we're going to Africa.

ROXANNA (*startled*). To Africa . . . I didn't realise.

MICK. Oh yes – and you know he's done this Albert Hall speech again about my designs, he's high-jacked several more occasions to do it.

ROXANNA (*dryly*). Played other gigs has he? (*Looking at model with professional eye.*) The wheels are a clever mechanism, but I think this machine has a perverse shaped front, this nose – it doesn't need to look like that, this is showmanship rather than streamlining.

DANNY. I'm still recovering from the Albert Hall, you could feel the resentment slowly growing stronger and stronger during Dad's speech – couldn't you?

FRANCES (*bustling with luggage*). No, because I was numb with terror, being made to go on stage and face all those managing directors. (*Laconic smile.*) A rotten audience too . . .

DANNY (*incisive*). There is something wonderful isn't there Roxy, comic even, in a person being *right* all the time, and people know he's right, but he appears so fucking rich at the moment – they hate him for it. They loathe Dad – and so they don't listen to a single bloody thing he says.

ROXANNA. Yes, a rich man who prophesies – who needs it! (*She moves.*) The worst possible combination.

DANNY (*sharp*). The more he does, the more they detest it. Especially as it seems to all come so naturally to him, everything, his instinctive taste about which innovation to back. (*Looks at* MICK.) Up to now anyway! The *money* . . . which he then says he doesn't care about.

MICK. They hate him – but they can't do anything about it! And his commitment is total. That's the great thing, he actually rings me in the morning and asks humbly if it just might be possible for him to come and see *me*.

MICK *with a bundle of things from pile, stuffing them into his bag.*

ROXANNA (*suddenly sharp.*) What are you doing with those things?

MICK. Oh he said come and collect what you want.

ROXANNA (*very sharp*). Did he indeed?

MICK. So I am . . . I've got a new flat to furnish.

DANNY. He's put many of his prodigies into first-class accommodation you see.

FRANCES. The very best working conditions. (*Sharp, to* MICK.) I hope they appreciate it.

ROXANNA. How very considerate of him. (*Swings round, loud at* MICK.) Those are my things you're taking you realise, you've even got some of my childhood books for chrissake – put them back at once!

MICK. Oh really – these are yours are they?

DANNY. And mine too.

MICK. I'll leave them – sorry. He said take *anything* you want. I've got to get another bag anyway.

Moves to exit.

You know your father's great – I thought I was a little sideshow, something he'd pick up and then drop just as quickly when he got bored, but I'm not! He's prepared to spend millions on it. (*He exits.*)

ROXANNA (*loud, to* DANNY). Is Dad trying to punish us, is this what this is about? (*Turns.*) Punish *me* anyway – is it?

DANNY. I'm not sure what he's doing.

ROXANNA (*furious*). It's really petty. (*Rattling suitcase keys.*) I ran things here once, after all.

FRANCES. He asks about you a lot Roxanna.

ROXANNA. Does he? Probably hoping to hear my marriage has disintegrated. And how are we coping Frances, with him, with all of this?

FRANCES. Me? I'm okay. It's exciting in many ways.

ROXANNA. In what way?

FRANCES. Moving with his ideas, following his projects, being close to it all. It's strange sometimes, but interesting. I spend my life now, long days, fielding his calls. He won't take any – unless they're from his prodigies, because he's only interested in their special projects, nothing else.

ROXANNA *moves over to pile of belongings, starts burrowing amongst them.*

ROXANNA. Jesus, I'd better find everything that belongs to me, before it's too late. You too, Danny.

DANNY *moving over.*

ROXANNA. There I am living in a filthy rat hole behind King's Cross Station, and Danny's not much better, are you?

DANNY. That's right, no.

ROXANNA. And there he is playing the great patron, making all this noise about discovering talent, trying to coax their ideas into existence by pampering them in a truly embarrassing fashion. Come on Danny, bring some boxes.

DANNY *and* ROXANNA *move urgently, finding their things, packing them away in boxes, old battered suitcases, which they empty, so they can put their things in them.*

DANNY (*as he does this*). This road-rail vehicle, Roxy will cost some colossal figure – he couldn't find anybody to come in with him, they wouldn't touch it, so he's doing it all on his own! He's either being extraordinarily clever . . .

ROXANNA. Or it's one gigantic ego trip.

DANNY. That's right, you know he's gone into property now?

ROXANNA. Property too, that figures.

DANNY. But not normal property, oh no, he's gradually acquiring a site, bit by bit, along the river, so he can build this hugely ambitious housing scheme using entirely new materials, and a so-called 'Invention Park' – Yes! – To show off his prototype . . . he's going to have all these machines buzzing around by the river.

ROXANNA *shutting bulging suitcase, strapping it shut.*

DANNY (*moves*). I want to be able to tackle him about what he's doing, but I find it so difficult still. (*Turning.*) He's spending so much Roxy, if he goes on at this rate – I mean it can't last for ever – he could easily go broke.

ROXANNA (*very startled*). Broke? . . . Really?

DANNY. Not immediately, but when –

BILL *enters, his jacket draped over his shoulders.*

Dad! We were just wondering where you were.

BILL (*warm, to* ROXANNA). So you decided to come after all Roxanna.

ROXANNA (*drawn towards him despite herself*). Yeah – I nearly didn't make it.

ROXANNA *changes, becomes animated as soon as he's there, sparring with her.*

BILL. You look like you're in mourning.

ROXANNA. You couldn't be further from the truth.

BILL. What's that mean? (*He grins.*) She's not, is she? You're not pregnant are you?

DANNY. Don't look at me – she never tells me anything.

ROXANNA. Not at the moment, wrong again.

BILL. I haven't seen you since the Albert Hall, what did you think? (*Surprised.*) People were enraged apparently, have you seen the papers?

ROXANNA. Has there been anything? I try not to read about you.

BILL. ' – Anarchic businessman lectures the captains of industry like they were a bunch of six-year-olds.'

ROXANNA. That's true for a start, you did.

BILL. I'm told I showed utter contempt for them.

FRANCES. I liked the bit about how he thinks of himself as a mixture of Isambard Kingdom Brunel and Billy Graham.

BILL (*lightly, fast*). I'm also meant to be intensely crude, impulsive and have impossible illusions of grandeur, the road-rail vehicle is a reckless imbecility, far from backing brilliance I'm funding eccentrics and losers (*Slight smile.*) and will become a laughing stock.

ROXANNA (*straight back*). Seems rather mild in the circumstances. (*She moves up to him.*) I've told you many times don't pay attention to what's being said about you.

BILL. If you don't read about me – how do you know?

ROXANNA. I know what some people think of you – you should be pleased they're talking about you, that's all.

BILL (*watching her*). One has to be aware of how one's regarded.

ROXANNA (*strong*). Why? What do you want their approval for, for fucksake? It shouldn't concern you at all.

BILL (*slight smile*). Of course Roxanna, I'll try to remember that.

ROXANNA (*loud*). I mean it. I don't know why I'm giving you free advice anyway.

BILL (*gently, closing in*). It's unstoppable, that's why.

ROXANNA *moving away.*

ROXANNA. Not any more. It isn't anything to do with me any longer. I forgot for a moment that's all. (*Tone changes, very sharp.*) Why are you giving away our things?

BILL. What things?

DANNY. There's been a muddle about some of the things –

ROXANNA. We had as kids, that belong to us. (*Straight at him.*) When we three were together remember, and you're letting anybody that walks in here take them.

BILL. That was a mistake obviously, I didn't mean that to happen.

DANNY. I knew it was only a mistake.

FRANCES (*trying to defuse situation*). Of course, and are you sure you've got everything now that belongs to you?

ROXANNA (*cutting in*). Trying to demonstrate something to us are you?

BILL. I told you it was a misunderstanding, for some reason Roxanna you want it to be more . . . we've been trying to contact you for weeks.

ROXANNA. Oh really – so what stopped you?

BILL. You never answer my letters.

ROXANNA. I tried ringing you, you wouldn't take my calls, you were permanently in a meeting, (*Louder.*) all my childhood you were in a meeting, but you always took my calls, always.

BILL (*lightly*). Yes, I remember your little voice jabbing out, in the middle of the financial crises.

ROXANNA. So you're trying to wipe Danny and me out of the picture? Is that it, disowning us?

DANNY (*sharp*). I'm sure it's not Roxy . . .

BILL. Don't be ridiculous. I'm just getting rid of all of this, because I'm moving again and going away too on this long visit to Africa.

ROXANNA (*looking across all the luggage*). It's like a missionary setting out, isn't it?

BILL (*forceful*). I'm going to be able to start building the first ever road-rail network, this is the biggest project I've had Roxanna.

ROXANNA. Clearly. Every time you've moved house so far it's been because you've backed something important. (*Quiet, to herself as she turns.*) Not this time.

BILL. I wish you'd spare a few weeks to come and see, watch the progress, see it grow, nothing more.

ROXANNA. *No*. I can't and you know I can't, *OK*.

DANNY (*quiet, slight smile*). I'd come.

BILL (*homing in on her volatile manner, tone changes*). What's the matter with you Roxanna?

ROXANNA. Who said anything was the matter?

BILL. You look so pale my love, where's Charlie?

ROXANNA. Who?

BILL. Your husband. (*Mischievous smile.*) Wasn't he called Charlie, where is he?

ROXANNA. Oh him. At home. And he's still called Charlie. And before you ask, everything's fine, more than fine.

BILL. Good. (*Up to her, touching her.*) And those aren't bruises are they, that you've covered with make-up? Caked here . . .

ROXANNA (*moving away*). No, of course not. Jesus that was cheap, a typically coarse suggestion. I told you everything's really good. (*Really sharp.*) Better than you can possibly imagine.

DANNY. Please come on you two, I hate it when you fight. Just leave it there, OK.

FRANCES (*unfurling sheet*). Yes, you've all got to help me with the packing, not getting off that lightly, come on.

BILL (*cutting in*). And that's the truth Roxanna? (*Looks at her.*) I'm glad then.

ROXANNA. Are you? (*Circling him.*) Now you're going to say – so what the hell have you accomplished, what do you do with yourself all day?

BILL (*straight back*). No, I don't need to know.

ROXANNA. No. (*Savage, mocking.*) Come to think of it, you're probably paying for 'research' to be done on me, people outside my window, under the street lamps watching for the first sign that you're going to be proved right, so you can move in, start reconstructing me.

BILL. Fine, Roxanna, right . . .

BILL *is moving to exit.*

ROXANNA. Where are you going? We have some business to do.

BILL (*turning in exit*). Business?

ROXANNA. I thought that might interest you.

Slight pause.

I want some money.

BILL *looks at her.*

A lot of money . . .

BILL. I see (*Quiet.*) If you need some, of course. I thought you always said –

ROXANNA. It couldn't matter less what I've always said.

DANNY (*to ROXANNA*). You should leave this for later – don't do this now.

BILL. Quiet Danny. You want it so you can really get away, is that it? From this, from me . . . ?

ROXANNA. No, you're wrong again. I don't want it all for myself. I want to be able to help the friends I've got, artists, with their music, painting, what you'd regard as all that shit, spend it on my project. (*Straight at him.*) I want some of your money before it all goes.

BILL (*dangerous.*) Before what?

ROXANNA. You heard – before you spend it all. Waste it.

FRANCES. Roxanna, don't do this, it really upsets me, please don't.

DANNY. Yes, stop it Roxy, don't push this now, this isn't the way.

ROXANNA (*moving, looking at* BILL). I don't believe in your present schemes, some of them may be of mild interest, no more, others are just fanciful. At first I thought if he has to be a tycoon, he might as well be a reasonably useful one. But that's changed. It's absurd vanity to think you, all by yourself, can make any difference to investment in new ideas.

DANNY. Roxy, this is not what you should be doing, not now, please, please.

ROXANNA. Most of this will fail, the housing project too. You're destroying your chance of doing something worthwhile, squandering it on the wrong things, on ideas that now have to be so ridiculously grand and long-term, which will lead nowhere. I'm sure we're never going to see the result of most of this . . . we're not –

BILL (*loud, furious*). That's enough Roxanna, don't you talk to me like that you understand.

Catches her by the wrist, pulls her close, as if he's going to hit her.

Because you know nothing about it now, *do you.* As you said you've forgotten it all – so don't you try to tell me anything, any more. Is that clear . . .

Pause.

(*Quieter, close, holding her*). Not a word out of you.

Slight pause.

ROXANNA (*quiet, defiant*). No. (*Being held close.*) So you're going to hit me, to show how right you are, are you?

Pause. BILL *looking down at her.*

BILL (*calmly, slight smile*). Not today . . . not now.

He lets her go, moves, takes out his cheque book, begins to write.

(*Slowly, as he writes.*) Since my daughter feels there will be nothing left – she better have it now.

Tears cheque out, gives it to her, moving.

FRANCES (*quiet*). Roxanna, this is shameful.

ROXANNA. This is not enough. (*Slight pause.*) Double it . . . at least.

DANNY (*to* ROXANNA). What are you doing for chrissake? Just stop this will you, now.

BILL (*staring at* ROXANNA). Fine. Do you want to dictate the amount. Come on Roxanna . . . I'll just write.

Silence.

ROXANNA (*very still*). I'll dictate. If you want. 'September 17th 1973, the city is surprisingly quiet, a sullen grey afternoon, a few days before my entrepreneur father is setting out on his great engineering adventure, . . .'

DANNY (*quiet*). What kind of cheque is this?

ROXANNA. . . . 'to my misguided ex-daughter Roxanna who I may not see for a little while (*Momentary pause.*) the sum of twenty thousand pounds.'

Pause.

BILL. There's a signed cheque, fill it up. I have no interest in how much. I don't expect we'll be referring to this again – Frances, come on, we have a great deal of work to do.

FRANCES *moves after him. Before they have exited* ROXANNA *calls out.*

ROXANNA. Dad – I don't know why it came out like that . . . why I said . . . (*Sharp.*) OK – I don't know . . . because I'm not used to asking . . . or something.

BILL *exits, she follows to call after him.*

ROXANNA. Just one of our normal fights (*Loud.*) wasn't it?

Turning to DANNY.

Danny, wasn't it?

DANNY. I don't know . . . maybe . . . It's like a marriage you two. You fight so hard, there's real blood flying around.

ROXANNA. Still – I got the money didn't I? I can get away now.

She sends a model of the road-rail vehicle rolling across stage.

I can get away from all this – I really can.

Fade.

ACT TWO

Scene One

1983.

ROXANNA *sitting on the pavement/floor front stage, smoking, older, her hair different, wearing a comfortable coat, shopping bags round her.* DANNY *leans against the wall of the stage, the side of the proscenium, ringing an entry phone and then staring up, as if looking up the wall of a building. We can hear a bell echoing inside the building. DANNY is holding a large brown paper parcel, and is smartly dressed, in a fine winter coat, sharp and efficient in appearance, he bristles with a new confidence.*

He is rattling his car keys as he moves, then listens to entry phone.

DANNY. Nothing, absolutely nothing, not even a crackle.

ROXANNA. How many times does that make?

DANNY. At least seven.

ROXANNA. Ring it again, we've hardly started.

DANNY. He was definitely expecting us, I made an appointment for 4 o'clock.

ROXANNA. He's not a great respecter of appointments these days, it just means we should be seen within a week or so.

DANNY. I'm sure he's in there – I saw some movement I think. (*Sharp smile.*) Will you recognise him do you think?

ROXANNA. Don't be ridiculous, I saw him recently.

DANNY. I was only kidding. (*He smiles.*) Half.

ROXANNA. I saw him just before Christmas, or rather a few months before Christmas (*Laconic smile.*) for 20 minutes. He sent the kids presents though, weird modules of some sort.

DANNY. Yes, my kids got the modules too. (*Surprised.*) They loved them. I think they were spaceships that could ski on water – no doubt a new project of his!

ROXANNA (*lightly*). Mind you, I don't think he'd recognise my kids, in fact I'm not even sure he remembers who their father is.

DANNY (*close to her, for a moment*). Are things good between you and Dave at the moment – are you happier?

ROXANNA (*smoking, laconic*). Sometimes yes.

DANNY (*moving, flicking keys*). I'm glad things are more settled with you Roxy, terrific . . .

ROXANNA. That's right.

DANNY (*ringing bell*). Maybe we should throw a few stones. Do you think he's staring down right at this moment, watching us. (*Looking up.*) After his restless moving from house to house settling down in this concrete block is a little weird – (*Turns.*)

ROXANNA (*smoking*). You can just see St Paul's, from one of the top lavatories apparently.

DANNY. *I* haven't seen him for over a year. (*Looking at* ROXANNA.) I haven't grown fatter have I? What do you think?

ROXANNA. A little rounder maybe.

DANNY. Really? You sure? I want to look good when I see him.

ROXANNA. Yes. I worry about that too. It's absurd isn't it.

DANNY. I have a lot to tell him, show him what's going on.

Sudden crackle out of entry phone.

What was that? (*Moving.*) Hello, this is Danny – Danny and Roxanna are here, Danny is outside! Down here. (*Loud.*) We're right outside.

Loud inaudible crackling answer from machine then silence.

Doesn't sound hopeful, does it! That noise hasn't unlocked the door. Either they're all still on the phone –

ROXANNA (*smoking*). – Or he wants to keep us waiting for a good while yet.

DANNY. You're being very calm.

ROXANNA. I smashed the doorknob last time this happened to me – so I thought I'd pace myself this time.

DANNY. Well I've got an appointment in town (*Pushing bell.*) and time is just beginning to be money – (*Sharp smile.*) One of the things I want to tell him. I wonder how his work is really going – what with delays in Africa, because of wars and other minor obstacles.

ROXANNA (*smoking*). And all the time that's gone on the electric car too.

DANNY. There's been a clever mix of small potential money makers and these great projects. (*Sharp.*) He kept that balance going longer than I thought. But the big schemes . . . we must be seeing the results soon, *surely*. (*Moving to machine.*) Can spare him one more ring. I really wanted to give him this.

ROXANNA (*looking at the parcel*). What is that?

DANNY. It's a surprise, but since he's kept us waiting.

He tears off paper to reveal a large virulent caricature painting of his father, dark and twisted like a Francis Bacon, on glossy hardboard.

ROXANNA (*startled*). Jesus, where did you get that?

DANNY. It's a blow-up – I had it done specially, a blow-up of the offending article, the cover, I thought he'd like it. Do you think it'll misfire? (*Sharp smile.*) Could enrage him of course.

ROXANNA (*staring at savage caricature*). There's a slight risk yes.

DANNY. I quite like it (*Sharp smile.*) I don't know why . . . (*Breezy, rattling car keys.*) Are you going to the trial? If they fix a date?

ROXANNA. I expect so, it may be the only chance I have of getting to see him.

DANNY (*lightly*). Yes – you know I think somebody got him to sue for libel, so all the people who want to see him will know

exactly where he is on a particular day. (*Looking at*
ROXANNA.) Court No.13 probably.

ROXANNA (*quiet*). The rich man's sport. (*Staring at the picture.*)
Were there two articles? I could hardly get through this one, it
was so boring.

DANNY. I think there were at least two, you know about him
having hired some people to force the remaining tenants and
little shopkeepers off the river site, because he'd had to wait
all these years to build his great housing scheme, that sort of
thing.

ROXANNA (*looking at picture*). I should read it obviously.

DANNY (*lightly*). There're a lot of other things of course, how he's
totally unqualified to make the judgements and attacks he has,
how his ideas are a sham, his crusade for investment in
innovation completely bogus, all the usual things! Very
unfortunately they have offered to settle out of court – I really
hope he doesn't accept, it could be fun.

ROXANNA. Maybe. (*Holding blow-up.*) Can I have this? I think
it's probably a better idea to give it to me than to him.

DANNY (*expansively*). Keep it. I knew you'd want one, so I had
three made. Mine's already hanging up in the hall, pride of
place.

ROXANNA (*sharp smile*). Thanks – I've been looking for a good
picture of him to show the kids.

DANNY. Time's up. No more rings. (*Into entry phone.*) If you're
there Dad – have to go now – I have another appointment.
Catch up with you soon. Your daughter – remember her –
wants to say something.

ROXANNA. Yes – I have to get back now to cook for the kids,
believe it or not. Bye. (*After thought, flashing out of her.*) And
you better bloody not be in there! You hear!

DANNY (*turning as he exits*). He really mustn't settle Roxanna. If
he does, we'll never get to see him.

Blackout.

Scene Two

The court environs, large emblem hanging near the back wall, staring down over the action.

There is a long line of seats, belonging to the court passages, front stage, leather high-backed chairs, beginning to split.

BILL, looking hardly any older, is sitting on one of the chairs, talking into a pay phone, he has slightly filled out round the waist, but his movements are full of energy. FRANCES looks distinctly older, tighter, spikier, less relaxed atmosphere to her than in Act One. She's busy with letters, files under her arm, loud buzz of conversation around passage.

BILL (*on pay phone, smiling*). No, no . . . I just wanted to know how you were doing, see if there were any unexpected signs of progress, the progress you keep promising . . . and of course to make sure you're working your arse off, you *almost* are . . . (*He smiles.*) what does that mean? Almost is a word I never use . . . what? . . . Torrential rain. So what's a little rain!

FRANCES (*bristling*). That's quite enough, come on, stop talking, we haven't got long.

BILL. No . . . I can't now. There is a trial apparently about to take place here. Yes I'm right there now.

ROXANNA and DANNY enter. They are out of their coats of previous scene, now in summer clothes.

(*In full flood on phone, doesn't appear to notice them.*) Yes, I've found a faulty telephone box – you know the sort that doesn't ever run out – so I thought I might as well phone Africa . . . of course (*Mischievous smile.*) I'm going to nip out regularly from the court and use it.

ROXANNA. Oh shit – he's on the phone.

DANNY. And then he'll be in court.

FRANCES. And there are two strangers to see you.

BILL (*into phone*). Yes, so you'll move quickly from now on, right?

BILL looking up to see ROXANNA and DANNY, then slight smile into phone.

As you know my patience isn't infinite.

BILL *rings off. He looks up at* DANNY *and* ROXANNA *for a split second not saying anything, then his tone is polite, but dead towards them, indifferent.*

Hi you two – how are you doing?

ROXANNA (*automatically*). Very well.

DANNY. Hello Dad, it's good to see you.

BILL. Yes. (*Immediately turning away to* FRANCES.) How long have we got?

FRANCES. Not long – how many times do I have to keep telling you. (*Bustling around.*) You can't keep a court waiting you realise, and you have a meeting with your legal team first, we ought to be there now.

DANNY (*to* BILL). We'd like to be able to take you out for a meal one day soon. Just for . . .

Phone rings.

ROXANNA. Christ, not the phone again.

FRANCES (*picking it up*). No, he can't take it.

BILL (*spinning round*). Of course he can take it.

FRANCES. Ring back later, he's completely unavailable now. (*Slamming down phone.*) He's only been here a few minutes and he's managed to give out this number to people! (*To* BILL.) And I don't know why you need conduct everything in the passage – we have a room.

BILL. It's full of lawyers, giving me instructions.

ROXANNA (*to* DANNY). Look at that – my hands shaking.

BILL (*suddenly looking at her*). Why? What's the matter? What you shaking for?

ROXANNA. Probably because I'm more nervous than you are.

BILL. About what? About the trial?

ROXANNA. Oh no, not the trial, the trial doesn't matter.

BILL. Doesn't it? I see.

ROXANNA. Of course not, I mean you can handle a small thing like that, I'm much more nervous about this meeting – seeing you again.

FRANCES (*busy, up to* BILL). Come on, I need you to sign these, give me something to do while you're entertaining yourself in there.

ROXANNA. The main excitement is not what you do in the witness box, but trying to catch you for a few minutes in these passages and see what you do then – (*To* BILL, *slight pause.*) isn't it?

BILL (*ignoring her, to* FRANCES). I need to change I think, the other jacket.

ROXANNA (*nervous smile*). Still the same taste in clothes I see, just a tiny bit behind fashion (*Sharp smile.*) but you're closing the gap I think.

DANNY (*as* BILL *puts on jacket*). Getting read for battle . . . You know in olden times if you lost a libel action you had a limb amputated. They literally were damages, maybe a hand, maybe a foot, and in a particularly bad case perhaps a whole leg. (*Jaunty smile.*) People would love to see that now, wouldn't they, entire legs coming off.

BILL. Thank you Danny – that's just what I was hoping to hear before I went in . . . (*Noise from passages.* BILL *smiles approvingly.*) People queueing already I see.

ROXANNA. Looking for a record turnout are you!

DANNY (*sharp smile*). Give people what they want and they turn up etc. etc.

FRANCES (*loud*). We've got to move now.

MICK *enters, as* BILL *moves.*

MICK (*calling out*). Bill – wait! Just came to wish you good luck.

BILL. Jesus – Mick! Look at him! (*With warmth, embracing.*) How fat he's got – encased now, in lard . . . look at this. (*Gives him a playful jab in stomach.*)

MICK. Just older that's all.

BILL. You're not old – you're just beginning still. (*Sharp look.*) Aren't you?

MICK. I'm more relaxed these days, that's for certain.

BILL (*broad smile*). I don't like the sound of that at all. (*To the others.*) You know what he's doing now?

MICK. I wasn't going to tell you that.

BILL (*warm, fast*). But I know! You didn't think I would but I do. This boy has lost his patents, all of them, except the one I've got. The development council let them lapse and he lost out to abroad so what's he doing? Tell them – he's designing parking meters, a new range of parking meters for Scotland. Can you believe that?

MICK. That's roughly right, yes.

BILL. Exactly right. Come with me. (*Warm.*) It's very good to see you you know, maybe we can reawaken something. (*Knowing smile.*) You never know, a few hours with me. I have news about your large baby, the road-rail vehicle, taking shape in elephant country as we speak. (*Sweeping him off.*)

ROXANNA (*loud*). Dad wait.

BILL *stops, she moves.*

ROXANNA. Your tie needs straightening. (ROXANNA *moves up to him. Pause.*)

BILL (*as she straightens his tie*). Don't give me any advice Roxanna, OK . . . (*He begins to exit.*)

ROXANNA. I need to see –

BILL *exits.*

DANNY (*moving after*). Come on! Come on, got to keep up with him.

ROXANNA. You go ahead, OK. (*As DANNY exits.*) I need a minute to myself.

GANT *enters briskly.*

ROXANNA. Not him as well. Really! (*She turns away.*)

GANT. Hello. (*Advancing towards her.*) We met once I think at your wedding, which I was lucky enough to attend.

ROXANNA. Oh yes, you were part of the innovation display at my reception, there were more machines than guests I remember.

GANT (*sharp smile*). I think I probably went as a guest (*Looking at* ROXANNA.) I've come to watch your father today.

ROXANNA. I gathered that.

GANT. I'm looking forward to it very much, extremely.

ROXANNA. I bet you are.

GANT. No, no, you've obviously been listening to things he's been saying about me – no I admire your father a lot.

ROXANNA (*sharply*). Really?

GANT. I think he's an extraordinary man – there're two ways of looking at him I suppose.

ROXANNA. Just two?

GANT. An inspired innovator taking risks, evangelical, ahead of his time – or somebody who's just turned into a slightly careless property tycoon . . . I favour the first myself. Yes. (*Moves.*) Have to get a good seat – (*As he exits.*) I'm taking an early lunch all week, so I can catch a bit each day.

ROXANNA (*turning, out front*). July 8th. Not so fast! We're not going in – not yet. I'm not sure I'm going to watch it all. The trial's an irrelevance.

July 9th to 14th. I keep coming back, a grown woman hanging around like a groupie, hoping to get him on his own, and all I get is this bloody trial! Not that I *need* to see him of course, just idle curiosity, and I'll be much too busy soon to keep on trying to see him. (*Tone changes.*) I've been in for a few short doses, and what hits you really strongly, there are no close-ups, you get so used to that from all the TV courtroom dramas, you really miss it, no giant close-ups of Dad, it's really disorientating. And there is no one-hundred-year-old judge asking 'Who were these men the Beatles?' etc., not in this trial anyway. Instead there is a very bland, younger than I expected judge, looking like he's made out of rubber, wearing a stupid pink sash and with this air of blubbery malice, and it's so hot in there I keep thinking he's about to melt.

Lights changing behind her.

And Dad has got what he's been hankering for – couldn't do without – a chance to flex his muscles, to perform in the heart of the Establishment, in this ludicrous setting, his two-tone voice ringing out.

And naturally I can't get anywhere near him.

Scene Three

JUDGE, *bland, rubberlike face, sitting high up staring down, wearing his pink sash and frilly cuffs, in front of the emblem.* BILL *standing in the witness box, moving restlessly as if the box is too small to hold him, and then forcing himself to keep still.* QC *moving in front of them, microphone suspended from ceiling, hanging above* BILL. *He occasionally almost hits it with his waving arm. Very hot, sticky, summer light, in two large pools, one round the* JUDGE, *one round* BILL.

QC. Mr Galpin, it is true is it not that you like to describe yourself as an engineer?

BILL (*rapid, light*). Yes, I have described myself accurately as an engineer, you're now going to say (*Very quick smile.*) but I have no formal qualifications as one, because I did not complete my training, and the answer to that is . . .

QC. Please don't try to anticipate my questions, that will get neither us or the court anywhere.

JUDGE *staring ahead.*

BILL (*waving his arm*). I apologise. Ask your questions, I'll answer anything.

QC. As it happens you were right about my next question, it is clearly something you are acutely conscious of – you did not complete your training as a civil engineer did you?

BILL (*rapid, quiet, moving in box*). We are all acutely conscious of where we have come from, how we began; (*To* QC.) are we not? I became involved in electrical ideas out of financial necessity but I did not lose my knowledge of engineering obviously, you are now going to ask but you have never built anything have you? The answer to that is literally true, although it won't be for much longer, some wonderful buildings are about to . . .

QC. You're doing it again Mr Galpin, you're trying to anticipate my questions and this time you are wrong.

BILL. Am I?

QC. These matters are obviously right in the forefront of your mind. Now I hope we won't have to fight over each question, be involved in a race to see who can get it out first.

JUDGE. Yes, it would help if you didn't try to cross-examine yourself Mr Galpin, however competent you may prove to be – try to desist.

BILL. Yes, (*Mumbles.*) my lord. (*Sharp smile.*) I will try to avoid seeing his questions coming.

JUDGE. And maybe you could do us another favour Mr Galpin and make a big effort to keep still.

BILL. Keeping still is what I'm worst at. (*Quiet.*) I will try . . .

QC. Nevertheless you are putting my case to the court very well so far, because one of the issues I want to examine is your professional qualifications. You have not hesitated in pronouncing on many public matters Mr Galpin, building, housing, for instance, and yet you are not an architect?

Pause.

BILL. Sorry, I didn't realise I was meant to reply.

QC. You are not an architect?

BILL. You know the answer to that.

QC. Please do not play to the gallery Mr Galpin, just answer the question please.

JUDGE. I know everybody considers themselves experts in modern architecture these days, but you have never trained as – you are not an architect?

BILL (*glancing around*). No – I am not. Nor am I a fully qualified engineer.

QC. Thank you. I'm glad we've established that. And indeed you made your fortune, your very sizeable fortune, out of a light electrical firm.

BILL. A lot of money, yes.

QC. A great deal of money.

BILL. If you prefer.

QC. And you made this money out of a breakthrough concerning gramophones, and since then you've multiplied your fortune many times. Correct?

BILL (*impatient*). A few times.

QC. And you've been anxious have you not, in the past, to downplay or even to disown this achievement. Why?

BILL (*lightly*). I don't consider it a particularly startling achievement. Once you've got some, any fool can double it.

QC (*sharp*). What did you say? Any idiot can do what?

BILL. No. (*Slight smile.*) Any fool. (*Lightly.*) It's no proof of intelligence, or even any particular skill, quite the reverse in fact in many cases. It was said of my father for instance he was too intelligent to be a rich man. (*He smiles.*) So you see what that says about me. Just to breed money once you've got some is nothing (*Slight smile.*) in my opinion.

QC. I see. And so you have used some of this money to very publicly sponsor a range of miscellaneous inventions?

BILL. Various innovative schemes and designs, yes.

QC. And how many of these varied innovative schemes and designs are on the market at the moment, can you tell us?

BILL. Most are still in development.

QC. How many?

BILL. A couple – I don't want to anticipate your question (*Quick smile.*) and I certainly cannot see it coming, but you are going to want to know a couple out of how many.

QC. Please tell us.

BILL (*lightly*). A couple out of over a hundred – but that is because . . .

QC. Because they're still in development – yes you told us. And some of them have clearly already failed, is that the case?

BILL (*lightly, but incisive*). No, none have failed so far. None. I want to make that clear, (*Slight smile.*) and they're all on schedule despite rumours to the contrary. They are long-term projects. They may take over a decade to come to fruition or more, (*Louder.*) that is why I was interested in them, that is why nobody else wanted anything to do with them. And that is why I decided to spend so much on . . .

QC (*cutting him off*). I see. And you didn't have experts, scientists, or experienced engineers to evaluate what was being offered to you?

BILL. No.

QC. You felt qualified to judge them all, you never delegated, because you have a profound belief in your talent for this – isn't that right?

BILL. If you have found you are reasonably good at spotting potential, you feel confidence in carrying on. You will want to know why in the case of the land acquisition I decided to delegate and . . .

QC. You're doing it again. Not so fast, don't be . . .

JUDGE (*cutting in*). You really must stop asking yourself questions Mr Galpin.

BILL (*giving it an odd emphasis*). Yes, my lord.

QC. You are fond of publicity, are you not?

BILL (*lightly*). No, that's not true.

QC. You are not claiming you are shy of it?

BILL. Nobody's ever called me shy – I admit that, but that's quite different.

QC. I shall rephrase. Over a period of time you have deliberately used your appearances on the media, especially television, for your own purposes?

BILL. Yes, of course. (*Slight smile.*) Doesn't everyone who appears on it do that . . . I wanted to try . . .

QC (*sharp*). I'm coming to that – you wanted to shake up the general approach to innovation and research. Act as a kind of catalyst isn't that so?

BILL. Yes. I wanted to express various ideas. I was certainly not the only one expressing them, but I wanted to broadcast them as widely as possible, popularise . . .

QC. Popularise, exactly. And that is why you sought publicity so avidly. Correct?

BILL. Sought no, accepted yes.

QC. And you 'accepted' opportunities, for instance, if we take a glance at a couple of these ideas, to castigate the record of British management.

BILL. Naturally, no sane person could do anything else, given the opportunity. Initially my interest, (*He smiles.*) my 'obsession', was in how many good ideas we were losing, wonderful notions slipping away, because of our terror of thinking further ahead than tomorrow afternoon, (*He smiles.*) to be deliberately provocative because I don't think it's changed – there's a lack of enterprise.

QC (*sharp*). You say initially this was your obsession.

BILL (*lightly*). Still is very much.

QC. But you underwent something of a conversion did you not about the kinds of ideas you wanted to invest in?

BILL. Yes. I began to see clearly we were over-concentrating on high tech at the expense of low, I've always found high tech products immensely exciting, but they are seducing us away from reality.

JUDGE. For the jury's benefit and certainly for mine, would you interpret that?

BILL (*animated, increasingly confident*). I'm sure they can understand, I can see they do. We're not changing our basic machines – that's what I mean – or building materials, that the ideal existence we are being offered to strive for is a house stuffed with home computers and video recorders and two ridiculously energy-wasteful cars in the drive.

QC. And therefore it has become increasingly important for you to create even more media opportunities for yourself, is that not true, in your campaign for instance to make 'engineering' glamorous again.

BILL (*in full stride*). Yes, that is vital for obvious reasons, because of the imminent collapse, literal collapse of our cities, and the simple question (*He smiles.*) if I'm still allowed to put any questions – who on earth will rebuild them? Because our young are not going into it.

I know from my own children, they turned their backs on all this, especially my daughter who was very gifted. (*He smiles.*) Of this at least I have direct experience, the right qualifications to speak.

But *I* on the other hand have become more and more involved in ideas that engineer our environment in a bold modern way, while helping preserve it at the same time, stopping its wholesale destruction.

JUDGE *moving.*

Do I have your attention my lord, I thought you might have been distracted for a moment? – Like the prototype I have supported of the road-rail vehicle, that's the vehicle with the strange snout some of you may remember, the notorious snouter, whose time has come now (*He smiles.*) I hope, and that will be followed by a new, powerful, and I think commercially viable electric car and then the buildings which –

QC. That's very interesting Mr Galpin. And these are exactly the ideas and projects you wish to popularise at the moment are they not?

BILL. Absolutely – and it's even more important than before, because we've now made it practically impossible for the single individual acting on his own to have ideas commercially accepted, as I'm sure you all know – and if history is anything to go by, we are excluding the very place where real progress has usually come from, (*He smiles.*) from . . . from the left of the field, out of nowhere, ideas that will change our lives, protect our planet –

QC. Right Mr Galpin now . . .

BILL (*carrying straight on*). And of course even when individual brilliance does somehow force its way to the surface, in this country, it's stamped upon, kicked in the teeth, oh yes, because just like the way we select our national sports teams jobbing mediocrity is always preferred to flair, so it is in science and technology, the commercial plodder gets the funding, the unadventurous idea, the one that can show the quick return. (*Lightly.*) And then of course if we are also underfunding our universities it makes –

QC (*loud*). Mr Galpin, please.

BILL *stops*.

I gave you the opportunity to make a speech for a very particular reason.

BILL. I never need a second invitation anyway.

QC. Exactly. That is my point. I put it to you, Mr Galpin, you have a thirst, an absolute compulsion to seek publicity.

BILL (*breezily*). No, that is not true.

QC. But we have just seen it in operation, have we not. We all saw how energised you suddenly became. I put it to you that many of your actions only begin to make sense when this need is understood?

BILL (*lightly*). No, that is not true.

QC. – and I further put it to you that you need publicity very

badly precisely at this moment on account of your delayed
projects which nobody has yet seen. And that is the main
reason for you bringing this action is it not? So it can become
a stage, as you've just demonstrated, for you to lecture and
promote your views to the court and the press.

BILL. I certainly don't think you can be right about that . . . it's
much easier to go on the BBC isn't it? (*Slight smile.*) A lot
cheaper too, I believe.

JUDGE (*bland, expressionless face*). I think it could be
lunchtime . . .

Blackout.

Scene Four

ROXANNA, DANNY *and* GANT, *in room downstage, chairs, wall
with a few wigs and gowns hanging up, small table, plates of food
covered with battered silver bowls. Very hot. Light, intermittent sound
of voices from passage.*

DANNY *moving, rattling car keys.* ROXANNA *smoking in her
summer dress, bare sticky arms.*

DANNY (*loud confident*). Come on – come on. Where is he? (*To
ROXANNA.*) You know I thought I'd be nervous about this,
it's a big surprise but I'm not, I'm fine, I really am . . .

ROXANNA. Are you? I'm not. I'm regressing fast, turning into a
jittery little girl which is absurd, because I was never like that
as a kid. (*Turning on* GANT.) You realise this is a private
lunch.

GANT. Yes – I just wanted to pay my compliments to your father,
I think I caught his eye in the passage, I have to see him
properly, no question, shake his hand.

ROXANNA. And then get the hell out of here, OK!

GANT. Along those lines, yes. You know we have only met a very
few times, your father and me, over the years, and each time
not for long, but the strange thing is, hardly a week goes by,

without me thinking about him, it's very curious.

DANNY (*sharp smile*). Tell him that – it'll make his day.

GANT. And it's extremely interesting to see him forced to be still isn't it, becuse he's usually always on the move, but to see him like this, under public scrutiny . . . don't worry, I'll be over here.

ROXANNA (*furious*). Jesus. (*Moving across.*) Danny this is going to be ordeal enough, without having to put up with that creep as well.

DANNY (*lightly, putting arm round her*). Calm down Roxy, it's OK. Quite OK. (*Looks at her.*) Things are less intense between you and Dad now, surely?

ROXANNA. Oh yes, only a small bit lingers on . . . if that. It's quite over really.

DANNY (*he smiles*). You're never nervous of anything, are you, anyway?

ROXANNA (*moving*). Dad's going to give me his own cross-examination I know and I have to be ready for it. 'Why you here?' reply 'Because I am!' (*Imitating withering tone.*) 'What are you doing with yourself these days?' (*She replies.*) 'Working three days a week in a bookshop and why not?' 'Spent all the money have you?' 'Yes – and things are pretty good too!'

DANNY. Just be yourself – what's so difficult? That's all that's –

BILL *enters, same clothes as in the witness box, but he's changed his shoes, fashionable footwear. He sees* GANT.

BILL. Ah it's my mate from long ago! (*He smiles.*) Isn't this marvellous – the place is full of enemies.

GANT. I just wanted to say hello.

BILL. It really is like my funeral, all of them uninvited, all of them staring down at me, people I'd forgotten existed coming running up saying 'We are watching you, we're having such a good time!' But this character here (*Indicating* GANT.) is different. (*Points.*) I've only met him a few times, but I've never forgotten him.

GANT (*smiling*). Really? I was just telling them how . . .

BILL (*cutting in*). A taste that keeps coming back. And how are things with you, has anything changed?

GANT. Oh yes, of course. It's a very exciting time, under this government we've changed our name, we have a new title and and we have a smaller staff, cleared out the dead wood.

BILL. *You* survived of course!

GANT. Naturally. (*Smiles.*) That was never in doubt. I've been given extra powers in fact. And we're full of new energy I hope. I'm still passionately committed to improving our success rate.

BILL. Still find making decisions rather tough, do you?

GANT. No, not at all. Looking into the future is never easy of course . . . (*Shrewd look.*) as you know – but for instance we've just moved on a revolutionary process for the manufacturing of a variety of fast foods – beat the Japanese to it for once. You see, I can make decisions! (*Provocative smile.*) Whether that particular project would meet with your approval or not, I don't know. (*Looks straight at* BILL.) How are things progressing with you?

BILL. Steadily, as I'm sure you know.

GANT (*shrewd sceptical look*). Steadily? . . . That must be encouraging. And I expect they will move quicker from now on. (*Sharp smile.*) Most things do. (*He moves.*) I very much like following what you've been doing, that's what I wanted to tell you. Just that. (*Shaking* BILL's *hand.*) Got to go. Of course I'm interested to see how all this turns out. Good luck. (*He exits.*)

BILL (*slight smile, watching him go*). Vermin. The extraordinary thing about him is he's bright enough to see the possibilities in ideas – and he still does nothing. A destroyer.

DANNY. Hi Dad.

BILL. Hello, you two.

Momentary silence. BILL *visibly begins to withdraw inside himself, suddenly alone with them, becomes vulnerable.*

DANNY. I think it's going great – you are doing very well, excellent.

BILL. Maybe. (*Not looking directly at* ROXANNA.) What do you think?

ROXANNA. You're doing OK. (*Slight smile.*) A little over the top.

DANNY. No, no, it's going fine.

ROXANNA (*warm*). And this room is terrific for us, the territory you've chosen, bits of judges hanging there, to stare at us, must everywhere, lawyers seething outside. (*Laconic smile.*) It couldn't be better. (*Warm.*) Your dream location, isn't it, to be able to eat here?

BILL. Always so impressed by anything institutional aren't you Roxanna. (*Watching her.*) So help yourself to some lukewarm food.

BILL *turns to trays of food, he seems more ill at ease than in witness box.*

ROXANNA (*suddenly moving right up to him*). I brought some pictures of the two boys, Mark and Nicholas. (*Nervous joky smile.*) Your grandchildren, in case you'd forgotten. Do you want to see?

BILL (*with tray of lukewarm food*). Of course – put them there . . . I'll look at them later.

ROXANNA (*instinctively flaring up*). What's that mean, you'll look at them in a couple of weeks? Look at them now!

BILL. I just had my hands full – I meant I'd look at them in a minute. (*Sharp.*) That's all I meant.

ROXANNA. Here they are. (*Showing pictures.*) Look.

BILL. Yes. (*Quiet, awkward.*) That's a very beady stare they're giving – quite big boys now – it's a long time since I've seen them.

ROXANNA (*pushing the pictures back into his hand*). Don't you want to keep them. (*More urgent.*) Go on, have them.

BILL. Yes. (*Taking the photographs.*) And Danny . . . (*Not looking straight at him.*) Are you . . . ?

DANNY. Everything's going exceptionally well, the family and (*Breezy smile.*) I'm making a surprising amount of money now, and got a new car, not a Porsche or a BMW you'll be pleased to hear, in fact I should be able to just about pay the expense of this trial if you lose. (*Sharp smile.*) That was a joke, heavily disguised probably, but it was one. I have some interesting clients at the moment. (*Serving himself food.*) I'm doing the books for Marwood and Price Ltd, you know the advertising agency, quite a newsworthy outfit at the moment, as well as Marwood (*Determinedly.*) we have Levant and Dorking, Parks and Greenwell, Petrie Associates, Kirsten and Bywater . . . the Gresham Company, T. Wyngate, that's another big one, Barbray and . . .

BILL (*very sharp*). Right Danny. (*Looking up at them.*) Why're you two here now?

ROXANNA. To see you.

DANNY. Yes, we felt we had some unfinished business.

BILL (*sharp*). What business?

DANNY. I mean we felt we were losing touch with one another – needed to straighten that out.

BILL. OK now, what do you really want?

ROXANNA. There's nothing else – isn't that enough.

BILL (*suspicious*). Is it?

ROXANNA (*warm*). Come on, let's eat, have you tried this wonderfully leathery meat, the gravy is like mud, repulsive over-cooked English food, it's perfect for this place – it's like eating the furniture.

BILL. You don't think I should be taking this libel action do you?

ROXANNA. Did I say anything?

BILL. I'm asking you and I want it straight Roxanna, as usual.

Momentary pause, ROXANNA responding like she used to be with him.

ROXANNA. OK then, you shouldn't. You should have floated above the gossip, especially as they were prepared to settle – amazingly. (*Looking straight at him.*) But you really wanted to have another go in public again anyway, didn't you? Because the results of your work are taking much longer than you expected, and you want applause for what you're doing. (*Warm smile.*) You shouldn't, but you do.

BILL (*watching her*). Do I?

ROXANNA (*lightly*). Why worry about anybody thinking you're failing – I couldn't care a fuck about that.

BILL. Go on.

ROXANNA (*animated*). In fact it's quite funny watching people block their ears in court, as you start spouting from the witness box, they practically duck down in their seats. (*Very warm.*) Often I think you sort of leave a trail of people doing that, wherever you go. (*She smiles.*) Are you going to erupt now, turn the table over? (*Slight pause.*) You are going to win the trial anyway, I just meant it makes your detractors extremely happy hearing those things said about you in court, but it's no big deal, this meeting is infinitely more important. (*Looking at him.*) How did I do? (*Lightly.*) Don't shrink back like that Dad, what's the matter?

Pause.

BILL. Please don't smoke in here.

ROXANNA. What?

BILL. I don't want to breathe your smoke.

ROXANNA. OK, I won't come near you – I'll sit over here. There'll be an exclusion zone right round you.

BILL. I'm asking you, please put that cigarette out at once.

ROXANNA (*startled*). OK . . . (*Moving away.*) Jesus, this is like having lunch with Henry the Eighth – (*Nervous.*) Just relax, OK.

Momentary pause.

DANNY. No, no, Dad she's wrong. I think you had to fight this action, you were absolutely right.

BILL (*quiet*). I'm glad somebody thinks so.

DANNY. Without doubt. And you're doing marvellously.

BILL. Yes, Danny, you told me. (*Slight pause, looking up.*) There's something else, isn't there?

DANNY. If I have one small criticism . . . (*Stops.*) No . . .

BILL (*calmly, not looking up*). Go on.

DANNY. It is – don't take this wrong – I think it's a mistake to keep on saying any idiot can make a fortune.

BILL. I didn't say that.

DANNY. Ridiculing financial security.

BILL. I have never done that.

DANNY. It's the most important aspiration for a great number of people, surely it drives everything . . .

BILL (*cutting him off*). Danny you don't have to tell *me* these things, (*Quieter.*) you really don't.

DANNY. I think you under-estimate how it looks coming from you, saying there's nothing to it, a million's a million, anybody can do it before breakfast, it can appear arrogant.

BILL (*dismissive*). You have misunderstood what I meant Danny. You can't have been listening. (*Quiet, withdrawn.*) But I hear what you say, I have noted it (*Sharp.*) OK . . .

ROXANNA. Why don't you ring a bell every time you want the subject changed. (*Lightly.*) He has a point after all. Come on you're not eating – the mushy sprouts are getting cold.

Pause.

DANNY (*staring straight at him*). But overall I think you've been really very clever.

BILL (*looks up*). Clever . . . in what way?

DANNY. In how you've managed things. Of course you believe in your building project, I realise, but some of the other things, most of the innovation schemes are deliberate tax losses, must be, and yet you have got all this publicity and kudos, in some quarters anyway, out of these schemes. It's brilliant, out of ideas that are going to be losers deliberately, like the extraordinary road-rail project.

BILL (*quiet*). So that's why you're here, you've come to provoke me, Danny.

DANNY (*determinedly, facing up to him*). Of course not, I'm just trying to make sense of your financial operation.

ROXANNA. Danny, maybe this isn't the time to try to have things out.

DANNY. I've been thinking about it so much lately and I believe I understand it now.

BILL (*quiet*). I don't think you probably have ever really understood Danny. (*His arm shoots out, catches* ROXANNA *by the wrist.*) While she . . . she on the other hand understands everything I'm trying to do, even more than she did before, but she pretends she does not, which is far far worse, (*Quiet, intense.*) and I expect what she's doing now, whatever it is, is not enough . . . is it Roxanna?

ROXANNA. Listen . . . (*Moving with plates.*) We're meant to be having a reunion. It's really hot, we're caged up in here – but we're going to make it work.

DANNY (*facing* BILL, *determined tone*). I did not understand I admit, how having made brilliant acquisitions earlier in your career being so far ahead of the field . . .

BILL. A little in front.

DANNY. No miles in front. I mean you had the chance, a real chance, of building a great consumer empire out of the cameras and gramophones . . . that sort of product – and now it could look like having made all your money out of these things you then promptly turned around and started attacking everyone for buying them. For possessing them. Couldn't it? I mean when you moved on to these visionary ideas – so long-term they don't even exist yet – I can't tell you how relieved people were, the people that had been the target of your criticism. They were jubilant, when you hit this visionary phase.

ROXANNA. Danny . . .

DANNY. But now I have a theory which explains all of this I think – which I'm trying to put . . .

BILL (*suddenly*). Danny – nothing you can say to me on this subject is of any interest whatsoever.

ROXANNA. This is lunch break in the High Court, we'll have lawyers running in here offering their services if we fight and I'm not paying! So please –

DANNY (*to* BILL). You can't say it's of no interest because you haven't heard it all.

BILL. Of course I can say that, because every time I look at you Danny, I see what I'm up against – you're a permanent reminder. Far too close to home.

DANNY (*sharp*). What do you mean by that?

BILL. I mean by that the sort of ignorance and pettiness, and lack of foresight, that is holding up a lot of my schemes.

ROXANNA (*loud.*) Don't talk like that – It's unforgiveable.

DANNY. It's OK Roxanna, I don't need your help, I can handle it.

BILL. It's true – you lack all curiosity about the ideas I'm backing, any sense of wonder, and you are quite, quite incapable of seeing their importance. Just like the people I have to deal with all the time.

DANNY (*strong*). That is not true and you know it.

BILL. Oh no? You think I should give up my projects, don't you. Go back into gramophones, into video recorders and all that shit. I CANNOT GO BACK. I WON'T GO BACK. And nothing I can ever do will make you see that – I've known that for a very long time now Danny.

DANNY (*sharp, facing up to him*). Really? I don't believe they're all without value anyway, your schemes, I think . . .

BILL (*savage smile*). You think one of them might show a glimmer of promise, do you Danny.

ROXANNA. This is my idea of hell, having this scene now, let's get out of here for fuck's sake, it's summer out there, break this up –

DANNY. You haven't allowed me to put my case, so you can't know what I feel about all your ideas. (*Straight at him.*) But I'll put it better at the end of today when –

BILL. There will definitely be no need for us to see each other at the end of today or indeed . . .

ROXANNA (*very strong to* BILL). That is enough – You *understand.*

BILL (*catching her by the arm*). As for you, I expect you put him up to this – this was all planned, my two children, conspiring to . . .

ROXANNA. You really think we'd do that – I think this is what *you* wanted to happen for some reason, so you needn't be bothered with us any more.

DANNY. What *I* was trying to do, if you'll let me finish for once in my life, I was trying to demonstrate something to you, that I'd made sense of your current situation, it came out wrong, but that doesn't mean –

BILL. No it didn't – it came out exactly as you meant it.

DANNY. Oh really, and how do you know that?

BILL. Because that's just the way you are Danny.

DANNY. Oh I forgot, you know everything about me of course even before I've thought of it! You're always right, whether it's the fucking road-rail vehicle or me, every time totally right. You say I don't listen, but you have never listened to anything I've said ever, never taken it seriously for a single moment . . . you made up your mind about me so early didn't you, I think you often couldn't even stand being in the same room with me (*Loud.*) could you?

BILL (*quiet, startled*). Danny . . .

DANNY (*near tears*). And I'm *not* going to let you make me cry either, you have never managed to make me – not going to let you now.

ROXANNA (*moving over*). That's right – why should we care what he thinks? Why should we worry for one moment? He just shrugged off his children when we didn't agree with him. (*Flicks the air.*) Surplus to requirements.

BILL. Roxanna – you know that's not true, that's not the case.

ROXANNA. We can do exactly the same, he never keeps in touch, he never tries to see us, scared to face his own children because they might tell him something he didn't want to hear – he couldn't care whether we exist or not. (*She moves.*) In fact it's really totally irrelevant what he says or thinks now.

BILL (*looking straight at her*). That's right Roxanna.

Pause. BILL sits in the middle of room eating a mouthful of his food. ROXANNA, watching him.

ROXANNA (*leaning by exit*). And unless I'm much mistaken, isn't there somewhere in this absurd building the audience you really want to be with, the court, waiting with baited breath for you, wondering where the hell you are?

BILL (*head spinning round*). Jesus, what's the time Roxanna?

Blackout.

Sound of passages, hum of hushed conversation mixed with footsteps hurtling down a long corridor.

Scene Five

The JUDGE staring down, round blubbery face, expressionless.
  QC stands waiting on the edge of the light staring into wings. Momentary pause. He glances up at the JUDGE.
  BILL arrives hurriedly by witness box, looks up at JUDGE, takes his place.

JUDGE. You are late. You are late back, Mr Galpin.

BILL. Am I? I was unavoidably detained . . . I apologise . . . my lord.

JUDGE. You have obviously found a class of catering in this building that I was unaware of. The whole process begins to disintegrate when lunch becomes more important than what goes on here – you will apologise to the court again.

BILL (*startled*). Again? Really? If that is considered necessary, I apologise to the court again. (BILL *glancing around*.)

JUDGE. Are you all right Mr Galpin?

BILL (*suddenly*). I'm quite all right.

JUDGE. Proceed.

QC. I want now Mr Galpin to move to one of the central issues of this case.

BILL (*cutting him off*). Good, about time, I had begun to think you weren't too keen to get there.

BILL's *manner abstracted, then suddenly focusing on* QC *then away.*

QC. It is true is it not that your large-scale building projects, the so-called road-rail network spreading over a piece of Africa *and* the controversial housing complex and 'invention park' in London have suffered massive delays?

BILL. Yes, yes, we know this. (*Sharp, correcting himself.*) But they are now back on schedule, very much so . . .

QC. That money, even your money couldn't make everything happen. That you were dependent on other factors, like the agreement of foreign governments and planning permission from local councils.

BILL (*not looking at him*). Yes, yes . . .

QC. And that you would very much like to quicken the process.

BILL, *a sharp mumble.*

I'm sorry. What did you say? I didn't hear that.

BILL. I said, you are stating the obvious.

BILL *gives the dangling microphone a shove – so it swings across like a pendulum.*

JUDGE. Mr Galpin, please try to keep still, and not disrupt the furniture.

QC. And in your attempt to speed up the process and clear the site in London of all the remaining tenants, we come to the moment when you hired Mr Hertie and Mr Clearsil.

BILL (*matter-of-fact*). Yes.

QC. Both of whom by an extraordinary coincidence are in Europe at the moment?

BILL (*hardly listening to him*). Means nothing, I asked them to come back myself.

QC. Now before we come to the strange sequence of events that followed, the fire in one of the shops, the breaking of windows,

BILL. That was kids.

QC. the late night phone calls, the spiral of alleged Rachmanesque behaviour . . .

BILL (*abstracted manner*). The alleged Rachmanism has already been examined by the police, at my request, and found to be groundless.

QC. I want to look at why you chose to delegate for the first time these –

JUDGE. Just one moment, for the benefit of the jury, I'm sure they know, but one or two of them are quite young, an explanation of the term Rachmanism is required.

QC. Of course my lord, Rachman was a slum landlord in the fifties and early sixties who employed men who used violence on his behalf to evict sitting tenants.

BILL (*suddenly focusing, provocative*). No, initially he was looked upon as a hero figure by the immigrant community, because housing conditions for them were so scandalously bad, he was one of the very few who would provide them with some . . . (*Stops.*) and it was only later –

QC (*sharp*). Yes, that's a very interesting interpretation Mr Galpin – why did you say that?

BILL. Because it's true.

QC. Is he a figure then with whom you identify?

BILL. That is not a serious question I hope, I was merely correcting a received opinion.

QC. And that is something you feel compelled to do in all your work is it? Provoking people out of complacency, correcting them when you feel they're wrong!

BILL (*beginning to lose patience*). I don't think I'm compelled – if I know about something, I say it. I've been looking into housing recently, so I naturally know about this.

QC. And just staying with this for a moment, would it be fair to say that you would like your name, obviously in a totally different way to Mr Rachman, but you would like it to be an ism?

BILL *mouths 'What' in astonishment.*

Become automatically associated in the public mind with something – in your case innovation?

BILL. Become an ism! (*Looking about.*) I can't answer such a dumb question.

QC (*sharp*). Put another way – you would like to be recognised as the ultimate patron of the age?

BILL (*flicking the microphone, letting it swing slightly*). Your questions are rapidly becoming complete gobbledegook. I've done what I've done partly because nobody else was doing it that much, OK? I don't know how on earth we got onto this.

QC. And just to complete the picture, you too, just like the figure we've been talking about, see yourself as a bit of an outsider . . . is that true?

BILL (*muttering out of the corner of his mouth, slight smile*). Can you believe this?

QC. In your case obviously an outsider in your own country – a person outside normal conventions?

BILL (*louder*). No I would have thought in almost every respect I'm a wholly conventional man. I've been married and divorced, I have voted Conservative nearly all my life, I have two troublesome children, one of whom is constantly telling me how conventional I am, despite my occasional exhibitionism in public. (*Looks around.*) I even watch a lot of television – an almost abnormally conventional picture.

QC. Yes – but you *also* see yourself as someone who has a lot to offer, isn't that the case? And someone who has not been listened to as much as he would like . . . ?

Silence. BILL *looks about, slight smile.*

JUDGE. Mr Galpin, will you please answer the question.

BILL (*dismissing the proceedings*). I'm not interested in that question. I don't think I can play any more I'm afraid.

JUDGE. What did you say, Mr Galpin?

BILL. I'm not going to play any more. Apart from everything else these questions have become absurd.

JUDGE. Your meaning is not clear Mr Galpin, are you dropping your action?

BILL (*glancing around*). No, I just don't want to continue for the moment . . . this interview is closed.

JUDGE. Mr Galpin you cannot just swat away the rest of your cross-examination, it makes a mockery –

BILL (*slight smile*). But I have to swat this round away. I must plead ill health or whatever you like, I don't care, it's extremely hot for a start (*Pointing at* JUDGE.) and you look as if you're shrinking in the heat (*Glancing about.*) and I don't see why you need worry, you're all getting paid enough! Right now, I just want to get the hell out of here as fast as I can – and I intend to.

ROXANNA's VOICE (*calling out angrily*). What on earth do you think you're doing?

Blackout.

Scene Six

ROXANNA *in spot front stage, standing between two models of the road-rail vehicle. The small model we have seen before, and a much larger model, at least five feet high, and twelve feet long, with its strange conical nose facing us.*

ROXANNA *is in dark colours holding a winter coat over her arm, smoking, music gradually building behind her, almost subliminal at the beginning.*

ROXANNA. November 6th – it's been weird watching it, ever since that gruesome meal, the trial spattering on for a few more sticky days, he refuses to quit, forces it to a verdict and loses.

She pushes the small model in front of her with her foot.

And people are naturally thrilled to see a rich man actually lose a libel case, who can blame them!

She moves forward with machine.

There are few more pleasurable sights in the whole world than a rich man suing and then falling resoundingly on his arse.

Moving forward, astride the small machine, ironic tone.

And there is even better to come – by coincidence or not, the Director of Public Prosecutions announces they are re-examining the evidence of suspected harassment on the site Dad bought. There is no real evidence. Dad, who had never delegated in his life, hired two morons to manage the site who then took the money and fucked off somewhere. He'd been too busy and had become careless, dumb even. (*With feeling.*) *That's all.* But the threat of prosecution is being stretched out, a lingering slur, far more effective than an actual trial.

ROXANNA *sends small model rolling into wings.*

For those who have always found Dad deeply suspect, insufferable in fact, the arrogant 'self appointed patron saint of innovation' – it's such comforting news. 'And he brought it all on himself'? It's wonderful!

ROXANNA *moving over to large machine.*

And pictures of the road-rail vehicle have started to reappear of course, with its eccentric nose. (*She gives the nose a sharp tap.*) The snouter, and the same jokes are bobbing up again. (*Moving along the machine.*) My kids now play with the model we've got – it fills up most of our tiny garden.

She climbs on top of the large model, her voice intense for a moment.

They travel on it fast through imaginary rain forests and up the sheer face of the Himalayas.

She sits astride large machine.

And Dad – is responding with a vengeance. To prove himself right.

She switches on the headlight on the model.

Working furiously to get the machines on the road. Trying to pull free. He won't shut up!

Holding her arms high over machine, she rides it as riding a bucking horse.

He is wounded and becoming more dangerous apparently, and therefore it would be quite interesting, even exciting to be able to talk to him wouldn't it? But it's impossible for me to get to see him.

She gets off machine, moving forward.

It's the most extreme it's been. He won't take my calls. And in these hustling times it seems not to be the atmosphere in which you just meet people you want to see by chance in the street.

Putting on winter coat, music getting louder behind her.

(*Sharp.*) It's ridiculous isn't it, comic even, here I am still hungry to see him, craving for that to happen (*Very sharp.*) which doesn't please me . . . and to have to go through moods, that change so violently, plunging about. (*Angry.*) But he'll be able to turn it round of course. All of this. For himself. And me? (*Loud.*) I can stop it too . . .

Music loud behind her.

But at this precise moment on this winter evening, I find I'm heading for a large dark concrete pub in South London, with sleazy music coming out of it, because I'm hoping to catch a glimpse of my father. One of the few chances I've got.

ROXANNA *turns as the large vehicle is taken off, the tawdry music loud round her.*

Red and blue lights playing on the back wall, shadows, a lot of the stage in darkness. In the pool of light near back wall, a single bare chair, and a large easel.

In a group downstage stand DANNY, FRANCES *and* MICK, *with* GANT *very slightly separate. All are looking inappropriately well-dressed among the smoke and coloured lights. They keep glancing towards the single bare chair.*

ROXANNA *moves towards them. The sound of disco music from the other side of the wall continues, mixed with drunken shouts and hand clapping.*

ROXANNA (*glancing around, startled*). You sure we're in the right room, is he really going to do it here?

FRANCES. This is where he chose, oh yes. (*Glancing at* ROXANNA.) You look so pale Roxanna. (*Touching her.*) You're wasting away like this – is anything the matter?

ROXANNA *moving, smoking.*

DANNY. It's so perverse him being here, this concrete hole, there are cracks in the ceiling even, (*Glancing up.*) might get hit by something. (*Running his hand along wall.*) And everywhere is coated in this layer of mashed up crisps and other junk.

Music behind wall rises and dips.

ROXANNA. Yes, not to mention the beer mats and old durex sticking to your feet. (*Staring into darkness.*) There're dark puddles over there, full of their own form of pond life.

MICK (*as the music pounds*). He likes all this. He's played the town hall, got that out of the way, now he enjoys doing the rougher venues too. But will he be able to drown out the sound of the stripper next door?

ROXANNA (*staring around*). And he's going to be watched just by us, is he, and kids with paint on their faces.

GANT (*sipping drink*). Isn't it strange, he won't see some of the people he used to know – but he comes to a place like this.

FRANCES (*looking at GANT, very sharply*). No, it isn't, he trying to get support from the community for one of his most important projects, his great housing plan. The public inquiry is starting any day now (*Closing in on GANT.*) and he's up against the full conservation lobby so it makes perfect sense for him to be doing this (*Loud.*) OK!

GANT *impassive*.

ROXANNA (*withdrawn*). What's so strange is all of us coming to watch.

MICK. We can't keep away from him, any chance and we take it! (*Sharp smile.*) This collection of odd creatures compulsively following him round at night. But he arrives in his limo at the door of the pub, does his gig, and slips away without anybody getting close to him.

ROXANNA (*quiet to herself*). I am *not* compulsively following him.

FRANCES. He won't see anybody – I spend my life lying to people.

ROXANNA (*looking up*). He'll see nobody at all?

FRANCES. It's like a disease – even with me whole days go by when he'll only speak through the intercom.

DANNY (*confident*). It's because of what's happened obviously.

FRANCES. I don't know – but I think people have enjoyed seeing it happen to him far more than some crooked city type being investigated.

ROXANNA (*quiet, withdrawn*). For me that is the single most striking thing.

DANNY (*authoritative*). Of course – they know where they are with straightforward monsters. They can't place Dad, he takes an odd delight in pouring his money away at the same time as lecturing people about forward-looking investment. (*He moves.*) People find these contradictions ridiculous.

ROXANNA. You mean you do, Danny – (*Quiet to herself.*) . . . he was right about you, really.

MICK. I think in a way, we've grown old, and he hasn't.

FRANCES (*sharp*). That's true of me. I age a year every week at the moment.

DANNY (*sharp*). Somebody described it as his 'maiming energy', he attacks without creating in its place.

Sound of glass breaking on the other side of the wall mixed with laughter and shouts.

ROXANNA (*turning towards the noise of glass being smashed.*) Jesus . . . what a place.

DANNY (*ignoring this, carrying on*). And those times have gone anyway, when he really stood out. I wished he still did! The world's crammed with far richer men now and he doesn't own newspapers, he doesn't own satellites, or TV stations. (*Slight smile.*) He wasn't even interested in going into compact discs, his natural territory. In the current climate he's without influence. But I'm not sure we know the whole story yet, there may be investments we haven't been told about, when he reveals these, people won't be able to say the things they –

GANT (*suddenly*). I don't think he minds what people say.

ROXANNA (*turning on him*). How on earth do you know that?

GANT. Your father is impervious, he doesn't care about it, he rises above it all, it's one of the things that's admirable about him.

ROXANNA. He didn't rise above it, that was his great mistake. You stupid man. He cared too much what all you fuckers thought. (*Bearing down on him in corner, threateningly.*) He needs to show some results now, doesn't he!

GANT. Yes he does. He really went out on a limb your father . . . but I expect this setback will only be temporary.

ROXANNA. Really! Is that so? And what are *you* doing here anyway?

GANT (*staring straight back at her*). It's a public meeting. It was advertised. I came.

ROXANNA. Come to have a gloat have you! Still passionately trying to make your mind up about one of his projects (*By wall.*) No doubt these smashed crisps everywhere are yours!

GANT. Mine? What on earth are you talking about!

ROXANNA. An achievement of your new fast food project, ending up smeared all over here!

She is in front of him. GANT *up against wall.*

GANT. Don't be absurd, it's something totally different (*Loud.*) that project – not remotely the same.

GANT *flinches away, as if* ROXANNA *is going to do him some injury.*

ROXANNA. Don't worry you're not worth it. (*Savage smile, leaning close.*) Or maybe you are! (*Dangerous, close.*) You know you remind me of one of those middle-aged women who go to boxing matches and try to get as close to the blood as possible while remaining totally safe, he horrifies you and he excites you at the same time, doesn't he? That's why you keep trying to see him, keep coming back for more. (*Savage smile.*) You need it.

GANT. You are wrong. (*Breaking away from her.*) You have never understood have you, my admiration for your father is genuine.

DANNY. Because that costs you nothing.

GANT. On the contrary you are wrong again, it has cost me my peace of mind. (*Moving into shadows.*) Quite substantially. Truly. There are moments when I see very clearly what I should be doing. (*Disappearing into total darkness.*) Oh yes!

He's gone.

MICK. That bastard will always survive!

Fluorescent lights flick off and on.

(*Agitated, looks at lights.*) Is this the two minute warning, for his entry? *I* get nervous when I'm near him, more than before in fact. Because I was one of his most perfect projects, his illustrations of finding brilliance that had leapt from nowhere – where of course he's always believed the most original ideas come from.

DANNY. His romanticism, yes. If it was ever true, it certainly isn't any more.

MICK (*smiles*). I had some good ideas – I really think I did, I was going to be his superstar innovator. And I betrayed it all by going off to do something utterly banal and lucrative.

ROXANNA (*very sharp.*) Of course – we've all done the wrong thing as far as he's concerned.

Something falls in the darkness, near DANNY, *like a light rain of plaster from a crumbling ceiling.*

DANNY (*loud.*) God, it nearly did hit me too!

ROXANNA *moving to* FRANCES *as music from the stripper on the other side of the wall getting louder.*

ROXANNA (*downstage, urgent to* FRANCES). Did you give him my message?

FRANCES. Yes, he just said tell her I'll reply . . . sometime.

ROXANNA. That's not good enough, not at all. You've got to get me in to see him.

FRANCES. It's impossible – he even resents me still staying with him. And the more his isolation grows, the more I turn into the bustling automaton secretary I wanted never to become.

ROXANNA. It's unforgiveable of him – he always swore he'd never indulge in this sort of Howard Hughes remoteness and now look at him.

FRANCES. And you Roxy, look at you, it's most unlike you to pine after anything.

ROXANNA (*furious*). Pining! I'm certainly not doing that for him. I assure you. (*Then urgent.*) Frankie you will do this for me though, won't you, I just need this, terribly badly, to be able –

BILL *enters from the side, carrying a large folder.* ROXANNA *startled, as he brushes past.*

(*Instinctively.*) Dad? (*As he moves.*) Dad!

BILL *gives them just an abrupt nod as he passes, he's dressed in a pale jacket, jeans and his distinctive shoes, moving upstage.*

MICK (*nervous smile*). You know I think he looks more at home in this place than we do.

ROXANNA. I expect you're right, he likes it here . . . for some strange reason.

BILL *standing upstage in spot, his manner direct and unapologetic, effortless, his best performance.*

BILL. I'd like to welcome you all here (*Sharp smile.*) to this dark cracked hole in the ground. It has a compelling odour all of its own doesn't it! And it was a new and shining structure so very recently.

Music pounding behind him.

To warm you up, before I show you the building scheme, as a curtain raiser I want to show you these pictures, an artist's impression of the road-rail vehicle in action.

Showing large picture on easel of the machine drawn in motion.

A great engineering achievement as you can see, and close, so very close, to being a reality.

Moving, getting next picture ready.

MICK. He makes me ashamed with his unflinching belief in my ideas. He never gives up, does he, he's got more of a creator's commitment than I have.

ROXANNA. He's doing it on purpose, bringing those with him.

MICK (*loud*). It doesn't alter the fact, does it.

BILL. And you will be able to see these machines right here, in this very city. (*He smiles.*) Oh yes. In the Invention Park that will be going up in your midst, (*Inviting.*) where you will be able actually to walk in among the inventions, (*He smiles.*) nothing between you and them, feel them, touch them if you want. Yes. Ideas that are not ephemeral. (*Pointedly.*) Definitely not ephemeral. And the park will be surrounded by these great buildings, using completely new materials.

Stripper's music really loud from next door. BILL holding up silvery drawings, we can half see in the light. BILL smiles.

I think they are probably reaching a climax next door, but maybe these are even more stimulating, I'll be handing round these beautiful pale drawings of the buildings for you all to see.

With power, across the depth of the stage, in the dark, smoky atmosphere, with the music behind him.

We're facing a very important public inquiry, people say these buildings are strange shapes, alien shapes compared to the hideous clutter around them, not safe, nostalgic shapes, nor are they pastiche post-modernist buildings, expressing nothing about ourselves. NOR WILL THEY FALL TO PIECES.

Sharp smile, music really loud.

They will be like nothing you have ever seen before.

Blackout.

Scene Seven

The music from the concrete pub continues, fading gradually away, as ROXANNA and DANNY stand together front stage, watching the back wall slide back.

The first thing we see is a great quantity of brown paper parcels, over two hundred spilled together, covered in different labels and stamps from all over the world. And then the large pile of unpacked belongings that dominated Act One, looking roughly the same as it did before, the suitcases packed up, the chairs, the carpets, except it now has many more old gramophones on it. It, too, has brown paper parcels littered over it.

DANNY and ROXANNA stand together, facing upstage, staring at the pile.

ROXANNA. Jesus! (*Looking at DANNY.*) Did you know about all this? (*Moving towards the pile.*) These are the old gramophones he used to make – what's he doing with them?

DANNY. I don't know. I had no idea he'd kept all this stuff still. (*Swinging his arms.*) It's so cold in here.

ROXANNA. Yes – it almost looks like he's trying to barricade himself in, high up in this terrible concrete slab (*Moving around.*) covered in scaffolding out there, damp on the walls here. (*Looks at DANNY.*) I don't know how he ended up living in such a place.

DANNY. It's weird isn't it . . .

Both of them moving along the base of the pile of belongings, picking things up.

DANNY. Some of my things are still here Roxy – from way back! A few of yours too. (*Pushing among parcels, curious.*) I'd heard about these, the brown paper parcels sent to him by crank inventors from all over.

Shakes one parcel, it makes peculiar rattling noise.

DANNY. Full of so called ideas. He's been bombarded by them. It looks like he doesn't want to open them.

ROXANNA. How's his financial position now?

DANNY (*briskly*). On the face of it, he's lost nine-tenths of his money, maybe more. He's been spectacularly extravagant on his projects just recently, trying to hurry them, complete them, selling his assets, going for broke. And of course since the trial and everything that's followed . . . he's finding it impossible to raise more money. That's totally out. (*Sharp.*) Remember this is on the face of it. (*Looks at her, touches her arm.*) You know Frankie's right, you don't look well.

ROXANNA. I'm OK, just about, I'm beginning to feel older that's all.

DANNY (*gently, near her*). Cultivating the gaunt and pale look? (*Shrewd smile.*) You've got to forget about him you know Roxy. (*Breezy.*) You see I'm fine now. Absolutely. (*He turns.*) I overheard something about you and him the other day . . .

ROXANNA (*startled*). About me and him?

DANNY. Yes – this guy was saying you could tell Dad was mad because unlike the normal run-of-the-mill millionaire who wants to turn his mistress into say a film star – Dad wanted to turn his *daughter* into an *engineer*!

ROXANNA (*icy*). Really?

DANNY (*gently*). Just lately I've been thinking about you and him a lot, wondering again if there was ever, long ago of course, this is difficult to put, but . . . (*Tentative.*) something going on between you?

ROXANNA. Going on? You mean sex Danny, something sexual between us. (*Loud.*) That what you mean? No, it was much more interesting than that – we had that relationship because I've felt his equal since the age of five. (*Quiet.*) Always knew it . . .

FRANCES *enters*.

ROXANNA. Well?

FRANCES. I've told him you're here . . . he may come out, I don't know.

ROXANNA. You've got to make him. If he doesn't – I'm never going to try again. You can tell him that.

FRANCES. That won't work, his moods are terrible at the moment, since he lost the public inquiry. (*With feeling, to herself.*) The scheme was far too unconventional for them of course. (*Instinctively tidying.*) I've given him the date when I'm leaving, he hardly seemed to notice at all.

DANNY. After all these years he didn't say anything? (*To* ROXANNA.) Look what's happened to Frankie – staying here –

FRANCES. He's always treated me well – though sometimes I had to ask him for a rise, and I've treated him well. But he wants me to go now, definitely. I remind him of the past. I like to think I've understood what he's trying to do, especially recently. This'll sound stupid, ridiculous even, but we had a kind of silent understanding, we did. I often knew what he was thinking. But now it's too late, I can't talk to him, shut up here, I can do nothing with him . . .

BILL has entered.

BILL. That's right. (*Moving past FRANCES, he touches her arm, matter-of-fact.*) That's exactly right.

BILL, appearance different. He's altogether more hesitant, suspicious, clenched. He sits upstage, a distance from them on a large chair at base of pile.

You wanted to see me?

DANNY. Yes.

ROXANNA (*looking over at BILL*). What's this? What you doing right over there, that's ridiculous.

BILL. What do you want?

DANNY. I just wanted to wish you Happy Birthday. (*He stops.*)

ROXANNA (*circling*). Yes, Happy Birthday. (*Matter-of-fact glancing up.*) I like the celebratory shoes.

BILL (*quiet, distant*). Thank you.

DANNY. There. I . . .

Pause. DANNY suddenly awkward, nervous smile.

Lucky I didn't bring a gramophone as a birthday present isn't it.

BILL (*very quiet*). Yes Danny.

DANNY. I want you to listen . . . I just want to say everything will come right. I know you've made very clear you think I'm not capable of understanding, I know you won't believe this, but I do admire a lot of what you're doing, and I know, (*Loud.*) and don't dismiss this, you're going to produce a surprise turnaround, a sucker punch – some investment we don't know about. Yes. And it's not all dark out there, there've been a few sympathetic articles about what you've been trying to accomplish.

Pause.

BILL (*very quiet*). Do you do this as some kind of revenge Danny?

DANNY. You see you've deliberately misunderstood what I'm trying to say, (*Loud.*) you do this to me again and again (*Really angry.*) don't you?

BILL. I'd be obliged if you'd leave. (*Icy, to* FRANCES.) Could you take him out of here please – right now.

DANNY. Don't worry I'm going, I'm getting away from here. (*Furious.*) I don't need this I can tell you! Any of it! (*Loud, with authority.*) And I won't be back . . .

ROXANNA. Danny!

FRANCES (*running after him*). I'll have to go with you otherwise you won't get out of here, all the security systems and locks he's had put in, (*With feeling at exit.*) it's typical of what's been happening.

ROXANNA. Frankie, get him back now, Danny! . . . (*Turning, loud.*) He's only trying to show you he exists for chrissake, because you've always made it so clear what you think of him – haven't you?

BILL *sits upstage, very still.*

BILL. And what do you want Roxanna? (*Sharp, flicking his fingers.*) Come on.

ROXANNA. So you're putting the clock on me already – 'granted' a few minutes in your presence and then out. (*Loud, moving.*) What's going on here anyway? These heaps of old gramophones, it's ghoulish – why've you shut yourself up like this, in this slab of a building, of all places?

BILL (*quiet, dangerous*). Roxanna – I want to know what you've come for?

ROXANNA. Stop doing that – I worked out what I was going to say, but it's gone now, (*Loud.*) completely vanished, this is not what I planned . . . (*Moving backwards and forwards.*) You see what happens – (*Really angry.*) and stop trying to make me so nervous, OK! Just stop it.

BILL (*quiet*). I know why you are here Roxanna, it's simple, you are going to tell me, you haven't decided how, but in a moment you will start telling me I haven't done what I intended to do (*Derisive.*) in your opinion, that I haven't begun to achieve what I set out to, you can't wait to list –

ROXANNA (*startled*). You think I came to do that? (*Sharp, dismissive.*) I don't care about any of the –

BILL (*suddenly lashing out*). Precisely. You don't care at all do you. That's absolutely clear.

ROXANNA. I didn't mean that, you know I didn't. (*Really nervous.*) Jesus, is this what it's going to be like trying to say anything to you now? If I say the wrong thing, I get attacked? (*She moves.*) I don't think you've failed, you clearly do, retreating up here, into this isolation ward. (*Looking at him.*) Are you going to scream at me now, go on, that should be worth one. Shouldn't it?

Turning to model of road-rail vehicle on pile.

You haven't done all you wanted obviously – sometimes you came very close, closer than I ever thought. (*Quiet, with model.*) For what it's worth now, I like some of the projects, the ones that disorientated people, this for instance with its nose, its fantastically perverse snout, like something out of a children's book, it's a wonderful idea this machine.

BILL (*very sharp, watching her*). Is it? You didn't always think like that Roxanna – and I'm not at all sure you do now.

ROXANNA. On to that now are you? Going to start throwing things back at me? You haven't forgiven me I know and I have *certainly* not forgiven you. (*Turns.*) Jesus you've hurt me.

BILL (*cold*). That's interesting. I've hurt you. What on earth do you mean? You turned away from everything you were good at, the work you should have done, from all the things –

ROXANNA (*loud*). I had to do that, of course. I had to get away from you.

BILL (*contemptuous*). That's rubbish – that's far too easy, and also totally untrue.

ROXANNA. How do you know? I don't want to go into this anyway. (*Turns suddenly.*) OK, I didn't want to be interested in those things but I was, despite myself, drawn towards . . .

BILL (*jabbing finger*). You were that's the point.

ROXANNA (*loud*). I didn't want to be!

BILL. Because for some unknown reason you were scared of it, that's what's unforgiveable.

ROXANNA. No. No, it was too much work or . . . I don't know, what does it matter now for chrissake. (*She moves.*) I probably wasn't any good really, you wanted to create a prototype out of me, set an example with your own daughter for the rest of the world to see, didn't you, at the very least create an apprentice for your work. You weren't right about me at all.

BILL. That's rubbish again. You could have done a lot more than me if you'd let yourself, maybe a great deal more, I was right without a doubt.

ROXANNA. Of course! Of course you were! You always are, I forgot, how stupid of me. (*Loud, provocative.*) We'll never know thank God anyway – will we!

She moves, strong.

Suddenly it all makes sense why you're here doesn't it, locking yourself up in decaying concrete buildings. It's to prove yourself *right* isn't it? You said this would happen, so you're inhabiting your own vision. (*Contemptuous.*) Naturally! Dwarfing yourself with all this junk.

BILL (*very quiet*). I don't advise you to go on with this Roxanna.

ROXANNA. Really – is that a threat? (*Moving.*) Trying to get rid of me like Danny . . .? I made a terrible mess of the break with you I know, I still dream about it sometimes. Trying to get away from you, I ended up thinking about you even more – that's what I didn't foresee. And it hasn't nearly healed, nearly stopped, but you know nothing about what's happened over the last few years, the moments of terror I went through because of what I thought I'd done to myself, the emptiness, till recently.

BILL (*quiet, straight at her*). I believe I told you what would happen if –

ROXANNA (*loud, mocking*). I thought you'd be able to resist

saying that, I really did, but no! Every time! (*Combative.*)
Come on – why don't you try some more . . . (*Suddenly
angry.*) You've made some mistakes as well, haven't you.
Plenty! – You got too impatient and careless didn't you,
because the work moved so slowly and you suddenly wanted to
make it all happen, show everyone, couldn't wait any longer
for the results, the ideas to be ready. (*With great force.*) Your
nerve should have held (*Loud.*) shouldn't it? I TOLD YOU,
DIDN'T I!

BILL (*sharp*). You see. You're doing it. You've started. Almost
exactly on time.

ROXANNA. Is that right . . . you sound so pleased. (*Moving,
upset.*) OK, I'm fucking all this up, being here . . . (*Quiet.*)
What do you want me to say, then?

BILL. I *knew* you'd come here to do this, you wonder now why I
kept away from you, because this is all you wanted, to come
and stare –

ROXANNA. That's not true.

BILL. To see me caged with all of this.

ROXANNA. You've caged yourself for a start.

BILL (*moving close to her, clenched*). Because this is all there is,
isn't there. As *you* know. (*Indicating gramophone.*) What should
have flowed from here, from these obsolete gramophones, from
all that junk, the ideas I should have made happen, they don't
exist. Not the important ones, nothing that really matters,
nothing that's finished. (*Close to her.*) I had the chance of
course, an opportunity like no other, but I can't make it
happen now. It's simple. It's gone.

ROXANNA. Yes.

BILL (*controlled, dangerous*). But of course that's no surprise to
you, because you always knew I was bound not to succeed,
didn't you?

ROXANNA (*quiet, watching him*). Yes.

BILL. But I don't believe that Roxanna, not at all. Not for one
moment.

He is very close to her, her head instinctively jerks back as if he is going to hit her.

What you doing that for? (*He looks at her, quiet, clenched.*) Why should I do that?

He moves her head, so she's facing him, holds it for a moment, his hands either side of her face.

ROXANNA. I don't know – because you want to. (*Staring straight back at him.*) Because I'm here now. (*She moves her head.*) Because you know you may not get another chance.

BILL. Probably not, no. (*Staring at her.*) I know that.

He holds her by one arm, very tight, he's hurting her, looking at her.

You're going to start telling me what people are saying about me, out there – just like Danny . . . The pleasure they're getting, from all of this. (*Holding her tight.*) Come on.

ROXANNA. You care about that!

BILL. Yes. (*Staring at her.*) Come on. (*Provocative.*) Start.

ROXANNA. Why should I want to do that? (*Slight pause.*) I came here . . . I couldn't stand what had happened between us any more. I won't put up with that any more, finding myself trailing after you, all over the city.

BILL (*moving off briskly*). I have things to do now, things to see to, Roxanna. So goodbye. If you find Frances, she should be able to show you a way of getting out of here.

ROXANNA (*furious*). Oh no, don't you walk away from this, don't you dare walk away from me now, just when I was telling you . . .

BILL is moving away, ROXANNA pulls at him fiercely as he goes, holding on, restraining him.

ROXANNA. Come back – don't you do this – come back here.

Forcibly, holding on to him, he turns, catches hold of her arm.

BILL (*with passion*). You should never have gone, you stupid, stupid girl – you wasted all that time, all those years.

ROXANNA *cries, angry tears, pushing her head at him.*

BILL. You don't realise how much you could have done.

ROXANNA (*angry, crying*). No, no . . . You're not right. You aren't. I'm not having you tell me this – it would never have happened . . . never . . . I'm sure . . . (*Pause.*) I am.

Pulling away, moving across.

Understand. *Understand that?*

BILL (*strong*). No. I don't.

Silence.

ROXANNA. That's what you mind most about, not making me do that . . . share your work.

BILL (*sharp*). Is it?

ROXANNA. I would have made absolutely no difference to all of this. (*Indicating models on pile.*) None. And you know it.

BILL (*watching her*). I thought you were just telling me how you would have changed everything, weren't you Roxanna, your fearless approach, how you would have made me . . .

ROXANNA. No difference. (*Louder.*) My advice from time to time would have changed nothing.

ROXANNA moving towards him, formidable.

BILL (*staring back at her*). Roxanna, we don't know that, do we?

ROXANNA (*by him, touching his face for a moment*). Even if I have always been older than you, don't you think? Since the age of five, or even three perhaps – and what good has it done me . . . what good at all. (*Looks at him.*) You frighten people you know, because you have this curious belief in oddly shaped machines, and buildings . . . and all the rest.

BILL. And I couldn't even make my own daughter see it – want to be part of it.

ROXANNA. Sometimes you did – isn't that enough?

BILL. No – *that is not enough.*

Slight pause.

ROXANNA. So what would be? (*She glances up.*) No, I didn't mean that, don't try, it's much much too late, I'm not coming to work for you – Jesus one is never safe with you is one! Come anywhere within range . . . ! We can't go back to that, you understand, it's impossible, I've forgotten everything I knew.

BILL. I could change that quite quickly.

ROXANNA. There's no chance. I'm not being pulled back. We can't.

Pause.

BILL (*flicking his fingers*). If, if I was to ask you . . .

ROXANNA. No. (*Moving off.*) *NO!*

BILL. – to stay a little longer tonight. Just . . .

ROXANNA *turns.*

ROXANNA. That's possible Dad. Of course. A little longer.

BILL (*sharp*). That's allowed is it.

ROXANNA. Tonight, yes. That's all. Do you understand?

Pause. Noise of creaking scaffolding.

Christ, that creaking, and the flapping plastic. You like that don't you? This place is really falling to bits, dissolving around us.

BILL. Its walls crack a little more each day. It's hardly lasted a handful of years.

ROXANNA. You're the only person I've ever met who finds quick decay comforting, that loves bits of loose masonry and wafer thin walls, you probably lean out of the window high up here and scrape another piece off yourself. (*Moving over to the pile.*) It's horribly cold though, the draught . . . and all these accumulated things here.

BILL (*moving towards pile*). Some of that is a reminder of better times. (*Straight at her.*) Isn't it?

ROXANNA. You should get rid of it all . . .

ROXANNA *begins to climb among the belongings and among the brown paper parcels.*

These are different of course – these parcels, you ought to open them, you can't just leave them, they're stranded up here at the moment.

BILL. They're all from lunatics.

ROXANNA. Probably, yes.

BILL. So it doesn't matter.

ROXANNA. Doesn't it?

BILL (*savage smile, animated, as he clambers among parcels*). It is deeply depressing opening one mad parcel after another I can tell you – this is exactly what my detractors would love to see Roxanna, me strutting about in an ocean of grubby paper parcels, becoming the king of the brown paper bags. Drowning in them. Some of them – look – even have strangely formed handwriting on them, huge childish handwriting, and they make weird sounds, or little bells start ringing when you turn them over with your foot. And in every one a crazy idea, a ludicrous notion about the future, a crank waiting for you, ready to leap out as soon as you raise the lid.

BILL *stands completely surrounded by brown paper parcels.*

This is not exactly what I had in mind.

ROXANNA. Fuck what anybody else thinks . . . we don't know what's here do we?

BILL. The only comforting thing is, they are really slowing down now, arriving in just a trickle.

ROXANNA. I don't think that's comforting, I think that's rather frightening. (*She's moving on pile.*) You're going to open some now, I think. I'll help until I have to go (*Firm.*) which is soon, very soon. (*Climbing on top of pile.*)

It probably is all junk . . . there're some really oddly shaped parcels here, but . . . Jesus, look at this! This one is eight years old, it's been sitting here for all that time. (*Lifting parcel.*) Here, catch, start on that one.

She stands on top of pile, BILL *watching her.*

ROXANNA (*warning*). Don't you look like that Dad . . . What you looking at?

BILL (*staring at her for a moment, slight pause*). Nothing, Roxanna.

ROXANNA. Good. Then get to work.

Sitting far apart on the great pile of brown paper parcels, they begin to open them.

Fade.

SHE'S BEEN AWAY

THE CAST

She's Been Away first broadcast by BBC-TV in autumn 1989.

LILLIAN	Peggy Ashcroft
HARRIET	Geraldine James
HUGH	James Fox
DOMINIC	Jackson Kyle
YOUNG LILLIAN	Rebecca Pidgeon
GLADYS	Rosalie Crutchley
MATILDA	Rachel Kempson
GEORGE	Hugh Lloyd
NURSE, (*Mental Hospital*)	Brid Brennan
DOCTOR (*Mental Hospital*)	David Hargreaves
LOUISE	Robyn Moore
HARLEY STREET DOCTOR	Richard Haddon Haines
YOUNG COUSIN EDWARD	Barnaby Holm
YOUNG LILLIAN'S FATHER	Donald Douglas
CITY FRIEND AT PARTY	Malcolm Mudie
MOVIE BUFF	David Timson
SUPERMARKET CASHIER	Anne Haydn
TRAFFIC WARDEN	Doyle Richmond
WOMAN IN HOSPITAL RECEPTION	Maureen Nelson
VICAR	Roger Davidson
YOUNG DOCTOR (*Baby Scan*)	Richard Huw
HOTEL RECEPTION CLERK	Jon Strickland
POLICEMAN IN NEWS ITEM	Nick Kemp
HEAD WAITER	Michael Carter
MAN AT DANCE	David Pullan
HOTEL PARTY GUEST	Graham Callan
YOUNG WOMAN AT RECEPTION	Claire Williamson
DOCTOR (*Country Hospital*)	James Griffiths
NURSE (*Country Hospital*)	Francesca Buller
1920'S DOCTOR	Hugh Ross
DIRECTOR	Peter Hall
PRODUCER	Kenith Trodd
DESIGNER	Gary Williamson
DIRECTOR OF PHOTOGRAPHY	Philip Bonham-Carter

Opening Title Sequence – Interior Mental Hospital – Day

The camera moves very slowly across a series of objects underneath the titles – old shoes, a model of St. Paul's Cathedral, some china figurines, covered in dust. They are evocative and strange.

Exterior: The Driveway; Mental Hospital – Day

A car approaches down a long drive, a silver Daimler passing ill-kept rhododendron bushes and piles of autumn leaves being burnt. Through the windscreen we see a large, shambling Victorian building.

HUGH is driving, he leans purposefully over the wheel. A man in his late thirties, he has a good natured face, exudes confidence, genial certainty. Next to him, HARRIET is smoking, looking at the great decaying building coming into view. She is in her mid-thirties, and is expensively, fashionably dressed. She has a sharp, ironic manner.

Exterior: Mental Hospital: Entrance – Day

They reach the building through a fog of builders' dust. As they get out of the car, sofas, chairs, boxes, old carpets, are being thrown from a first floor window down into a massive skip. From several other windows roundabout in the building, pale faces stare down, mostly old people, one or two much younger. They watch carefully as HARRIET and HUGH get out of the car.

HARRIET (*almost being hit by the builders as she climbs out of the car*). This can't be the right place, can it?

HUGH. Of course it is. How could I come to the wrong place? I've been here before.

HARRIET watches the faces staring out of the window, through the haze of builders' dust. One of the builders has a radio blasting out Radio One, as they chuck the contents of the building out.

HUGH. Do you think I should take the chair? (*He is fiddling with a shiny new wheelchair from the boot of the car.*) I don't know if she needs it, it may not be the thing to do . . .

HARRIET. How do I know what the thing to do is. . . ? Let's get it over.

HUGH (*decisively, straightening out wheelchair*). I'll take it – she might appreciate it.

Interior: Old Mental Hospital: Corridor – Day

A NURSE *is heading down a passage clouded with builders' dust, leading* HARRIET *and* HUGH. *The* NURSE *is walking very fast,* HUGH *pushing the empty wheelchair racing along, and* HARRIET *half having to run to keep up with them.*

NURSE. There's no easy way of doing this, no rules, there's almost nothing you can do wrong in these circumstances . . . or right for that matter.

HUGH. Yes, it's not exactly the sort of thing you do everyday! Collecting somebody who's been shut up for –

NURSE (*cutting him off*). But don't expect reactions. She's a very docile sort of person, passive creature now, she could have been let out of here a long time ago really.

HUGH. I know, my mother wouldn't try to get her out. . . (*Hurrying after the* NURSE.) my mother's dead now, so –

NURSE (*cutting in*). Don't expect her to respond at all, she doesn't really understand anything that's going on round here, just wants to be on her own.

They have come to a barrier in the passage, a makeshift wooden barrier, that they have to get through and squeeze the wheelchair through.

The NURSE *guides an old man who's got through the barrier and is glancing around the doorway, back into his part of the building.*

This is meant to keep them out of the builders' way. (*To old man.*) But some of us get through don't we?. . . (*Firmly to old man.*) I don't know why, because there's nothing to see.

HARRIET (*squeezing last through the barrier*). You seem to be knocking the place down around them –

NURSE. There's a deadline by which time the building has to be empty. So they had to start on this wing – nothing we could do.

Interior: Mental Hospital: Ballroom – Day

Cut to the NURSE, HUGH *and* HARRIET *crossing a large room, like an old ballroom, now full of split leather armchairs and a central table completely covered in belongings, old clothes, shoes, handbags, old pocket mirrors, hats. Several of the inmates are sitting round the room in corners, peering through the dust filled air, for the builders' dust has permeated into this part of the building.*

We can see workmen and builders' machinery outside the window of the ballroom.

NURSE (*marching across the room indicating the people in the shadows as she moves*). All of these will be leaving in the next three months, they all have to be gone by then. (*She points to an old man in the corner sitting alone.*) That's George, used to spend a lot of time with your Aunt once, but I haven't seen them near each other for several years.

HARRIET *stops by the table of belongings, as the* NURSE *begins to sweep on.*

Those are all belongings of people that died here, over the years. (*Pointing at the inmates.*) We're trying to encourage any of these to take what they want – some of them may really need it. (*She smiles pleasantly at one of them.*) It's their own antiques road show, isn't it? (*Sharp.*) Come on, the doctor's waiting.

HARRIET *is staring at the evocative spread of belongings including small china figures, some of them quite beautiful.*

HUGH *moves up to the belongings breezily, pleasant smile.*

HUGH. Isn't it odd what some people want to keep. Careful darling, we don't want to break anything.

NURSE (*not unkindly*). Anything you want – just grab it. We've got literally rooms full of that stuff.

Interior: Mental Hospital: Corridor – Day

HUGH *and* HARRIET *sitting obediently on very low chairs in the passage, as a* DOCTOR *holding a file leans against a door opposite them. The* NURSE *is also there. The* DOCTOR *is leafing through the file and swinging on the door. As he swings on the door, they can just catch a glimpse of an old lady sitting with her back to them in the far room.*

Next to them in the passage is a line of three fish tanks, full of weeds, dark green water, but still with quite large fish in them.

HUGH (*pleasant smile*). I remember the fish from last time.

DOCTOR. Yes, we tried to brighten the place up. (*He glances at the dark fish.*) But we seem to have all lost interest after a time, didn't we . . . when we knew the building was going. (*The DOCTOR gently swings on the door.*) She won't remember your last visit.

HUGH. I know.

HARRIET *is looking at the dishevelled paper chains and other efforts to brighten the place up, now shrivelled. There are also some paintings and drawings stuck on the wall further down the passage. HARRIET's gaze settles on a striking almost cartoon version of a middle aged man's head.*

DOCTOR. She doesn't remember anything, but you'll find she's very easy. She likes doing her own cooking . . . that was a new development about 10 years ago, simple things like sausages, scrambled egg. She never watches TV, she's in a totally insulated world, in fact, very little, if anything, gets through. . .

HARRIET *finds she's staring through the crack of the door at the back of the old lady, and then at the strange shaped fish right beside her in the tank.*

You have to remember she's been in institutions for over sixty years, there's not much left when that's happened.

HUGH (*earnestly*). Of course, I meant to do this gradually, take her out to tea, on trips, have her come to stay for weekends, but with you closing her ward, it –

DOCTOR (*pleasantly*), Yes, yes. It wouldn't have made any difference. Good. (*He closes the file.*) She's all yours. Take care of her, don't let her out of the house on her own, that sort of thing. Use your common sense (*he smiles straight at them*) which I'm sure you possess. Otherwise she'll be as good as gold, won't she sister? (*He begins to move off down passage, then turns, pleasantly.*) I'm getting my release too this week, early retirement (*as if answering an enquiry from them*) mixed feelings, really – (*he smiles*) but basically I can't wait.

Interior: Mental Hospital: Ward – Day

LILLIAN *sitting in the foreground of shot in deep old chair, alone, right close to the window overlooking a courtyard. As she senses them approaching, she closes her eyes.*

NURSE. Have you got everything now Lillian? (LILLIAN's *eyes still shut.*) We packed, didn't we. Come on, you are not really asleep are you? It's the day we've been waiting for.

There are two old battered suitcases, with Lillian's name written on them in girlish handwriting, standing among the empty beds in the wards. Some of the beds have already been stripped of their mattresses.

HUGH (*crouching down by* LILLIAN *so his head is close to hers*). Aunt Lillian – we've come to take you home. Do you remember me? . . . Hugh, Margaret's son, I've been before to –

HARRIET (*turning away, staring about the empty ward*). She doesn't remember, Hugh, they told us.

LILLIAN *staring straight back at* HUGH.

LILLIAN. Is he here to clean? I'll move then, if he's going to clean.

NURSE. Don't be silly – it's your big day today.

LILLIAN (*to* HARRIET). Have you got some clean sheets at last? (*Sharp.*) Have you brought them? You can make my bed then.

HARRIET. I'm Harriet. Hugh's wife. I've come to . . . (*she stops, embarrassed*) help on the journey (*she smiles*) be in the way.

LILLIAN *stares back at her, there is something direct and unsettling in her look,* HARRIET *moves, glances out of the window at the view* LILLIAN *has been staring at. The window overlooks a grubby courtyard, with a large white tiled wall directly opposite. The courtyard is full of old pieces of furniture and other junk.*

NURSE (*in background of shot, as* HARRIET *is looking*). Say goodbye to your seat Lillian – this is where she's spent years just sitting. Only wants to look at the wall, quite happy if she can do that. (*Warmly.*) Silly girl, it's not the best view around here.

HARRIET (*staring right down into the bottom of the courtyard*). Jesus, what a dump.

Interior: Mental Hospital: Corridor – Day

The NURSE, HUGH *and* HARRIET *move along the long passage with* LILLIAN. HUGH *pushing* LILLIAN *in the wheelchair,* HARRIET *carrying the suitcases.* LILLIAN *is clasping a small bag. They pass through the barrier.*

LILLIAN. We are going the wrong way. I'm not meant to be going this way! This is not right!

NURSE. I've been telling you for weeks Lillian, come on now. You are going outside.

LILLIAN. I'm going to walk. Let me walk. (*She gets out of the wheelchair, she stays close to the wall. Sharp, to* HUGH.) You don't know where you're going do you?

Interior/Exterior: Mental Hospital: Entrance – Day

Cut to LILLIAN *standing facing the large main door. The camera is behind her, as the door opens, and she steps out. A wall of dust greets her and the builders standing on top of the great pile of rubble and junk already filling the drive, seen from* LILLIAN's *point of view, look strange and slightly threatening. All round the building, faces are staring from windows, as some of the remaining inmates watch her.*

HUGH (*taking her by the arm*). This way, this is the car. (*Gently.*) You don't mind riding in one of those do you? Let's sit in the front.

LILLIAN *tenses slightly at the sight of the car. She lets herself be put in the car, but she insists on the back seat, automatically moving there, she is not looking at anyone.*

Exterior: Mental Hospital/Interior: Car – Day

The car moves off, HUGH glancing at her in the mirror, as she sits on the back seat.

HUGH (*slowly, as if to a child*). When was the last time you went outside? (*Gently.*) When you were outside the home?

LILLIAN *seeming not to listen, she is staring back at the receding view of the home, the large Victorian building, gradually disappearing behind trees.*

HARRIET. She hasn't been out for a long time we know that, the doctor said –

HUGH (*firmly*). Yes, but I want to know how long.

LILLIAN *has suddenly started burrowing among her belongings in the bag she is clasping, hunting furiously for something.*

LILLIAN (*Loud*). Stop. Stop it. (*Catching the door handle as car is moving.*) Stop at once . . . stop it.

HUGH *brakes sharply, they have just turned onto the main road.* LILLIAN *very agitated, searching.*

I lost it.

HUGH *gets out, leans through the back door to help her.*

HUGH. Now, it's alright Lillian. Calm down, tell me slowly, what have you lost?

He starts going through the belongings, a seemingly random selection, in bag. Slow tone.

The apple is here, that's not it is it? The gloves . . . the tin plate? Not that? Your greeting cards, and this old picture book, that's not it is it?

LILLIAN *suddenly looks relieved. She's holding a pair of silver sugar tongs, now freckled with black.*

Is that what it was? Those tongs. Hold onto them now. Everything OK? . . .

HARRIET *whispers to him as he climbs back into the driving seat.*

HARRIET. We haven't even *started* Hugh . . . it's too sudden doing it this way, it's crazy, I don't think she's ready for it. (*Even quieter.*) *I'm* not anyway.

HUGH (*reassuring, confident*). Everything's under control now . . . sit back and relax Lillian. We can all enjoy the drive, lots to see.

HARRIET (*sharp smile to* LILLIAN). He'll call out some of the sights I expect.

Exterior: London Suburbs/Interior: Car

Vivid shots of coming in to London, motorways, large vehicles, juggernauts, speeding coaches, past the airport, with a 747 coming in to land, very low, seemingly about to scrape the tops of houses, a huge DIY store in the middle of a traffic interchange, pylons marching across the landscape, and then sudden unfamiliar palm trees clustering round a mosque in Surrey with its golden dome shining in the sun.

HARRIET. Have we got lost? This doesn't look right at all. We're going round in circles Hugh!

And then onto LILLIAN's *eyes, a distant stare, confused by all she sees outside the window, she looks away, shutting it out, starts scrabbling amongst her things.*

Exterior: Street Outside London House – Day

The car rounding the corner into leafy residential street in Holland Park.

HUGH. This is it Lillian. We're home. Do you remember this street? Do you recognise the houses? There's the family house! It's still the same one you were brought up in.

LILLIAN *is not looking, staring down at her things.*

The door knob! Remember the door knob?

There is a striking door knob of a lion's head on the door of a substantial early Victorian house, set back from the road.

LILLIAN *looks up for a second.*

HARRIET. Leave her alone.

LILLIAN (*pulling her belongings close to her*). I don't know why you've brought me here. I'm going to be late back. You're going to get me into trouble because of this.

Interior: London House: Hall – Day

Subjective shot as LILLIAN enters the house. Her point of view moving into the hall, as a small reception party stands waiting for her. A young English nanny, LOUISE, and a Portuguese cook, THERESA, are standing with an eight year old boy DOMINIC. LILLIAN is looking neither left or right.

HUGH's voice cutting into her point of view.

This is my son, Dominic and Louise who looks after him . . . and Theresa, Lillian, where you going?

LILLIAN *not stopping, moving slowly but purposefully, ignoring everyone.*

Things have changed of course since you'll remember the house, but there's still a lot the same. Your rooms are through here, in the new extension –

A small frisson crosses LILLIAN's face as she moves past some pictures, portraits of relatives, but we can't tell if she has recognized anything or just uneasy with her surroundings. She shuffles out of the hall.

LILLIAN (*muttering*). This is all wrong . . . you've brought me to the wrong place.

Interior: London House: Granny Flat – Day

HUGH guides her through the large house to a self-contained granny flat at the back.

HUGH (*gently enthusiastic*). This is your flat, you see completely self-contained, bathroom . . . what estate agents would call luxury kitchen, small but it's got everything, and there's food in the fridge, patio out there. (*Correcting himself, in case she's unfamiliar with the term.*) Little paved garden, it's about 20' by 20', you can sit out there . . . flowers from the garden.

LILLIAN *has been standing in the middle of the bedroom while he's been saying this, a look of incomprehension in her eyes. She picks up some of the flowers out of the vase.*

LILLIAN (*holding the flowers*). When do you come in here to clean?

HUGH (*patient smile*). I told you I don't clean – but if you want it cleaned, I think it's spotless, but –

LILLIAN. If you clean it *now*, I can have my rest.

HUGH. It *has* been cleaned.

LILLIAN (*pushing the flowers at him*). Take the flowers, I'm not allowed any flowers.

HUGH (*slowly*). You are here now, this is home, there are no rules.

LILLIAN. And I'm not allowed two pillows (*handing him pillows*) and these are breakable, I'm not allowed them, take them away. (*Indicating china ornaments.*)

HUGH's *arms are now full. Piled high, from things to remove.* LILLIAN *staring at him.*

How much time is there left now?

HUGH. Time till when?

LILLIAN *looks cross at him not understanding.*

LILLIAN. Time till you have to switch off all the lights of course.

Interior: Dining Room – Evening

HUGH, HARRIET *and* DOMINIC *are sitting round the dinner table, staring at the celebratory meal prepared for* LILLIAN, *a fine fresh salmon lies in front of them, and some beautifully prepared salads. Candles are flickering on the table. They are eyeing the empty chair at the head of the table.*

HUGH. We were told this would happen . . . take no notice. She'll come when she's ready. We *must* leave her alone.

DOMINIC *is twisting his chair, staring down the passage that leads off the dining room. There is a curl of smoke visible, coming from round the corner.*

DOMINIC. There's a terrible smell. Can't you smell it? It's horrible. . . (*He twists round.*) It's disgusting.

HARRIET. Dominic you always state the obvious – just eat up, and keep quiet.

HARRIET *though is also eyeing the passage, where the smoke is visible.*

DOMINIC. If she sets the house on fire, will they blame you? (*He looks confidently at* HUGH.) Are we insured for any damage she does?

Interior: Granny Flat – Night

Cut to the interior of the little kitchen, LILLIAN *with grilled sardines, smoking, burnt. She is just taking them off the grill, and putting them on a tin plate, the same tin plate we saw in the car.*

We see LILLIAN *staring down at the modern gadgets, waste disposal, coffee maker, Magimix, that* HUGH *has put in the little kitchen for her. A moment of her alone among the alien machinery, touching it.*

Then we cut to her sitting alone in her room, eating off her tin plate on her knees, determinedly.

We see that her room is now completely empty, except for the bed, and the chair, and her two suitcases.

Interior: Main Bedroom – Night

HUGH *and* HARRIET *lying in bed, it is dark.*

Close up of HARRIET *as she lies there, wide awake. There is a strange noise from downstairs, something rhythmically banging, again and again, like something knocking against a pipe or a radiator.*

HARRIET. Do you hear that?

HUGH. Of course I hear that. (*The knocking is even louder.*) It's Lillian, naturally.

HARRIET. The whole street must be able to hear. They'll think we've got a trapped animal in the house, or something.

HUGH (*switching on side light*). It's OK. The first night was always going to be difficult.

HARRIET (*quiet*). It's not OK . . . I don't want her breaking anything down there.

HUGH. We just couldn't put her straight in another home, without her having a chance to see outside. I feel very strongly about that, don't you? (*With feeling.*) She is family after all. Anyway Aunt Sarah said she would have her next year, when she's finished the conversion in her basement. Its only for a little while darling . . .

Close up of HARRIET as the unsettling noise continues, in fact seems to be getting louder.

HARRIET. This isn't going to work Hugh. (*Quiet.*) There isn't a chance in hell.

Interior: Granny Flat – Night

We see LILLIAN from the back. She is sitting up in the dark room on single chair, rocking backwards and forwards, banging her radiator with her tin plate, not in a desperate fashion, more as if she's just occupying the time. We move closer to her, as she sways on the chair.

Exterior: London Street – Night.

Shot down into the street, the night world LILLIAN is staring at. We see two kids riding by on bicycles covered in luminous lights, glowing back at LILLIAN.

We cut back to LILLIAN's face.

Then back into the street, a car draws up, its engine running very loudly, doors slamming, loud Kensington voices shouting in the night streets, oblivious.

We cut back to LILLIAN *swaying in her chair.*

Interior: Main Drawing Room – Day

Bright sunlight in the main drawing room. LILLIAN *is sitting bolt upright in a chair facing* HUGH *who is just completing drawing a family tree on a blackboard.* LILLIAN's *demeanour is peaceful, but totally impassive, one can't tell if she's taking in a single thing* HUGH *is saying. But her eyes are very watchful.*

HUGH *making a scratching noise with the chalk as he completes the diagram.*

HUGH. I haven't written on a blackboard for some time, forgive the squeak. NOW, Lillian. (*He points to the top of the family tree.*) This is Grandfather Edwin sitting up here, he had two children, one of whom was your father, Gerald, he married Letticia, your mother, you see I've underlined them in red, can you see that?

LILLIAN *watching but not responding.*

And there were eight children, yes eight. You were fifth, my mother third, can you remember your sister Margaret? My mother? (*Curious.*) Got any feeling about her?

HUGH *is using his patient slow tone, as if to a small girl. He spreads some photos in front of* LILLIAN *on the table.*

(*Sitting opposite her at the gleaming mahogany table.*) Can you pick out the photo of you as a young girl?

LILLIAN *surveys the pictures, her hand moving over them for a moment, hovering. Then, like a small child, as if taking her cue from his tone of voice, she flicks the pictures onto the floor.*

(*Watching her closely.*) You don't remember anything do you? (HUGH *takes her by the hand, looking very directly.*) Do you like to be called Lillian or *Lilly*? They used to call you Lilly as a girl, didn't they? (*He calls her name.*) Lilly? Lillian? (*Decides on Lilly*). *Lilly.*

LILLIAN (*staring straight back at him*). Can I go to my room now? I don't think I'm allowed out of the room for this long.

HUGH. I told you you can do whatever you like now, Lilly.

LILLIAN (*sharply*). And there is no pot under my bed . . . it's been forgotten.

HUGH (*smiling*). I'll see to that.

HARRIET *is standing watching from the stairs.*

(*Turns.*) She doesn't remember anything, they were right.

HARRIET. We know that for chrissake. And stop drawing her diagrams, she's not come here to be made to work. Have you?

LILLIAN *and* HARRIET's *eyes meet.* HARRIET *disconcerted by her look.*

Interior: Harley Street Consulting Room – Day

HARRIET *lying prone, her face in close up, her dress rolled up, as she's examined out of frame. We stay on her face, she's rolling her eyes with impatience.*

DOCTOR. Everything's fine. In spanking order.

We see him, moving over to desk, fine Harley Street interior. He is about 40, but seems older.

HARRIET. You took your time – I thought you'd got lost down there.

DOCTOR (*sitting down at desk*). We have to be thorough naturally, when –

HARRIET. When the mother-to-be is as ancient as this one you mean.

HARRIET *lights a cigarette.*

DOCTOR. No, no, plenty of time for you to have at least four more.

HARRIET *looks horrified, blows smoke.*

HARRIET. What a terrifying thought. (*She takes an ostentatious drag, as if daring him to tell her to stop smoking.*)

The DOCTOR *is writing, with a stylish gold pen,* HARRIET *watches it slide across the paper.*

DOCTOR. Everything nice and normal at home? Not having to rush around too much I hope?

HARRIET (*lightly*). Everything's fine. We have a crazy aunt of Hugh's staying with us, who was shut up in a loony bin for over 60 years, and makes strange smells all over the house (*the* DOCTOR *not looking up, not reacting*) and she lies awake every night banging a tin plate against a radiator while making a whining noise, otherwise everything's perfectly normal.

DOCTOR (*not looking up*). Relatives tend to come in all shapes and sizes don't they? Turn up at awkward moments, too, always happening. (*The* DOCTOR *looks up.*) And how has your husband greeted this happy news? The baby coming? Is he as pleased as he should be?

HARRIET. He doesn't know.

DOCTOR (*startled, for the first time letting his cool be ruffled*). He doesn't know! Why?

HARRIET (*ironic laugh*). He doesn't need to know, does he?

Interior: London House: Hall – Day

HARRIET *comes through the door into the hall, to be greeted by a strange sight. The house is absolutely full of flowers, large bouquets and bunches of freshly cut flowers.* HARRIET *moves through the hall in surprise.* LILLIAN *is sitting among the flowers on the half landing, staring out of the window. On one of the bouquets hanging over the bannister is a large greeting card saying 'well done, my darling'.*

HARRIET. What's going on? (*To* LILLIAN.) What's all this about? Did you see who did this?

LILLIAN. They told me not to touch.

The phone rings. HARRIET, *with her carrier bags, has to squeeze past* LILLIAN *on the half landing, to get to the phone. She answers the phone on the main landing, close enough for* LILLIAN *to be able to hear.*

HARRIET. Yes!

HUGH'S VOICE (*loud, excited*). Am I right? I guessed right, didn't I? It's true, isn't it?

HARRIET (*very sharp*). Guessed what?

HUGH. We're going to have a baby! You've done it, my darling. Haven't you?

HARRIET. How on earth did you know?

Interior: HUGH's Office – Day

We see HUGH *in impressive city office with glass walls onto larger open plan office. The telephone conversation is intercut.*

HUGH. I guessed from the number of times you were going to the doctor.

HARRIET. You guessed from me going to the doctor! Really? I thought you'd been following me for a moment.

HUGH. I don't need to do that!

HARRIET. What if you'd been wrong Hugh, what if I'd got AIDS or something? (HUGH *doesn't seem to hear, she shouts down the phone.*) AIDS!

LILLIAN *staring at her.*

HUGH. Harriet really! Don't make jokes like that, it's not like you! Got to go now. Congratulations my love. (*He whispers.*) Our long wait is over!

HUGH *replaces the receiver in his comfortable glass-fronted office in a merchant bank. He turns, smiling broadly to a young secretary in the room.*

I was right. (*The girl smiles.*) I knew I was, I was right. Come on – get some glasses. (*He goes into the open plan office to tell some more people.*) We're going to celebrate!

Interior: London House: Hall/Landing – Day

Rain flicking down the window, LILLIAN's face in profile, staring benignly out through the rain spattered window, watching the blank wall opposite with interest as if watching a film screen.

HARRIET moving past, dressed to go out, catches her coat on the chair. LILLIAN has positioned her seat directly in the middle of the passage.

HARRIET turns, suddenly surprises herself by being really sharp with LILLIAN.

HARRIET. Do you have to sit there – of all places! It's a big house, you don't have to sit right here, you're in the way of everybody. It's really dumb – putting yourself there.

LILLIAN continues to stare out of the window, not even registering HARRIET's presence. HARRIET stands there rattling her car keys.

What's so interesting down there anyway?

For a second, both of them stare at the blank wall.

HARRIET *(as she stands, staring at the blank wall)*. We're having a party apparently – quite a big one, celebrating something or other, and I have to go and do the shopping. Hugh has made a list, surprise, surprise . . . *(She begins to go, then turns.)* You don't want to come, do you? *(LILLIAN very slightly turns.)* You haven't been out since you arrived here – I think you better come. OK? *(HARRIET bends over LILLIAN their faces close.)* Was that a nod? Just a tiny hint of a nod? Was it? Can you understand what I'm saying?

LILLIAN stares back out of the window.

HARRIET suddenly takes her by the arm, and begins to lift her out of the chair.

Come on, you're coming anyway.

Exterior: London Streets/Interior: Car

HARRIET *driving in HUGH's silver Daimler, LILLIAN trussed up in her seat belt next to her, her head right back in the seat, as if she is riding on a roller-coaster.*

The car radio is on one of the pop channels – a guess the mystery voice competition, callers trying to identify the name of some actor.
HARRIET *hunched over the wheel, smoking.*

HARRIET. I should stop smoking for the child, shouldn't I? (*To* LILLIAN.) I should stop.

HARRIET *takes another drag,* LILLIAN *staring ahead, her head pressed back.*

Why you sitting like that? We're not about to break the sound barrier or something. (*Warm smile.*) You look as if you want a crash helmet. (HARRIET *is hardly looking at the road.*) *Don't worry.*

LILLIAN's *eyes are half shut.*

Don't you want to take a look? Have you really not been out for all those years? I don't believe it. So what do you think of everything, Lillian?

Shots of young girls walking along the streets, kids in groups moving down the pavement, the car is travelling behind a large paper lorry, pieces fluttering out of it towards them. HARRIET *swings the car round a corner rapidly.*

If you really hadn't been out, you'd be overwhelmed by all this wouldn't you? (*Glancing at* LILLIAN.) Things have changed haven't they?

As they round the corner, they are greeted by brewery wagon, drawn by black horses moving at a stately pace down the road, the wagon ridden by liveried men in top hats.

(*Laughs.*) That's just an advertisement, take no notice of that.

LILLIAN *staring at the horses as they over-take, a private, contained look in her eyes.*

HARRIET *putting her foot down, car roaring down the street. She's calling out at the radio mystery voice competition.*

Ronald Colman . . . Errol Flynn . . . It's one of those

Hollywood gents, who do you think it is? Do you recognize it? (*Lightly, glancing at* LILLIAN.) I used to be an actress, you know a sort of part time, very tiny roles kind of actress . . . before I met Hugh. Would you have ever guessed that? (*She laughs.*) Used to play the bitches that get killed off halfway through the first act in Agatha Christie. Type casting, don't you think! (*Sharp laugh.*) I expect I was awful really . . .

HARRIET *brakes violently.* LILLIAN *has taken her safety belt off, and is making a movement, as if she's about to open the door.*

What the hell are you doing?

LILLIAN. I don't think I'm allowed to be here, it's not permitted. I will get into trouble.

HARRIET. You can't get into trouble anymore, relax.

Exterior: Shopping Centre – Day

Outside large concrete shopping complex, in the car park, HARRIET *trying to squeeze the car into a small space.* LILLIAN *standing on the pavement, watching her.*

HARRIET (*shouting out of the window*). Have I got room . . . have I got enough room?

LILLIAN *stands watching, she moves her head slightly.*

(*Shouting.*) Is that a nod?

There is a crunching noise.

(*Sharp laugh.*) Oh to hell with it. (*Gets out, starts to walk away.*) This is Hugh's car, I shouldn't be using it for shopping. I'm not even going to look! Come on.

Interior: Supermarket – Day

HARRIET *and* LILLIAN *moving through a sizeable upmarket supermarket.*

They are both pushing large trolleys in front of them. HARRIET *scrambling around for* HUGH'*s list.*

HARRIET. Hugh's lists are always so beautifully planned, they
follow the layout of the shop exactly. It says 'start at the cheese
counter . . . and then move in a clockwise direction. . . ' Which
is clockwise? Where's the cheese? (*She goes over.*) Here we go . . .

HARRIET *starts to order at cheese and delicatessen counter. She
doesn't notice that* LILLIAN *has wandered off on her own.*

(*To an empty space.*) I hope you are not going to find this party
too much of an ordeal Lillian . . . I mean all the surviving
family being there.

The shop assistant looks at her oddly.

We cut to LILLIAN *wandering down the aisles of the supermarket,
staring intrigued at all the stacks of goods. She moves closer to a tall
pile of biscuits, being marketed in tins with evocative nostalgic period
pictures on the front, and called 'Old English Biscuit' selection. She
takes several tins and puts them in her trolley. She takes them from
the middle of the pyramid display of tins, and moves off, leaving it
standing incredibly perilously balanced on one tin.*

LILLIAN *picks up large 'Special Offer' signs, plucking them off the
rows of food and cans and 'New Range' of pre-cooked meals, and
drops the signs into her trolley, until she has quite a pile of them,
wheeling them along the aisles as if about to purchase them. People
are eyeing her oddly, but* LILLIAN *is moving on, oblivious, pushing
her trolley.*

*She stops at the frozen meat counter, and surveys a display of frozen
joints of beef, lamb and whole ducks. She picks up a frozen duck
from the fridge, then another, then another. We cut back to*
HARRIET *still ordering from* HUGH's *list, totally immersed in it.*

We cut back to LILLIAN, *she has about eight or nine frozen ducks
now in her trolley, she has put a couple of biscuit tins in the fridge,
to make room for them. She also drops most of the pile of 'Special
Offer' signs into the fridge, leaving only two small signs in among the
ducks.*

*People are standing watching her, out of the corner of their eyes,
having stopped their own shopping.*

We cut to LILLIAN *waiting patiently in the check-out queue, a benign innocent look on her face, with her great pile of frozen meat in her trolley.*

LILLIAN *gets to the cashier, it is her turn.*

CASHIER (*lifting the 'Special Offer' signs out from amongst the frozen ducks*). You don't want these I don't think, do you? Must've fallen in somehow. But you'll need the trolley I expect.

LILLIAN *watches intrigued as the total is rattled up on the cash register, a second assistant helpfully puts the meat in bags and puts them back in the trolley.*

LILLIAN *smiles at them, a slight, peaceful smile. The receipt is snaking its way out of the machine.*

That'll be £122.53 pence please love.

LILLIAN *nods sweetly at them and, without making any move to pay, pushes her trolley straight on through the check out and towards the automatic glass doors, that hiss open, as she approaches with the vast pile of frozen meat.*

Immediate alarms go off, and assistant and shop managers converge from all corners of the shop and surround LILLIAN.

We cut to HARRIET*'s head spinning round, in her part of the shop.*

HARRIET. Lillian?

HARRIET *runs across the shop, shouting 'wait, wait, she's with me, don't do anything, she's with me'.*

She passes the pyramid of biscuits, that collapses as she runs past scattering across the aisle.

She reaches the group, just as they're escorting LILLIAN *towards an office.*

Exterior: Shopping Centre – Day

Cut to LILLIAN *sitting on a bench outside, totally impervious, sitting watching the cars.*

Interior: Supermarket – Day

We cut inside the shop, HARRIET is standing surrounded by assistants, and the trolley of frozen meat. A little man is remonstrating, jabbing his finger at HARRIET. She is bright red with fury, and is waving a frozen duck round in her hand.

HARRIET (*shouting*). Why do I have to buy it? I'll put it back! If you let me for chrissake. The meat's begun to defrost? That's rubbish! That's because we've been standing here for twenty minutes, you idiots! (*She grabs a biscuit tin, waving it furiously.*) The bloody biscuits haven't begun to defrost, have they?

Exterior: Shopping Centre – Day

We cut back to LILLIAN sitting blissfully on her seat. She is watching some kids weaving their way through the cars, trying the door handles of the parked cars. They get to the Daimler, try the door, and then break the back side window with expert ease. One of them looks up at LILLIAN just as he is reaching in to unlock the door. LILLIAN continues to watch, even gives them a little smile. The kid smiles back, and gets inside to steal the radio.

HARRIET comes out of the shop wheeling the frozen ducks, just as the kids scamper away from the car. HARRIET sees them go with the radio.

HARRIET. I don't believe it. I just don't believe it! (*To LILLIAN, furiously.*) Why didn't you tell me, you idiot! You just watched, did you! (*She begins to run towards the car.*) Hugh will kill me. (*She turns in the car park and yells back at LILLIAN.*) This is the last time we ever go shopping you hear! (*Really loud.*) You understand!

Exterior: London House – Day

LILLIAN *by window, overlooking the street, staring down as Bentleys, taxis, one or two BMWs and Porsches are rolling up into the short drive in front of the house.*

People getting out, dressed smartly for a party, a chauffeur being told when to come and pick up a couple of guests. LILLIAN looking tense as she watches them all arrive.

Interior: Drawing room – Day

Cut to subjective shot, LILLIAN's point of view, the door opening into the main reception rooms. A large buffet party is in full swing – a magnificent spread of food, dominated by all the duck LILLIAN bought.

There is a range of people present, spreading from HUGH's relatives to some of HARRIET's friends, a couple of people that could have been actors with her. But mostly it is LILLIAN's surviving family, the relations, old ladies, elderly stout men with jowelly faces, and their offspring. The room is ringing with small talk and the sound of eating, people are also spilling into the ample garden.

DOMINIC is standing staring carefully at the guests, dressed in smart little suit, he surveys everything with a cool stare, sucking a drink through a straw. He moves up to two city friends of HUGH, still sucking out of the straw.

MAN (*patronising smile*). Hello Dominic, we were just . . .

DOMINIC. Talking about house prices. Yes I heard. Please carry on, it's one of my best subjects.

Nobody seems to notice LILLIAN for a moment. She stands on the edge of the room, for a moment watching them all, her old family, spread out before her.

She sees two old ladies talking in a corner, looking in her direction, and exchanging knowing looks.

HARRIET suddenly appears by LILLIAN's side, she is strikingly dressed and in a febrile, extrovert mood.

HARRIET. You're going to eat something aren't you Lillian? (*She smiles.*) You see all the ducks here! (*She turns to one of the guests.*) The food is largely Lillian's contribution . . . she chose most of it.

LILLIAN is watching her.

You must drink Lillian. (*Pouring her some champagne.*)
Celebrate, and really enjoy yourself, there are lots of people
here who want to meet you, they're already queuing up.

LILLIAN *flinches away.*

*The two old women she saw gossiping about her in the corner, bear
down on her.*

One of them pushes her face right up to LILLIAN, *as if addressing
a very deaf child.*

MATILDA. You don't remember me, I'm sure. I am Matilda . . .
do you remember? You came to stay with me in Horsham, one
summer holiday, when *I* was a girl.

MATILDA *looks older than* LILLIAN.

And we quarrelled the whole time.

The other woman, GLADYS, *sharp faced and smaller, pushes in.*

GLADYS (*to* MATILDA). She doesn't remember. She can't
remember, don't you understand? (*She moves* MATILDA *away
for a moment whispering loudly.*) She isn't even able to remember
who she is. Poor dear . . . you can't ask her questions, there's
no point, she's just like a gentle vegetable, shut up all that time
. . . in that building.

GLADYS *then returns, to talk to* LILLIAN *herself, she speaks
slowly, too, and for some reason feels she has better chance of
making herself understood, if she traces the shapes of the words in the
air.*

I came to visit you once . . . and you look just the same *now* as
you did then (*She smiles.*) Isn't that nice? (GLADYS *moves off.*)
Must just get myself some of that duck pâté.

LILLIAN *begins to move away, but suddenly* MATILDA *appears
again, pushing her face towards her.*

MATILDA. Must find somewhere to sit down.

MATILDA *looks at* LILLIAN *as if she expects her to find a
chair.* LILLIAN *does not move.*

No, don't you do anything, I'm sure I can manage myself, I've not been too well recently, had to keep on going to see the doctor.

LILLIAN (*looking straight at her*). Why? Is it because you've got AIDS?

MATILDA *looks astonished.*

If you've been going to the doctor a lot, it could be AIDS.

LILLIAN *begins to move off.*

MATILDA (*calling after her*). Whatever they've been trying to do to you in that place Lillian, it certainly hasn't worked.

We cut to LILLIAN in another corner of the room. She stands watching two fleshy-faced, plump elderly men who look like brothers, one only slightly older than the other, in conversation with a rather elegant woman who is nodding vigorously.

We track in on the jowelly faces of the two men, then back onto LILLIAN's eyes. One of the men has noticed her watching, and instinctively, turns away. Like they have been talking about her. The other brother then glances in her direction, uneasy under her stare, and then looks away. The noise of the party getting louder.

We're back on LILLIAN's face, sudden churning flashbacks begin, like a stream of thought inside her has suddenly been uncorked. Rapid glimpses, piling vividly on top of each other.

Flashback: Interior London House – Drawing Room – Day

We see a young, vital, slightly wild looking girl of about fifteen, a sense of trapped energy, in contrast to the plush upholstered worlds we see her passing through.

We see her face in close up watching through a crack in the door, staring into a large drawing room in the twenties, watching her family at a formal tea party with guests. A subjective shot of her entering the room, her clothes and hair are wet, her legs bare, people looking at her, very disquietened by her entrance.

We see she is holding a dead hedgehog, she lifts the silver cake cover up

*and places the hedgehog next to a walnut cake. Then she walks across
and sits down.*

YOUNG LILLIAN (*watching the startled guests*). Somebody trod on
   it in the garden. I thought you'd like to see it.

*We see LILLIAN's spiky faced sister MARGARET watching her,
appalled.*

Flashback: Interior: London House – Day

*We cut to another plush interior and see YOUNG LILLIAN jumping
up and down on an ornamental sofa, a powerful unstoppable, surge of
energy as she sings, almost chanting rhythmically, a song of the period
again and again, getting faster with each jump. Till she's leaping like
on a trampoline.*

Flashback: Exterior: Alleyway – Day

*We then see her in an alleyway with two boys that look like brothers,
one slightly older than the other. They are standing in the rain, the
older boy tells the younger one to get lost. And then the remaining
brother and the YOUNG LILLIAN are passionately kissing. Slipping
down in between a crack in the wall, and water streams from gutters
round them, and people watch from a window opposite, but they are
oblivious, rolling in the mud and the water.*

COUSIN EDWARD (*laughing, close to her face*). You do it so well,
   Lillian!

   YOUNG LILLIAN's *face in profile, water dripping off her.*

YOUNG LILLIAN. You think so? (*She kisses him passionately.*) I
   have been practising – just for you. . . (*Another sensual,
   experienced kiss.*) . . . only for you.

Flashback: Interior: Drawing Room – Day

*We cut to the YOUNG LILLIAN watching a recital, a concert in the
drawing room, a relative or member of the family is intoning a poem of
his own composition, with suitable music on a gramophone behind him,*

creating the right ambience. But YOUNG LILLIAN is suddenly laughing in the hushed atmosphere, at the reverential delivery and the solemn music behind, a loud spontaneous laugh. Each time he does another line, she laughs louder, she gets off her chair, onto the floor repeating the last line he's just recited and dissolving into shrieks of laughter.

Flashback: Interior: Drawing Room – Night

We cut to a large room after a party, covered in paper streamers, and crushed party hats and food, YOUNG LILLIAN screaming and shouting as the brother we saw her kissing walks past her. He is getting his hat and coat, she tears his scarf away as he passes her and then starts breaking glasses, throwing them in several directions at once, like a catherine wheel going off, as she implores him not to leave.

Flashback: Interior: YOUNG LILLIAN's Room – Night

We cut to her father coming into her room, her own little room, with the curtains drawn, a dark private space, where the walls are covered in weird pictures of distorted faces, forming strange patterns across the wall. Her father, a straight, comfortable looking man, stares at her and then at the faces on the wall. Among the faces is one very obviously of him, looking grotesque and comic.

The same picture HARRIET saw on the wall of the mental hospital when she was waiting in the passage.

FATHER (*staring down at her*). What on earth are you doing in here Lillian?

YOUNG LILLIAN (*looking up, staring directly at him*). Nothing. Enjoying myself. (*She stares at the grotesque picture on the wall.*) Reminding myself what you really look like.

Flashback: Interior: Drawing Room – Day

Then we cut to the two brothers entering a room and walking past her, towards a row of seats where a formal group photograph of the entire family is about to be taken. There are thirty individuals present, all dressed up. The older brother passes YOUNG LILLIAN and fails to respond to her calling his name. As he moves to try to take his seat, he is caught by the YOUNG LILLIAN, *holding onto his leg, and she won't let go. As he moves away she continues to hold onto him, and as he walks across the room, he drags her along the floor behind him for a few paces, incredibly embarrassed, as the whole family looks on.*

Her sister MARGARET *is looking particularly stunned and appalled.*

YOUNG LILLIAN (*calling out passionately as she holds onto him*).
Look at me, PLEASE. Just look at me. (*Yelling from the heart.*)
Why are you doing this to me? I'm not going to go away. I'M
GOING TO MAKE YOU LOOK AT ME!

The Party: Main Drawing Room: The Present

We cut back to the party, and the present, and the fleshy faces of the two men, the two brothers as they are now, one of them is shovelling a piece of celery into a cheese dip, gulping it up, and talking vigorously at the same time, how he 'always knew the hovercraft would never be much of a success . . . how he'd told everyone, but nobody had listened'.

LILLIAN *watches the two brothers.*

LILLIAN (*to nobody in particular*). I think it was the older one
. . . I'm not sure . . . (*Louder.*) I can't remember which was the
one I liked. I don't remember! (*Slight smile.*) Can't tell them
apart now, anyway.

The sharp faced old woman, GLADYS, *is passing at this moment, half overhears.*

GLADYS. What dear? You don't know which is your glass? (*As if to a child.*) Just take another, that's what we do at a party like this. (GLADYS *starts pouring her another glass.*) You're allowed to drink all this are you?

LILLIAN *turns, watching the champagne fill the glass − a sudden swift flashback as if her thoughts have started again.*

Flashback: Interior: London House, Nursery – Day

A high shot of YOUNG LILLIAN, lying as if after sex with the elder brother, on a carpet somewhere, surrounded by toys, like they are in LILLIAN's old nursery. Both of them are laughing, and she's kicking in a lazy, sensual way at an old rocking horse in front of them.

YOUNG LILLIAN (*her spontaneous laugh*). They think this is where I belong still. (*She looks serious for a moment, an intense stare.*) Nobody knows what to do with me . . . (*She begins to draw idly, sensually with a piece of charcoal on his bare back.*) Don't move, don't move . . .

The image begins to cloud, as if this is where she's beginning to lose the clarity of her thoughts . . . the image burning out to white, as HUGH's voice cuts in and we land back at the party with a jolt.

The Present: Interior: Drawing Room – Day

HUGH (*smiling*). Can I have your attention please. (*Mock authoritarian.*) ATTENTION PLEASE, there at the back.

HUGH *standing on a chair, surveying the family gathering, contented faces, now just beginning to get drunk.*

We're here on this happy occasion – for three reasons.

Calls from some of those watching 'only three' 'Hugh you're slipping' etc.

Apart from seeing all of you of course (*loud*) the *first* reason – this is Harriet and mine, this is our tenth wedding anniversary. This very day.

Applause, calls of 'fifty more to go', 'is it only ten years, seems much longer' etc.

Second – to welcome my Aunt Lillian back – her return from (*he stops*) a long time away (*with feeling*) an unnecessarily long time – to put it mildly.

A ripple of 'Hear hears', people not quite certain how to react, looking at their feet embarrassed; one or two people glance in her direction and give little nods, and half-toasts with their glasses. But

LILLIAN *has her back to all of them, seemingly oblivious, eating a piece of duck.*

And thirdly (*he smiles*) we mustn't forget thirdly (*he touches* HARRIET) because there's a little bulge down here. Yes, we're having another baby. (*Smiles.*) At last –

Applause and some drunken Ahs!

HARRIET (*slightly drunk smile*). No need to start telling them how often we've been trying.

HUGH (*lifts glass*). Well we've made it.

As long as I don't let Harriet go out in my car anymore – you should see what Lillian and she managed to do to it!

Cut to HUGH *blowing out candles on a cake marked 'H and H – the first ten years'.* HARRIET *is brandishing a large knife, miming slicing off* HUGH's *head as he blows the candle, people clapping and laughing.*

Interior: Basement Room – Evening

We cut to much later in the party, evening in the basement room, HARRIET *and* HUGH, *some of her friends and one or two of the elderly relations are playing charades.*

HARRIET *is acting out the film title 'Splendour in the Grass' gesticulating, acting smoking dope, writhing in the grass etc. Her mimes are full of vitality, and quite original. People are calling out 'Venom', 'The Snake Pit', 'Jaws III'. One of the elderly relatives pipes up with 'Dr Zhivago'. There is a pebble-glassed,* MOVIE BUFF *type crouching in the corner, quietly calling out fairly obscure movie titles.*

MOVIE BUFF. Closely Observed Trains. (*As* HARRIET *writhes on the floor.*) The Cow – it's an Iranian movie you know. (*Slowly intoning.*) Woman of the Dunes.

HUGH *is enthusiastically belting out film titles and clapping loudly at each of* HARRIET's *moves. His eyes are shining full of pride at* HARRIET's *acting. He is also holding a stop watch, and calling out every ten seconds how long they've got to get it.*

DOMINIC *is watching his mother objectively, like watching a stranger.*

LILLIAN *is sitting on a high-backed chair in the middle of the room, watching them all. MATILDA and GLADYS, having drunk rather a lot, are sitting on the floor a little way away, GLADYS has kicked off her shoes. LILLIAN overhears them.*

MATILDA. She seems very peaceful doesn't she . . . almost happy I think . . . you wouldn't know anything just looking at her would you . . . And to think of the things she did.

GLADYS. I always used to say she's got a skin missing . . . a whole skin wasn't there – she felt everything so *extremely*.

MATILDA. Part of her brain missing I would say. Its marvellous how Hugh and Harriet treat her so normally.

HARRIET *has stopped – somebody has at last guessed the title.*

As HARRIET *moves to take her seat,* HUGH *catches her by the wrist.*

HUGH. That was good, the Hippy you did, that was especially funny.

HARRIET *(embarrassed in front of her friends).* Yes, OK darling, alright.

She pulls aways, but HUGH *hasn't finished.*

HUGH. No, no, the dope smoking and everything was really effective, really gruesome. *(To somebody sitting next to him.)* It was almost up to professional standard, wasn't it. Yes I thought so . . . *(He smiles.)* She hasn't forgotten it all yet, acting. *(Knowing tone.)* Far from it, I can tell you, when she really wants something. *(Very warm smile at* HARRIET *who has sat down by now.)* Well done darling.

HARRIET *stares back at him across the room. She catches* LILLIAN's *eye, watching her closely. The* MOVIE BUFF *who is very drunk says without thinking.*

MOVIE BUFF. Why doesn't Lillian have a go? It's Lillian's turn now?

HUGH *(embarrassed, jumps up immediately).* No – I think we've had enough now. The game's over. Let's see who's left upstairs, see what they are getting up to.

As HUGH *and some of the other guests begin to leave the room,*
LILLIAN *suddenly starts singing . . . in a quiet hoarse voice, an*
obscure song of her childhood, that is a little difficult to make out,
but quite tuneful.

HARRIET, HUGH *and the others all stop at the door, watching this.*
It doesn't last long. LILLIAN *stops in mid verse and stares back at*
them.

HUGH (*with feeling*). That was very nice Lillian . . . excellent.

HARRIET *is staring straight at* LILLIAN *with a shrewd look.*

Interior: Basement Room – Night

Cut to the empty downstairs room, drinks, party hats, streamers,
squashed food all over the floor.

HARRIET, *rather drunk, is crouching on her hands and knees on the*
floor, tidying up. LILLIAN *still sitting in the same chair.*

HARRIET. Aren't people pigs! . . . look at this mess. (HARRIET
surrounded by the remains of the party.)

HUGH *enters, picking his way gingerly over the mess.*

HUGH. You haven't got very far, have you? (*He looks at the*
smashed food, the half eaten plates of leftovers.) Maybe we can use
some of this again – must try to salvage some of it. Be pity to
waste it all.

He begins to move to go, LILLIAN *and* HARRIET *watching him;*
he turns.

You haven't been smoking again Harriet?

HARRIET. Hardly.

HUGH *picks up fag ends that she has left in a line, standing on*
their ends on the mantlepiece.

HUGH. Are these yours? This looks like you.

He pulls a plastic bag out of his pocket, a see-through plastic bag
and starts dropping the fag ends into it, one by one.

You *know* its stupid, but you still go ahead and do it. (*Sorrowful tone.*) Amazing obstinacy. (*Dropping the last one into the bag.*) I'm going to keep these as a reminder, hang them up in the bedroom (*closing bag*) – no, I am. Now hurry up, its extremely late, you don't want to be up too late darling, do you?

He leaves.

HARRIET. What are you looking like that for? (*She stops.*) Aren't you going to help?

LILLIAN *staring at her.*

Sorry – I didn't mean that. (*Loud.*) Yes – maybe I *did* mean that. (*She moves up to* LILLIAN *on all fours.*) Because you don't fool me – do you Lillian? You haven't fooled me – from the start.

LILLIAN *impassive,* HARRIET *crouching by her on the chair, their faces very close.*

Because you know far more about what's going on than you pretend – don't you. You understand *everything* don't you but you're refusing to show it. (*Drunken smile.*) You prefer to seem an idiot . . .

LILLIAN *giving her nothing, staring straight back at her eyes.*

I know you don't like me – but I want you to know. (HARRIET *puts her hands on either side of* LILLIAN's *face.*) I've seen through you – do you understand my dear . . . maybe you're having a little laugh at me right at this moment.

HARRIET *and* LILLIAN's *faces together in close up.*

You're a fraud Lillian – quite a good one, but a fraud. Aren't you? Give a little nod, go *on*.

LILLIAN's *head remains completely still. A direct completely neutral stare straight back at* HARRIET.

It's OK, I don't mind, nobody else need ever know.

Interior: The Dining Room – Day

We cut to HARRIET, *tottering down to breakfast in her dressing gown.*

DOMINIC *is sitting at the table eating two fried eggs on fried bread.* HARRIET's *stomach practically turns over on seeing this. She sits looking fragile, rather beautiful, her face very pale, sipping her coffee, and watching huge dripping mouthfuls go into her son's mouth.* LOUISE *is there too.*

DOMINIC. You look terrible mummy, you look like you are going to be sick any minute. (*Putting another mouthful in.*) Are you going to be sick any minute?

HARRIET. Dominic please . . . (*Glancing over at* DOMINIC.) How did I produce such a crude specimen? Where did you come from? I don't know . . .

THERESA *coming in with another plate of eggs.*

Not more. Don't have some more please. Theresa take it away.

DOMINIC (*firmly*). Theresa put it down. (THERESA *hesitates.*) At once.

THERESA *puts it down hastily and moves to start cleaning in the background.*

HARRIET (*watching this*). Nobody listens to me in this house at all!

DOMINIC (*with egg*). It's great. (*He starts eating, with relish.*) You are always cross with me – do you know that, mummy? I've been counting – its 160 days since you last said something nice.

HARRIET. Is that all? (*She smiles.*) I had no idea we were getting on so well lately.

DOMINIC. It's at least 200 days since you said something nice – and *meant* it. (*Another mouthful of egg.*) I bet you've been counting the days till I go back to school. (*He glances up.*)

HARRIET. That's right – I cross them off each day. (*Lightly.*) It's a huge relief when the end's in sight.

DOMINIC (*busying himself with his plate*). For me too . . .

HARRIET. Don't be silly darling. (*Her voice matter-of-fact.*) I hate it when you go back. You know that.

DOMINIC *not looking at her.*

(*Suddenly her head turning*). Where is the smell? (*To* LOUISE.) The horrible fishy smell Lillian is always making at this time – where is it?

LOUISE. Oh Mrs Ambrose – Lillian went.

HARRIET (*startled*). What do you mean, went?

LOUISE (*very agitated now*). She said she had to do it, she had to go. She had to leave.

DOMINIC (*eating a piece of toast now*). Oh yes, she went about 10 minutes ago – didn't I tell you? I meant to – she just walked out of the house. Didn't even say goodbye. (*Bites into toast.*) Can't blame her really.

HARRIET (*jumping up*). She can't go out on her own. DON'T YOU SEE! That's the one thing we were told about! . . . She can't even cross the road . . . ! (*Really alarmed,* HARRIET *moves backwards and forwards, by the table.*)

Theresa – ring Mr Ambrose, tell him what's happened – tell him to get back here *now*. (*Shouts.*) Right *now*, don't accept any excuses, get him here now!

HARRIET *opens the door and runs out into the street in her dressing gown.*

Exterior: London House – Day

HARRIET *stands for a moment on the pavement, shouting back at* DOMINIC *and* LOUISE *watching her from the front door,* HARRIET's *dressing gown and nightdress blowing about.*

HARRIET. She can't have got far! I'm just . . .

Exterior: London Street – Day

HARRIET *runs down the street, she turns the corner into the main road.*

There is a row of shops on the corner and an office of a design consultancy with several men sitting at desks in front of the tinted glass window which is at street level.

HARRIET *runs into the office in her dressing gown. Two of the men look up at her very startled.*

HARRIET. Did you see an old lady pass by just now? (*They look blank.*) An old lady . . . on her own? About this high? Looking lost, looking like she'd never seen a car before – DID YOU SEE HER? (*She's furious, looking at them.*) Jesus, what you all staring at? Nobody see her? She must have come by here? . . .

MAN AT DESK. If we see her. . . ?

HARRIET. Call the police if you see her! Is that simple enough for you to understand? And all of you watch, watch OK – she may come back this way!

HARRIET *goes out into the street. Glancing around anxiously. Wherever she looks, she sees old ladies. Sitting on a bench, standing at a zebra crossing, walking along slowly in front of the shops.*

HARRIET *goes up to a bus queue, who watch her approach with some amusement.*

Did you see an old lady pass by here . . . ? (*They stare at her,* HARRIET *looks rather wild in her dressing gown.*) She would have looked like she was completely lost – in a daze, wandering about? (*Really angry as she sees somebody smirking.*) Don't laugh – just answer a perfectly simple question, did you see somebody? (*Blank faces staring at her.*) Jesus, what a wretched collection of people.

Thanks very much.

HARRIET *turns, runs along the street a little way.*

This is ridiculous, I'm never going to find her like this.

HARRIET *sees a male* TRAFFIC WARDEN *standing there.* HARRIET *grabs him by the arm.*

You've been keeping an eye out no doubt – have you seen an old lady?

WARDEN. An old lady? No, I'm only looking at vehicles I'm afraid.

HARRIET (*very sharp*). Great! (*She looks about the street, heavy lorries on the road, she's suddenly really worried.*) How am I going to find her for Chrissake!

Exterior: London Roads/Interior: Car – Day

HARRIET *driving in* HUGH's *car, the Daimler, driving fast. She dressed so quickly she's still straightening the sweater she's wearing as she drives, she's also talking into the car phone at the same time, waving the phone about. We intercut with* HUGH, *in his glass office.*

HARRIET. Hugh – have you got through to the home yet? (*Loud.*) You know the *HOME*! The hospital, whatever you call it . . .

HUGH. There's no answer, I've tried several times.

HARRIET *driving erratically with one hand – sometimes no hands.*

HARRIET. We've got to get their help, they'll know what to do . . . I'm going to go there.

She puts her foot down in the car.

HUGH. Going there! Don't be stupid darling.

HARRIET. Be quicker than waiting for you to get through! And what about the police?

HUGH (*patient tone*). I don't want to bring them into it yet, darling.

HARRIET. Why not for chrissake!

HUGH. This is something we can do. We don't want Aunt Lillian involved with the police, there might be publicity.

HARRIET. Publicity! Who the hell's interested in Lillian – or the family for that matter?

HUGH (*firmly*). She's only gone for a walk Harriet – that's all that's happened – I'm going now to look in Holland Park, because that's where she'll be. That's where I told you to look.

HARRIET *driving faster and faster.*

HUGH's *voice.* I don't know why you haven't looked there. She's not capable of going any further . . . And take care of the *car* won't you.

Exterior: Drive of Mental Hospital – Day

High shot above the drive of the mental hospital, as HARRIET roars through the gates and up the drive, bouncing on the uncertain surface of the cracked, ill-kept drive.

She brakes fiercely as the car heads directly towards the skip and the builders, she practically knocks one of them over as the car pulls up.

HARRIET *leaps out and runs through the clouds of builders' dust, even thicker now than it was, into the building.*

Interior: Mental Hospital – Day

HARRIET *runs through the main entrance, at the reception there is an elderly woman watching an old black and white TV. She looks totally blank when HARRIET calls out to her.*

HARRIET. Is Lillian here? Lillian Huckle. Has she come back? I thought she *might* have come back.

ELDERLY WOMAN. I don't deal with the patients.

Interior: Mental Hospital, Corridor and Ward – Day

HARRIET *runs down the passage which is deserted, she smashes through the makeshift barrier sending bits of it scattering all over the place. She runs past the green fish tanks, and turns into the ward, which has now only one bed left in it, and a chair by the window.*

On the chair, LILLIAN is sitting, staring out of her usual window.

HARRIET (*shouts with relief*). *Thank God* you're here, Lillian.

LILLIAN *with her back to HARRIET. LILLIAN's head moves, but she doesn't turn round.*

We were so worried . . .

HARRIET's *relief turns quickly to fury, as* LILLIAN *hardly acknowledges her presence.*

Don't you ever, *ever* do this again. Leave without telling anybody. DO YOU HEAR?

HARRIET *moves up to* LILLIAN *really shouting.*

Do you hear me? (*Loud.*) We didn't know what had happened to you!

LILLIAN. What's going on? I don't know why you're shouting.

LILLIAN *turns her head, leans round in her chair.*

Why is she shouting? Do you know?

HARRIET *suddenly sees they are not alone, three old people, two old men and a woman are sitting on the one remaining bed in a corner. All with coats on, like they have travelled back too. One of them is* GEORGE, *the old man we saw in the ballroom at the beginning of the film.*

HARRIET (*staring at them*). They came back as well did they? (*Quiet.*) None of you can keep away . . .

She stares at them.

The NURSE *comes into the ward.*

NURSE (*as she enters*). No – they've been drifting back over the last few days, as soon as we get one to leave, another one tries to come back. (*Looks at* HARRIET *sharply.*) Glad you have come for her anyway. If they all had somebody it would be easier. Now Lillian – you *know* you shouldn't be here.

LILLIAN *absolutely still, not going to move.*

Interior: Ballroom – Day

Cut to HARRIET *and the* NURSE *trying to coax* LILLIAN *through the door of the ballroom, and across the room towards the main entrance, but* LILLIAN *is holding on tightly to the side of the door, calm expression, but very determined. She doesn't want to be moved.*

NURSE. She'll come . . . don't worry . . . Just a little reluctant, but she'll come. Won't you Lillian . . . Just let go, come on love.

HARRIET (*pleading*). Please, Lillian, you can't stay here, the ward's closed, they've closed *your* ward, its gone. I know you can understand that. (*To* NURSE.) I'm sure she can understand a lot more than we realize. . .

NURSE. Well we can't have her back, whatever happens. (*Loud.*) Do you hear that Lillian? (*Sharp.*) We don't want to have to use force. . .

LILLIAN *calm but still holding onto the wall tightly. They could easily overpower her, but they are trying to coax her instead, gently taking hold of her arm, then letting go.*

LILLIAN (*simply*). This is the place I want to be.

HARRIET. I'm sorry about what happened last night – I didn't mean it, OK. Is that what you want to hear?

LILLIAN *looking away.*

Is this what this is about? I was drunk, I was really pissed, and I'm saying I'm sorry, OK!

NURSE *watching this, rather intrigued.*

(*To* NURSE.) How did she get here anyway?

NURSE. By taxi.

HARRIET (*pleased smile*). By taxi. I knew you could get around if you wanted. How did she know the address? Does she know where this place is? (*She smiles at* LILLIAN *warmly, her face close.*) I would love to have overheard you giving directions to the cabbie. . .

The NURSE *unclasps* LILLIAN's *hand.* LILLIAN *is grasping tightly one of the labels from her suitcases, with her name and the address of the hospital on it. The label looks extremely old.*

(*Approvingly.*) That's clever.

LILLIAN *gives her a sharp suspicious look, as if saying 'are you trying to get round me this way'.*

NURSE. She didn't pay though – we had to. (*Handing* HARRIET *the bill.*) It was over seventy pounds.

HARRIET *sees* GEORGE, *the old man, lurking in the shadows, in the doorway behind them.*

HARRIET. I'll take your friend too. We'll give him a lift home. (*Sudden smile at both of them.*) I'll take you both out to tea if you like.

Interior: Fortnums – Afternoon

LILLIAN, GEORGE *and* HARRIET *eating ice-creams at Fortnums or similar luxury tea rooms.* LILLIAN *and* GEORGE *tucking into their large ice-creams.* HARRIET *watching them closely, just dipping into hers with small spoonfuls.*

GEORGE *is talking at the top of his voice, a stream of things, jumping in the middle of sentences making only partial sense. His voice switching from matter-of-fact to real intensity and back.*

People staring from other tables, at some of the things he is saying and at his erratic behaviour, blobs of ice-cream fly around, as he waves his spoon about. But HARRIET *finds herself strangely unembarrassed.*

GEORGE. I escaped twice – I did – under the river, there's a pipe, I knew it was there, I had known about it for a long time. They use it for all sorts of things, my God, if people knew what went on there, who I'd seen going through that pipe. Faces you'd know, oh yes! Household names. Before I used it, I'd seen them from the window, going down to the river. I kept on trying to get away from that, but they were always watching me. (*He turns to* LILLIAN, *suddenly much more coherent.*) I used to get the pillow, the punishment they gave us – I said I'll tell the prime minister what you're doing here, I'll tell Winston Churchill, he was prime minister then, they said go ahead, I wrote about twenty-five letters.

LILLIAN. I remember the letters. They didn't work.

GEORGE (*his voice rising*). They never posted them – because they thought I was dangerous. (*He smiles.*)

Faces turning from their tea and cakes.

(*Loud.*) You know what they did with the pillow, they held it, the held it over your mouth till you were purple, till you could hardly breathe, you were kicking, you were fighting, you were tearing with your hands, but they kept on holding it right there. (*To* LILLIAN.) We both got it, didn't we?

LILLIAN (*eating ice-cream with great poise*). They used to sit on me, two or three of them used to sit on me . . . when I got the pillow.

GEORGE (*suddenly to* HARRIET). And I'll tell you the really interesting thing – they were terribly *bad* at everything they did. They couldn't even do *that* properly. Amateurs . . . (*Bangs table.*) They were hopeless.

LILLIAN. Don't shout like that, eat your ice-cream.

LILLIAN *has authority over* GEORGE.

GEORGE. Don't shout, don't shout, don't shout, don't shout . . . etc.

HARRIET. If you could keep your voice down just a little.

GEORGE. After the pillow . . . (*Chants.*) Get it in the morning, get it in the evening, get it, get it, get it, get it . . . etc.

A rhythmic chant, oblivious to the noise he is making. LILLIAN *joins in with him staring at* HARRIET. *Both of them trying to unsettle* HARRIET. HARRIET *deeply embarrassed for a moment, but then stares directly back at* LILLIAN.

LILLIAN (*to* GEORGE). Eat your ice-cream.

HARRIET. Thank you, that was almost as good as Lillian's song at the party. Do you know any more?

GEORGE (*looking at* HARRIET). You are having a baby?

HARRIET. How did you know that?

She looks at LILLIAN. LILLIAN *pointedly looks away.*

She told you, did she? She won't talk to me . . . but she'll talk to other people.

LILLIAN *not looking up.*

Been gossiping about me, have you?

Exterior: Outside seedy Bed and Breakfast – Afternoon

HARRIET *and* LILLIAN *inside the Daimler, watching* GEORGE *walk up the steps of a really seedy Bed and Breakfast hotel in some back street behind Paddington. Peeling paint, and feel of decay and filth from the building; one of the windows is boarded up with hardboard.*

HARRIET. Does he really have to stay here?

LILLIAN *watching him go.*

It's an even worse dump than that home you're so fond of. (GEORGE *turning to wave.*) Will he be alright? (LILLIAN *glances at her.*) I can only deal with one of you Lillian, OK! Is that a terrible thing to say? No, – anyway it's true.

GEORGE *is standing with his plastic bags, waving, and then sticking his stomach out, making himself into the shape of a pregnant woman, and then giving the thumbs up sign. Pushing out his stomach rather grotesquely.*

What on earth is he doing? He's not going on about the baby again is he? Jesus.

HARRIET *watches him with a slight smile.*

He'll get us all arrested doing that.

Receding shot of GEORGE *on hostel steps.*

Interior: Hospital: Baby Scan – Day

Close up of the scan image, the foetus at 16 weeks, moving, HARRIET *lying staring at the image of her baby from the scan, with a slightly detached stare.*

HUGH *and* DOMINIC *are there too, and a young male doctor murmuring in the background.*

HUGH. Amazing sight, isn't it. That image. It's beautiful. (HUGH *smiles gently.*) He looks just like you.

HARRIET (*lying there, staring at it*). How do you know it's a he?

YOUNG DOCTOR. We don't normally specify the sex at this stage – unless we get a very good shot of the . . .

HUGH. Of the relevant area! Naturally.

HUGH *peers closely at the image trying to make its sex out.*

I just can't quite see . . .

DOMINIC (*to doctor*). I can understand you being cautious, I mean if people painted their room for the baby, pink and then it turned out to be a boy, or painted a whole part of the house blue, the nursery and everything and then it was a girl, they might *sue* you mightn't they?

The doctor looks very startled.

If they'd spent a great deal of money on it I mean . . . they might demand compensation. I think you are being quite wise.

HARRIET. Alright Dominic, you can stop handing out legal advice please for once, just be quiet.

HUGH *moves into a corner of the room, starts talking to the doctor in a confidential whisper, but HARRIET can just about hear.*

HUGH (*conspiratorial tone*). She is doing everything right is she? I mean the right diet and everything. (*Thrusting a piece of paper at doctor.*) I've brought a list of a typical few days' meals, that she's eating. (*Pointing at paper.*) Just to interpret, the asterisks mark the dishes she's particularly prone to, and the question marks things that might be of concern. I mean my wife can be, how can I put it? (*Calling back.*) Be with you in a moment darling – my wife can be just a tiny bit scatty sometimes, so you should tell *me*, you know, if everything's being done properly.

YOUNG DOCTOR (*having looked at list*). Looks fine . . . excellent . . . no, she's in splendid condition.

HARRIET *staring at them and then the image on the screen.*
HUGH *again looks at the scan.*

HUGH *moving close to HARRIET, his face is shining with delight.*

HUGH. Isn't it marvellous?

Suddenly HARRIET *pulls him down towards her holding onto the back of his head – her tone strangely intense.*

HARRIET. I'm so pleased *you're* so happy my love. . .

Shot of the image of the child on the scan, we move close into it.

Interior: Drawing Room – Day

Slow dissolve from the image of the foetus, to HARRIET *much much larger, 6½ months pregnant. She is sitting sweating profusely in a large chair.*

Across the other side of the room is LILLIAN, *sitting in another chair, not looking at her, her back turned towards* HARRIET.

HUGH *and* DOMINIC *playing with a new computer, giggling and laughing together in another corner of the large room.*

HARRIET *from her position staring out of the window can see* THERESA *busy cleaning the Daimler down in the drive.*

HUGH (*calling over from the computer*). Everything alright my love?

HARRIET (*watching* THERESA *cleaning the car*). Everything's thrilling over here . . . Lillian and I are having such an interesting little talk.

LILLIAN's *head twitches slightly, but she remains sitting with her back to* HARRIET, *not looking at her.*

HARRIET *watching* THERESA *clean the Daimler, it is shining brilliantly, she begins to mutter under her breath.*

I mustn't panic . . . I mustn't panic . . . I mustn't panic.

HUGH's *face suddenly appears beside her, his face pressed close,* HARRIET *very startled, not sure if he has overheard or not.*

HUGH. What love?

HARRIET. Nothing . . . just talking nonsense to myself.

HUGH (*watching her closely*). Some kind of list was it darling? (*His face really close to her.*) A list you were making?

HARRIET. That's right.

HUGH (*whispers*). I don't want Lillian to hear this, but Edward has died. Cousin Edward . . . Lillian was very close to him a long time ago, he and his brother, I'm sure she doesn't remember, but just in case, we're going to have to break it gently to her.

Exterior: Cemetery – Day

Cut to the whole family gathered, many of the same faces as at the party, now all dressed in black standing in a windswept cemetery. They are arranged in two large clumps near the grave.

We see first the one remaining brother, his jowelly face, staring in dignified plumpness. And then we see LILLIAN standing with GLADYS and MATILDA and HARRIET staring across at him. HUGH is there looking serious, tall and upright amongst his family. DOMINIC is also there, standing still and serious, watching them all.

HARRIET. It's quite frightening seeing the whole family in black, it doesn't really suit them, to put it mildly.

HARRIET *surveying the massed ranks of HUGH's family.*

GLADYS. I hate funerals. (*She glances around at the faces of the family.*) Who'll be next?

MATILDA. Poor Lillian – look at her . . . she doesn't remember him obviously, doesn't realize what's going on at all.

LILLIAN *standing as the funeral service drones on, she has a smile on her face, which increases until she is positively beaming.*

At the end of the service the surviving brother passes LILLIAN, and gives her a little patronizing nod of recognition. LILLIAN shows no sign in return. As he moves just past her, LILLIAN announces to anybody who is listening.

LILLIAN. I'm very glad that this has happened.

People look astonished.

It's much less confusing now there's only *one* of them left.

GLADYS *turns to* HARRIET.

GLADYS (*rolling her eyes at* LILLIAN's *behaviour*). Can you help me get away from this dear as quickly as possible. (*She takes* HARRIET's *arm as they move off down the path.*) Next time we meet will be under much happier circumstances, I hope. (*She gives* HARRIET's *stomach a little playful tap.*) Don't forget to invite me to see the baby.

HUGH *sweeps up behind them on the path, puts his arm round* GLADYS.

HUGH. Don't worry, Gladys, you will be in the very first batch, one of the very first visitors. Won't she darling? And that's a promise!

Interior: The Bedroom – Night

Cut to bedroom, HARRIET *in nightdress, sitting on the edge of the bed, staring at herself in the full length mirror with a deep intense stare. We move close in on her eyes.*

HUGH *is in the bathroom, washing himself, brushing his teeth, he has a tape playing, the Eurythmics, humming along to them.*

HUGH. I don't know why I feel so good . . . funerals shouldn't make one I know, it's perverse.

Music, HUGH *calling out over the top of it,* HARRIET *staring in the mirror.*

HARRIET *turns her head and stares up at the plastic bag of cigarette ends, hanging from the ceiling, slowly revolving in the light, like some strange piece of decor, the dead cigarettes clearly visible through the plastic. It is suspended over her side of the bed.*

Doesn't Gladys look incredibly young still? Must be over eighty. It's probably because she's never had a worry in her life. (HUGH *looks at himself in the bathroom mirror.*) That doesn't apply to me does it? . . . Would hate it if somewhere somebody was saying exactly the same thing about me. I really don't think its true, it's been bloody in the city this winter. (*He smiles.*) Trench warfare.

HARRIET has moved slowly across into the bathroom. HUGH singing along to the track.

HARRIET switches off the music, watching HUGH dry his feet.

HARRIET. You're always so clean, Hugh.

HUGH. Am I?

HARRIET (*very precisely*). You're an above average washer, no question.

HUGH (*with a gentle smile*). Was the music annoying you? I'm sorry love . . . I don't know why I feel so full of energy. It's you that's meant to have a sudden burst of energy when it gets close.

HARRIET. It's not that close yet, not for two months.

HUGH. No. (*Drying himself.*) It's been such a warm winter, maybe that's something to do with it. (HUGH *rubbing his feet vigorously.*) That reminds me – it's a silly time to mention it now – but don't you think we've been over-heating the house? I keep on having to go round switching off radiators. Try to watch out for that darling, OK? (*A big, broad smile straight at her, as he dries himself.*) It's so lovely and mild at the moment!

HARRIET (*watching him in mirror*). There's a woman in our ante-natal class . . . who's suddenly decided she doesn't want the baby.

HUGH. How extraordinary . . . just like that. (HUGH *carefully putting the top back on the toothpaste.*) What did her husband say?

HARRIET. She came home, didn't say anything, started giving him these little cuffs.

HUGH. Cuffs. What you mean cuffs?

HARRIET. Like this.

She starts giving him cuffs, on his face, at first gently, playfully, hardly touching him, but then getting stronger and stronger, glancing blows on his cheek, till she's slapping him.

HUGH (*catches her hands by the wrist, laughing at this horseplay*). OK – OK – I get the idea. Always the actress.

HARRIET *doesn't stop for an instant, and* HUGH *has to really hold her tightly by the wrists.*

I get the idea Harriet. (*He stares into her eyes.*) Nothing wrong is there?

HARRIET (*straight back at him*). Wrong? What could be wrong?

It's as if HUGH *senses something about her for a moment.*

HUGH. You don't want to see the doctor or anything?

HARRIET (*sharp*). No.

HUGH. Fine . . . splendid. (*He touches her neck, then kisses her on the ear.*) It's funny how funerals always make you appreciate what you've got.

Close up on HARRIET.

HARRIET. That's right.

Interior: Main Staircase – Day

We cut to shoes being hurled out of the bedroom, followed by various other objects. HARRIET *emerges out of the bedroom.*

HARRIET. Where the hell has he put all the cases? (*She really yells.*) Where are the bloody suitcases? (*Calling down the stairs.*) Louise! Theresa! (HARRIET *stares down the bannisters, the only person she can see is* LILLIAN *sitting below in her usual place on the half landing.*) Where is everybody?

HARRIET *moving with great, furious determination, despite her heavy size, she climbs onto a box on top of her chair to reach some high cupboard on the second landing on the staircase.*

She totters perilously on the chair, seemingly completely oblivious of the danger, the box on the chair at an alarming angle. HARRIET *gets the cupboard open.*

There's the bloody thing! (*Pulling at her suitcase, buried amongst other suitcases in high cupboard.*) If Hugh has locked it . . . ! (*She pulls at case trying to get it out.*) What a ridiculous place to put a load of suitcases.

The phone begins to ring.

(*Calling out.*) Don't anybody answer that – don't you dare to try to answer that Lillian, OK. It's Hugh, I know.

She manages to pull the suitcase out and the rest of the suitcases rain down around her, smashing several ornaments below her on the landing, and causing considerable devastation in the passage.

HARRIET *gets off the chair, seemingly oblivious to the mess, and moves off with her suitcase.*

We cut to HARRIET *standing by the answering machine, playing back the message.*

(*Staring down at the machine.*) If he mentions . . . if he mentions the CAR just *once*. (*To machine.*) I warn you.

HUGH'S VOICE. Hello darling . . . this is Hugh, of course. Where are you? Are you in the bathroom or something? Why didn't you answer the phone? Sometimes you must remember to check if the volume on the ringer has been turned down. There's a little knob on the phone – do you see it? – marked 'Ringer'. Check it now darling, just move it sideways if you need to, that's right.

HARRIET *not moving, poised over the answer machine.*

Now, I'll be dropping by later this afternoon, because today is the day the car has to go in for its quarterly service, so since no one else can take it in – I'll . . .

HARRIET (*triumphant*). He mentioned the car! (*Calling down to* LILLIAN.) Did you hear? He mentioned the car! Right!

We cut to HARRIET *going through her wardrobe grabbing dresses.*

Then we cut to her by the front door, opening it. She is dressed in a long coat, holding two suitcases, LILLIAN *is staring at her from the half-landing.*

HARRIET *looks embarrassed for a moment, holding the suitcases.*

I am just popping out – just for a moment.

LILLIAN. I think I could pop out too . . . be nice to pop out.

HARRIET (*impatient*). I'm only going round the block, to the shops.

LILLIAN. I'll pop out to the shops too.

HARRIET (*sharp*). I'm not going far – you'll see. (*Their eyes meet.*) If you *have* to come – come on then! Get ready! Hurry up!

Exterior: London House – Day

HARRIET *and* LILLIAN *walking along the cars in the drive. HARRIET carrying three suitcases now, including LILLIAN's battered one, with its labels from the mental hospital still on it.*

LILLIAN *clasping the bag she had at the beginning of the film.*

HARRIET. We ought to take my car of course – because we're only going to the shops, take five minutes at the most. (HARRIET *stops at the Daimler.*) But what the hell!

She starts unlocking the Daimler.

Where are you going?

LILLIAN *has decided to sit in the back, stands determinedly by the back door.*

You don't trust my driving I see . . . I can't think what gave you the idea. Reckon you're safe there do you? I wouldn't bank on it. (*As* HARRIET *gets behind the wheel.*) We're only going for a little spin, that's all.

Exterior: Street outside London House – Day

Cut to the Daimler setting off at speed down the road – HARRIET's foot really down on the accelerator, she scrapes the car on a bollard as she goes round the corner, quite a bad scrape, more of a gash along the wing.

LILLIAN *sitting in stately splendour in the back, rolls her eyes at HARRIET's febrile driving.*

HARRIET. Don't know what you're doing making faces like that . . . If you're going to be back-seat driver you can walk! Or you can drive! Can you drive?

LILLIAN. I don't remember.

HARRIET (*smiles*). Very convenient loss of memory! I'm going to start making a list of those, the things you choose not to remember. (*She puts her foot down again.*)

Anyway Hugh is already going to kill me for that, for that scrape . . . he will cut me up into little pieces . . . it's the only thing that really enrages him . . . maybe he'll wait for the baby before he starts dismembering me because of the car. (*She smiles.*) I don't know. I'm not at all sure which means more to him . . . (*Her tone suddenly serious.*) It's going into service today, this car . . . I mustn't forget. I must get it back in time for that. We're only going round the block after all, we got plenty of time . . .

Exterior: Confectionery Shop – Day

Cut to the car pulling up outside a large confectionery shop.

HARRIET (*looking at LILLIAN in the back seat*). Do you want to make a pig of yourself?

Interior: Shop – Day

Cut inside the posh confectionery shop with HARRIET buying a large pile of chocolates, luxury boxes stacked on top of each other.

HARRIET. How much? £60!

There is a very poker faced middle aged shop assistant serving them.

You got it Lillian?

LILLIAN *shakes her head.*

LILLIAN. I have no money at all.

HARRIET. Oh yes of course I forgot. (*To shop assistant.*) She doesn't believe in paying for things.

LILLIAN *is pointing at something.*

What do you want? What are you pointing at?

LILLIAN. I would like that bird please.

LILLIAN *is pointing at a large chocolate chicken.*

HARRIET. You want that! It's about the most hideous thing in the shop. You sure? (*To assistant.*) She's been away for a long time, you have to forgive her a few things.

LILLIAN (*very determined*). I WANT THE CHICKEN. (*Sharp.*) PLEASE.

HARRIET *totally unabashed in front of the shop assistant.*

HARRIET. Didn't people bring you things like this in the loony bin? I would have thought it was just the sort of revolting present people would have shown up with.

LILLIAN. Apples. I got nothing but apples. Very unripe apples too.

Poker-faced assistant watching, getting agitated now.

HARRIET (*turning*). We'll take the ghastly chicken too then.

Exterior: London Street/Interior – Car

LILLIAN *sitting in the back in splendid isolation nibbling little pieces of chocolate off the chicken.*

HARRIET *also munching chocolates compulsively as she drives.*

HARRIET. We'll just go round the block once more then . . . OK?

HARRIET *watching* LILLIAN *in the driving mirror.*

Was that a nod? I wish your nods would get a bit bigger. You're quite capable of saying yes. (*Slight smile.*) What's it to be? Once more round the block?

Pause.

LILLIAN (*quiet*). Yes.

Exterior: Country Motorway/Interior Car – Day

Cut to wide shot of the car travelling through rolling countryside in Oxfordshire, ripe landscape, they are travelling along the motorway.

HARRIET. What do you think of it so far Lillian?

LILLIAN sitting in the back, the chicken is now half eaten.

Our little spin! Do you think it's time to go back? (*LILLIAN licking her fingers, of chocolate!*) Or do you think we should go round the block one more time?

The red petrol light is flashing on the dashboard. HARRIET is oblivious to it, she just doesn't see it.

(*Smiles.*) Could have a picnic if we wanted, do a spot of fishing. I haven't the slightest idea where we're going . . . isn't that marvellous?

Red light flashing, then becoming permanent.

(*Warm smile.*) I wanted to show you there was still some country left, that it wasn't all swallowed up while you were in the bin.

LILLIAN glances briefly out of the window.

I suppose last time you were here, this was full of nice young boys in boaters driving about in their jalopies making honking noises at each other. Just country lanes and . . .

LILLIAN grabs her arm from the back seat.

What on earth are you doing Lillian? What are you poking me for?

LILLIAN. There's a nice light that has come on down there. The red light, see . . . does it matter?

HARRIET sees the red warning light.

HARRIET. Oh Jesus Christ. The bloody petrol, got to get off this road – or we'll be smashed up by juggernauts.

There is a juggernaut behind them, HARRIET watches it looming up close to them.

Where the hell is there a bloody turn off?

HARRIET takes the next exit off the motorway.

(*To car.*) Come on, come on, don't run out, get us somewhere, OK! (*Furious.*) It's typical of Hugh, he never fills the car right up, he's too mean, he has some theory or other about wastage, the last two litres in the tank being unnecessary or some shit.

She hits a bollard at the side of the road, as she is saying this. The car is now badly dented.

They are travelling down a quieter country road. The engine stops.

The car has stopped Lillian, we're out of gas.

HARRIET *turns off the road, and lets the car slip gently down a dirt track in a wood, until it comes to a halt. The light is just beginning to close in, evening falling fast. Silence, the car has stopped.*

It looks like we're here for the night.

LILLIAN (*quiet surprise*). You want me to sleep here?

HARRIET. Yes! I'm in no condition to run around the country with petrol cans, but you can if you like. (*Slight smile.*) Can change a wheel or two if you like, and give the engine a little tuning.

LILLIAN, *not amused, sitting in the back.*

If we are here for the night, can you do me one very big favour? Don't bang tin plates around, *please*. You can take one night off can't you? OK?

LILLIAN *throws a box of chocolates at her.*

Lillian, don't do that. You have to behave yourself. There's no room for you to do anything else. Understand?

LILLIAN *throws another box.*

Lillian please! It's not my fault we're here and there's nothing else we can do.

LILLIAN. I'm not meant to sleep outside.

HARRIET. I don't care what you're not meant to do.

LILLIAN. It's not allowed, it's forbidden.

HARRIET. You're not in the home now for chrissake! And this is what happens when you're not. OK? OK? I'm going to have a cigarette now too.

LILLIAN *coughs in protest.*

If that's you acting, it's very bad acting. I know I shouldn't but I deserve one. And we can feast on chocolates, nothing else to eat here.

HARRIET *lies back in her seat but is hit in the side of the face by another box of chocolates that* LILLIAN *has tossed from the back seat.*

High shot of the car with its lights on now, in the middle of the wood, as the night closes in.

Interior: London House – Hall and Landing – Evening

Cut to HUGH *walking back into his house.*
LOUISE, THERESA *and* DOMINIC *are all standing waiting for him in the hall.*

HUGH. Louise, Theresa, what's the matter!

LOUISE. We found the place like this. When we were out . . . something terrible's happened.

HUGH. Terrible, what you mean? Where's HARRIET?

HUGH *running up the stairs, to the second landing where the smashed china is all over the floor, the shoes thrown everywhere, and the chairs lying at crazy angles.*

LOUISE (*calling up*). Miss Harriet, and Miss Lillian are not here.

HUGH. Not here? (*Staring at the broken things.*) Have you called the police? We must call the police at once!

LOUISE *has come up the stairs, kneels and starts to pick up things.*

Nobody touch anything. (*Sharp.*) Put that down at once, Louise. Everything must stay exactly as you found it. (*He picks up the phone.*) They took Lillian as well . . . Jesus. (*He dials emergency services.*) Can I have the police please!

Exterior: Wood – Day

Cut to the morning light. LILLIAN stretches in the back of the car, then peers through the window at the early morning wood.

She stares out at the winter trees, and the undergrowth. She's surprised to see two boys staring back at her, from the darkness of the wood, then another pair, then another, we see there are nine or ten kids, both boys and girls, standing in the shadows. They are dressed in an amalgam of clothes, post punk, weird clothes. Two of them have dirt smudged on their faces, like they have camouflaged themselves like combat troops.

They look quite frightening as they stare back from the edge of the trees. To LILLIAN's eyes they appear to be like Amazon Indians in a forest, their faces half obscured by branches, wild exotic people.

One of the boys moves closer. HARRIET opens her eyes, slumped across the front seat, to see these faces staring at her through the windscreen. She yells out and jumps up.

LILLIAN gives the boy a ferocious look from the back seat, and he retreats slightly.

HARRIET. Lillian for chrissake, we've got to get out of here. (*She instinctively tries to start the car, then remembers.*) Come on, out, out . . .

The kids standing, a little distance off, wary of this odd couple they see emerging from the car.

HARRIET gets out, and in her haste her dress gets caught in the door, and part of it is torn off.

(*Furious.*) That's all I need! About to get murdered and look what happens! Come on Lillian let's get out of here.

HARRIET takes the suitcases. With difficulty, they move away watched by the puzzled kids.

(*Shouting back at them.*) Plenty of chocolates in the car, they're all yours! (*An afterthought.*) And the car for that matter!

HARRIET turns to LILLIAN who is moving very slowly, not trying to rush at all.

LILLIAN. Who are those natives?

HARRIET. Natives! Not quite. Just kids living rough . . . in these pockets of woods between the motorway. Nobody disturbs them here, obviously. (*Watching the kids close round the car.*) The wildlife of the area . . .

HARRIET *stops behind a bush.*

Anyway I got to change if I'm going to have to hitch, I've got to look respectable.

Exterior: Wood – Day

We cut back to the car, the kids are falling on it ravenously tearing at the seats, grabbing the remaining chocolates, smearing them on the upholstery, tearing out the radio cassette, the cigarette lighter, the telephone, the whole car being devoured. They also tear out some of HARRIET's clothes from the one suitcase she was forced to leave behind.

Exterior: Country Roadside – Day

Cut to HARRIET sitting looking resplendent in the fine Ascot-like dress, sitting on her suitcase, with LILLIAN next to her sitting on another suitcase.

In front of them is a strange telecommunications tower.

HARRIET. Lovely spot isn't it?

LILLIAN *calmly sitting on her suitcase, watching the tower.*

LILLIAN. It's quite nice here.

HARRIET (*lightly*). Yes, well we know how fond you are of staring at blank walls Lillian, but I'd like to move on.

LILLIAN *staring at the strange tower, and all its electrical antennae.*

LILLIAN. When does that work?

HARRIET. What do you mean?

LILLIAN. When does it work?

HARRIET. I don't know. All the time. I don't know. It's telephones or a listening thing or . . . God knows.

Lorry appearing, moving down the road towards them.

HARRIET *hitches with a languid movement of her thumb. Lorry passes and stops.*

Got one. (LILLIAN *looks dubious.*) It's not great, OK, I know. But girls like us can't be too choosy. Come on.

Interior: Lorry – Country Road – Day

In the cab of the lorry, Scottish driver, HARRIET and LILLIAN. Lorry driver studying them, with an amused smile.

LORRY DRIVER. And where are you two heading for?

HARRIET. I don't know, that's an exceedingly good question. (*To* LILLIAN.) Which way are we going?

LILLIAN *nods in the direction they are heading.*

It's OK, we're going in the right direction. (HARRIET *smiles a radiant smile at the driver.*) She hasn't a clue of course – but that doesn't matter.

Exterior: Modern Hotel – Day

Cut to the lorry moving into the forecourt of a large Holiday Inn-style modern hotel. The lorry moves in amongst the Mercedes and BMW's parked outside.

HARRIET (*calling down from the cab, with great style,* LILLIAN *peering next to her.*) Porter – get us out of this vehicle please.

Interior: Hotel Reception – Day

We cut to HARRIET and LILLIAN at reception checking in. HARRIET looking down at the form she has to fill in. HARRIET is full of provocative, dangerous energy.

HARRIET. Name? (*To* LILLIAN.) What are we called? (*She looks at the reception clerk.*) What are we calling ourselves?

(LILLIAN *about to reply.*) No don't answer that, it's alright. (*To clerk.*) Only kidding . . . we're Mrs and Miss Dickens. (*Indicating* LILLIAN.) She's my mother, she's the Miss. (*As* HARRIET *fills up form.*) I'm giving her a holiday.

RECEPTION CLERK. That's nice. There's lots to see in this area as I'm sure you know.

HARRIET. There'd better be. She hasn't had a holiday for over fifty years.

Reception clerk looks startled, then recovers his cool.

RECEPTION CLERK. Really, that's (*searching for the right words*) that's rather a longer pause than most of our guests take between holidays. (*He smiles.*) I hope we'll make up for it.

LILLIAN *staring at the airport-lounge-like interior.*

HARRIET. You bet we will, we'll make sure of that. (*Picking up the plastic key-card.*) What's this?

RECEPTION CLERK. Your door key.

HARRIET. This is a key Lillian. You see they look like this now. (*Dangerous smile at reception clerk.*) What entertainment have you got? We want to sample everything. We're looking for pleasure. You understand.

RECEPTION CLERK (*eyeing them warily*). We have some dancing, of course, and all the usual amenities. (*Pushing leaflet at them.*)

HARRIET. Hear that Lillian. (*Looking at leaflet, sharp smile.*) Saunas . . . disco . . . adult TV channel, that means porno channel. Great. We were hoping for one of those, weren't we.

RECEPTION CLERK *staring at them, rather alarmed.*

Exterior: The Wood – Day

We cut to the wood, the abandoned Daimler, the place is swarming with police, and police cars in the wood. Blue lights flashing, officers moving through the undergrowth, finding the piece of HARRIET's *torn dress. We see it being put in a plastic bag. We see policemen examining the car, with its torn seats, the havoc the kids have caused, that looks as if some violent act has taken place inside the car, the stains of smashed chocolate, and the broken windows. We see beyond the trees there is a small lake and police frogmen are getting ready to search it.*

Hotel: Bedroom – Day

We cut to LILLIAN *sitting on one bed in the hotel room just making herself comfortable,* HARRIET *lying on the other, sweating profusely. It is a horrible room, full of plastic looking fittings. But trying to be luxurious.*

HARRIET (*is shouting down the phone.*) You can't believe how hot it is in here, we spend £120 quid a night – and we get punished like this, roasted alive! What you mean switch it off – I can't switch it off, there's nothing to *switch* . . . this is the fifth time I've called, . . . you better bloody send somebody. The engineer's gone home? Then find another one. (*Slams down the phone.*)

Self-mocking smile.

I suppose I deserve this. . .

She climbs off the bed, with difficulty, feeling her pregnancy, her size.

Come on – let's do what rock stars do (*she smiles*) wreck the place. . .

She moves over to the heater . . . which runs along the wall with a grid along the top. Trying to find a way of switching it off. She's really sweating. The plastic key, which she's waving around in one hand, slips through the grid running along the top of the heater.

(*Smiles*). Great! Might as well get everything I want to get rid of – and feed it into this heater. (*Starts burrowing in her bag.*) Get my dental reminder . . . in it goes. Some pills. The car keys. Some of Hugh's credit cards. (*Laughing.*) Shove my whole life down there, and maybe stop this heater as well! Clog it up.

LILLIAN *watching* HARRIET's *febrile mood, as she shoves things down the heater.*

LILLIAN. Are you not feeling well?

HARRIET *looks up in surprise.*

HARRIET. She asked me! She spoke! (*She smiles.*) Thank you for inquiring, but I'm fine. Really. And isn't this great? Nobody in the whole world knows where we are. I have no idea why I find that so exciting right at this moment, but I do.

Interior: HUGH's House, Dining Room – Night.

HUGH *eating just a bowl of soup,* DOMINIC *tucking into a large plate of steak and potatoes.*

HUGH (*quiet*). Your mother will be fine . . . I know it. I'm going to keep talking about it, because I think we should.

DOMINIC. Yes, Daddy.

HUGH. It's a kidnapping and God knows anything can happen, but I do feel it will be alright . . . in the end.

DOMINIC (*calmly eating*). Will you pay the ransom?

HUGH (*sharp*). Dominic! It hasn't come to that. Of course I will, if that's what's required.

DOMINIC. Yes, I think you're right to do that. You're not insured of course but –

HUGH (*sharp*). Dominic!

DOMINIC (*unperturbed, eating his steak*). – But that doesn't matter. I hope the police look around here, that's where they should be concentrating their effort . . . in a lot of cases kidnap victims are held very close to where they were kidnapped, maybe as close as half a mile. I hope they realize that.

HUGH. I'm sure they do Dominic – if it's true.

DOMINIC (*cross*). Of course it's true.

HUGH. OK, I've made a note of it. (*Trying to sip his soup.*) I hate to think of your mother frightened, Lillian will be alright. Probably doesn't realize what's going on, but your mother, . . . she always thinks she likes drama and . . . but she doesn't.

HUGH *unable to bear the sight of* DOMINIC *eating with such relish any longer.*

How can you sit there eating like that? (*Sharp.*) It's unnatural.

DOMINIC (*looks up calmly*). You *sure* they really have been kidnapped?

HUGH. Of course. The signs of the struggle here, the condition the car was in when they found it. Nobody saw anything here but –

DOMINIC *finishing his plate, chewing the last piece of meat.*

DOMINIC. After dinner we should look at the clothes that were taken . . . there will almost certainly be a clue there. Don't you think? (*He looks up at his father.*)

Interior: Hotel Bedroom – Evening

Cut to HARRIET, *leaning over the washbasin in the bathroom, splashing cold water over her face, again and again, almost feverish movements.*

LILLIAN *is sitting at the end of the bed, staring at the television, the nine o'clock news, the sound is on quite softly. An item of world news gives way to a piece of home news.*

As LILLIAN *is sitting on the bed she idly begins to draw on the wall with some of the leftover chocolate eclairs they have had for tea.*

'Police are investigating the disappearance of the wife of city financier, Hugh Ambrose, from his Kensington home on Wednesday night. There were signs of a struggle in the house, and Police later found Mr Ambrose's car in a wood near the M40 in Oxfordshire. Pieces of women's clothes were found in the undergrowth nearby' etc. . . .

As the images come up to illustrate this news story, the house, the car in the wood, LILLIAN *is watching fascinated, but gradually getting impatient when there is no mention of her.*

LILLIAN. Where am I?

Then a picture appears of both of them. A flattering, recent picture of HARRIET, *and a completely unrecognizable one of* LILLIAN, *and the commentary continues.*

'A second person has also disappeared from the family home on the same day, Miss Lillian Huckle an elderly aunt of Mr Ambrose, recently returned from a period spent in hospital.'

LILLIAN'*s eyebrows raise at this description.*

The picture of her shown on the screen is several years out of date, and looking like a police photo, of a mad axe-woman.

LILLIAN *stares with some digust at the picture, and then stirs herself, to attract* HARRIET'*s attention.*

LILLIAN *gets off the bed, as the commentary continues to roll with a short interview with the policeman in charge of the investigation.*

She goes into the bathroom, where HARRIET *is by the basin.* LILLIAN *tugs at her sleeve.*

LILLIAN. Come and look what's on the machine . . . come and see. You must see it.

HARRIET. What's this? What's the matter with you?

HARRIET *moves into the room, but the item has changed by then, the news has moved on to an item about the Royal Family.*

HARRIET (*looking at the picture of the Queen*). I had no idea you felt so strongly about the Queen, Lillian. (*She smiles.*) I've learnt something about you . . . (*She turns.*) NOW, I'm going to get us dressed for tonight!

Interior: Hotel, Corridor – Night

LILLIAN *and* HARRIET *come out into the hotel corridor in their evening dress. We see them in long shot coming towards us,* HARRIET *looking dazzling, and* LILLIAN *in one of* HARRIET'*s dresses, looking very striking too. They move along the passage, with a little difficulty.* HARRIET *because of her great size.*

HARRIET. OK, let's slay them shall we!

Interior: Hotel Dining Room – Night

HARRIET *and* LILLIAN *enter the dining room, large modern dining room with cascading glass decorations, and a dance floor. Two or three couples are taking part in a modest genteel disco. There is a band dressed in red and white playing versions of current hits.*

The head waiter approaches HARRIET *and* LILLIAN *as they stand on the edge of the dining room surveying the scene.*

HEAD WAITER. I am sorry, madam, but the food is all finished.

HARRIET (*startled*). Finished?

HEAD WAITER. 9.30. It finishes at 9.30. It is now (*he holds up his watch*) 9.35 .

HARRIET. I don't believe this – you are not serving food any more? (*Loud.*) Can you believe this place, Lillian?

HEAD WAITER. Everything is finished – except the carvery. (*He indicates joints of meat, in a side area marked 'The Great British Carvery'*)

The carve yourself meat . . . that is available.

HARRIET (*tottering slightly, being made to stand like this.*) Carve yourself?

HEAD WAITER. Yes – it is meant to be shut too . . . but I think we can make exception. (*Glancing at a manager standing in the shadows.*) Can we let these ladies use the carvery?

HARRIET (*dangerous smile*). We're being punished Lillian – it's like Hugh planned this – and said 'do this to them' – (*She moves.*) OK. (*She grabs two plates.*) They've asked for it, let's do it!

We cut to HARRIET *carving the meat, hacking into it, giant slices onto both plates. A ferocious amount of meat.*

They're going to see some champion carving tonight . . .

Then we cut to LILLIAN *and* HARRIET *moving to their table, the only one that is empty, moving across the dining room, with their plates absolutely groaning under the weight of the meat, the size of the portions. HARRIET has taken most of the Great British Carvery with her.*

People can't help but look, glancing stares, as HARRIET and LILLIAN cross the dining room.

(*To LILLIAN, indicating the stares.*) Don't take any notice of them, they're just jealous.

They reach the table.

(*Sinking into her seat.*) Let's tuck in shall we?

She picks up a piece of meat in her hands and starts really ravenously tearing into it, oblivious of the people watching.

LILLIAN *sits watching her for a moment. She is smiling at HARRIET.*

(*Looks up at LILLIAN, meat over her chin.*) Well, I'm glad I've made you smile.

Interior: HUGH's Bedroom – Night

Cut to HUGH and DOMINIC sitting on the floor of the bedroom, clothes spread out all around them. HUGH holding one of HARRIET's dresses.

DOMINIC. You see . . . her favourite dresses have gone, haven't they? Of all her clothes . . . (*They stare at the cupboard with all HARRIET's many dresses.*) . . . she's taken four of her favourite dresses. (DOMINIC *watches his father.*) If she was being kidnapped – it's unlikely that would have happened, isn't it?

HUGH. You sure those are her favourite dresses?

DOMINIC. Yes Daddy – even I know that, it's what she wears for really special occasions. And she's taken her own suitcase too – that Italian one she likes.

HUGH. The police say they must have made them grab a few things before they took them out . . . But maybe they let Harriet choose her best clothes . . . gave her time to pack.

DOMINIC. That wouldn't make it a very normal kidnap would

it? Mummy wouldn't take her best clothes for that. (*Calmly.*) It would be unnatural. (*He smiles.*) Even for mummy.

HUGH (*sitting on the floor with* DOMINIC). Maybe. So what do you think it means?

DOMINIC (*suddenly looking embarrassed*). I don't know Daddy – what do you think?

HUGH. It can't mean she just left (*he gropes for the words*) left of her own free will. (*He gets up, pacing.*) I mean it would be terrific of course – I mean it could be she's safe, but . . . (*Silence, he looks at* DOMINIC.)

DOMINIC (*quiet*). I can't imagine why either Daddy. (*Genuine.*) I've been thinking, and I can't.

HUGH. Maybe Lillian did something to her. I'm beginning to think it was a mistake bringing her here. (*Suddenly urgent, picking up the phone.*) I'm going to get the police to bloody find them! Now it's time we took a hand. They've had long enough!

Interior: Hotel Dining Room – Night

Cut to the disco, the plump figures of the prosperous of the district, dancing, some even gyrating, on a Friday night. There is a birthday party group with party hats just finishing their meal, and some coloured lights are playing across the walls as the band plays.

HARRIET *pours the last drops out of a wine bottle into* LILLIAN's *glass. It is obviously not the first bottle they have finished between them.*

HARRIET. I know you don't like me still.

LILLIAN *shakes her head.*

What does that shake mean? Do you mean you do or you don't?

LILLIAN. It's getting better.

HARRIET *smiles.*

HARRIET. Of all the people to be lumbered with – you come out of that hospital after 50 years and you get stuck with me! (*She*

drinks, her tone light but direct.) A spoilt ex-bit part actress, who
couldn't act, and is a lousy mother. (*Amused smile, totally
without self pity.*) Worthless, not an idea in my head, no real
knowledge, no political views, (*she smiles*) nothing. (*Her tone
changes.*) I know that.

LILLIAN *watching her, a little nod.*

(*Sharp laugh, touching her a moment.*) Don't be in a hurry to
contradict me will you. (*She looks down for a moment.*) Hugh
thinks I'm a kind of scatty flighty creature – doesn't he – that
has to be trained, *really* trained, but who sometimes can act
being hostess of his dinner parties surprisingly well –

LILLIAN *lifts empty wine bottle, catches a passing waiter by the
sleeve, presents him with the bottle.*

LILLIAN (*to waiter*). More. Lots more.

The dancers dancing, the music loud.

HARRIET. I mean Hugh is a good man. He is. (*She laughs.*)
That is what's so terrible – he tried so hard, for both of us, he
really tried. He is the perfect provider, he has a strong sense of
family and all that (*she smiles*) and we loathe him for it.

LILLIAN *smiles at this too.*

You see you do! (*She looks at* LILLIAN.) It's unforgiveable isn't
it?

HARRIET *is tapping the cutlery to the awful music, the dancers
swirling round them, very close to the table.*

(*Lightly.*) The English trying to be sexy. (*She laughs.*) It's really
gruesome, isn't it?

We cut to the dancers, then back to LILLIAN *and* HARRIET.

I bet you must be thinking I wish I'd stayed away for another
fifty years!

*As they talk the plump dancing couples do take on a ludicrous,
complacent, grotesque appearance.*

HARRIET *leans across the table as the dancing couples get closer and closer, jostling their table, brushing nearer and nearer, as they spread out from the main dance floor. HARRIET shoves her fork into a couple of bottoms that come too close, she gets some very strange looks. LILLIAN smiles, delighted at this. But HARRIET's face, complexion, is looking different, flushed and ill, although her eyes are shining.*

It's very unattractive I know – to be so full of hate. (*Staring straight at LILLIAN's eyes.*) Is there anything worse, any worse feeling in the world than hating the child you're about to have? . . . and not really knowing why. (*Matter of fact.*) That's terrible isn't it? And I have no excuses . . . One of the simplest things isn't it, that feeling, (*looking at LILLIAN*) and it really is quite horrible (*quiet*) scary . . . And I don't know what to do about it. (*She leans very close to LILLIAN.*) What about you, going to say anything to me?

LILLIAN. I don't think so.

HARRIET. Why not? It's just us here. (*Catching hold of LILLIAN's wrist, very direct.*) You despise us all, I know, don't you? (*LILLIAN looks away.*) Yes you do, you can't forgive, why should you? (*Direct.*) You can only start again, that's the only thing you can do, Lillian. Start again from scratch. But I haven't got the guts to do that. I'm much less brave than you were. (*Loud.*) I can't even leave him for chrissake, can't make myself. (*She pours LILLIAN some more wine.*) *You* did what you had to, you followed your feelings, or instincts or whatever you'd call it. I'm guessing you did of course – because you won't tell me about it!

LILLIAN looks away.

(*Warm smile.*) Didn't exactly get you very far did it! But that's something else. . . .

LILLIAN stares across at TV.

Are you listening to me? I may be drunk but I demand your full attention, Lillian. I *know* I shouldn't be drinking, for the baby, but I *am*.

As she has been saying this, LILLIAN is pointing. Above the bar,

*behind the barman is a television, and their pictures are on the
television again, in a brief resumé of the news. Seen through the haze
of the dancing figures, nobody but LILLIAN seems to notice.*

(*Following LILLIAN's pointing.*) If I wasn't so pissed, I'd say
they look a lot like us.

The picture has gone now.

LILLIAN. It was. We're wanted on the television.

HARRIET. Wishful thinking Lillian! You want to be famous do
you?

*A MAN comes up to the table, looking down at her as dancing
figures jostle round the table.*

MAN. What a dance love? (*He is leaning close.*)

HARRIET. You won't want me when I stand up.

*She stands up, she looks enormous now. She moves with much
heaviness like a tank towards the man, he backs away, and the
dancers try to avoid her, spreading out before her, a little exclusion
zone breaks out around their table. HARRIET's bulky shape moving
to the music.*

(*Calling down to LILLIAN as she moves.*) I have a funny feeling
of getting bigger and bigger. (*She laughs.*) Swelling by the
minute . . . (HARRIET *calling down to LILLIAN indicating the
scene in front of them.*) Think Lillian, what would happen if we
did go away for another fifty years, what would we come back
to? How would it look then?

*They both stare at the cramped, plump dance floor under the
cascading glass.*

You know what I think, we'd come back to exactly this! The
muzak might have changed of course. (*Staring at them.*) But not
much else.

Interior: HUGH's House – Night.

HUGH *on the phone,* DOMINIC *by his side, with maps spread out of
England.*

HUGH (*to the police on the phone*). We have drawn up five areas here, radiating out from where the car was found – and a list of the hotels, and (*snaps*) are you listening to me? I want you to check the following hotels, yes hotels – because I believe my wife and my ageing aunt under whose influence I believe she's acting – are staying normally – in some hotel. People should be able to spot them a mile off! And we're going to find them tonight – do you understand that, (*savage down phone*) because you've made a proper balls up of it so far. FIND THEM.

HUGH *slams down the phone, looking at* DOMINIC, *sudden doubt in his voice.*

I hope you're right about her favourite dresses. I've only got *your* word for it.

DOMINIC. Yes Daddy. Don't worry, I'm right.

HUGH (*more dangerous*). Then where the hell are they?

Interior: Dining Room and Dance Floor – Night

Cut to the dining room deserted covered in crushed streamers and squashed party hats. Two diners left, HARRIET *and* LILLIAN, *and all the waiters standing round impatiently.*

HEAD WAITER. Come on please – come on ladies! Time for bed.

HARRIET. We'll come when we're ready! (*Her face close to* LILLIAN, *urgent tone.* HARRIET's *face very red and looking strange, but she seems oblivious. She puts her hands either side of* LILLIAN's *head.*) Lillian . . . tell me, what it was like being shut away like that. I often think about it. The whole of the war for instance, must have been just a series of distant rumbles and bangs which nobody explained to you, was it? Going on somewhere far away. Tell me. Just *one* thing about it all. I know it's difficult for you, I know you find it hard to talk.

LILLIAN. I can't.

HARRIET (*strong*). Yes you can.

LILLIAN. I can't, Harriet . . . (*She turns her head.*)

Pause.

It was, every little year, every little year that went, I shut things away some more . . . because I'd shouted so much and then one day you can't anymore.

And you just grow smaller and smaller, tighter . . . until even very ordinary things become so . . . difficult. It all stops working . . . (LILLIAN *looks up, straight at* HARRIET.) Will that do?

HARRIET (*laughs*). Was that the real thing, Lillian? Or just manufactured for me? I can't tell with you!

LILLIAN *stares back not indicating either way.* HARRIET *touches her.*

That's what I like about you, I really do. (*She touches her.*) You're so hard, Lillian.

Interior: Hotel Lifts – Night

We cut to LILLIAN *standing by a row of modern lifts pressing the buttons.*

HARRIET. Come on let's climb, otherwise we'll be here all night. Somebody's hired all the lifts for tonight, probably have to pay extra to use them!

A couple of girls pass them.

GIRL. Oh yes, didn't you know you ought to have special lift vouchers.

The two girls giggle and exit.

HARRIET (*very sharp*). Thank you.

HARRIET *and* LILLIAN *move off towards the stairs.*

They begin to move up the stairs.

We cut to them on a landing about to move up the second flight. When HARRIET *suddenly collapses, breathing rapidly, her blood pressure very high, she looks very ill.*

HARRIET. I can't move Lillian, I don't know what's happening, I can't move.

LILLIAN *begins to move down the staircase.*

LILLIAN. I will get them, stay there.

HARRIET (*recovering her normal self for a second*). I'm not going anywhere am I!

Interior: Hotel Corridors – Night

LILLIAN *now suddenly on her own, wandering down a passage, in the enormous hotel, looking for somebody. There is a faint sound of music, she follows it, and opens a door. There is a small private party going on in the 'Waterloo Suite'. A crowd of people laughing inside, there is a man inside the door, one of the guests.*

GUEST. This is a private party, you can't come in.

LILLIAN *suddenly finding she can't get the words out quick enough.*

LILLIAN. You must. (*Very urgent.*) You must . . .

GUEST. Sorry, private party. (*He closes the door.*)

We see LILLIAN in a maze of identical passages, moving past the hideous decorations.

Interior: Hotel Staircase – Night

We cut back to HARRIET lying on the stairs breathing with difficulty. She tries to move down the staircase on her bottom with great difficulty.

HARRIET. What's happening to me? Who's doing this? Did Hugh arrange this too? Did you? (*Really loud.*) Is this what I deserve? (*Screams.*) Is it? Could somebody . . .

She collapses at the bottom of the steps.

Interior: Hotel Reception – Night

We cut back to LILLIAN who has found the reception, the reception clerk and two young women standing there. The receptionist casually chatting them up, as he watches TV simultaneously, 'Pillow Talk'.

FIRST GIRL. No, we haven't finished for tonight. You shut down so early, we're going off to the Casablanca, it's new, just opened.

LILLIAN *gets up to the desk.*

LILLIAN. You must come at once.

RECEPTION CLERK. Just one moment madam.

LILLIAN. You got to come . . . (*Fighting the words out.*) She's, she's . . . she's on the stairs. She . . .

RECEPTION CLERK. You want the stairs madam? I'll be with you straight away.

LILLIAN. You'll be with me now!

RECEPTION CLERK (*rolling his eyes at the girl, as much as to say 'I've got a right one here'.*) Excuse me a moment, now madam is it your key that you've lost, or your room?

LILLIAN. Bloody fool. (*She makes a jabbing movement, with the heavy ashtray that is on the desk, she hits the fire alarm, not hard, but hard enough to break the glass, and the whole hotel is ringing with alarms.*)

Interior: London House – Night

HUGH *sitting in the shadows in the darkened sitting room, DOMINIC watching. During his speech, HUGH is flicking magazines off the coffee table with an increasingly sharp flick.*

HUGH (*his tone suggests he believes DOMINIC*). If you're right . . . if she and Lillian went off (*his voice rising*) leaving *NO NOTE*. (*He makes it sound a threat.*) I will never *understand*, never, how she could. . . . (*He stops.*)

DOMINIC (*watching in the shadows*). No Daddy.

HUGH. To cause all these problems, all these people running around the country, it's even been on the television.

DOMINIC. You have to expect that.

HUGH. On the national news for chrissake, everybody will have

heard about it. (*Loud.*) What *do I tell them*? What? (*Furious.*)
She never showed any sign at all that something was wrong.

DOMINIC. No Daddy.

HUGH. None. Just remember that! (*He begins to pale.*) My God,
she'll have to explain a lot . . . these last weeks till the baby is
born, she'll never be out of my sight. I mean it! (*His voice really
tense, really loud, his face full of incomprehension.*) I want her
back for godsake! (*He turns, he cries out.*) Dominic – I want her
here!

Exterior: Hospital – Night

*We cut to HARRIET being carried out of an ambulance now barely
conscious, and rushed through the glass doors, her face distorted in
pain.*

Interior: Hospital – Night

*HARRIET being sped along hospital corridors on a trolley, doctors
running alongside and nurses, the whole atmosphere surrounding an
emergency case.*

Interior: Operating Theatre – Night

*We cut to HARRIET being taken into the operating theatre, the whole
ritual of an operation spinning into life, the oxygen mask, the
equipment closing around HARRIET. Her face looking very different,
very ill.*

Hospital Corridors – Night

A DOCTOR emerges into the passage, where LILLIAN is standing.

DOCTOR. You're the person with her are you? (*The DOCTOR
looks at LILLIAN.*) Are you the patient's mother?

LILIAN. I . . . (LILLIAN *hesitates, not wanting to be told to
leave if she gives the wrong answer.*) I, not . . . not quite her
mother I . . .

DOCTOR (*looks knowingly at a nurse standing there*). OK, we'll deal with that later. Now, she's suffering from Eclampsia, that is rapid rise in the blood pressure, general swelling, excess water in the body . . . it is extremely dangerous for both the mother and the child, so we have to get the baby out, *NOW*.

LILLIAN. I must see her.

DOCTOR. I'm afraid that's impossible, just wait here.

LILLIAN (*with real force, not trusting him*). I must see her . . . (*She thinks quickly.*) I have something to give her. (*Stamping.*) I *must* see her.

DOCTOR (*sharp*). You don't seem to understand that young woman could easily die, now stop wasting our time, and wait over there.

He takes her firmly by the arm, and guides her forcibly across the passage. LILLIAN pulls away from that grip on her arm, automatically tearing herself away, she's been guided like that so often.

We see a sudden torrent of thoughts, flashbacks being unleashed. Like at the party, gradually gathering in intensity.

Flashback: Interior, Mental Hospital Corridor – Day

We see her as a young girl being guided down a passage, with exactly the same grip on her arm, each time she moves her arm, the grip tightens. We don't see the man who is holding her, just the shoulder, and the arm. And the grip tightening.

Flashback: Interior, Harley Street Consulting Room – Day

We then see the YOUNG LILLIAN in a large room facing two doctors, one a woman, across a smart consulting room. YOUNG LILLIAN is pacing backwards and forwards, remonstrating at them with real force.

YOUNG LILLIAN. You don't know what you're talking about, that's the trouble, and I *know* you don't. That's what you don't like.

And she moves across the room and tugs at one of the curtains, the large curtains come crashing down, the whole curtain rail.

Flashback: Interior Mental Hospital Office – Day

Then we see YOUNG LILLIAN *sitting across a polished desk, sitting bolt upright very much the same way we see her sitting opposite* HUGH *in front of the blackboard at the beginning of the film. A very correct male doctor faces her.*

DOCTOR. Now do you understand Lilly? The answers you give to these questions are very important. A lot rests on what you reply now . . .

We see a beady look in YOUNG LILLIAN's *eyes, determined to give deliberately perverse answers.*

DOCTOR. Who is the Prime Minister of this country?

YOUNG LILLIAN (*very deadpan*). A kind of monkey.

DOCTOR. What do we call a man that looks at our teeth?

YOUNG LILLIAN. A bloodthirsty man.

DOCTOR. What is the name of this country where we live, what do we call it?

YOUNG LILLIAN. I don't know. Black Island, some name like that. A place that you fall through.

DOCTOR (*writing*). Fall through?

YOUNG LILLIAN. Fall right through – and come out the other side.

DOCTOR. Why do you think you are here?

YOUNG LILLIAN. Because I'm cleverer than you . . . because I'm meaner than you, because I see through you, and it would be much easier if I wasn't around. (*She smiles sweetly.*) Wouldn't it? And because you don't feel anything. (*She suddenly tweeks his hand across the desk.*) You don't feel this, or this, or this. Just like my father.

Flashback: Interior London House, Drawing Room – Day

We cut to close up of YOUNG LILLIAN *and the cousin* EDWARD *in their love scene on the nursery floor, a sensual erotic kiss, as they lie among the toys, it's as if it's a continuation of the moment that burnt out to white in the party scene, in the middle of the film.*

YOUNG LILLIAN. They'll come soon, find out where we are. Can we stop them? (*Urgent.*) Stay with me? (*A passionate kiss.*) Stay. I can make you stay forever.

Flashback: Interior London House, Drawing Room – Day

We then see her facing her father, in front of a large ornamental mirror.

YOUNG LILLIAN. I want to explain why it's not possible for me to listen to you any more – it's because I've stopped believing.

FATHER. You're talking nonsense Lilly.

YOUNG LILLIAN. I can no longer believe you exist. I have lost my faith, I can't believe such a boring, small-minded, lumpy man can be my father. (*She stares into his eyes.*) So I've decided you aren't my father. You have ceased to be.

Flashback: Interior London House, Conservatory – Day

Then we cut to a conservatory, heavy with flowers and tea things, a scented place. And YOUNG LILLIAN *is being approached by a man and a nurse, talking to her in gentle tones.*

YOUNG LILLIAN. Get away from me!

A terrible fight ensues as they try to catch hold of her, tea things being broken and smashed, glass being smashed as the sharp face of her sister MARGARET *watches terrified, totally uncomprehending.* YOUNG LILLIAN *kicks and screams and when finally they have got hold of her, she picks up the nearest thing at hand, a pair of silver sugar tongs, and slices the man repeatedly across the face.*

Very quick images follow of YOUNG LILLIAN *in the institution*

being held down, crying uncontrollably, then being examined by
doctors strapped down to a table.

Then a shot of the OLD LILLIAN *being held down too in a chair,*
followed by GLADYS's *face approaching her with apples, and then*
a room full of some of the relatives we saw at the funeral
approaching LILLIAN *across a room, looking deeply embarrassed,*
keeping their distance.

OLD LILLIAN (*whispering to herself*). What a miserable bunch, I
had forgotten how awful they looked.

Flashback: Interior Mental Hospital, Cell – Day

And then the YOUNG LILLIAN *being shut up in a small room and*
screaming passionately and repeatedly through the grid in the door.

YOUNG LILLIAN. I don't know what's the matter with me, but
it's nothing compared to this place – what's wrong with all of
you. You can't even do this properly, (*screams*) can you?
Bastards. (*Screams.*) Bastards – DON'T DO THIS TO ME,
YOU BASTARDS . . .

Her face ferociously crying by the grid. We stay on her – she screams
through the grid. Desperate screams, that shake right through her
body.

Interior: Hospital Corridor – Night

We cut back to the present. LILLIAN *standing by a window in*
profile, beginning to shake very slightly.

Interior: Operating Theatre – Night

We cut to HARRIET *being operated on, close up of her face,*
unconscious.

Interior: Hospital Corridor – Night

Cut back to LILLIAN *by the window, staring at the traffic moving on*
the night roads, and the office blocks lit up opposite the hospital. She
stares at this contemporary view, her body shaking.

LILLIAN. I don't know what happened to all that time . . . it was just taken away . . .

In the corridor there is a woman of about fifty, sitting with two young children. She nods at LILLIAN, not knowing what LILLIAN's talking about, but nodding pleasantly.

I can't forgive, she is right about that you know . . . and to have to start again . . . (*Tears pouring down LILLIAN's face, but her voice is tough.*) It's a bit late . . . a little too late . . . and it's so tiring now . . . (*Her body shaking.*) It frightens me, it frightens me so much.

The woman in the passage smiles at her, nodding. LILLIAN's body really shaking, then she turns.

I don't want her to die. (*Loud, dangerous to woman.*) Do you hear? I DON'T WANT HER TO DIE.

Woman nods sympathetically.

I expect they'll bungle it up, don't you . . . make a bad job of it . . . better go and make sure they're doing it right. (*LILLIAN sets off down the passage muttering.*) They aren't doing it right. (*LILLIAN shuffling along.*) They'll make mistakes like they always do.

Interior: Operating Theatre and Corridor Outside – Night

We cut back to the operating theatre, doctors working on HARRIET surrounded by machines, HARRIET buried amongst it, her face looking very small.

Then we cut to LILLIAN trying to enter the operating theatre, people closing round her, pulling her back, restraining her.

LILLIAN. I *must* see her. I don't want her to die . . . I won't let them. (*Loud.*) I don't want them to kill her.

We cut back to HARRIET. Her figure fragile among the blood and machines.

Then we see LILLIAN staring through the window in one of the doors at the back, watching intensely, apprehensively, every move.

To her eyes the modern operating equipment takes on a futuristic, menacing aspect.

(*At first quiet, but growing more and more insistent.*) You do it right. You do it right. You hear me. Do you hear me. *You do one thing properly*, understand. YOU DO THIS RIGHT.

We cut back to the operating theatre, getting closer and closer to HARRIET's face. We hear her breathing on the sound track.

Interior: Incubator Room – Night

Then we cut to LILLIAN staring down, with a nurse beside her, at a tiny premature baby in an incubator, fragile, covered in wires, just clinging onto life. LILLIAN staring down at it with grave fascination.

Hospital Room – Night

We cut to HARRIET lying in a small cubicle room, nurse just coming out, LILLIAN moving up to the door.

NURSE. You can't go in there, now.

LILLIAN (*taking no notice*). Rubbish.

She goes through the door without looking at the nurse.

NURSE (*moving off*). I'm coming right back in a minute to get you out of there.

HARRIET (*staring at LILLIAN, quiet, Pause.*) There you are. They say it may live and it may not. The baby. I don't know if I want it. Still. Isn't that terrible?

LILLIAN. No.

HARRIET (*slight smile*). I could be dead apparently, nearly was.

LILLIAN (*staring down at her*). Yes.

Exterior/Interior: Hospital Entrance – Night

HUGH *arriving with* DOMINIC *marching through the electric doors with tremendous determination.*

HUGH (*to* DOMINIC). Stay there. (*Indicating seats.*) I need to do this on my own.

Nurses bearing down on HUGH *to stop him getting past reception at this unusual hour.* HUGH *brushes past them, walks literally through them, sending them scattering, and hitting a trolley that rolls into a wall with a crash.*

HUGH (*as he does so*). Out of my way ladies – thank you.

HUGH *marches on, out of sight down the passage.*

DOMINIC *sits coolly on a bench against the wall, stretching his arms along the back of the bench nonchalantly.*

DOMINIC (*to nurses*). Don't worry – he'll pay for any damage he does. (*Calmly.*) He's collecting my mother you see.

Interior: Hospital Room – Night

We cut back to HARRIET's *room.* HARRIET *moving with difficulty in bed, staring back at* LILLIAN *in pain.*

HARRIET. Jesus, it hurts.

LILLIAN *moves slowly towards her and leans over* HARRIET, *brushes her cheek clumsily with her mouth, a strange form of a kiss. She does this for quite a long moment, then moves away.*

HARRIET (*laughs*). What's that meant to be? (HARRIET *leaning back in the bed.*) So what the hell do we do now, Lillian? (*She laughs at herself.*) Listen to me – I'm asking *you* that.

LILLIAN. Yes! (*Watching her.*) I don't know why you're laughing.

HARRIET *leans back, slight smile.*

Interior: Hospital Corridors – Night

We cut to HUGH *marching down the corridors, now with a flotilla of doctors and nurses, surrounding him. They round a corner, and move towards us down another corridor, getting nearer and nearer* HARRIET's *room.*

Interior: Hospital Room – Night

We cut back to HARRIET's room, just as LILLIAN is pushing a chair, or a small cupboard with great difficulty and effort so it bars the door, forming a kind of barrier. It requires a lot of effort from LILLIAN but she gets it into place.

LILLIAN (*turns to HARRIET*). Go to sleep now. Go on.

LILLIAN is by the door, staring out of the glass, standing guard.

I'll tell you when they're coming.

Close up of HARRIET, she smiles, her point of view of LILLIAN standing guard by the door, then she leans right back in her bed, and half closes her eyes.

Interior: Hospital Corridor – Night

We cut back onto the corridor – we see HUGH come round the corner with all the doctors and nurses bearing down on HARRIET and LILLIAN.

Then we suddenly see apprehension and doubt come into HUGH's face, into his eyes. His pace falters.

For he sees LILLIAN, standing guard, massively determined. A face he has to get past, staring through the glass directly down the corridor at him. HUGH's pace slows almost to a standstill as do the doctors and nurses round him.

We cut to LILLIAN's face, staring out at HUGH and us, in giant close-up, full of power, unmoveable, staring directly into us.

CENTURY

Century opened in the UK on New Year's Eve, 1993, with the following cast:

PROFESSOR MANDRY	Charles Dance
PAUL REISNER	Clive Owen
CLARA	Miranda Richardson
MR REISNER	Robert Stephens
FELIX	Neil Stuke
MIRIAM REISNER	Lena Headey
MRS WHITEWEATHER	Joan Hickson
JAMES	Carlton Chance
THEO	Graham Loughridge
MRS PRITCHARD	Fiona Walker
THOMAS	Alexis Daniels
MEREDITH	Ian Shaw
EDWIN	Joseph Bennett
KATIE	Liza Walker
DR MAKIN	Michael Burrell
INTERROGATOR	Bruce Alexander

Directed by Stephen Poliakoff
Produced by Therese Pickard
Director of Photograpy Witold Stok
Production Designer Michael Pickwoad

A BBC Films Production in association with Beambright.

Pre-credit Sequence

A photograph of a New Year's Eve party, from 1899, the Reisner family group staring out at us, slightly stiffly.

MR REISNER, PAUL *and* MIRIAM, *surrounded by various Christmas decorations and Happy New Year signs.*

One of the servants is giggling in the back of the photograph, and an old woman in an enormous hat, and leaning on two sticks, is peering out at us ferociously.

As we slowly move towards the image, we hear the VOICE-OVER. *The photograph grows larger and larger, grainier and grainier, as we move across from the old woman, to the laughing servant, to* MR REISNER's *confident stare, until we are peering straight into* PAUL's *eyes.*

The VOICE-OVER *is an elegant old man's voice, crackling slightly as if from an old fifties-type recording.*

VOICE-OVER. I think it's best to start with Father's New Year's Eve party, a really memorable occasion . . . His party to celebrate the beginning of the new century . . .

We are closing in on PAUL's *face.*

At least *we* all thought it was the beginning of the new century.

We mix from PAUL's *eyes staring at us to a wide shot of a clump of trees opposite a row of substantial houses, near a river in a small provincial town.*

My father was Romanian by birth, but had arrived as a young man in Scotland, where he brought us all up after the death of my mother. Before bringing us and his building contractor's business down south, to England. We were living in a small town about fifteen miles outside London. It was a rather horrible, smug little place, with a very surprising smell that everybody pretended not to notice. I think it was a mixture of horses and the local brewery . . . Anyway, sometimes I think I can still smell it on my hands. In fact, it's difficult to convey how much I was really *dying* to leave home.

The credits begin over the following sequence:

MR REISNER *is standing at the foot of the trees, a solitary figure watching a group of* MEN *bearing down on him like a posse, one man on a horse, the rest walking.*

Suspended in the trees above MR REISNER'*s head is an enormous sign:* HAPPY NEW YEAR – WELCOME TO THE 20TH CENTURY.

The leader of the group of men closing in on MR REISNER *is calling out as they approach:*

FIRST MAN. Mr Reisner, you can't do that. We *told* you you can't. Take it down at once. What on earth do you think you're doing?

The MEN *reach* MR REISNER; *the sign is swinging above their heads, covered in little bulbs; strange cables run down behind.*

MR REISNER *is an impressive, prosperous-looking man.*

MR REISNER. What do you mean, what am I doing? I'm celebrating . . . It looks good, don't you think? A special electrical sign, people will see it for miles.

FIRST MAN. This is *not* your land. Didn't you listen to the Council resolution? We've told you again and again, we are celebrating next year in this town. The century doesn't start till next year – everybody agrees that.

SECOND MAN (*shouts from back*). It begins next year. Next year!

Interior: Passageway – Day

MIRIAM, *a dark-haired girl of seventeen, is staring out of the window, watching this scene from a first-floor landing.*

MIRIAM. *Paul*, Paul, come here quickly. (*She presses her face against the window.*) Oh my God, they are not going to pull it down, are they?

Exterior: Reisner House – Day

Shot from the window, of MR REISNER *waving his arms, two of the* MEN *in the group begin to pull on the electrical cables.*

PAUL *joining* MIRIAM *at the window; he is a man in his mid-twenties, with sharp, quick-witted eyes.*

The two of them watch as their father grabs the other end of one of the cables, holding it taut between him and the two MEN.

MIRIAM. I don't understand why it doesn't begin tomorrow – it's New Year's Eve 1899! That must be the end of the century, how can it not be?

PAUL. Because they say you're not one year old till your first birthday, so the century is not 100 till next year.

MIRIAM. That's stupid.

PAUL. Nearly every country, every town, has decided to celebrate next year.

MIRIAM (*staring at her father tugging on the cable*). Except Papa.

PAUL (*quiet*). Except Papa. (*To himself.*) So determined to be among the first.

Exterior: The Road – Day (Reisner House)

We cut back under the trees.

MR REISNER. I hate to disagree with you, gentlemen. (*Staring at the plump, hostile faces.*) But I am holding a party to celebrate *now*, this very day, and nothing will stop that, absolutely nothing.

FIRST MAN. And we have to enforce the wishes of the town, and this *isn't* your land.

MR REISNER. But it's my sign, and it is doing no harm, indeed you'll all agree, I'm sure, it's a rather wonderful sign.

Interior: Reisner House: Passage – Day

PAUL *and* MIRIAM *watching now, surrounded by four or five of the* SERVANTS.

PAUL (*to himself*). Papa, just leave it. You've made your point, please just leave it.

Exterior: Road – Day (Reisner House)

We cut back under the sign, MR REISNER *standing guarding it, the* MEN *circling him.*

FIRST MAN. Why on earth are you celebrating New Year anyway? It's not your New Year! Your New Year is different, because of your religion, isn't that so?

MR REISNER. But I'm also a Scotsman, as you probably know – and no Scotsman has ever not celebrated New Year.

FIRST MAN. We're going to have another meeting about this – I warn you Mr Reisner.

MR REISNER *smiles warmly, feeling he's won.*

MR REISNER. Have a meeting by all means. Have twenty-five meetings.

The MEN *begin to move off.*

And then come to the party. You'll have a tremendous time, I can guarantee. I'll see you all there, gentlemen. (*Calling after the* MEN.) You do have all your invitations, do you? Good. Till tonight.

We cut to the sign glowing into life, just as the light is falling, its orange and pink bulbs flickering on: WELCOME TO THE 20TH CENTURY.

End of credit sequence.

Interior: Reisner House: Reception Room – Night

The main reception room of the Reisner house, completely covered with Christmas and New Year decorations and lit by candlelight.

The Reisner family standing in a group: MR REISNER *and the children,* PAUL *and* MIRIAM, *all very formally dressed.*

The SERVANTS *are standing in another group a little apart.*

And then we see the mass of empty chairs they are looking at: the room is completely empty of guests, except TWO YOUNG GIRLS *sitting in a corner and giggling to themselves.*

THREE MUSICIANS *are playing grating party music in a desultory fashion in a far part of the room.*

A shot outside of the sign glowing, among the trees, visible from miles away, dominating the scene.

We cut back inside the drawing-room, the empty chairs, the GIRLS giggling, the MUSICIANS' embarrassed glances over their shoulders, the faces of the children, very strained.

MR REISNER (*defiant, lifting his glass*). A little too early – a little too early to welcome everybody, but there is still a quarter of an hour to go to midnight.

There is a loud crunching noise of something being knocked over in the hall, then a further sound of breaking. They all stare at the door.

A FAT LADY in a strange mauve dress and enormous hat appears, using two sticks to walk on. She stops in the doorway and growls in an earthy voice.

FAT LADY. So where's the party then?

PAUL (*whispers to his father*). Who the hell is she?

MR REISNER. I have no idea – I don't think she can have been invited.

Interior: Reisner House: Passage – Night

Cut to PAUL and MIRIAM by a window, and the sign glowing out from the trees through the window.

MIRIAM (*running her finger down the window*). I'm still excited – it's still a great night, despite everything. A great, great night.

PAUL. Despite this appalling town.

MIRIAM (*touching PAUL's face*). It's all very well for you, I'm going to miss you terribly. (*She kisses him on the nose.*) You don't deserve to be missed as much as I'm going to miss you.

PAUL (*smiles*). Rubbish, you won't notice I'm gone . . .

MIRIAM. Going to London, oh, Paul, if only I could come.

PAUL. You *will* come, I'll make sure.

MIRIAM (*staring at the sign, then at him*). If some people think this is the end of the century and some don't, maybe this next year doesn't really exist. It's a sort of island all on it's own. (*She laughs.*) We can do anything we like!

Interior: Reisner House: Drawing-room – Night

We cut back to the main room. The family and the tiny splattering of guests are standing, poised, as the last chimes of midnight ring out, then there is applause and 'Happy New Year's.

MR REISNER (*steps forward*). The toast, welcome to 1900, a New Year, a new century . . . (*Staring at the empty chairs.*) . . . and a new start in our little town.

PAUL (*under breath*). No speech, Papa.

MR REISNER. And a celebration too of my son Paul, my doctor son, going off to work with the new pioneering medical research Institute, soon to be world-famous I hope. The Whitelion Institute.

PAUL (*correcting*). Whiteweather, Papa.

MR REISNER. Yes, I knew it had a funny name, like a public house. And he's going to study enokinkology.

PAUL. Endocrinology, *glands*, Papa.

MR REISNER. Study all our glands, yes. And by God we're going to give him a big send-off, especially after tonight, a carriage with six horses –

PAUL (*muttering*). Not six, Papa.

Cut to shot of MIRIAM *kissing the younger* SERVANTS *Happy New Year and then her father.*

MR REISNER. I'm not sure you should kiss the servants, Miriam, even on New Year.

MIRIAM. Don't be silly, Papa, and don't worry. Forget about the idiots that live in this town. You look magnificent, like a member of the House of Lords.

The OLD WOMAN *is wolfing a lot of food, moving quite easily now without her sticks.*

MR REISNER. She seems to manage without her sticks when she wants to eat! But she came after all, so whoever she is –

We cut to a shot of MR REISNER *dancing with the* FAT LADY, *who is still wearing her huge hat.*

They swing round the room in a stately dance as the SERVANTS *smile and clap.*

Exterior: The Road – Day (Reisner House)

The great sign lying in the grass covered in crawling CHILDREN, *stepping on the words 'Welcome', '20th Century', little pudgy hands exploring the electric bulbs.*

Interior: Reisner House: Sitting-room – Day

The sitting-room absolutely caked in mess, the food and decorations squashed everywhere.

MIRIAM *is lying spread-eagled on the sofa, her dress all ruffled. Bright sunlight on her face, she opens her eyes, turns her head and lazily scoops up some cream from a nearby bowl.*

MIRIAM. Welcome anyway, even if you aren't a new century. (*She stares at the sunlight everywhere and licks her fingers.*) Whatever you are, you certainly taste good.

PAUL *is lying nearby curled asleep in a chair. He opens his eyes dreamily to see through the hall: the front door is opened by a* SERVANT *and a large horse-drawn van marked* NATIONAL TELEPHONE COMPANY *pulls up to the front.*

MIRIAM (*following his stare*). Papa has bought a telephone.

PAUL. So I see.

MIRIAM. He means to begin this year in style.

Close-up of PAUL *suddenly staring closely at the van.*

Exterior: The Road – Day (Reisner House)

Cut to the whole family (except MR REISNER), *and the* SERVANTS *standing on the steps to see* PAUL *off.*

They are staring at the huge telephone van, with PAUL *standing beside it, waiting impatiently.*

PAUL (*exasperated*). Where is Papa?

MIRIAM. He's using the telephone apparently, talking to the local newspaper.

We see MR REISNER *in the shadows of the hall in full flood on the telphone.*

They wanted to hear about his sign and his party.

MR REISNER (*emerging on to the steps*). That's put that quite straight. The record is straight, it's the last we'll ever hear about not being able to hang signs where we want to.

PAUL (*embarrassed*). Yes, Papa, but we've been waiting for . . .

MR REISNER. I don't know why you want to sneak out of town like this, it's absolutely wrong.

PAUL. I'm not *sneaking* out. It's best this way. (*Facing up to him.*) You wanted to hold your party and I want to leave as simply as possible. So goodbye, Papa.

MR REISNER. It's not what I had planned for you. I've already booked the six horses. Look at this ridiculous vehicle.

PAUL *is squeezing through the small door which has a grid in it, at the back of the van.*

PAUL. It's absolutely fine. There's plenty of room. (*He is squashed inside, with his luggage and all the telephones around him. He hits the roof of the van with two sharp taps as if he was in a hansom cab.*) I'm ready, driver, drive on.

We cut to PAUL's *P.O.V. as the telephone van moves off, but incredibly slowly.*

The SERVANTS *begin to wave goodbye, and* MIRIAM.

PAUL's *father's face appears at the grid, large and forbidding.*

MR REISNER. I'll walk a little way with you.

PAUL (*under his breath to the van*). Can't you go any faster.

Wide shot of the telephone van going slowly down the street with the big figure of MR REISNER *right up to it, talking expansively to the metal grid in the door of the van.*

MR REISNER. Remember you can ring me whenever you want.

PAUL (*crouched among the telephones*). Yes, Papa.

MR REISNER (*easily keeping step with the van*). I am not going to give you advice, because you can look after yourself. But this professor, whatever he is, *Mandry*, do what he says, because he's in the forefront of his field.

PAUL. Absolutely. (*He catches glimpses of the town through the grid, and a board on a condemned building saying* REISNER BUILDING CONTRACTORS.)

MR REISNER. And remember if you go out at night be armed, with at least a sword stick.

PAUL. I'm only going to London, Papa!

MR REISNER. No, no, there are at least four murders a night, keep a sharp stone in your pockets, those are recommended, you can lash out with that any time if you're attacked on the streets.

PAUL (*smiles*). Don't worry, I'll keep an eye out.

MR REISNER *catches sight of* TWO MEN *from the New Year's Eve group standing in the early-morning street.*

MR REISNER. Glad you could come to the party!

The MEN *stare at him.*

You missed something special!

PAUL. Ssh, they are not worth it. (*He looks around him.*)

MR REISNER (*right up to the grid*). I am not going to say don't let me down, because I know that is impossible, quite impossible so I will just say . . .

The van suddenly picks up speed. Receding shot of MR REISNER *through the grid, getting small and smaller, as he stands in the middle of the road, being enveloped in dust.*

I will only say – be the best – (*Shouting.*) – and why shouldn't you be? (*Shouting through the dust.*) The absolute best. (*Calling.*) And of course you will be a success!

PAUL (*watching him get smaller*). Oh, Papa.

Interior: The Van – Day (Countryside)

We cut inside the van as it bumps along, full of jingling telephones, PAUL nestling back among them, looking at the different species of telephone, weird shapes and sizes and strange instruction-panels.

Then a wide shot of the van passing a solitary building in the middle of the country, like an old deserted mill; the walls of the building are covered in large advertisements for various household items, including the National Telephone Company. The horse-drawn van is dwarfed by the large, peeling notices, with the green hills stretching behind.

Interior: The Van – Day (The City)

Cut back inside, PAUL asleep slumped against the ornamental telephones.

Suddenly violent noise, sounds from outside.

Exterior: City Streets – Day (PAUL's P.O.V.)

We see from his P.O.V. a strange YOUNG MAN's face looking through the grid, running with the van and making faces through the grid, then a YOUNG GIRL pushing, moving close, looking down at PAUL.

He presses his nose against the grid, and sees a group of SLUM CHILDREN running after the van, banging on the grid, and then smoke and WORKMEN's faces glistening with sweat.

All the time a deafening noise of shouting and road noises.

Exterior: The Square – Day

We cut to a wide shot of a large, imposing Victorian building seen across a square, with some roadworks going on in one corner, sending dust and smoke blowing across.

The van has slipped into view on the other side of the square from the building.

PAUL *squeezes with difficulty out of the back door of the vehicle, and stares across the wide expanse of the square to the building.*

DRIVER (*looking across at the building*). Is that it? What is it? A hospital?

PAUL (*patiently*). No, no, it's a new institute, which has moved in here; there are no patients, only doctors and volunteers.

DRIVER. Volunteers! Really! (*Glancing at building.*) Well, let me know if they need a telephone . . .

Exterior: The Institute: Front Door – Day

PAUL *rings the bell, by a great door.*

A YOUNG BOY opens the door and PAUL passes into a beautiful hallway, full of imposing pictures and fresh flowers everywhere.

Interior: Institute: Hall – Day

The hall is half in darkness, with corners illuminated by the afternoon sun.

Facing him across the hall is a woman with heavy jewellery, sitting behind a desk.

In one of the corners of the hall, sitting on a mahogany bench, is a MIDDLE-AGED WOMAN in a magnificent fur coat sitting waiting with a very sick-looking YOUNG GIRL next to her.

PAUL *approaches the desk. MRS PRITCHARD, the woman, who is writing on small pink pieces of paper, does not look up. Her heavy jewellery clanks in the silent hall.*

PAUL (*coughs*). I'm Doctor Reisner.

No reaction.

I have come . . .

MRS PRITCHARD (*not looking up*). You are early. You are not meant to be here till tomorrow.

PAUL. I apologise. (*Instinctively sliding into a slightly posher accent.*) My transport arrangements . . . there was a sudden change. (*He smiles embarrassed.*) And I seem to be . . . here.

MRS PRITCHARD *does not look up.*

Can I see my room?

MRS PRITCHARD *looks up sharply.*

Interior: Institute: Passage – Day

They move through glass doors on the first floor, from a landing full of flowers and portraits to a ruined passage, shabby walls, covered with a little graffiti, and ivy and weeds growing through the window. The contrast is dramatic.

PAUL *stares at the passage, very startled.*

A woman, CLARA, of about thirty takes two of his bags.

PAUL *is so surprised by his surroundings, he hardly acknowledges her presence.*

They pass further ruined rooms, with rubbish piled up in them.

CLARA *walks in front of him, carrying the two heavy bags, seemingly effortlessly.*

MRS PRITCHARD's *jewellery clanging, humming to herself unconcerned.*

Interior: Institute: Dormitory – Day

At the end of the passage is a large room containing seven beds; one of these is in a little room of its own, partitioned off, with a muslin curtain in its doorway. The other beds are arranged as a dormitory.

PAUL *is truly taken aback.*

PAUL. I think there must be some mistake . . . a mistake here. I am *Doctor* Reisner. I am not . . .

MRS PRITCHARD (*very sharp*). Not what?

PAUL (*embarrassed*). Not a volunteer or . . . (*He stops.*)

MRS PRITCHARD. We had realised you were not a volunteer, believe it or not. You are Doctor Reisner, and *this* is Doctor Reisner's bed, and these are all the other little doctors' beds.

CLARA *is taking off the counterpane and smoothing the pillows, her hands moving across the sheets.*

PAUL *watching this.*

During the following exchange, CLARA idly plucks a piece of ivy which is growing round the window-pane and drops it on to the pillow, as she straightens the bed.

PAUL. For some reason I was expecting a room of my own. (*Self-mocking smile.*) I don't know how I got that idea, very eccentric of me.

MRS PRITCHARD. Yes, it was. (*Sharp.*) Now there's nothing useful you can do here – Clara will unpack. You will find the others across the street, you can talk about your bed to them if you like.

Interior: Coffee-house – Day

PAUL *pushes open the door into the coffee-house; tawny late-afternoon light.*

A resplendent group of five young men in magnificent formal clothes are sitting round a bar at the end of the coffee-shop: FELIX, EDWIN, THOMAS, THEO and MEREDITH. They are in dark suits with stiff, high collars, and some have added a touch of dandyism – rich silk scarves and canes with sculptured heads of lions and tigers.

PAUL *advances on them warily; they are a formidable-looking group.*

PAUL. Good afternoon, my name's Reisner, Doctor Reisner.

Amused smile from a couple of them.

Are you doctors? You're not doctors? Sorry, I'm looking for the doctors from the Whiteweather Institute.

There is a group of YOUTHS *in working clothes sitting in a far corner in a haze of smoke;* PAUL *half turns towards them instead.*

FELIX (*charming smile*). No, no, *we're* the doctors.

EDWIN (*holds out his hand*). Bacteriology.

THEO (*introducing himself*). Cardiology.

PAUL (*introducing himself back*). Endocrinology.

PAUL *looks at* FELIX, *who hasn't introduced himself.*

FELIX *has a long, thin face, very pale, but blazingly bright eyes, and constantly flapping hands.*

FELIX. Endocrinology.

PAUL. Oh, good, you too . . .

FELIX (*casually*). Yes, Endocrinology, Bacteriology, Cardiology, and a little rheumatic fever thrown in as well.

Their eyes meet.

He doesn't believe me.

PAUL (*smiles*). Not yet, no.

FELIX (*shaking his hand*). I'm Felix Russell. (*Pleasantly looking down at* PAUL's *arm.*) Don't worry, we'll get you some clothes. (*Examing* PAUL's *clothes.*) Because you're absolutely naked like that, aren't you?

Exterior: Street – Evening

FELIX *and* PAUL *moving past a wall with advertisements for different forms of food, shoes, and a display of magic in St George's Square.*

Dying light, smoke drifting from the roadworks, sense of excitement as PAUL *moves with* FELIX.

FELIX (*talking dramatically*). *He* makes us dress like this, the *Mandry*, the professor, and it's sensible too. You know how research is regarded – I don't know what they think of it where you come from. (*Pointed smile.*) Wherever that might be – but here in London it's regarded as the lowest form of life (*Mimics.*) because 'medicine's an art', you see, not a sordid science where people work in *laboratories*, with machines'. (*Mimicking astonishment.*) *Machines.* (*Mimicking.*) 'That's so vulgar!'

PAUL. So if we look magnificent it helps.

FELIX. It's a necessity.

PAUL (*sharp smile, watching* FELIX *striding along*). Quite an enjoyable necessity.

Interior: Institute: Passageway and Rooms – Evening

Cut to FELIX *and* PAUL *passing from the flower-strewn beautiful landing down a second shabby passage towards the laboratories.*

Just before they leave the landing FELIX *looks at* MRS PRITCHARD *below them in the hall, writing on pink paper, never looking up.*

FELIX. She never looks up on purpose – that way she makes sure she doesn't see things she wouldn't approve of. (*He smiles knowingly at* PAUL.)

They move down the ruined passage.

We can't afford to use most of the building yet . . . one day it will be full! And we'll be able to cure everything!

PAUL. But why does he let it look like this – if *Mandry* cares so much about how we dress?

FELIX. Because nobody from outside sees these passages and because he spends the money . . . where it *really matters*. Brilliantly.

Interior: Institute FELIX's *Laboratory – Evening*

FELIX *on saying this bangs through a door into a room which is very sparsely furnished, but contains gleaming microscopes and other equipment.*

PAUL *moves among the gleaming equipment, touching it with wonder, almost sensually, spellbound by it.*

FELIX (*watching PAUL's excitement, pleasantly*). It's the best train set anybody ever had to play with!

PAUL *smiles.*

(*Pronouncing his name thoughtfully.*) Reisner . . . are you Jewish? It makes no difference to me, I just wanted to know.

PAUL. Yes, I am. (*Looking round.*) Who's laboratory is this?

FELIX. Mine, of course. That's yours over there. (*He indicates a small, cell-like room through an adjoining door, completely bare except for one microscope.*)

PAUL *looks at it in dismay.*

Nobody knows how good you are. So you get the smallest.

PAUL (*glancing at FELIX's room, smiles*). Things can always change I assume.

FELIX. Of course. (*Charming smile.*) But to get me out of my lab won't be easy, Reisner, not easy at all! Or anybody else for that matter.

PAUL (*grinning*). I don't expect it will.

Interior: Institute: Dormitory – Night

We cut to a model of a strange machine the size of a toy, by FELIX's bed.

FELIX. It's an electrical chair that turns into a horseless carriage. You can join up with your friends, each in a chair, and ride six-a-breast down the street!

PAUL *picks up the toy.*

I collect them. Everybody's selling them this year, models of machines of the future . . .

PAUL *is lying in bed, trying to keep warm. All around him the others are getting ready for bed, MEREDITH staring at his rather beautiful face in a mirror.*

EDWIN *putting on stylish pyjamas. They seem very confident, and at ease despite the extreme cold.*

FELIX *is sitting up in bed next to PAUL, working on a mass of papers.*

PAUL *staring at the partitioned room near the stove.*

Only the keenest sleep on the premises.

PAUL. Or those that have to . . . Who gets the little room?

FELIX (*casually*). We all do, once a week. *You* have to wait a little longer though.

THEO *enters busily at that moment with a young working-class GIRL, muffled up against the cold.*

THEO *and the GIRL move across the dormitory to the partitioned room, ignored by everybody but PAUL. He stares fascinated as he sees THEO and the GIRL embrace behind the curtain that covers the door.*

The GIRL chatters lightly as THEO begins to undress. The GIRL begins to undress, and plays with the curtain. PAUL can't stop himself watching.

GIRL. It ain't very private in here, is it! Oh, well, you're all doctors. You all know what a lady looks like, at least I hope you do! This gentleman I went to visit, he was an officer. Maybe I shouldn't say that. Anyway, he had a few rude things to say about doctors – but then two of his brothers died last year.

PAUL *blows out the candle next to his bed. We cut to him lying in bed watching the partition transfixed, where THEO is making love to the GIRL, their entwined bodies glimpsed through the wafting curtain.*

Next to PAUL, FELIX is still sitting up working on his papers, completely oblivious, disregarding a routine event.

PAUL *stares back at the figures behind the curtain. He can't stop himself moving to get a better look and then we see the GIRL's eyes catching a glimpse of him watching in the small mirror on the wall in front of her.*

The GIRL smiles at PAUL in a carefree, abandoned way, totally unbothered.

Interior: Institute: Dormitory – Morning

Morning light on his face, PAUL's eyes spring open. Shot of the window with the ivy, and just glimmers of light, first signs of dawn. PAUL's head twists round in surprise.

Sitting at the end of his bed is the tall, imposing figure of MANDRY. He is an elegantly authoritative figure, but with boyish charm, sudden, surprising informality.

He is sitting at the corner of the bed, as if he's been waiting for a moment for PAUL to wake. The others are still curled up, slumbering.

MANDRY. Welcome to the Institute.

PAUL (*startled, sitting bolt upright in bed*). It's an honour, sir, I didn't realise you were there, I . . .

MANDRY (*pleasantly*). Don't be silly, it's not an honour to be woken at this hour. I just wanted to catch you before you begun your first day. We start early here.

PAUL. Of course, sir. Normally I wake pretty early too. I have a very good body clock, it fails very rarely.

PAUL's eye is caught by the GIRL in the cubicle lazily getting out of bed naked, standing by the window, slowly beginning to pull on some clothes, very casually.

PAUL's eyes flash back to MANDRY, who is sitting with his back to the GIRL.

MANDRY. There is only one thing you have to realise about being here . . . You are *free*. There is no daily supervision, no firm structure, you follow your instincts. (*Sharp smile.*) If you have any. *You* decide how to spend your time and I judge the results – (*Charming smile.*) – which may happen at any time, I warn you. I remember your interview . . . Endocrinology, much to find out there. (*He smiles.*) You are all explorers, are you not . . . venturing into the unknown. What could be better? No need to wish you good luck. (*Pleasantly.*) Of course you are here on a temporary basis only, until I decide otherwise.

Close-up of PAUL. He looks very surprised at this.

MANDRY *moves off the bed; the* GIRL *is by the window.* PAUL *cannot tell if* MANDRY *has seen her or not as he sweeps out.*

Interior: Institute: Hall – Day

The group – THEO, EDWIN, THOMAS, MEREDITH, FELIX – *are spread out at one end of the hall in their splendid formal clothes, poised, waiting.* PAUL *stands slightly upright in his plainer clothes.*

A tall BLACK BOY *of about twenty-one comes up to him.*

EDWIN (*introduces him to* PAUL). This is your laboratory assistant, James.

PAUL *is startled, and shows it for a second, before trying to cover it with a smile.*

Russell, me and you share him, he works for *all* of us, remember that.

JAMES (*stretching out his hand*). Is this your first day?

PAUL. Yes. (*He takes* JAMES's *hand with just a momentary hesitation.*)

EDWIN. Don't worry, he is surprisingly good at his job.

JAMES *flicks a sharp look at* EDWIN *and moves off with a smile.*

The great door opens and a group of about FIFTEEN VOLUNTEERS *file in. A strange collection, upper-middle-class and working-class people mixed together, bringing in with them a strong sense of the contrasts in the world outside. Some with disfigurements, a girl of sixteen with premature ageing looking startling and haunting, a woman with a thyroid problem, massively obese, and two very pale and anaemic-looking young men, staying close together. The* MOTHER, *in her fine clothes who we saw in the hall before, comes in with her diabetic daughter* CHRISTINA, *who looks very ill indeed.*

JAMES (*to* PAUL). They come here because nobody else can help them.

They all take their places on the mahogany benches as if they are used to the routine, and then call out to the doctors, 'I am here today, please can you use me, doctor', 'Doctor Russell, come to me', etc.

FELIX's *name is called a lot. They are all uninhibited about offering themselves to the doctors.*

In the series of images gathering in intensity, we see PAUL *going into action, moving among the* VOLUNTEERS, *selecting one, feeling the glands of the massive* OBESE WOMAN.

PAUL *quickly becomes conscious that whatever he does, wherever he moves, he is being watched, evaluated.*

MRS PRITCHARD *watching him out of the corner of her eye and making a secret note.*

THEO *and* MEREDITH *watching him sideways, even the* YOUNG BOY *that opened the door to him seems to be judging his performance.*

There are faces everywhere.

PAUL (*glancing at* JAMES, *who is watching him*). Are you marking me as well? (*He smiles.*) My God, this is like some gigantic exam!

Exterior: Back of the Institute – Day

Cut to PAUL *moving, with his clothes already messy, past the hedge at the rear of the Institute. We see the building backs on to a public park.*

PAUL *catches fleeting glimpses of* WOMEN *in fine clothes promenading together, laughing together, as he passes the hedge. A sense of the outer world being very close.*

PAUL *running down some stone steps.*

Interior: Institute: Basement – Day

PAUL *passes into a dark subterranean world, with young women laboratory 'assistants' working in cramped and badly lit conditions. There are lines of cages disappearing into the shadows, with rats, dogs and monkeys in them.*

We see some dead rats lying on a table, half cut up, with women mashing the black thyroid paste; we see clearly where it came from.

PAUL *moves past the pale women, who are talking together, laughing heartily.*

*He moves into a white tiled room where there are two large cages with
monkeys in them and a wall of glass bottles with various solutions in
them.*

CLARA *is standing against the white tiles in a pale red dress, cleaning
some bottles. She has a natural confidence, despite her surroundings.*

PAUL (*not noticing who it is*). I need some alkaline solution . . . and
some thyroid extract. And hurry please.

CLARA *moves to get it, opening a grim-looking jar.*

Oh, it's you – (*Very surprised.*) – I didn't realise you worked here.
I thought . . .

CLARA. I made the beds. I do make the beds three times a week.

PAUL. But you shouldn't, should you, do both?

CLARA (*spooning thyroid extract, a thick, ugly-looking paste, from a
large bottle to a smaller one*). Are you worried I'm a health risk,
sir? You want to make your own bed in future? (*She smiles.*) I
promise I won't object if that's what you want.

PAUL (*lightly*). I'll consider the offer and let you know. (*Pleasantly
but very firm.*) You do realise it can be very dangerous down here,
the risk of infection is extremely high; you must make sure you
keep everything as clean as possible. You understand? Including
yourself.

CLARA. Yes. (*Nods.*) Thank you, sir.

PAUL *moves off.*

I *did* wash myself thoroughly before I unpacked your luggage, sir.
So you shouldn't catch anything, you see. Not from me, anyway.

PAUL (*stops*). Good. (*Self-mocking.*) That's reassuring. (*He leaves.*)

CLARA (*under her breath*). And I have managed to survive a whole
year in this place, without your advice.

FIRST GIRL. Which is more than he will.

Interior: Institute: Passage – Day

FELIX *and* PAUL *working side by side*, FELIX *holding ornamental handkerchief to his mouth. They are examining a small boy who has a skin disease.*

PAUL *starts staring at* EDWIN, *who is treating a volunteer further down the passage, a boy of about fifteen.*

EDWIN. This is a pancreatic extract to treat the diabetes. I am going to inject it.

> *The boy looks nervous.*

> Don't worry, young man, look at the ceiling. This will stop you losing your sugar.

> PAUL *has been walking down the passage towards* EDWIN. *He reaches him just as* EDWIN *is about to inject the boy.*

PAUL. Are you mad? What do you think you are doing? You can't inject him with that!

> EDWIN *continues to prepare injection.*

> *We notice* CLARA *standing in the passage, watching* PAUL.

EDWIN. Excuse me – this is my volunteer, this is my treatment. You must *never* interfere with a colleague's work here. Do you *understand?*

> PAUL *knocks the syringe out of* EDWIN's *hand.*

PAUL. You can't do that – it can do him immense damage.

> EDWIN, *furious, makes a grab for* PAUL, *grapples with him, pushing him against the wall.* PAUL *has to fight him off.*

Interior: Institute: MANDRY's Study – Night

PAUL *facing* MANDRY *over a polished table*, MANDRY *stirring lemon tea in an ornamental glass.*

MANDRY (*casually stirring*). What on earth do you think you were doing, Reisner? Assaulting a colleague, that has never happened before.

PAUL (*watching the spoon go round and round*). He was giving the wrong treatment, sir, which could have been fatal in my view. The theory that you can inject *untreated* pancreatic extract is totally discredited.

MANDRY (*piercing look*). Discredited by whom?

PAUL. By . . . By . . . (*Thinking quickly.*) . . . all the authorities I respect.

MANDRY (*staring at him*). And that is your explanation?

PAUL (*hesitates*). Yes, sir.

MANDRY (*very sharp*). You've had an interesting first day, Reisner.

PAUL *begins to look very nervous.*

There is a knock on the door and MRS PRITCHARD's *face appears round the door.*

MRS PRITCHARD. There is a call on the telephone for this gentleman. (*She pronounces the word oddly.*)

PAUL. I won't take it now, thank you. Tell the party I'll telephone them later, please.

MANDRY. No. You might as well take it now. (*Sharply dismissive.*) I have nothing further to say to you.

Interior: Institute: Passage – Night (Intercut with Reisner house)

PAUL *grabbing the ornate telephone on the wall without waiting to hear who it is.*

PAUL (*really sharp*). Yes, Papa, what is it?

MR REISNER. How on earth did you know who it was?

PAUL. Who else could it have been? So what do you want?

MR REISNER. What do *I* want? What do you think. To know how you are getting on. How does that place with the strange name seem?

MANDRY *appears.*

PAUL. This is not a good moment, Papa.

OPERATOR'S VOICE. You have been on the telephone for exactly one minute, one minute.

PAUL. Oh, shut up!

MR REISNER. I can't hear you.

PAUL (*shouting*). Everything's very good, wonderful in fact.

MANDRY listening before he sweeps on. PAUL incredibly embarrassed, wishing his father would stop asking questions.

MR REISNER (*loud*). Now give me some details, Paul, *details*.

MANDRY sweeps past PAUL without saying anything and disappears into the darkness of the hall.

PAUL. But this is just about the worst moment of the day. So I have to go. I have to go *now*!

PAUL rings off. He stares at the noticeboard in the passage by the telephone. Somebody has stuck up a notice saying just 'Reisner?' The question mark is huge – and stares back at him.

Interior: Reisner House: Reception Room – Night

We cut to MR REISNER replacing the receiver, sitting across a table in the window of the sitting-room. MIRIAM opposite him.

REISNER. He's very well. Everything is splendid. And you see even the telephone works over the long distance.

MIRIAM. Yes, Papa. I wish one didn't have to shout so much when one uses it.

MIRIAM and MR REISNER both glance out of the window.

Over by the trees, where the sign was, opposite the house, two of the MEN are standing talking, giving surly looks towards the house.

REISNER gives them an uninhibited wave. Calling through the window:

MR REISNER. No hard feelings about the sign, I hope. (*Indicating himself.*) There are none here anyway! Absolutely normal relations can be resumed I'm sure. I will be attending all Council meetings again from next Tuesday onwards.

The MEN *stare back at him.*

See you all then! (*Smiles at* MIRIAM.) You see, it's all forgotten!
They can't think of a single thing to say.

Interior: Institute: Dormitory – Night

Cut to PAUL *lying in bed, tense.*

EDWIN *sitting up in bed, confidently smoking.*

FELIX *is in the cubicle with another working-class girl, who's talking
lightly in the background.*

FELIX, *holding a fistful of papers, shuts the curtain. He grins at*
PAUL *as he does so.*

THEO (*to* PAUL). Don't worry, you don't get to use that place for
several weeks.

MEREDITH. Will he still be here by then?

THOMAS. Rumour has it he will not . . .

    PAUL *watches* FELIX *as his arms go round the girl and he gives her
a gentle kiss.*

    PAUL *glances sideways at the picture of his family on his bedside
table. He looks very worried.*

Interior: Institute: Laboratories and Passage – Day

We cut to PAUL, *trying to look confident, walking up to the door of his
laboratory. He turns the handle; it is locked. He looks round in alarm.
He tries it again. It won't open.*

JAMES's *head appears round a doorway further up the passage.*

JAMES. Come here . . . (*Louder.*) Come on, come here.

Interior/Exterior: Institute: Room – Day (Courtyard)

We cut to PAUL *and* JAMES *standing by the window overlooking the
courtyard.*

EDWIN *is marooned in the middle of the courtyard, with all his luggage piled up, waiting for transport.*

PAUL. Poor Edwin.

JAMES *smiles cynically.*

PAUL. No, I mean it.

JAMES. Why? He was no good – so now he's gone. That's the way it works here. (*He gives* PAUL *a friendly smile.*) I ought to mention, sir, in case you didn't know, you *are still* on trial, so to speak.

FELIX *comes through the door, exuberant smile.*

FELIX. You're going to be after *me* next!

Exterior: Institute: Terrace – Day

We cut to FELIX *and* PAUL *moving down the passage and out on to the terrace, really animated, laughing together.*

FELIX. It's going to be exciting between you and me, Reisner . . . You're so ambitious!

PAUL (*laughing*). Of course! This is an amazing place to be, Felix. (*Seeing women in park and lab equipment on terrace.*) But I'm not at all sure I'm safe yet.

FELIX. You're not!

They see MANDRY *passing along the path below them, walking with two fine women wearing huge hats.*

MANDRY *looks back at* PAUL *over his shoulder, giving him just a hint of a smile of acknowledgement.*

PAUL. Did he smile at me?

FELIX (*teasingly*). No, you imagined it.

We stay on MANDRY, *as* PAUL *watches him on the path below. A young woman turns her head, glancing back at* PAUL. *He stares back at this world, coveting it. Excited look in his eyes.*

Interior: Institute: Dormitory – Day

PAUL *is in front of a mirror, pulling on some fine clothes, like the others wear, except his are just a tiny bit more flamboyant.*

Interior: Institute: Passage – Day

Cut to PAUL *moving down passage in his fine clothes.* MANDRY *is coming towards him.*

PAUL *looks a little less confident than he did in front of the mirror.*

MANDRY (*passing without stopping*). Admirable, Reisner.

PAUL. Sir . . .

   MANDRY *turns.*

   Can I just ask how I'm doing?

MANDRY. You can – but you won't get an answer today.

   PAUL *gulps.*

Interior: Institute: PAUL's *Laboratory – Day*

PAUL *and* JAMES *working together, their faces close, as they weigh some samples.*

PAUL (*whispers as* JAMES *is up close*). James – this is a very indelicate matter, but I am going to broach it all the same, while I'm still here. You know the room, the cubicle in the dormitory? . . . Well, it's my turn tonight.

JAMES. Yes, I was wondering when you'd ask about that –

PAUL (*looks back down microscope*). I was thinking, you might know a companion, a female who . . .

JAMES. It's funny, isn't it, everybody is talking about sex at the moment. You know last year there were two thousand pamphlets published on heterosexual activity, sexual habits among the different classes.

PAUL. That's very instructive, James, and no doubt I will be reading them, but they are not much use . . .

CLARA *is moving down the passage with a tray of glasses, which are tinkling. She passes the door without looking at them.*

JAMES. I *may* know someone, yes.

PAUL (*watching her receding figure in the dark, shabby passage. He ponders the prospect*). Maybe . . . So what do I do?

JAMES (*grinning*). You want me to do everything?

PAUL (*lightly*). Not everything, no, only the difficult part.

JAMES. You have to take her out. For at least a walk.

PAUL (*watching CLARA disappear, quiet, embarrassed*). Do I pay her? Will she expect that?

Interior: Institute: Passageway – Day (Intercut with Reisner House)

The group – FELIX, PAUL, THEO, THOMAS *and* MEREDITH *– moving towards the sunlight down a passage.*

CLARA *is bringing up the rear.*

A telephone rings just as they are about to pass out of the passage into the light.

THEO *answers the telephone.*

THEO. It's for you, Reisner.

PAUL (*taking it, warm smile*). Yes, Papa.

We intercut with MR REISNER talking on the telephone in his ornamental bathroom, sitting deep in a scented and soapy bath, and PAUL in the passage.

MR REISNER. You do it every time. You know it's me. It's uncanny.

PAUL (*affectionate smile*). Not that uncanny.

CLARA *has remained in the passage, leaning against the opposite wall, watching him.*

Noticeboard now says: 'Reisner???' The question marks are even bigger.

MR REISNER. So – have you got the job permanently yet?

PAUL. It's all in the balance at the moment.

MR REISNER. So things are not *that* wonderful. But Paul – you'll never guess where I am – I can work from the bath! Isn't that an astonishing piece of progress? I'm calling you from inside the bath.

PAUL (*lightly*). Yes, Papa. I can smell the soap. Don't get all your papers wet.

CLARA *leaning against the wall, in her independent way.*

PAUL *is unwittingly beginning to jingle coins in his pocket.*

MR REISNER. People actually visit the bathroom – just to look at the telephone! I promise you they do. We're entering a new age, my boy, do you realise? It completely changes your life.

PAUL. I realise – (*Genuinely warm.*) – Papa, it's wonderful to hear from you, but I have some urgent business to attend to.

CLARA *watching him.*

MR REISNER. Of course – (*Smiles.*) – I mustn't stand in the way of medical science. Goodbye, my son.

PAUL *replaces receiver.*

CLARA. You didn't have to hurry because of me . . . sir.

Cut back to MR REISNER *in the soapy bath, a few letters and papers around the bath.*

MR REISNER (*to himself*). Surprisingly little mail for this time of year. (*Lying back, contentedly.*) No doubt a temporary lapse. They are all going to do business on the telephone from now on . . . I'm sure that must be it.

Exterior: Park – Day

The group moving towards us. A sense of the young men erupting into the outside world.

FELIX *is setting a tremendous pace, his hands flapping.*

PAUL *watching* CLARA *closely.*

The atmosphere in the park is immediate, rather dangerous, and extremely sensual. A sharp glimpse of a society with few places for people to meet privately, so all over the park are couples, intimate, in love, flirting, or conducting agonising partings, hovering, close to sex, kissing and breaking apart, entwined together half masked by bushes. An erotic, vivid atmosphere, but with litter blowing along the paths, nannies hurrying children past couples in the grass. A sense of release too, people wearing new, daring clothes, drunken men coming straight towards the camera.

And some fine women promenading, heading towards us, glancing at the group of young men out of the corner of their eyes.

We see PAUL *staring at these women and then at* CLARA, *who's walking close to him. Should he make a move?*

We then cut to the group laughing together, moving deeper into the park, CLARA *just a few steps behind, watchful.*

FELIX. Here – see what they are after.

   He points through the bushes; three or four children move off, like animals surprised in a forest, scuttling away.

   FELIX *moves towards what the children were doing. Among the bushes is a compost heap covered with a whole range of litter, lots of old bottles of pills and patent medicines.*

   FELIX *watches the children emerge from the bushes; they run down one of the broad avenues of the park, towards what looks like a distant rubbish heap situated on scrub land.*

Those are children from the City of Rubbish, as I call it. People living rough.

PAUL *watches the children weave past two women in gorgeous coats, and run on towards the hill, which is clothed in dust. Glimpses of people living rough, like the edge of a shanty town.*

CLARA (*following his gaze*). I'll take you there one day if you like.

PAUL (*without enthusiasm*). Yes, why not?

We cut to the group spread out on a grass slope, overlooking a broad path in the park.

FELIX *spotting passers-by and merrily nominating illnesses they've got. (A long lens shot of the unsuspecting people.)*

PAUL *lies down next to* CLARA.

FELIX. Look at those. (*Pointing at three incredibly elegant women moving very slowly.*) The one on the left is in the middle of her period and having great difficulty with the towel.

PAUL. Felix, please. There is company present.

THEO *and* MEREDITH *exchange amused looks at* CLARA *being called this.*

CLARA. Thank you, Doctor Reisner, but I'm interested. (*At* FELIX.) Do you think they'll find an easier way of dealing with periods?

FELIX. It must happen. Ladies going out now, during their periods, it's an incredibly perilous business making sure nobody sees anything. Somebody must come up with a better sanitary invention. It's just because nobody has applied themselves to it.

PAUL (*sharp*). Is that what you're working on then, Felix, your private schemes?

FELIX. No, certainly not. Not yet. (*He secretively pushes papers deep into his pocket.*) Who said I was working on anything, anyway.

Combative smile.

You can't know *everything*, Reisner.

The others in the group continue spotting things on the path below them, as the world brushes past, and they stare at it with a mixture of excitement and slight superiority. They good-naturedly try to name

*people's ethnic backgrounds: 'Look, that face, Spanish extraction',
etc. 'A Jewish face' somebody else calls out.*

PAUL *moves close to* CLARA; *she shifts away.*

THEO (*spotting* MANDRY *in park, calls out*). A leading figure in
medical science who had already done brilliant work by the time
he was our age.

THOMAS. Rumour has it he is about to make some more changes.

Below them, on the path, MANDRY *is moving with two women,
laughing and talking with them.*

PAUL *watches* MANDRY, *fascinated as he moves past them.*

Then a close-up of MANDRY, *as he glances at his boys sprawled
together on the hill.*

PAUL (*looking down at* CLARA, *straight into her eyes as she's
stretched out on the grass*). This evening, are you busy this evening?

CLARA. Busy? No. Not particularly, sir.

PAUL (*sounding rather casual*). Can we . . . Can we meet, do you
think?

CLARA (*her eyes narrow*). You mean meet – or *meet.*

PAUL (*deeply embarrassed*) I thought we would just meet.

CLARA. Meet, where?

PAUL. If you didn't go home after work, I could take you for a
meal and . . .

CLARA. And what? (*Sharp.*) Suddenly not worried about infection
any more?

The others are listening now.

MEREDITH (*calls out*). Go on, Clara . . .

THOMAS (*murmuring to himself*). A lady of experience . . .

PAUL. I do just mean for a meal. We could have a feast and . . .

CLARA. And then I'd be booked for the little cubicle, would I?
(*Looks at him.*) You know it may seem strange and old fashioned,

but I think I prefer meals I don't have to pay for. (*She drops some grass casually on to* PAUL's *face*.)

Interior: Institute: Hall – Day

Various quack medicines hit the floor: vividly coloured pills, potions, strange gold powders. PAUL *is pulling them out of a capacious bag of one of the volunteers and throwing them away.*

PAUL. We don't need any of this . . . wild animal extract . . . no, no, no, this is quackery.

Volunteers calling out: 'Doctor Reisner, Doctor Reisner, work with me, *please use me* . . .

A shot of MRS PRITCHARD *and* MANDRY *watching* PAUL *closely.*

Interior: Institute: Basement – Day

PAUL *coming down steps into the dark subterranean world where the girls work. He looks rather grand now in these surroundings.*

PAUL (*handing one of the girls a glass jar*). We need some more of this please, and quickly.

CLARA *is there, mashing more thyroid, the dissected bodies of animals lying in the shadows.*

(*Warmly.*) If you're going to wear gloves to do that work, it is advisable for them not to have holes.

CLARA's *eyes narrow.*

JAMES (*appearing behind* PAUL, *urgently*). Sir, sir! You're *late* for your appointment, the widow, the Patroness. Don't you remember?

PAUL *startled, hesitates.*

She really *matters*, she has enormous power over what happens to people here.

PAUL. Oh, my God. (*He spins round in the basement, looking at his watch.*)

CLARA (*beadily*). The quickest way out is that way. (*Points into the darkness.*) It's a short cut, I promise. Go on, go on, it's by far the best way out.

PAUL *runs down the dark, low passage.*

He soon finds himself battling through stacks of old bottles covered in cobwebs, skeletons of animals, specimens in jars; his notebook is knocked out of his hands and falls into the grime. Past decaying files, old urine and blood samples, skulls sitting on shelves, dust everywhere, quickly covering his clothes. He curses CLARA *as he fights his way through the clutter.*

Exterior: Back of the Institute – Day

PAUL *emerges out of the darkness, up some stone steps, into the blinding light of the square.*

Exterior: London Streets – Day

A dark-haired, poorly dressed girl, KATIE, *of about sixteen, standing with a group of poor children, watches* PAUL *pass.*

PAUL *rushes past. He has to cross the roadworks, deafening noise, smoke and dust getting into his eyes.*

Interior: Cake Shop and Tearoom – Day

Cut to PAUL *approaching twelve or fifteen women in heavy dresses and massive hats sitting at little tables surrounded by oozing cakes, the cakes piled high in the window and along shelves. A long incredibly ripe interior, the tearooms dripping with affluence as well as cakes.*

There is a hushed atmosphere as PAUL *moves towards the ladies, because in the background a* BALD MAN *is addressing them, a teatime lecture on eugenics, as the ladies fill themselves with cake.*

One of the feathers on a lady's hat regularly spikes the cream cake on the shelf above her head. A rich, succulent atmosphere.

The man's speech runs on in the background through the scene.

BALD MAN. As we have found recently with the quality of recruits for the war now sadly going on in Africa, people are *unfit*

. . . physical deterioration in the breeding stock . . . We are addressing this question with what we call the science of 'Eugenics'.

PAUL *sits opposite* MRS WHITEWEATHER, *an old lady determined to look much younger, with a very refined voice, spooning in apricot cake.*

MRS WHITEWEATHER *has a small lap-dog with her and is feeding it little pieces of cake.*

PAUL, *who is famished and is eyeing the dripping cakes, is oblivious to the lecture. His manner very confident and unembarrassed as he brushes the remaining cobwebs off his coat.*

PAUL. My deepest apologies.

MRS WHITEWEATHER (*hard smile*). Are they all as young as you?

PAUL. I am not *that* young.

PAUL'*s eye is caught not just by all the cream cakes but also by a plain woman sitting in an extraordinarily lovely dress. He looks at the dress.*

MRS WHITEWEATHER. My husband imagined, I'm fairly sure, men in beards.

PAUL. Excuse me?

MRS WHITEWEATHER. When he left the money to fund the Institute, he meant there to be distinguished professors, like in Germany, with beards – and instead there's *one* professor and a lot of little boys.

PAUL. It's a new science, a whole new field, so –

MRS WHITEWEATHER (*sharp*). A 'science', is that what it is?

The BALD MAN'*s speech running on.*

The dripping cakes all around, the ladies sinking their teeth into the cakes.

BALD MAN (*running on in background*). The decline of the Empire and the decline of the breeding stock inextricably linked . . . The chance to take the principle from agriculture where a race of improved plants can be bred . . . Can the desirable multiply and the inferior be decreased? Can we improve the human breeding stock, improve their genes, produce *better* people? . . . How to achieve the BEST BREEDING COUPLES . . . human poverty still a desperate situation . . . People breeding who cannot support themselves . . . A cycle of poverty and it is infectious. Even in America they are asking these questions.

MRS WHITEWEATHER (*leans forward during the speech and whispers loudly at* PAUL). I hope they are keeping to the rules at the Institute . . . the animals are not mistreated, I hope.

PAUL. Absolutely not. (*He stares at the cakes, starving.*)

MRS WHITEWEATHER. Rats are not a problem . . . You can do anything you like to rats, boil them alive if you want – but not higher animals, no monkeys or dogs – (*Strokes the dog.*) – or rabbits – the highest beasts. There shouldn't be any on the premises.

PAUL (*lying convincingly*). There are no higher beasts there, I promise you.

PAUL *and* MRS WHITEWEATHER's *eyes meet.*

MRS WHITEWEATHER. Good.

The BALD MAN's *speech running on:*

BALD MAN. Hunger and famine . . . statistics to prove . . . Can we use our knowledge, can a scientific approach be brought to bear, ladies – not just for the mentally ill, and hereditary diseases . . . but plan for the whole population? etc.

MRS WHITEWEATHER. I hear you are the very best they have got. You and another boy, but you are even better than him.

PAUL (*startled*). You heard that? From whom?

MRS WHITEWEATHER. Don't pretend you didn't know . . . the very best.

PAUL. I . . . I didn't know! (*Leaning forward, animated.*) It's wonderfully exciting, being part of an élite group, in the forefront, feeling you can discover anything. (*He can't stop himself*

*scooping up the last remaining piece of cream cake from her plate. He
smiles at MRS WHITEWEATHER.)*

MRS WHITEWEATHER. At least I think it was you. Reisner . . .
maybe I have got the wrong person.

Interior: Night: Institute: MANDRY's Study

*Cut to the faces of the group sitting around MANDRY in a circle, a
pool of light in an otherwise dark lecture theatre. They're drinking
brandy and smoking cigars, having an extra session after a meal.*

CLARA is moving round filling their coffee-cups.

They take no notice of her – except for PAUL.

MANDRY. I want some more predictions. I like predictions.

THEO. Cancer cured by . . . (*Stops.*)

MANDRY. Yes?

THEO. By nineteen . . . fifty-nine.

MANDRY (*sharp*). *All* forms of cancer?

FELIX (*dismissive*). No, no, it'll take much longer, another seventy
years at least.

THOMAS. Many viruses conquered . . . the familiar cold will be
defeated undoubtedly – (*Smiles impishly.*) – by August 1940.

FELIX (*bangs the table, really trying hard*). No, no, there will always
be more viruses, annihilate one – and another will appear.

*CLARA reaches PAUL; he watches her fill his coffee, the dark
coffee, her hair almost touching him.*

PAUL (*slight smile, whispers*). That was a very good short cut you
gave me.

CLARA. I thought you'd appreciate it, sir. (*She moves away into the
dark.*)

THEO. Diabetes. I'm not sure that will be solved, how to treat that, not in this century.

MANDRY (*laughs*). Which century are we in?

FELIX (*emphatically*). I disagree.

PAUL *watching* CLARA.

I think that will be one of the first to go.

MANDRY. Reisner, you're being very quiet? (*Stares at* PAUL.) Do you really think we can make people live longer, healthier lives, or will we always be degenerate?

For a moment PAUL *seems caught out. During his speech,* FELIX *waves his hands and makes faces, trying to put him off.*

PAUL (*calmly poised*). I think if we look back fifty years ago, it seems like a medical dark age. And it was. We knew nothing. Since then we have come further than anyone dreamed possible. And now with organised research for the first time, I think we are poised for the most extraordinary advance. We live in a civilised age, with a hugely successful economy. I think to get even close to what will happen we have to predict the wildest leaps of knowledge imaginable. And then double those. The expectation of life will increase over the next half-century to 130 years, maybe 150 . . . at least. I predict.

MANDRY (*watches* PAUL *closely*). You can all go except Paul.

FELIX *looks up in surprise.*

They leave PAUL *and* MANDRY *alone.*

MANDRY (*smoking, using an ivory cigarette holder*). Here. (*He passes the brandy bottle across the table.*) I approve of you, Reisner.

PAUL. Thank you, sir.

MANDRY. And from relatively humble origins, too, aren't you? (*Blows smoke.*) Scottish Jewish, originated from Romania?

PAUL (*blows smoke too*). That's correct.

MANDRY (*pleasant smile*). I think you may even have some flair. (*Warmly.*) Don't for heaven's sake get even more arrogant now than you are already.

PAUL (*having a drink*). What do I say to that? (*Glancing at* MANDRY.)

MANDRY (*boyish smile*). You can try answering me this.

PAUL *tenses.*

How would you like to come and work with me?

PAUL (*stunned*). With you, sir? (*Thrilled, suddenly loud.*) *Working with you!*

MANDRY (*amused, gently*). I assume that means yes . . .

Interior: Institute: Room by MANDRY's Office – Day

We cut to PAUL working in a large room, directly next to MANDRY's office. The same shabby walls as his other lab, but with three splendid chairs and a fine desk.

We see PAUL trying out the chairs.

Interior: Institute: MANDRY's Study – Day

We then see PAUL working closely with MANDRY. MANDRY's immaculate research notes spread all over the desk, exquisitely drawn diagrams, MANDRY amused at the extreme respect PAUL shows in handling the pages, like they are something holy.

Interior: Institute: Passageway by MANDRY's Study – Day

THEO *and* FELIX *pass in the passage seeing* MANDRY *and* PAUL *working so closely together.* THEO *looks jealous,* FELIX *just smiles.*

CLARA *is working in passage.* PAUL *reluctant to acknowledge her while working with the Proffessor.*

Exterior: Lake – Day

We then see PAUL fishing, with MANDRY, both of them in less formal clothes, PAUL echoing MANDRY's taste.

MANDRY *casting his fishing-line with a flourish,* PAUL *following him.*

MANDRY (*lightly*). You don't have to do everything exactly the way I do it, Paul.

PAUL. No, only the things I've never done before!

MANDRY (*glancing at PAUL, a moment of warmth between them*). My father used to take me fishing; he was a very mundane little shipping clerk.

PAUL *looks very surprised at this.*

It was the only thing we ever did together, those fishing trips. But he never spoke to me at all while we were there. He thought that *must* be how *proper* gentlemen fished! In total silence!

PAUL *smiles. We stay on his eyes as his voice-over starts.*

PAUL (VOICE-OVER). Dear Papa, we find ourselves immensely busy, with very little time for anything else . . .

Interior: Institute: Bedroom and Passages – Day

PAUL (VOICE-OVER). Especially time to get home.

We see PAUL lying in the new bedroom, in the summer heat, his shirt undone. The young men have taken over the other ruined rooms in the heat, and turned them into individual bedrooms. A sensual, uninhibited atmosphere. We see them half naked, larking around in the tiled passage, teasing a young chambermaid as she passes. PAUL has been given by far the biggest bedroom.

CLARA is stacking a pile of sheets at the end of the passage, PAUL watching her, her head bending. We hear his voice over images of CLARA.

PAUL (VOICE-OVER). I have been seeing a little of the daughter of a Russian Count, in the very few hours I've had off. She is quite beautiful, rich, tempestuous.

Exterior: Garden – Day (Reisner House)

We cut to MR REISNER reading the rest of the letter to MIRIAM while sitting on a child's swing in the garden.

MR REISNER. 'She has large feet and lives in an enormous house in Richmond.' (*He looks up.*) His handwriting gets worse! But his news gets better.

He waves at a next-door neighbour over the hedge, who promptly turns away and scuttles into his house.

We see MIRIAM minding.

(*To neighbour.*) You must have some fruit from the garden this year, Mr Willet. (*Calling after the disappearing figure, totally oblivious, not seeing WILLET's hostility.*) Come round and make your own selection. (*To MIRIAM.*) We'll make our own selection for him, woodland fruits – when he tastes those we'll never be able to get rid of him!

We stay on WILLET for a second and hear him muttering 'Nasty little Jew'.

MIRIAM (*hating the neighbours being so rude*). Just read the letter, Papa!

MR REISNER (*turning to the letter*). 'But the great news is . . .

Exterior: Edge of Park – Day

We cut to PAUL and MANDRY moving into the City of Rubbish. MANDRY's tall figure, striding ahead, an imposing sight.

PAUL (VOICE-OVER). The great news, the really first-class news, is my extraordinarily good relationship with Professor Mandry. It improves with every day. I think it's likely I will be judged top of the Institute, ahead even of my friend Felix. I am no longer just a pupil of the Professor, but a colleague, nearly a friend. I can say anything to him! He is a proud and a private man, and a great man, who takes an interest in all aspects of society. I am privileged to be with him.

They are crossing into the heart of the City of Rubbish.

Every week, he goes to work amongst the poor, and I'm allowed to accompany him.

We move with him through the dust. It is a shocking, immensely vivid, hallucinatory place, a shanty town of makeshift shelters, boxes, built round abandoned drainage pipes instantly reminiscent of the shanty towns of the Third World.

Faces of children and women staring back among the flies and the washing. The people have accumulated a weird jumble of belongings, collected from the environs of the park.

We see PAUL *staring around him in shock; it is like entering another land – an alien place.*

We then cut to PAUL *and* MANDRY *working with these people, treating their ailments.* MANDRY, *in his fine clothes, examines the people. He notices* PAUL's *expert work.*

We glimpse from amongst the squalor, on the edge of the park, through a wall of dust, a party of young things on bicycles, in fashionable clothes, trailing a giant floating cherry behind them, laughing together, oblivious of the world around them.

The cries and noise of the babies in the squalor grow louder surrounding MANDRY. *We stay on* MANDRY's *face, as he listens to the cries of the babies.*

Interior: Institute: MANDRY's *Office – Day*

We cut to MANDRY *dropping exhausted on to the window-seat, stretching his long body out, his fine clothes covered in dust.*

PAUL *flopping down on the other window-seat, his legs dangling casually; he dares to treat* MANDRY *as an equal.*

MANDRY. What a day! (*Stretching out.*) They go *on* having children they can't support.

PAUL (*helping himself to a biscuit*). I know . . . well, they can't be stopped by force.

MANDRY (*in the window-seat, light behind him*). No, of course not. (*Staring at* PAUL.) No, Paul. (*He gives* PAUL *a very searching look.*)

PAUL. No, I mean of course you couldn't do that.

They are staring down through the window at heads of people moving on the path, a weird collection of heads.

(Confidently.) The only answer is education and it *is* what you do best, isn't it? After all, better than anybody in London.

MANDRY. According to whom?

PAUL *(without thinking, teasing him)*. According to you!

Pause. PAUL tenses; has he gone too far? MANDRY is turned away from him.

MANDRY. I don't think we should go there for a while. *(Suddenly his tone changes, he turns back towards PAUL.)* Maybe we're working too hard, Paul!

PAUL *(immensely relieved)*. That's more than possible – sir.

Interior: Institute: Passage and PAUL's Room – Evening

CLARA *is walking directly towards us down the passage; she is wearing her best dress, slightly shabby but an attractive one.*

PAUL *is standing in the door of his room, in evening dress, very impatient.*

FELIX *(also in evening dress)*. Why haven't we left yet?

PAUL *pulls CLARA into the bedroom. There is something very obviously concealed under the counterpane of his bed.*

PAUL. I didn't think you'd come.

CLARA. I nearly didn't – *(Staring round.)* – but my curiosity got the better of me – sir.

PAUL. Don't call me sir. *(Turns.)* This will seem very, very rude – in fact practically the rudest and most inept thing anybody could do. *(He throws back the bedcover; there is an identical dress to the one he saw in the tea rooms.)* I got this not because I didn't think you'd look nice – but because.

CLARA *(lightly)*. You didn't want me to show you up.

PAUL *(with feeling)*. No, no, *no* – because I liked it so much. *(Smiles.)* And since *I* can't wear it myself – at least not tonight.

CLARA (*smiles at this*). You're right – it is amazingly rude. (*Moves over, touching dress.*) But it is also really quite nice. How did you know my size?

PAUL (*looks at her figure*). I used my medical knowledge, told at a glance.

CLARA. We'll see if you're right, shall we?

Interior/Exterior: Institute: Hall – Evening

FELIX *and* PAUL *in the hall with umbrellas, front door open, rain pouring down.*

FELIX. Right! I'm not waiting any longer.

PAUL. Just two more minutes.

FELIX. What's she going to do with her own dress, anyway? Where's she going to leave it?

PAUL. I don't know. Somewhere . . . In a cupboard.

CLARA *appears on the stairs above them, listening.*

FELIX. A cupboard! In *your* room! You can't allow that.

PAUL. No, no, in the passage, I'm sure.

CLARA *descends the staircase, looking startling. She reaches them.*

CLARA. You were wrong. (*She smiles.*) It doesn't fit.

PAUL. Really? (*Self-mocking smile.*) I can't have been wrong. (*As* CLARA *gets closer.*) It is *hired*, you know, that's the other unforgivable thing I had to tell you.

CLARA. Oh, I never thought you'd bought it. (*She just brushes him as she passes.*)

FELIX *watching, surprised at* PAUL *letting her be so familiar.*

After all, you have no idea how tonight is going to turn out, do you?

Exterior: Warren of Alleyways Leading to Courtyard – Evening

Pouring rain, FELIX *and* PAUL *with large umbrellas,* CLARA *with a smaller one. They are moving towards the camera down the maze of alleyways; old awnings and advertisements wave their heads in the rain, washing being pulled in to dark windows. They are in an excited, exuberant mood.*

FELIX. We're ridiculously overdressed for where we are going.

CLARA. I don't know where we're going. (*Laughs.*) Do we even need to get there?

FELIX stops suddenly, pulls out a piece of paper and, pressing himself into a tiny dry corner, starts making notes.

PAUL. Felix, this is unendurable.

He catches FELIX by the arm and pins him to the wall.

I've got to know and I'm going to know – what are you working on?

The rain getting stronger.

FELIX, PAUL and CLARA are outside a small clothes factory. Inside, three Oriental girls are working at sewing-machines, and garments are being dipped into vats of blue, yellow and red dye. The water that is gushing out of the drainpipes into the courtyard is also coloured by the dye.

What is it, Felix? (*Half mock, half serious.*) If you value your life, you'd better tell me, because you are pursuing something nobody else knows about, *aren't you?* (*Holding him.*) Deny it and you die.

FELIX (*smiles*). I deny it.

PAUL (*really tightening his grip very hard*). It's about diabetes, isn't it?

FELIX. More, much more, hormones and glands, everything in fact. (*Staring at PAUL, water gushing down.*) If each gland produces a substance.

PAUL. A substance?

FELIX (*exhilarated*). Listen and don't just moronically repeat things.

FELIX moves off with PAUL, puts his own umbrella and PAUL's on the ground to form a diagram in the courtyard. Suddenly he comes back for CLARA's *and takes* CLARA's *umbrella as if he doesn't notice she is there.*

CLARA *getting soaked in the summer rain.*

CLARA *is advancing towards them through the incredibly heavy rain.*

We can hear FELIX's *speech, but we see the whole sequence through* CLARA's *eyes as she gets nearer and nearer to the two boys, totally absorbed in their work.*

A substance which is then released into the bloodstream and which then travels to a *different* part of the body where it takes effect and if they all form a co-ordinating *system*, which they do.

PAUL. Do they?

CLARA *nearly up to them. In the rain, the dye is running in rivers of yellow and red all around them.*

FELIX. *Yes!* And what if there was one master gland in the brain that controls the function of all the others, which I think I can prove it does, and *also*, I think I've found a way, given enough resources, to chemically isolate the internal secretions of the pancreas, and that would mean of course we could treat diabetes properly for the first time –

Just as CLARA *reaches them, they disappear round the courner of the building.*

PAUL (*stumbles back into the courtyard, stunned by the idea*). That's extraordinary, Felix.

FELIX. It is revolutionary, yes of course!

CLARA *and the magnificent dress are completely soaked, the Oriental girls laughing.*

So what do you think, Paul? Tell me.

PAUL. I'm thinking . . . I'm not even going to say I wish I had thought of it myself, because –

FELIX (*lightly*). Because you couldn't have thought of it, that's why.

PAUL (*decisive*). I have to be convinced it's even worth considering and at the moment I'm *not* convinced. (*Suddenly.*) What do you think, Clara?

They look up to see her totally soaked, leaning against the wall, not bothering to shelter.

Oh, my God, Felix, look at the dress! (*Warm smile at* CLARA.) I forgot about the *dress*.

Interior: Stairs, Club Theatre and Gallery – Night

Cut to FELIX, PAUL *and* CLARA *running up steep steps towards a club theatre and art gallery.*

FELIX (*as they run up stairs*). Come on, Paul – you're not still trying to convince yourself?

PAUL. I'm thinking, Felix – I promise you!

We cut inside. The whole space is full of an extraordinary exhibition of prophesies and models of the future.

Along the stage a display of glass tanks with models of the cities of the future, some submerged with fish swimming around them. There are models of flying machines, vehicles, houses, clothes; live models are dressed in the clothes of the future, wearing them around the exhibition. Everywhere there are imaginative glimpses of the future. A notice says THE EXHIBITION TO RIVAL PARIS!!

A fashionable, avant-guarde audience is mingling around the exhibition. We see a bedraggled PAUL, CLARA *and* FELIX *staring in wonder at the models.*

PAUL *keeps looking at* CLARA, *getting closer and closer to her, until he is very gently touching her.*

The atmosphere is strangely erotic and warm.

In the corner simultaneously with them staring at the exhibitions, a PERFORMER *is conducting a one-man show in a little side room, his show running on in the background.*

The PERFORMER *is doing his show in front of a rather striking erotic backcloth.*

THE PERFORMER. So let's talk about sex, the subject you've all been waiting for.

People laughing, answering back.

Will women – the *new* women – live in cities of their own? Will special trains carry breeding males to these cities and then straight out again, will the males have to compete against each other for the *right* to mate? Will they wear amazing sexual shoes like they used to do in the Middle Ages? (*He begins to strap on very peculiar and alarming shoes.*) Or will there be tolerance and gentleness, even a little love.

Audience calling out.

We are of course all very tolerant now. (*Ironic smile.*) There is no race hatred here, no religious persecution, no hounding of perverts, and Europe itself is a perfect haven compared to anywhere else in the world. (*He smiles.*) We're safe here, aren't we?

CLARA (*next to PAUL, staring at a submerged city*). You'd have to really like fish, I suppose.

FELIX *seeing a couple of small models he likes and merrily slipping them into his pocket.*

We cut to the three of them standing in front of a wall, in another part of the exhibition. A notice says: WRITE YOUR PROPHECIES FOR THE NEXT CENTURY AND COME BACK AND SEE IF YOU ARE RIGHT.

People are writing and drawing on the wall, the camera gliding over this mosaic of prophesies.

PAUL. Somebody's put a moving staircase – but the first one's already been exhibited in Paris this year! Things move so fast . . .

FELIX. Actually there is one in Harrods already! Look, the famous men's corner.

Line-drawings of some distinguished men's faces and their prophesies.

Professor MANDRY is staring out.

FELIX *reads his prediction.*

A drug – to stop your hair falling out. That's not very good! (*He turns to PAUL.*) Come on, I'll cap anything you can think of.

How about a tunnel under the Atlantic with vehicles speeding at 100 miles an hour.

PAUL. How about free doctors.

FELIX *rolls his eyes at* PAUL.

No, no, listen, a doctor on every train and every bus in the morning, to check the workforce.

CLARA (*reading off the wall*). 'This is the year of magic!' What about balloon holiday villas –

FELIX. – floating on wires 2000 feet above the City, so you can go for an aerial vacation.

CLARA (*moving her hand gently over the wall*). What if *all* of this came true.

PAUL (*begins to write decisively on the wall*). I prophesy a visual telephone with a picture. (*He laughs.*) That will please my father.

FELIX (*grabbing his hands to stop him writing*). But my idea is here *now*, Paul, you must be convinced.

He sees PAUL *watching* CLARA.

Stop thinking about her. I'm really surprised at you, she's so way beneath you, Paul. (*He stares at* PAUL.) Even for just one night . . .

Exterior: Courtyard – Night

Cut to FELIX, PAUL *and* CLARA *crossing the courtyard.*

It's stopped raining; puddles stained with blue, yellow and red are dotted across the yard.

A high shot of CLARA *holding her shoes and stockings and spinning round barefoot in a large puddle.*

A sense of excitement and energy in all of them.

CLARA (*spinning in her dress*). The smell of summer, it's so warm. The last year of the century and it's so hot! (*Laughs.*) And I'm holding part of a city of the future in my hand.

PAUL (*suddenly, solemnly*). Felix, I *am* convinced. Just now, it happened. It's not easy for me to admit, because I thought *I* was going to be assessed top of the Institute. But if you let me, I'll work on it with you, help you present it to Mandry.

FELIX (*turns*). *All* my ideas? It has to be all of them.

PAUL (*smiling*). If you must, all of them! (*Up to* FELIX.) And I'm going to say something terribly dangerous and unoriginal.

FELIX (*charming smile*). But you're always unoriginal, Paul.

PAUL (*lightly*). I *was* going to say, this is the most exciting night of my life.

FELIX. Yes, I really believe it is!

PAUL (*laughs*). Oh, you've had better, I suppose!

CLARA (*to* PAUL, *quiet*). Will you be seeing me home?

PAUL *looks round.* CLARA, *holding her shoes, is drifting along the wall.*

I don't mind that much either way, but you can come.

PAUL *sees her standing in the mouth of the alleyway, with the sordid signs and bits of washing hanging out in the night air.*

PAUL. It's down there?

CLARA (*mimicking him*). Down *there*, yes. And there is no other way to get there.

PAUL (*obviously torn, watching* CLARA). I don't think I will, thank you. I have to talk to Felix.

CLARA. Of course. I understand. Thank you for tonight. (*Moving to take it off.*) Do you want the dress back right now?

PAUL. Don't be stupid, please.

CLARA (*lightly*). I really hope you won't have to buy it now. (*She moves back into dark alleyway, turns.*) Just remember you had the chance.

Interior: Institute: MANDRY's *Study – Day*

Close-up of MANDRY *flicking through the pages of their work, a file of about ten pages.*

PAUL *and* FELIX *standing a respectful distance from his desk, looking anxiously at him.*

Silence except a clock ticking.

MANDRY *takes out a pen, makes a mark on the page and resumes.*

MANDRY. Some of this is misspelt.

PAUL. We must have written it down too fast, but – (*Stops.*)

MANDRY. And there is a great deal of it. What do you think, Reisner? (*Pleasantly.*) I'm very interested to hear what you think.

FELIX *looks at* PAUL *respectfully.*

PAUL. I think they are extraordinary ideas, which we should concentrate on with as many resources as possible. It could be something very important, I really mean this, not just for all of us, but the Institute. It will get us serious attention from the newspapers, help us raise more funds.

Clock ticking, pause.

MANDRY. At first glance, I have to say . . .

PAUL's *and* FELIX's *faces really tense.*

. . . they do seem rather intriguing, maybe remarkable. (*Leans forward.*) I will talk to you about this soon – don't mention it to anybody till then.

Interior: Institute: Laboratory/Passages – Day

MANDRY *moving down passage; both* PAUL *and* FELIX *stick their heads out of the door, eyes full of expectation.*

MANDRY *is walking with two older men, one short and fat, one stooping.*

MANDRY (*pleasantly*). This is Doctor Makin from the United States of America and Doctor Leisen from Germany . . . Good morning, gentlemen.

PAUL. Sir, sir . . .

MANDRY (*sweeps on; he looks back*). Soon, Paul, very soon.

Interior: Institute: By Window – Day

CLARA *by herself, humming by a window, holding one of* FELIX's *models, watching it spin and turn in the draught.*

PAUL *suddenly moving past her in a rush.*

PAUL (*as he passes*). Nothing yet . . . No news about Felix's idea *at all.*

Interior: Institute: Hall – Night

FELIX *and* PAUL *working with the volunteers, the vivid selection of faces turned up to them, seeking help, their diseases visible on their faces.*

MANDRY *is moving above* PAUL *and* FELIX *on the first landing. He does* not *look in their direction.* PAUL *seems more exasperated by this than* FELIX.

PAUL. Professor Mandry . . . *Sir.*

MANDRY. Not just now, Reisner . . . this is not the moment. (*He disappears from view.*)

Interior: Institute: Passage – Night

Cut to PAUL *getting some new gloves from a broom cupboard. We see him pausing to see which colour he will choose, black, white or brown. He tries one on for size.*

Suddenly his eye falls on a pile of books and files right at the back of the cupboard, among the blankets and brushes, and beginning to be covered by dust is their submission, their file.

Interior: Institute: MANDRY's *Study – Day*

The group is sitting around a table with MANDRY, *just finishing Sunday lunch, a fine spread of summer fruit, cherries, raspberries, melon and ginger.* JAMES *serving coffee.*

In the background we can see the trees of the park and hear bands playing and bells ringing out, golden light.

MANDRY *laughing, cracking jokes at the head of the table, all the boys dipping into the fruit, a meltingly hot summer's day.*

PAUL (*watching MANDRY entertaining at the head of the table, his boyish charm*). I don't know why you are not responding to our report, sir?

MANDRY (*looking up*). Not responding? What do you mean?

PAUL. To our submission.

MANDRY (*lightly*). There's a lot there, Reisner. (*To the others.*) This is the potentially interesting work I've received from Reisner and Russell. (*To PAUL.*) It's only been a few weeks and I've had to read it three times so far. It *is* extremely novel. I don't want to discuss this further in company. When I'm ready you will hear from me, you can be assured. I am giving it my full consideration.

PAUL. Is that why it's being kept in the broom cupboard?

Pause. All the others fall silent. PAUL staring at MANDRY down the table.

MANDRY (*lightly*). That's why I couldn't find it the other day. The cleaning arrangements have become ridiculously sloppy. I will look into the matter. (*Smiles to PAUL.*) You didn't leave it in the 'broom cupboard', I presume?

PAUL. No, I did not.

MANDRY. Good. Then I can get it back from you, can't I. Thank you.

PAUL. With due respect, sir, I don't know why you seem to be deliberately not giving the ideas the consideration they deserve.

FELIX. Paul, stop it. Please, don't do this.

MANDRY. That was unpardonable, Reisner. Everybody present knows I have shown support for your ability, advanced you further than anyone at the Institute. I don't advise you to say another word on this subject. You understand.

PAUL (*unable to stop*). I just feel we are entitled to know why there has been such a delay – we're owed an explanation, sir.

Silence.

'Entitled' may be the wrong word, but I want to know . . .

MANDRY (*calmly*). Reisner, stand up please. Go on, stand up.

PAUL *stands, all the others watching him, very nervous.*

You will not set foot in this building for one whole month. You will also receive no pay for that time. You will lose your laboratory. When you return you will have to use the one you began in. I don't want to see the slightest sign of you till then . . .

Their eyes meet, PAUL *terribly shaken.*

PAUL. Sir . . . Sir, please can I have a moment alone with you. (*He stares at* MANDRY's *eyes, searching for his special relationship.*)

MANDRY. No, you certainly cannot. (*He snaps his watch open.*) Four weeks precisely from today. Don't you dare try to reply to this. Now get out of here.

PAUL *looks stunned, he half opens his mouth to reply.*

No.

Interior: Institute: Basement – Day

PAUL *runs down the stairs into the basement, past the dissected animals. He moves into the white tiled room, the women in there busying themselves preparing various substances.*

PAUL. Where is Clara? (*He looks around.*)

FIRST GIRL. She's not here.

PAUL. Not here? She's always here.

FIRST GIRL. She's got a week's holiday. I don't know where she is.

PAUL. You must know.

FIRST GIRL. She could have gone anywhere.

PAUL (*urgent*). Where's her home? Her room? Where she lives?

Exterior: Alley and Courtyard – Evening

PAUL *moving down alleyway, towards a derelict-looking arch at the end. A balloon is bumping along the pavement towards him.*

PAUL *passes through the arch into a courtyard with high, crumbling tenement flats all around. The yard is full of large gas-filled balloons, some caught in the balconies, the rest drifting across the ground, festive balloons that have come to rest in the yard.*

PAUL *crosses the yard, staring up into the windows and the washing hanging around.*

Interior: CLARA's Room – Evening

Cut to PAUL pushing open a rickety door, and moving down a very narrow passage which opens out into one large room, full of clutter, and a bed on the floor, and a tiny kitchen in one corner.

CLARA *is standing in the middle of the room.*

PAUL. You're here – thank God. (*He corrects himself.*) What I mean is – I'm glad I got the right address. You were really difficult to find.

CLARA (*amused smile*). I thought for a moment you were pleased to see me.

PAUL. Of course I am.

CLARA (*lightly*). You must be in trouble of some kind, Doctor Reisner, or you would never have come.

Interior: CLARA's Room – Evening

Cut to coffee boiling in lab equipment. We see her room is partly furnished with tubes, jars and other medical equipment taken from the labs. Here they are full of flour, herbs and other household goods.

PAUL *and CLARA are both standing, watching the coffee dripping through the tubes.*

PAUL. It's just a little local difficulty with the Professor. I overstepped the mark. Because I seem to be his favourite pupil, I thought I could – it's an easy mistake to make. Everything will come right, I'm sure, because he likes me. (*Watching* CLARA *bent over the coffee, he smiles.*) Did you steal all this equipment?

CLARA. No, I did not! What do you take me for? (*Lightly.*) I stole half of it. The rest is cracked or wrong in some way.

PAUL *touches her arm, as they watch the coffee run down the tube.*

What are you doing?

PAUL. Can I kiss you?

Short pause.

CLARA. You may, Doctor Reisner.

PAUL. You must stop calling me that.

They kiss among all the glass tubes.

I have been waiting to do that ever since I saw you.

CLARA (*lightly, touching*). That is a total lie for a start. You're still not sure if you should really touch a laboratory worker. (*She laughs.*) I think you'd really like to be doing this wearing gloves. 'The lowest form of animal life', that's what you doctors call us, isn't it?

PAUL. You certainly don't look like the lowest form of life right at this moment.

CLARA. I suppose that's a compliment.

PAUL (*more earnest*). Clara, you are –

CLARA (*closing* PAUL's *lips*). No, no, don't say any more. No serious words. (*She slips her hand under his pristine shirt.*) Do these clothes ever come off – or do you keep them on for *all occasions*?

We cut to PAUL *making love to* CLARA *among the tubes and the medical jars.* CLARA's *eyes, full of detached, amused sensuality.*

(*Teasingly, as* PAUL *kisses her shoulders.*) Am I clean enough for you? Now you are able to see all of me?

PAUL (*lightly, as he kisses*). I see no areas for real concern.

CLARA. Thank you, Doctor Reisner. (*Moving her hands over him.*) But what about *you*? That's much more to the point. (*She turns her head.*) I said I'd stop doing this, I did, especially with doctors.

PAUL. Really? (*Self-mocking smile.*) That couldn't possibly apply to this doctor, not *now* . . .

CLARA (*laughing*). You're so vain – you really are. *A* doctor, there was only one.

Interior: CLARA's Room – Evening/Night

PAUL *and* CLARA *half dressed, bare legs, very hot, sitting in the middle of the floor with a large frying-pan and two plates. The window behind them, dusk just creeping up.*

CLARA. This is something exotic I have made. We used to have an Oriental volunteer at the Institute and he taught me . . . This is *Chinese* food, a sort of Chinese food. See if you like it.

PAUL (*dubious, looking down at his plate*). What peculiar-looking stuff. (*Munching.*) It's surprisingly edible. But a very acquired taste, though.

CLARA (*laughing*). You mean it only appeals to the very best palates, like yours, of course!

PAUL (*beginning to wolf it*). That's right.

CLARA. I expect we're the first people in this whole district to eat this food.

She laughs as PAUL *gobbles the bizarrely shaped food.*

Maybe you should give up medicine . . . get a job sampling the foods of the future.

Her face close to his and the food dangling.

Exterior: Courtyard below CLARA's Room – Evening/Night

In the yard below, balloons are drifting, and two young men are weaving among them singing a strange song, a song that continues through the scene.

Interior: CLARA's *Room – Evening/Night*

CLARA. They're a couple of opium addicts, they make a lot of noise. This place is full of bohemians and drifters. (*She smiles.*) Doing terrible things without drawing the curtains.

We see behind them the lights coming on in interesting rooms, glimpses of people leading unconventional lives.

PAUL. I want to ask you one thing, Clara.

CLARA. Just one! (*She eats her Chinese food very delicately.*)

PAUL (*watching her closely*). Why is somebody like you –

CLARA (*self-mocking*). Somebody as bright and interesting as me, working in the bowels of the earth as a laboratory worker? Where I may not even survive much longer unless I take your advice. (*Pause.*) Because I had a baby, and absolutely no husband, and then no money, and eventually there was no baby. And for somebody like me . . . where are you welcome? A very normal story really – except I refuse to behave like some wretched grateful creature who's lucky to be *allowed* into the Institute.

PAUL. What happened to the baby?

CLARA. It died. It caught influenza and eight hours later it was dead.

PAUL. I'm sorry. (*Touching her gently.*) I am very sorry, Clara.

CLARA. I used to think it was the one thing I'd ever created in my life – but it's bad to think like that. (*She smiles, touching him.*) It makes me live very much in the present. All the time like now – this moment.

CLARA *curls her bare legs round* PAUL, *and kisses him strongly.*

You have to stay here, don't you, because you have nowhere else to go? (*She undoes his shirt, curling around him.*)

PAUL. Nowhere, that's right – I can't go home.

CLARA. And I have five whole days of holiday left – I don't think we ever need go out, do you?

PAUL. And then?

CLARA. Oh, don't think about 'and then'. (*Humorous smile.*) And it's still the year of magic. (*Touching his lips.*) Isn't that right?

Exterior: Courtyard below CLARA's Room – Day

Cut to children playing with the balloons, kicking them along the ground, jumping on them.

The opium addicts curled up asleep in the sun.

Interior: CLARA's Room – Day

CLARA is standing by a mirror putting on her working clothes.

PAUL dressed in casual clothes, baggy trousers and shirt, obviously not his own. He is barefoot and unshaven.

PAUL. And you'll check, check the slides James has got, see they are being kept properly. And you should know the volunteers I'm particularly interested in . . . maybe you can make some notes, you know, secret notes; if there have been any dramatic changes, bring them back to me.

CLARA. I do know what to look for. I have picked up *some* knowledge while being here.

A voice shouts from down in the courtyard, 'Paul, Paul'. He goes to the window. FELIX is calling up.

FELIX. How is everything? Forgotten it all yet? (*Smiles.*) You'll never catch up.

PAUL (*lightly*). Go away. Get away with you, we shouldn't even be seen talking! I'll surprise you when I get back, and the Professor! (*He turns to CLARA.*)

CLARA (*light laugh*). You look wonderful in those clothes.

PAUL. Yes. Why won't you tell me whose they are?

CLARA. Because it's none of your business, and don't you start getting jealous. (*She opens the door.*) You going to be all right?

PAUL. Absolutely. I'll cook us a meal. (*Points to the glass tubes.*) I will work with these.

We cut to PAUL, washing his own shirt in a large bowl and mooching about idly, inspecting CLARA's clothes in the wardrobe, with some approval.

The bell clangs loudly again.

PAUL rushes over to the window with a jug of water.

PAUL. I told you to stop it! Don't gloat. Get away from here, or I'll . . .

PAUL finds himself staring into the eyes of his father, MR REISNER, standing below in the courtyard with MIRIAM.

MR REISNER. I thought we must have the wrong address – but very obviously we have not.

Cut to PAUL opening the door of CLARA's room, MR REISNER looking with intense surprise at the unconventional surroundings, at PAUL's bare feet and stubble.

What an extraordinary place to find you.

PAUL. Yes, of course it is. But the explanation is simple. I . . . I – (*Staring at his father.*) – I tend these people as a little extra service, a little medical care and they allow me very kindly to wash myself here.

MR REISNER (*staring hard*). Go on.

MR REISNER sits with MIRIAM on a low box against the wall, because there are no chairs. Both stare at the glass tubes.

PAUL (*waving his arms*). And this room . . . belongs to a woman . . . an elderly woman, who used to be at the Institute – and does some of her own research as you can see in her spare time. Once you've got a taste of it, it isn't easy to let it go.

MR REISNER. And why are you dressed like that?

PAUL (*staring back at his father*). I find it easier to dress like them – while among them.

MR REISNER. That is not a good policy. I can assure you.

PAUL. Yes, Papa.

MIRIAM. You look ridiculous, Paul.

PAUL (*relieved*). Now, let's forget about explanations, I will take us all out for lunch. (*Remembering, feeling in his pockets for money.*) Or maybe a cup of coffee would be best, the coffee in London is wonderful.

MR REISNER. No, no, no.

PAUL. What do you mean?

MR REISNER. You are going to show me all round the Institute, of course.

PAUL. What? (*Sharp.*) That's totally impossible. It's shut.

MR REISNER. Rubbish. I've just been there. One of the boys told me where you were.

PAUL (*startled*). You went there . . . ? What did they say?

MR REISNER. What do you mean what did they say? They told me you were visiting patients here . . .

Close-up of PAUL.

Now for God's sake put on your shoes, I can't stand seeing you with no shoes. And shave yourself, and we'll get off at once!

Exterior: Park – Day

PAUL *in his formal clothes,* MR REISNER *and* MIRIAM *moving across the park.*

PAUL *leading them through the back parts, hidden by bushes.*

MR REISNER. There is so much litter everywhere. It is ridiculous. There won't be any grass left soon. (*He picks up litter, handing it to* MIRIAM. *He also lifts his hat to any passing woman, as if they were walking down a village street.*) Good morning, how are you?

Two women pass in extraordinary, brightly coloured dresses of an unusual design, wearing some of the futuristic clothes that were being modelled at the gallery; there is a general air of exhibitionism.

MIRIAM. What terrible clothes! Aren't they ashamed to look like that? (*Watching* MR REISNER.) I'm a little worried about Papa, Paul. I think he's troubled by something . . . maybe it's his work. Paul . . .

PAUL (*not listening, watching the women with their new fashions in the park*). People are trying out all sorts of dresses ready for the great celebrations.

Then PAUL suddenly sees the fat figure of DOCTOR MAKIN coming towards them. He pulls his father and MIRIAM through some bushes.

MR REISNER. Where is the Institute? Where are you taking us?

Exterior: Park – Day (City of Rubbish)

We cut to them skirting round the edge of the City of Rubbish. There is a scattering of people moving amongst the pipes and makeshift shelters.

We see the dark-haired girl who hid from PAUL watching them.

On another part of the hill, we see a coffin being carried down among the boxes by four men in black. We see them through a haze of dust.

MR REISNER. Why are we going this way?

PAUL. This is a short cut.

MR REISNER. We're going round in circles. This is ridiculous! I will find it.

Exterior: The Institute – Day

We cut to MR REISNER ringing the bell at the great door.

Interior: Institute: Hall – Day

PAUL, *seeing the door is ajar, pushes it open and hustles them across the hall.*

MRS PRITCHARD *is sitting in her usual place. She does not look up.*

Two volunteers are sitting on the benches. One of them calls, 'Doctor Reisner, where have you been?'

Cut to PAUL pulling them along the passage outside the laboratories.

JAMES. Hello, Doctor Reisner, you're back already!

PAUL (*waving frantically to him to be quiet*). Yes, yes. Get back to work, James.

MR REISNER. Which is your laboratory?

PAUL. My laboratory?

PAUL *realises he doesn't know, he half turns to his special room next to* MANDRY, *then realises he can't go there. He looks urgently at* JAMES.

JAMES *smiles, and indicates his old laboratory is still available.*

Interior: Institute: PAUL's Laboratory – Day

We cut to MR REISNER *standing in the laboratory, staring around at the equipment.*

MR REISNER. Why on earth is there some dust here?

PAUL. That's good – for certain experiments, we need to make tests in all conditions.

MR REISNER (*rolls his eyes at this*). And where is your bedroom and bathroom?

Interior: Institute: Summer Bedroom – Day (Passage)

We cut to PAUL *dragging them very fast down the bedroom passage. He is very angry at having to go through this. Nevertheless he moves ahead, to scoop up some women's clothes that are lying in the passage.*

MR REISNER *staring in surprise at the shabby walls.*

FELIX *appears in the passage.*

FELIX. What on earth are you doing here, Paul? Have you gone completely mad? Mandry's not fooling, you know.

PAUL. No, no, I finished much earlier than I expected. Felix is our resident eccentric, take no notice.

He sees MRS PRITCHARD *and* DOCTOR LEISEN *at the other end of the passage coming towards them.*

Come on, we'll go this way out . . . (*He angrily pulls his father on.*)

Interior: Institute: Basement – Day

We cut to the basement, the subterranean area among the women.

MR REISNER *holding his handkerchief over his mouth.*

PAUL (*totally furious at being put at risk like this*). It's good, the smell, isn't it? I thought you'd like to savour it before you went.

CLARA *looks up from where she is working. She stares at PAUL alarmed, and starts signalling. PAUL ignores her.*

MIRIAM. There is a woman over there, waving at you.

PAUL. Oh, is there? Yes, she does that to everybody, take no notice. This way. (*Starts to pull his father on down the dark passage.*)

CLARA. Doctor Reisner . . . wait a moment. (*Then very urgent, loud.*) Paul, not that way, Paul. (*Shouts.*) Paul!

PAUL. Take absolutely no notice of her.

PAUL *rounds the corner with his father and MIRIAM, to find MANDRY standing there in the basement passage, looking at some files.*

MANDRY. Reisner?

PAUL. Sir . . . sir . . . good afternoon. Let me explain. I am not really here at all. This is my father, he just wanted to see the Institute. (*Staring at him.*) *I am not here,* sir.

MANDRY (*leaning forward, taking MR REISNER's hand*). I'm delighted to meet your father.

MR REISNER. The pleasure is all mine.

MANDRY (*looking straight at PAUL*). A word with you, young man.

Interior: Institute: MANDRY's *Office – Day*

Cut to PAUL facing MANDRY across his desk.

MANDRY. What did I say to you?

PAUL. I know. *I know, sir*. But I have explained. I really feel I have an excuse.

MANDRY. You have been away merely a week. Do you think I didn't mean what I said?

PAUL. Of course you did. You think I'm a fool? My father insisted, really insisted, and it's incredibly difficult to stop him doing anything, if you knew him . . . (*Quieter.*) And I'm also very sorry I was so rude to you before. I had no business to sound like that.

MANDRY (*flicking something on his desk*). That's quite gracious . . . really quite an elegant apology – (*Gently.*) – as I'd expect from you – (*He leans back.*) – I might even allow you back here even sooner . . .

PAUL. If you could – (*Adds quickly.*) – sir.

Pause.

MANDRY. But you will have to realise the matter of your research, your submission with Russell, that cannot be raised under any circumstances, until *I* raise it.

PAUL. That's a strange condition, when will that be . . . sir?

MANDRY. When it has been considered. No exact time limit can be put on it. There is nothing unusual in that. (*Looking straight at him.*) Paul, just listen for once in your short life. I am offering you another chance. It's not even your own work we're talking about here.

PAUL. Sir – if you don't believe in the work, give it back to us and we can publish it elsewhere.

MANDRY. You know that's impossible, all work done here belongs to the Institute.

PAUL. For how long?

MANDRY. For ever. (*Leaning towards him.*) Paul, you have to realise I will only allow you back to the Institute on these terms, and that is final, no further discussion is possible. (*More gently.*) You must listen to me.

PAUL. I have to say I think it is a rather monstrous condition. You must give that work a chance, give us the resources for it.

MANDRY. If I could be certain Russell and you would work on it quietly, then perhaps.

PAUL. Quietly? So when?

MANDRY. One day, when it has been considered.

PAUL (*enraged*). One day, *one day*! What does that mean? I think you're jealous, aren't you? *Aren't you*? You're far too good not to have seen the potential in that work. You are jealous of it, because *you* didn't do it and you want to destroy it. And that's unforgivable!

Interior: Institute: Hall – Day

We cut outside into the hall where MR REISNER *is sitting patiently with* MIRIAM.

MR REISNER. This is much more how I imagined the place to be. With good furniture like this. (*He gets up, touches some decorative pieces on the mantelpiece.*) Some good taste here. I must compliment Professor Mandry on these pieces. Sit still, Miriam, they are obviously deep in conference.

Interior: Institute: MANDRY's Study – Day

We cut back inside MANDRY's *study,* PAUL *very pale, but still furious, staring at* MANDRY.

MANDRY (*calmly, very hard*). I warned you and you took no notice.

PAUL. I'm sorry about the tone of what I said. That happens with me. I'm sorry. You have to accept that. (*Loud.*) But you must *not* delay this work.

MANDRY. Be quiet. (*Calmly.*) It's too late, Reisner, you are finished here. *If* I ever see you again, and I mean this, I will make sure you will never work as a doctor anywhere again. You will also keep away from the other doctors here; I will *not* have you stirring them up. And I don't threaten lightly. As it is you will never work in medical research again, that is over for you. I will see to it.

PAUL. You can't do that.

MANDRY. Paul – ssh . . . keep quiet, if you ever want to practise again. Remember – how shall I put it? – you are an outsider. Just remember who you are. I shouldn't have to remind you what certain people think outside these walls. You have no contacts, nobody to help you. Remember that. I advise you to leave this room without saying another word.

Pause. PAUL completely stunned.

PAUL. You know I'm good. You know that. You liked me. I was even a favourite. We agree on so many things. Why are you doing this? I thought – I can't believe you're being so . . .

MANDRY (*suddenly exploding*). You see, you don't take my advice, do you, about anything. You arrogant boy. Get out of my sight, out of the Institute, go on.

Interior: Institute: Hall – Day (Front Downstairs)

PAUL *goes into the hall, sees his father and* MIRIAM *sitting waiting expectantly.*

PAUL (*loud*). Come on, both of you.

MR REISNER. No, no, wait a moment.

He goes up to MANDRY's door.

PAUL (*shouting*). Papa, no. (*He frantically tries to stop his father.*)

MR REISNER (*waving through the door*). I hope to see you again, Professor Mandry, very soon, you must come down and visit us in the country, we've some wonderful fruit this year.

MANDRY. What a charming idea, Mr Reisner. *If* I'm ever in that part of the world . . . I believe your son may have something to tell you, just waiting to tell you.

MR REISNER. I just want to say how pleased I am that my son is doing so well here –

PAUL (*grabs his father and drags him from the door*). Papa, *for God's sake!*

Pulling and yanking him across the hall, really yelling.

You've got to come now, got to come right away from here. Just stop talking . . . (*Really screams.*) Stop, *do you understand me*. You should never have *come!*

Exterior: Square – Day

MR REISNER (*totally amazed*). What on earth did you do that for? I demand an explanation. What happened in there? Did you argue – you must never argue with him. What is it?

PAUL (*leaning against the wall, his head turning away, almost vomiting; desperately trying to stop himself crying*). No, no, it's nothing like that.

MR REISNER. What is it?

PAUL (*turns, staring at his father's face*). I, I . . . I . . . I . . . may be about to be promoted, my own research unit, maybe. Maybe. It's a nerve-racking time. I just didn't want you to complicate things. You are. By talking to him . . . (*Loud.*) . . . you'll see. I have to go now. Bye.

MR REISNER. No, don't be stupid. You can't go! You have to come to Uncle Isaac's children's party, of course. That's why we're here.

PAUL. *Children's party?* No, no.

PAUL *walks off, dazed. He looks back: his father is staring after him.*

PAUL *walks hurriedly away, not daring to look back again.*

Interior: Institute: Hall – Evening

A shot of MANDRY *sitting in the hall, late-evening light, some volunteers sitting opposite, hoping to be seen.*

JAMES *appears with a tray of tea.*

MANDRY (*leaning his head back, his eyes half closed, a gentle smile*). Take tea with me, James, please.

JAMES, *surprised, sits next to him, and since there is no cup he eats a biscuit.*

Interior: CLARA's Room – Night

CLARA *and* PAUL *in her small bed, naked, hot and sticky in the humid night.*

Strange calls and fragments of songs from the opium addicts.

PAUL (*burying his head into CLARA's shoulders, seeking to curl up with her, away from everything*). Am I finished, Clara? I can't believe it. Me, Paul Reisner! Do you really think *Mandry* can stop me working everywhere?

CLARA. I don't know. He is a powerful man. (*Gently.*) You shouldn't have ignored me, when you were with your father and I was warning . . .

PAUL. It would have happened anyway. He is so jealous. The Professor . . .

The shadows in the darkened room, the glass equipment, the sound of the opium addicts.

I am not going to end up like them, am I? That is a terrifying idea.

CLARA. Who knows?

PAUL *looks startled.*

I'm already like them, aren't I? That's how most people regard me . . . 'Clara has fallen over the edge.'

Shot of the men below doing a strange ragged dance. Then intense close-up of CLARA.

PAUL. *You* are all I've got now.

CLARA (*very firm*). No you don't – don't you say that, because that's not true. That is absolutely not what is happening. (*Staring into his eyes.*) Is it? I know as soon as your trouble is over . . . you will leave me, very quickly.

PAUL. No, I won't. Why on earth do you say that?

CLARA (*running her fingers over his mouth*). Because, Paul, you are who you are – you can't help it, can you? You'll never be satisfied with someone like me. Can you see yourself ever introducing me to your father?

PAUL's *eyes flicker.*

Anyway, I don't expect anything, so long as you don't lie to me.

PAUL. If I'm not allowed to use the word love –

CLARA *is watchful.*

– then I'm addicted to you, Clara, I am.

CLARA (*touching him*). We'll see . . . I manage my life in a funny way, perhaps, but at least it's *me* doing it. (*Her face close to his.*) And I will not allow you to take away from me. Ever.

PAUL (*slight smile*). I couldn't, even if I wanted to.

CLARA. Oh, *yes*, you will. (*Touching his lips.*) If I ever let myself care too much. So – (*She rolls on top of him.*) – since neither of us can sleep . . .

PAUL. You are incorrigible, Clara!

CLARA (*lightly*). There, you see you've started already. (*Kissing him along his neck.*) I must be some sort of grotesque, because I like sex rather a lot, and I don't pretend otherwise. (*Teasing smile, looking down at him.*) There, you did it again, I'm not even allowed to say it.

PAUL (*lightly*). You shouldn't talk about it, no . . .

CLARA (*bending over him, giving him short kisses*). You're not paying me any rent, after all, I do deserve some other payment.

He opens his mouth to reply; she shuts it, her hand brushing across his lips, the glass equipment tinkling.

PAUL (*catching hold of her*). Before we start – if you can resist for one (*Teasing smile.*) more moment, if that is physically possible – what do I do next, Clara, about Mandry, in *your* opinion?

CLARA. If you insult people, you can beg forgiveness. It's simple, that's what you've got to do with the Professor. You go down on your belly, but it will have to be *right, right* down, and say I was wrong about everything. (*Very warm.*) But I'm not sure you can get down that far, Paul . . .

Interior: Day: Institute: MANDRY's Study

A shot of MANDRY sitting in one of his suite of rooms by the window, as two fashionable young women are playing a duet on a piano; they are giggling together because the Institute piano is out of tune.

MANDRY is staring down at the people below. His eyes settle on a group of destitute people living rough, camping along the park wall, close to the Institute.

Exterior: Day: Back of the Institute

Then we cut to MANDRY walking up to them, looking at them, deep disquiet at the signs of their poverty, their bad complexions, the children's faces.

He bends close to them. A long moment as he stares at them.

We stay on his face.

Exterior/Interior: Coffee-house – Day

The group, FELIX, THOMAS, MEREDITH, THEO and a young newcomer, DANIEL, sharp-faced, twenty-one, all stare at PAUL as he approaches through the smoke of the coffee-house.

PAUL is dressed in his casual, baggy clothes, unshaven, his hair longer than before.

The tables are scattered with pamphlets about preaching, prophecies and fortune-tellers.

FELIX (*tugging at PAUL's sleeve as he gets up to him*). Look at you, what's this? Mud on *you*, Paul, mud.

PAUL (*lightly*). You get muddy in this city – didn't you know? (*He is totally unselfconscious about his appearance.*)

MEREDITH. A wild and primitive costume, it's good, Paul.

PAUL (*catching hold of one of the boys, showing stain on shirt*). It's ridiculous working in these clothes, look at this. How many times do you have to change a day? We should have overalls, work in overalls to do research.

FELIX (*horrified*). Overalls! I know we work in a modern, eccentric place, but that's ridiculous! He's gone insane, clearly, while he's been away.

PAUL. What does the newest worker think?

DANIEL (*very sharp, arrogant*). I think that idea is balderdash.

FELIX. You really are managing reasonably well, are you? In exile?

PAUL. Yes. (*He smiles.*) It's interesting, in a way, a different view of things. But Felix, I am thinking of retracting, going to Mandry and saying I was wrong, and I will never mention Felix's idea again, I solemnly swear it.

MEREDITH. I'm sure that is the right thing.

FELIX. Yes, yes, absolutely. Don't worry, I have moved on to other things, other interesting ideas already.

PAUL. You would have!

FELIX. It was too ambitious anyway.

PAUL. I don't believe that.

THEO. We need you back, Paul.

FELIX. We do, we do. It's undeniable, much as I'd like to deny it.

We see Professor MANDRY in the street, walking with the little American DOCTOR MAKIN. He stops, watching PAUL talk to the other doctors, through the window.

THEO. Then we can be one of the most advanced groups there are. (*Suddenly loud.*) Careful. Look who's coming, take cover.

PAUL looks up. He sees MANDRY at the window with DOCTOR MAKIN. PAUL ducks down just as MANDRY glances in. PAUL is not sure whether MANDRY saw him.

PAUL. Oh, my God. That's all I need! He didn't see me, did he? I'm sure he didn't. He'll think I'm plotting something if he saw me. (*Watching the receding figure of* MANDRY.) He didn't see me . . .

Interior: Reisner House: Hall – Day

The telephone ringing. MIRIAM *moves up to it, she hesitates for a moment and then answers.*

A man's voice, a farmer's voice with a country accent, blurts out very loudly:

MAN'S VOICE. Is that the Yid's house? The one who insulted us all in the local papers? Well, we don't want your sort telling us how to run *our* affairs, so my best advice to you is –

MIRIAM. Oh, shut up, you stupid little man, go to the devil.

MR REISNER *comes into the hall.*

MR REISNER. Was that another one?

MIRIAM. Yes, it was. They always seem to call at teatime. We should get it taken away, Papa, the telephone.

MR REISNER. No, no, it doesn't matter, everybody gets them, those strange calls. It comes with the machines. If you own one that's what happens. It makes life more interesting. Now I need you.

MIRIAM (*muttering, under her breath*). If *only* you hadn't spoken to the local paper and said those things about the town being run by vegetables. (*To the younger brother, a* TEENAGE BOY.) Papa doesn't notice. People are scuttling away from him, all over the place. He must see it. What are we going to do with him?

MR REISNER. Come on, come on. I want you to help me with the invitations for the New Year party.

MIRIAM (*to the* TEENAGE BOY). This party will never, never work. It'll make the last one look a success. (*She moves towards her father.*) Already? Invitations now? It's not nearly time.

MR REISNER. Yes it is. I have to send them off in good time . . . before other people do. I have had the invitations specially designed. (*Holding up a lovely-looking card.*) What do you think?

MIRIAM (*stares at her father*). Oh, Papa!

Exterior: Courtyard below CLARA's Room – Day

PAUL *moving along the street, loping along, smoking, glancing round.*

He stops by a wall covered in large posters for public meetings: 'The New Tomorrow, is there one?', 'What's going to happen? – come to St John's Hall and find out', 'All the way from India, prophecies of doom and salvation', etc.

PAUL (*reading posters*). Buy your guide to the next century now.

Two MEN come up to him as he is reading, tap him on the shoulder.

STOCKY MAN. Doctor Reisner?

PAUL (*turns*). Yes.

STOCKY MAN. Doctor Paul Reisner?

PAUL (*slightly suspicious*). Yes, what is it?

STOCKY MAN. Will you just come with us, please, we need to talk to you.

PAUL. Talk to me?

STOCKY MAN. Yes, just a little interview. Nothing out of the ordinary, sir, absolutely not.

Interior: Police Building – Day

Cut to PAUL being led along a passage painted in three different colours. Stripes of paint.

PAUL. Where are we going?

STOCKY MAN. Nearly there, sir. We're painting the building in time for the celebrations, of course. (*Indicating walls.*) And this helps us to decide on the right paint. What do you think?

PAUL *is led past a cell with two tramps sitting in it, and then a cell with four dogs in it, yapping away. One of the dogs, a poodle, has ornamental clothes on, a gold coat.*

People have been losing their pets like nobody's business. Their minds must be on other things.

They come into a large room with uniformed police in it, pictures of ripe chorus girls and Queen Victoria. Piled all along one wall and over the floor is a great mass of lost property: fur coats, scarfs, shoes, even underwear.

This is all from the great Devonshire ball this weekend – what they must have got up to!

Two aristocratic women in stunning dresses, rich colours against the grubby walls, have come to look through the belongings for what they have lost. Their manservant is looking and they are giving instructions.

(As he passes.) Found what you're looking for, ladies?

We cut to the women eyeing PAUL.

PAUL is led into another room separated from the passage by a wall with windows and a glass door. The INTERROGATOR looks up as PAUL is led in.

INTERROGATOR. Good afternoon, Doctor Reisner . . . please sit down. We are just doing a little research . . .

We cut outside to the women watching PAUL through the glass door.

FIRST LADY *(whispers, laughing)*. Shall we take *him* home with us? Maybe he can be hired for the day?

We cut back inside the room – the STOCKY MAN and the POLICE CONSTABLE standing behind PAUL.

INTERROGATOR *(politely)*. As you may be aware, there is a strong likelihood of this Alien Act coming into force very soon . . . to stop the flood of undesirable aliens we are having to endure at the moment. *(Looking up politely.)* And we are just compiling a few documents of our own, to be in readiness . . . *(Shuffling papers.)* Now your father, despite having a German name, was born in Romania –

PAUL. I know where my father was born!

INTERROGATOR. People often pretend they don't, isn't that strange? *You* were born in Scotland, then a short stay in America with your family as an infant, before you went back to Scotland, and then at last came down south to us.

PAUL. How do you know all this?

INTERROGATOR. We just want to trace the journey your family made, and make sure the right procedures were followed . . . at every stage . . .

PAUL. This has all been arranged by him hasn't it? By Professor Mandry?

We cut to the fashionable women waving to people waiting for them on the pavement outside.

We cut back to PAUL.

This is the result of a personal vendetta – you have no legal right to do this. Your job does not entitle you to detain me in these circumstances for a single moment. As you well know. (*He gets up, pushing his chair back sharply.*) Goodbye, gentlemen.

PAUL *knocks into the* STOCKY MAN *with his chair as he gets up. The* STOCKY MAN *smashes him across the face.*

You bastard!

He is bleeding vigorously; he hits back, grabbing the STOCKY MAN *against the wall.*

STOCKY MAN. Don't you dare tell us how to do our job!

The POLICE CONSTABLE *pulls them apart.*

The women, their faces pressed against the glass door, watch, enthralled.

INTERROGATOR (*watching this calmly*). Now, now, gentlemen, please. Let us have none of that. (*Calmly, unbothered, handing* PAUL *a handkerchief.*) If you want to leave us, Doctor Reisner, please do. (*Looks up beadily.*) This is only our first meeting after all. We'll be seeing each other again.

Interior: CLARA's *Room – Day*

PAUL *coming down the narrow passage into* CLARA's *room. She's standing right at the other end of the room.*

CLARA (*with real passion for a moment*). Paul, what on earth has happened to you? What have you been doing? Are you all right, Paul?

Her hands go up round PAUL's face, holding his shoulders hard, tight, then her normal detached tone returns.

What on earth did you walk into?

PAUL. Just something Mandry arranged for me . . . I think it can safely be said, he truly hates me.

Cut to PAUL sitting in a chair in the window, overlooking the courtyard, CLARA poised with sponge, and a bottle of blue ointment.

PAUL staring at the ointment with great alarm.

CLARA. Do you trust me? You have to trust me.

PAUL. I don't. What is that stuff? I have never seen it before.

CLARA. Something we use at the Institute. It was developed there.

PAUL. I'm the doctor and I have never heard of it.

CLARA (*smiles*). You see, you don't know everything.

PAUL really yelling with pain as she expertly dabs the ointment on his wounds.

Come on, brave boy – don't worry, I know what I'm doing.

PAUL. This stuff will never become popular! (*He turns his head.*) I ought to get back to being a doctor, Clara . . . he can't stop me being a doctor everywhere.

Exterior: The Park and City of Rubbish – Day

Cut to PAUL moving purposely through the City of Rubbish. He is carrying his doctor's bag, CLARA carrying dressings, following him.

The startling poverty all around them, but the faces of the people are very hostile. They shift into the shadows, some of the women hide their faces, covering their eyes.

We cut to PAUL treating a young man. While he is doing so, his stare travels back into the shadows of the man's shelter.

The shape of a woman lying curled up, breathing poorly, her face in pain, her hands stretched down across her body.

PAUL moves into the depth of the shelter, examining her. We stay on his face, on his gathering disquiet.

We then see a sequence of shots of women, mostly young but some in their thirties, being examined by PAUL. We only see their faces, their eyes in pain, their faces turning away in shame, and with a great sense of loss.

We see PAUL examining them; some of them are extremely ill.

They answer his questions, shaking their heads and crying, telling him repeatedly they never asked for anything to happen to them.

CLARA *watching closely, both their faces in shock.*

PAUL (*to CLARA*). They've all been sterilised . . . some of this has been very clumsily done. (*Very quiet.*) They've suffered terrible harm. (*To the women.*) We will come back with more medicine – I will try to get you into a hospital.

We cut to PAUL and CLARA moving into a fly-infested shelter.

In the back corner, in the shadows, lie the bodies of three dead young women, awaiting burial. The flies all around.

PAUL *and* CLARA *staring down at them; PAUL bends close to the women.*

CLARA (*very quiet*). Has the same thing happened to them? Did they die because of it?

PAUL nods. The sound of the flies everywhere. PAUL deeply shocked.

Then we cut to KATIE, the dark-haired girl who was watching PAUL by the Institute.

KATIE starts to move away from PAUL, but he catches up with her.

PAUL. *You* tell me. Who did this to you? . . . Who was it?

KATIE (*whispers; PAUL has to bend very close*). The head one. The one who came with you.

PAUL. The Professor?

KATIE. He said he'd give us an operation to make us not get ill.

We stay on PAUL's face.

Exterior: Edge of Park – Day

We cut to CLARA and PAUL on the edge of the park, the Institute in the distance.

The passers-by swirl all around them – oblivious.

PAUL is pacing furiously, he is almost in tears, startled and confused.

PAUL. I cannot believe . . . a man like him . . . that he would do this. It's against everything he ever said.

PAUL and CLARA moving on the path, long lens shot of the promenaders in the park, brushing past them.

CLARA. I know, I know.

PAUL (*angry, near tears*). They wouldn't have known what was happening to them!

Interior: CLARA's Room – Day

We cut to CLARA's room, the floor covered in newspapers, articles, scientific journals, pamphlets about eugenics. Both CLARA and PAUL are on their knees on the floor, voraciously reading everything they can find.

PAUL (*reading out a fragment*). 'Good genes must be encouraged . . . bad genes eradicated, otherwise we will be overrun by the degenerate.' 'The underclass must be stopped from breeding.' (*He looks up.*) Does that mean we kill them!

CLARA (*reading out*). 'The feeble-minded should be sterilised, never allowed to breed . . .' This is an American journal.

We see a headline of a pamphlet: 'Mental Patients Should Be Terminated'.

PAUL (*reading*). 'Worthless genes must be stopped from spreading.'

We see more weighty articles in German, Italian, French and American, all of them discussing ways of breeding better, purer humans, stopping the 'population problem' and avoiding being overrun by inferior humans.

We cut to CLARA pinning some of them up on the wall.

(*By the window, watching her do this.*) I mean, I thought he never paid attention to this rubbish . . . he knew this was just for cranks and ladies' discussion groups and a few very conservative scientists. (*Loud.*) He had contempt for all of this, Clara, total contempt.

The camera gliding across the newsprint on the floor, it comes to rest on an article in an American pamphlet: 'Society's failures should be discouraged from breeding, by Professor C. Mandry'.

We cut to PAUL lying on the floor exhausted, surrounded by paper, CLARA kneeling near him.

He thinks somehow he is taking action over the population problem. He must think he's conducting some kind of controlled experiment with those people on the rubbish heap . . . choosing who can breed.

CLARA (*deep in thought*). He didn't want you interrupting life at *his* Institute, with Felix's idea. It would have caused a lot of attention from the outside world. He has *his* work to do . . .

PAUL. He must have been just starting this 'Sterilisation Programme' when we came rushing in with Felix's idea! (*He pauses.*) He knew what I thought. (*Loud.*) He lied to me.

CLARA (*watching him*). We'll never be able to prove it anyway, they'll just say –

PAUL. The women gave their consent. I know.

CLARA (*mimics*). And you can never tell what those kind of people want anyway . . . (*She sighs deeply.*)

PAUL (*suddenly*). I'm going to *stop him, Clara*, find witnesses and . . .

CLARA. You can't even get near him, Paul, just think for a moment, you –

PAUL. I am going to get him!

Exterior: The Square – Day (The Institute)

PAUL *approaches the great building with* KATIE, *moving across the main square, the workmen still working, watching them go by.*

CLARA *is pacing backwards and forwards by the steps where the subterranean passage emerges into the square.*

CLARA. I can't let you in this way. It's impossible. It's not going to work. Doctor Leisen is down there. And there are other people too, we can't get by them.

PAUL. Let's try the front, then. Sometimes the most obvious route is also the most successful.

He walks up the steps with KATIE *and rings the great bell.*

CLARA. I have to get back, I'm not allowed out at this time. (*She disappears back into the darkness.*)

Interior: Institute: Hall – Day

The main door is opened by the YOUNG BOY, *just as it was that very first day. Inside the hall we see about five young women giggling in white dresses, and rows of food set out on a long table.*

MRS PRITCHARD *is standing up, directly facing the door.*

PAUL. Not here too! Everybody is already having a party.

The BOY *stares at him with a direct, hostile stare.*

BOY. You can't come in here . . . you are never going to come in here again. (*He slams the door shut.*)

Exterior: Institute – Day

PAUL. I'm very sorry, Katie. (*He looks back at the Institute and then across the square.*)

KATIE. I wasn't looking forward to it very much, sir, anyway.

KATIE *and* PAUL *move down the steps together, into the wide square.* PAUL *suddenly stops.*

PAUL. He gives a lecture. A Christmas lecture. He does. He must. Everybody does. He will do it this year. He'll be in public.

Interior: Institute: Passage and Small Lecture Hall – Day

We cut to PAUL and KATIE moving down a passage heavy with Christmas decorations and bits of the new-century decorations plastering the walls and hanging from the ceiling.

CLARA is by the door of the lecture theatre, as if she has been taking tickets.

We can see MANDRY in full flow through the glass door, the small lecture theatre crammed with young men, their backs up against the glass.

PAUL catches glimpses of MANDRY through the standing figures.

CLARA (*whispers*). Good luck.

She gives him a kiss.

PAUL. I need it. We need it. I don't think I've ever dreaded doing something more in my whole life. Do you think I can do it?

CLARA. Of course you can do it.

PAUL (*to* KATIE). I'll speak and then you speak, and if you forget anything, I'll just prompt you very calmly. There'll be no hurry, once we start.

KATIE and PAUL pass into the hall, squeezing into two bench seats at the back.

There are only about three other women there, very posh in appearance compared with KATIE. They are wearing huge playful hats with models of the future dangling off them.

On the blackboard are beautiful futuristic drawings of machines and people.

MANDRY is in tremendous form, his boyish charm, his charisma, his effortlessness. There's an end-of-term feel, a populist tone to this public lecture.

MANDRY. So will man evolve physically in relation to these machines, will we have long spidery hands that can touch and caress these machines into life? Because everything will be run by machines, and our strength, will we need our strength any more? Will we need to lift heavy objects ever again? Or will we possess eventually beautiful drooping limbs that can flick and twist knobs and our toes will be used to switch machines on and off too . . . to order them around.

PAUL *ducking behind people whenever* MANDRY *looks up towards the back of the hall.* PAUL *clears his throat, ready to speak, to interrupt.*

MANDRY (*his speech moving on all the time*). And what about women? Could women ever develop differently in this respect? Women who are beginning to make quite a noise for themselves, will they evolve too into the physically stronger sex . . . (*Smiles.*) . . . should we even worry about that? Will they become dominant as in some other animal species?

KATIE *glances at* PAUL. *He is staring at* MANDRY, *unable to speak.*

Paul (*whispers*). Any moment.

MANDRY. More seriously, and in conclusion, should we worry about physical degeneracy at all in our society? Because we all realise it's happening. There are so many diseases we haven't conquered contaminating whole sections of the population . . . How difficult is it to stop this cycle? When we are constantly creating an underclass which cannot support itself, and yet continues to multiply regardless. Or should we try to plan, and influence nature, to control and use *science* to improve the society we are giving birth to?

PAUL *opens his mouth, trying to force himself, lifting his arm.*

But these are such weighty questions. I think we have to resort to something we have created in the Institute to help us solve it.

There is a trolley covered in a sheet standing beneath the blackboard.

MANDRY *whips back the sheet.*

MANDRY. Home-made fudge! Yes. Chocolate and vanilla fudge. Created in this very building in our laboratories here, and highly delicious it is too. The Whiteweather present to all of you! I even have to admit I've created some of it myself.

There is delighted laughter and clapping at the revelation of the fudge. The audience start buzzing with conversation.

MANDRY (*passes the trays to the first row*). Pass them back, pass them on, let everybody get some.

PAUL staring around furious as everybody is talking, the audience scrambling, moving clumsily over the benches to get to the fudge. The noise level is suddenly deafening.

As people move around, PAUL is more exposed at the back.

He suddenly finds MANDRY is staring directly at him. Their eyes meet.

KATIE ducks down in the bench.

PAUL stares at MANDRY.

From MANDRY's viewpoint we see PAUL.

MANDRY (*with a charming smile, looking at both PAUL and KATIE*). I think the home-made fudge should travel to the back. There are some very hungry mouths to be fed there.

Interior: Institute: Passage – Day

Cut to PAUL, CLARA and KATIE moving down the passage outside the lecture theatre.

People in high spirits all around them, with drinks, laughing, making arrangements.

PAUL. I couldn't do it. I just couldn't do it. I missed the moment and then, I don't know, I wasn't brave enough. I saw him there, and I thought, I really like him . . . he looked so good.

KATIE. I'm glad, I don't think I could have done it either.

PAUL. It's not fair on you, I know.

CLARA (*quiet*). *I* couldn't have done it, it seems so simple, but . . .

FELIX suddenly appears, moving in the opposite direction, his arms full of Christmas presents.

FELIX. There you are! When are you coming back!

He is carried on down the passage by the weight of people.

When *are* you, Paul? (*He disappears.*)

CLARA. There'll be another chance for this I'm sure.

PAUL. When? I don't see when. Mandry's gone back behind closed doors.

He stares at the people coming down the passage towards him, brushing the decorations.

The whole city is having a festival. Who wants to listen? Nobody will want to stop in the middle of all this.

CLARA. And this is only Christmas – God know what New Year will be like.

A shot of PAUL moving through all the decorations in the passage, and futuristic drawings on the wall, and Christmas festivities. He moves on and on through the celebrations and laughter as they close around him.

A very powerful sequence, the luminous, beautiful decorations, the girls' faces in their dresses, the oblivious laughter.

Interior: Institute: Backstage of Lecture Hall – Day

A shot of MANDRY taking off his gown. JAMES is with him.

MANDRY. Did you see Paul? I think I saw Paul Reisner in the audience. (*Pleasantly.*) I hope he's well.

Interior: Reisner House: Bathroom – Day

MR REISNER *is sitting in his dressing-gown, alone, by a dressing-table and wash-basin. His head is slumped, as if he is deeply thoughtful and depressed.*

MIRIAM *comes in, startled to see her father like that.*

MIRIAM. Oh, Papa, I'm sorry, I didn't realise you were in here.

MR REISNER. Not at all. (*Recovering his composure.*) Come in, my dear.

MIRIAM. Is everything all right, Papa?

MR REISNER (*concealing his worried state*). Everything is absolutely . . . splendid. As always.

MIRIAM (*gives him a searching look, takes his hand*). As always . . .

We stay on them for a moment.

Interior: Cake Shop and Tearoom – Evening

Sudden quiet of the tearooms, the winter light moving in very fast. A rich, heavy atmosphere all around, the cakes' snowy winter scenes. The icing beginning to melt at the end of the day.

The tearooms are almost totally empty. PAUL moves past the deserted tables, awash with leaflets, the aftermath of another eugenics lecture.

The last two ladies are just finishing their cakes, watched over by a couple of waitresses.

And in the distance MRS WHITEWEATHER is being helped towards the exit by a stone-faced young woman.

PAUL (*running up to her*). Please wait. Please could you wait, Mrs Whiteweather.

MRS WHITEWEATHER *turns.*

Just for a moment. Please.

MRS WHITEWEATHER. I do not possess a moment. I am going to the theatre, there is a gala performance, and I cannot be late.

PAUL. Don't you remember me? We had tea . . . I was covered in dust.

MRS WHITEWEATHER. Yes, yes, I remember you. I remember you quite clearly. (*She sits at a table piled high with golden cake boxes. She has her dog with her on her lap. She takes out a large round watch from her bag and flicks it open.*) You have forty-five seconds.

PAUL. I don't know if I can do it in that time. It is about the Institute, everything is going wrong . . . Professor Mandry, while ignoring important work, is . . .

MRS WHITEWEAHTER. What important work?

PAUL. It doesn't matter the exact nautre, I can't explain now, in the time, but –

MRS WHITEWEATHER. You think I'm stupid? You think I wouldn't understand?

PAUL. No, no. It's just a little technical, I shouldn't have mentioned it. (*He leans over and clicks her watch shut.*)

MRS WHITEWEATHER. A doctor with bloodshot eyes, never trust a doctor with bloodshot eyes.

A cat is moving among the empty chairs, licking plates. It jumps on to the shelves among the cream cakes.

PAUL. *Please*, let me begin again. Let my time start again.

MRS WHITEWEATHER. I heard something else about you, I believe. You are the foreign name, aren't you? Reisenberg – I must say you do not look it particularly. But nowadays one never can tell . . . (*Calmly.*) I am not anti-Semitic myself, though some of my friends have their own opinions. (*She flicks open her watch.*)

The stone-faced woman watching PAUL. *The winter cakes melting.*

PAUL. I'm starting again, from *now*, you understand . . . (*Very firmly.*) Professor Mandry, the head of your husband's Institute, is sterilising people, without their consent. People who are living rough near the park, poor people, some very young. *Many* have been sterilised and some of them have died. Yes, Professor Mandry has become deeply involved with eugenics, improving the genes, and preventing certain people from having children.

MRS WHITEWEATHER (*watching him closely*). If Professor Mandry sees it as part of his work, so be it. We have had our talks here about eugenics; I rarely listened. It doesn't sound at all sinister to me.

PAUL. But he is sterilising people against *their will*, while pretending to give them medical care.

MRS WHITEWEATHER. How do you know it's against their will? They no doubt gave their consent.

PAUL. I knew you'd say that, I have witnesses who –

MRS WHITEWEATHER. They are probably trying to get money, everybody these days is trying to get money. You are growing tiresome, young man, this is a time of celebration. Haven't you noticed? I have every faith in Professor Mandry.

PAUL. People have died. Directly or indirectly they have been *killed*.

MRS WHITEWEATHER. People are dying all the time, unfortunately. Sometimes I think medicine is killing as many people as it cures. Your time is over, young man.

PAUL (*really urgent*). You have to listen – beacuse I know you wouldn't like what's happening. I *know* that.

MRS WHITEWEATHER. Don't be so presumptuous. You have no idea about my feelings, don't you dare tell me what I'm thinking or feeling. *Now* I know why you lost your place at the Institute.

She begins to hobble away with the stone-faced woman.

Let us be on our way. I have to change for the theatre.

PAUL *watches her go in her massive hat.*

His eyes settle for a second on the cat moving in the empty tearooms, licking at the left-over cakes.

PAUL (*suddenly calling after her*). You know he's using monkeys to experiment on. Professor Mandry. He is, and dogs. All the time.

MRS WHITEWEATHER *stops, her back to him.*

Higher animals, I should have a look if I was you.

MRS WHITEWEATHER (*turns, quiet, dangerous, holding her dog*). What did you say? Monkeys and dogs, is that what you said?

(*We stay on* MRS WHITEWEATHER'*s face for a moment.*)

Interior: Institute – Day

FELIX *moving through the Institute, the camera moving with him, as people pass him all the time in the opposite direction, carrying boxes, equipment, trunks, pictures off the walls, even vases of flowers, taking all of them out of the building; we see the medical machinery being wheeled out too.*

In the shadows in the hall sits a pathetic group of volunteers, calling out 'Doctor Russell, Doctor Russell, can't you use us today? What is happening? Where will we go after this?'

We see the other members of the group, THEO *and* MEREDITH, *watching from a distance. A powerful sense of desolation.*

MRS PRITCHARD (*moving in circles on the landing, muttering to herself*). There was no warning, we, we were given no warning. Shut down just like that, no warning at all. Without the Professor, what will I do? (*She bursts into tears by the window, stifles them when she sees* FELIX.)

Interior: Institute: MANDRY's *Study – Evening*

MANDRY *sitting in his study with* JAMES.

JAMES *looking very upset.*

Sound of the building being vacated around them.

MANDRY. Please be so kind, join me in a drink, James.

JAMES. Of course, sir. (*Pouring himself a drink.*)

MANDRY (*gentle*). Tell me, have I showed any prejudice towards you, James? Tell me honestly.

JAMES (*very surprised*). Of course not, sir. Less than anyone I have ever met. I mean not at all, you have always encouraged me.

MANDRY (*looking vulnerable and solitary*). I hoped you were going to say that. I have tried to encourage deserving talent wherever I have found it.

JAMES. And you have! It's a great gift . . . to encourage others.

We move closer to MANDRY's *face; he is deeply thoughtful.*

MANDRY. You see, James, it is my job to be aware of the problems of the future, to be ahead of the current thinking, and sometimes that is a difficult job, because so few people are equipped to do it, at the moment. (*We are right up to his face, quiet.*) So very few. (*Suddenly he looks round, really energised.*) And we have to fight for this place!

Interior: Institute – Evening

PAUL *pushing the door of the Institute open, evening light. He stares round at what he's caused to happen. He sees* FELIX.

FELIX (*shouting at the removal men*). You can't take those papers, those are mine. My own work, give them back! (*He grabs them back, he is stuffing as much as he can into a battered suitcase. He sees PAUL.*) Do you see what you've done?

PAUL. Yes, I'm sorry. But you know what we found out, it had to be like this.

FELIX (*really angry*). You sound so smug. You had no proof, no proof at all.

PAUL. I did, I did, Felix.

FELIX. I hope this isn't purely your revenge, because he threw you out.

PAUL. You know that's not the reason, Felix. You can't believe that.

CLARA *is coming towards them.*

FELIX. Does your father know what you've done?

PAUL. I telephoned my sister. But I can't tell my father. One day he'll know.

FELIX (*sitting on the bulging suitcase*). What a way to spend New Year's Eve! The New Century is coming and we're here. I haven't even got a party to go to now. There was going to be one here, but look at it. (*Waving at packing-cases.*) The most important New Year's Eve for one hundred years, and nowhere to go.

PAUL. Come down with me, come to my father's party. Please come, Felix, I would love that.

FELIX. Maybe . . . maybe.

CLARA. Can I come too? To your father's party?

PAUL (*looks at her. For a moment we see the definite hesitation in his eyes*). Yes . . . Yes . . .

CLARA (*looks startled for a moment. Then her anger really beginning to mount*). You see. You see what you did. You hesitated.

Near tears, FELIX *moves away.*

Already, it's starting.

PAUL. Clara . . . don't do this . . . (*Loud.*) What's the matter with everyone, for heaven's sake. (*He catches hold of* CLARA.)

CLARA (*really enraged*). Let go of me – let go. The day after – one day and it starts. Don't you touch me. I helped you, I helped you survive for God's sake! And the first opportunity you get, you begin to get rid of me.

PAUL. Clara . . .

CLARA (*savage*). 'Addicted' indeed, some kind of addiction that vanishes overnight! Why did I ask to come? I was mad to do that. To ever come near you. To expect anything different. *You* – who wanted to say you loved me. (*She rains blows on him with her fists.*)

PAUL (*catching hold of her fists*). Clara . . . I only meant . . .

CLARA. I know what you meant. Don't lie to me. You don't want to introduce me to your father.

PAUL. No – that's not true. I promise I'll prove it to you. You've got to come. You have to be with me, tonight of all nights.

CLARA. I do, do I? (*Then softer.*) Paul . . . that hurt so much.

PAUL *touches her.*

You're not much different to the Professor really, when it comes down to it.

PAUL *shuts her lips, gently.*

Shot of THOMAS *watching this from passage.*

PAUL. Don't say that. (*Turns.*) I have to find him. He's somewhere in this building, isn't he?

Interior: Institute: MANDRY's Study – Evening

PAUL *walks towards MANDRY's study, a curl of cigarette smoke coming out through the half opened door.*

JAMES *is sitting at MANDRY's desk, smoking. He stares with hostility at PAUL.*

All around them they can hear the sound of carriages setting off, and the bells ringing out across the city.

JAMES. Pleased with yourself?

PAUL. Don't you start too.

JAMES. This place meant a great deal to me. More than you can imagine.

PAUL. I'm sorry, I'm very sorry, James. Where is he? (*Looking down at MANDRY's things on the desk, his crocodile cigarette holder.*) He must be nearby, his things are still here.

JAMES. He's set off for a New Year's Eve party. The one he's chosen. He was invited to nearly every party that matters in London, and many outside.

PAUL. Really? (*Staring at the hundreds of invitations.*) So which one has he picked?

JAMES. Oh, don't you know? (*He leans forward, with the invitation card. We recognise it.*) Your father's. (*He stares at PAUL.*) He had a mission to accomplish.

PAUL (*really startled for a moment*). Of course. He would do that, wouldn't he. (*Very quiet.*) Oh, my God . . .

Exterior: The Road Approaching the Reisner House – Night

Cut to PAUL, CLARA and FELIX riding on a rickety cart, children with lanterns running behind them.

They are approaching PAUL's home, the house seen across the river.

PAUL (*to the driver*). Please. Come on, come on, can't you go any quicker?

We see, standing outside the house, the great sign with all its flickering pink bulbs: WELCOME TO THE NEW CENTURY – AGAIN.

As they reach the house, a group of people is standing in the street, curious, straining their necks to see.

Exterior: Garden and River – Night (Reisner House)

A boat is coming towards them, towards the house, down the river. The boat is covered in lights and candles, a shimmering vessel of light.

PAUL *and* CLARA *watch it bear down towards them.*

At the front of the boat stands MR REISNER.

PAUL. Oh, Papa, isn't that too vulgar. Far too vulgar. (*He glances around the faces of the people to see if they are laughing.*) Why did you do this?

MR REISNER *alights from the boat below the house and climbs up steps towards it and the people waiting. We see he is wearing the most extraordinary fancy dress costume, deliberately perverse, a costume with a tail and grotesque reptilian spikes and fins.*

MIRIAM *comes towards* PAUL *and* CLARA. *She's also dressed in a bizarre costume. And gradually* PAUL *sees all the children and servants are in ferociously defiant and eccentric costumes.*

What are you all dressed like that for?

MIRIAM. It was my idea. To show *them* all! Papa is some sort of sea monster. Doesn't he look good? And I'm some sort of mosquito sucking blood and biting people. I can bite people all night. It's to show we don't care if they come or not.

PAUL. This is Clara, who is, who I hope . . .

CLARA. What do you hope?

MIRIAM (*taking her hand with a broad smile*). Delighted to see you. We met once in a basement full of rats, remember? (*She moves, urgent.*) You must come and see this now.

Interior: Reisner House: Dining-room – Night

MIRIAM *pushes open the door of the dining-room of the house. It is full of packing-cases. She walks across it in her extraordinary costume.*

Outside we can hear music, the New Year's party.

MIRIAM. You see, we are going to have to move. Leave this house.

PAUL. Move, why?

MIRIAM. Because there is no business for Papa in this town. They
are all boycotting him. They won't use him, he can't get any
building work.

PAUL. Why didn't he tell me? Why on earth didn't he say?

MIRIAM. They want to drive him out of town and they have
succeeded.

PAUL. They can't do that. They can't. (*Very sharp.*) This is turning
into a great night.

MIRIAM (*touching him*). I'm sorry about everything, going wrong in
London, for you I mean.

PAUL. Yes, I have come to see that man. Where the hell is he?

Interior: Reisner House: Sitting-room – Night

PAUL *moves through the sitting-room, followed by* CLARA. *A sense of
excitement and fear. They move through a series of strange hoops that his
father has erected, covered in lights and weird decorations, keeping the
sea monster motif, and towards the marquee.*

As PAUL *and* CLARA *move through the hoops, his father approaches
in his extraordinary costume.*

PAUL. Papa, you look truly bizarre. (*Slight pause.*) And rather
wonderful.

MR REISNER. I do not dare catch a glimpse of myself, in case I
lose my nerve and take it all off. On the boat I was worried in
case I saw my reflection in the water. Your poor dead mother
would not have approved, me dressed like this! But Paul . . .
(*Pause.*) . . . you will never guess, there is the most wonderful
surprise tonight, who on earth do you think has honoured us, has
come to my party?

PAUL (*steely*). I know, Papa.

Interior: Marquee – Night

PAUL *moves very determinedly through the marquee, which is decorated
inside with some strange furturistic décor mingled with flowers and
lanterns. He sees in the far corner* MANDRY *is sitting, surrounded by*

an admiring group, asking him medical questions. He looks wonderfully elegant sitting there.

PAUL *walks right up to* MANDRY, *and interrupts the conversation.*

CLARA *next to him.*

PAUL. You shouldn't have come here. I must ask you to leave here immediately. You understand, *now.*

MANDRY (*gently*). Paul, is that all you have to say to me? (*He extends his hand to shake in reconciliation.*) It is New Year's Eve, you did what you thought was right, I understand that. But you can't stop progress.

PAUL. Progress? Is that what it's called?

MANDRY (*straight at him*). And you are intelligent enough to know progress can initially be unpleasant. But for everybody's sake, to stop poverty, to stop us being engulfed, an approach has to be found –

There is a strong contrast between the guests watching this in a festive mood, nodding in a bemused way, and the real tension between PAUL *and* MANDRY.

PAUL (*steely*). An 'approach'! Why are you here, anyway?

MANDRY. I was invited by your father. I wanted to see *you.* We couldn't leave it messy and disagreeable between us. I'm fond of you, Paul. (*Staring at* PAUL *with a warm smile.*) And of course I would quite like you to retract what you said, to say you were mistaken, so the funds can return to the Institute. A lot of good work has been stopped, Paul, because of what happened. Hugely important work.

PAUL (*really tense*). Of course, I know that! But that's hardly my fault.

People crowding round watching the scene, the two men oblivious.

MANDRY (*close, confidential*). I want to explain, Paul –

PAUL. You can't explain . . . (*Straight into his eyes.*) I *know*, remember.

MANDRY. Then let the Institute continue without that work. You *must* think about it. (*Suddenly urgent.*) I *need* that place, I *really* do.

PAUL's *eyes hesitate.*

(*Genuine.*) Paul, do this for me, we agree on so much.

PAUL (*flaring at this*). You may have forgotten but you tried to get me thrown out of the country, my own land. Tried to turn me into an undesirable alien.

MANDRY. I was angry with you, for a time, Paul, because you *wouldn't listen*, and you were angry with me. But that's over.

PAUL (*face very close*). We belong as much as you do. Say it. We *belong*. Say it. *Go on, say it.*

MANDRY (*quiet*). Of course, Paul. *You* belong. (*Stares at* PAUL.) Now, it's New Year's Eve now, and we should . . .

PAUL (*clenched*). Will you get up, Professor Mandry, and go from here. I'm not going to ask you again.

MANDRY. Let's leave this for a while, then. Your father thinks everything is absolutely splendid.

Shot of MR REISNER *in the distance.*

PAUL *watching for a moment, hesitating.*

MANDRY (*stares straight into* PAUL). Why spoil his night? It's very important to him. Let us enjoy your father's party.

CLARA. Don't talk to him any more, Paul.

She throws her drink over MANDRY, *across his clothes and face.*

Leave us, go on, get away from us!

Surrounding guests astonished.

MANDRY *gets up a little awkwardly; he stumbles slightly.*

PAUL *stares at him, shock in his eyes.*

MANDRY. I just . . . I . . . I won't be a moment.

He moves across the marquee, mingling among the guests.

Exterior: Garden – Night (Reisner House)

We cut to FELIX *with his case of papers being pursued across the grass by children.* FELIX's *battered suitcase has burst open, and papers are blowing out of it.*

FELIX *trying to catch the papers. Also all the little models and inventions have escaped, and are blowing across the grass.*

CHILD. Tell us more, Mr Russell. Please, go on, about the machines of the future. Will there be shops on the moon? Will we be able to eat strawberries there? Will there be trips to the stars in balloons that travel as fast as fireworks?

Papers blowing everywhere. The little machines whirring and flying.

FELIX. Help me catch these papers, then I'll tell you. *Please* catch them. My ideas are here, come on, get that one, catch it. Faster.

The children and FELIX *chase after the papers.*

PAUL *sees his father doing a dance with* MIRIAM *in their extraordinary costumes, a startling, defiant dance watched by a group of the towns people we saw at the beginning of the film. They keep their distance, but they are unable to stop staring at the bizarre, uninhibited costumes.*

MIRIAM *and* MR REISNER *thrust their costumes out as they dance.*

MANDRY *is watching; we keep cutting to him as he begins to see his last chance go.*

PAUL *accompanied by* CLARA *moves up to his father as he finishes his dance. Music playing all the time. A sense of midnight being very close. A powerful mix of excitement and tension.*

MR REISNER *standing sweating in his sea monster costume. As* PAUL *nears him, he realises his father knows something.*

MR REISNER. Miriam has told me the unbearable news. Can it be true?

PAUL. Papa, yes. I closed the Institute. I arrived to conquer London, to be the very top of the Institute, and I ended up being responsible for it being shut down. (*Dryly.*) Some achievement

. . . (*Quiet.*) That's what your son did . . . (*He stares across at* MANDRY.)

MR REISNER (*shaking his head*). I don't know . . . I can't believe a man of his distinction, a good man in many ways, could do such things. You will have to persuade me you weren't wrong. I can't even think of it now, Paul . . . it is such a business. He is our guest tonight.

PAUL. And it doesn't stop there, Papa. This is Clara, a laboratory worker from the Institute. I have been *living* with her for the last few months.

CLARA (*goes up and shakes* MR REISNER's *hand through one of its reptilian pieces*). Hello.

Pause.

MR REISNER (*his face beyond shock*). Clara. It is New Year's Eve. I may be dead tomorrow. In fact I possibly will be. I will just say, she is beautiful anyway. (*He shakes his head.*) What is happening tonight?

The townspeople watching.

PAUL. Look at those bastards, they were all going to boycott the party, but they couldn't keep away. They came out of curiosity, to gloat or . . . They don't know what to do. They don't.

The younger children of the family in their weird sea monster costumes dancing on the grass, dancing in front of the townspeople.

(*Staring across at the townspeople and* MANDRY.) But you can't leave this town, Papa, you can't let them win. I might even stay here a while. They look so unhealthy, there will clearly be plenty of work.

MANDRY *suddenly appears at* PAUL's *side. He looks very vulnerable, suddenly uncertain, a haunted figure.*

MANDRY (*with real feeling*). We won't forget each other, Paul, I hope.

Before PAUL *can reply,* MANDRY *has moved off, moving through the guests and the children. People are beginning to chant a countdown to the new century.*

We cut to PAUL *moving up to* CLARA, *who is standing under the sign with all its bulbs shining.*

PAUL (*very urgent*). Clara – will you stay here, with me? Decide before midnight, tell me!

CLARA. It's not going to work. It won't work between us, Paul.

PAUL (*very forceful*). You don't know that. You don't *know*.

CLARA. I do know.

PAUL. No you don't . . . (*Catching hold of her.*) You'd keep everything, you'd keep control over your life, yes. You would be the same Clara.

CLARA. It won't work.

PAUL (*very close*). Say you don't know for sure, say it, say it, before midnight.

He kisses her. The countdown is continuing.

CLARA. I do know it, very surely.

PAUL. You can't be so sure – you used to love me a little, I know. I shouldn't use that word, I know, but I am, I will.

CLARA (*calmly*). There are moments when I've been terribly in love with you, Paul.

PAUL. Only *moments*.

CLARA (*laughs*). You're *so* vain!

PAUL. Say it, Clara. (*Very strong.*) You don't *absolutely* know it won't work. Say it. Before midnight!

CLARA *hesitates, the children running round them in their extraordinary costumes.*

I'm not going to let you go.

CLARA (*smiles, slowly*). I'll say that – I don't *absolutely* know it won't work.

PAUL (*very close*). It *will* work, my love.

The sound of the gunfire in the distance, the salute for the New Year. MANDRY walking at the very edge of the party. The countdown has finished.

MR REISNER. Oh, my God . . . I don't know why I'm crying . . . all the things I haven't done in my life. Is there time? I don't know. Will it change? What will happen? It was some party, wasn't it! It was a truly great party, wasn't it at least!

The clock beginning to strike midnight; they are all grouped round the sign.

PAUL. Felix, a prediction . . .

FELIX. We will be able soon . . . we will . . . we will . . . (*Laughs.*) I don't know.

As the clock strikes, we stay on their faces, a mixture of elation and a few tears. Each of the main characters is staring out, as the chimes ring out through the night air. A sense of both hope and fear.

It is midnight. They cheer.

The OLD PAUL'S VOICE *that began the film starts, and we see shots of the family and party as he speaks.*

VOICE-OVER. My father was obviously given a tremendous boost by this party, because he lived for almost another twenty years!

Shots of the little machines flying across the grass and FELIX *and the children dancing with them.*

Felix did some very fine work on diabetes a few years later, but I remain convinced if that year had gone differently he would have been the first to discover insulin.

A shot following MANDRY *walking into the night, away from the glow of the party; we move with him, his tall figure.*

Often at night, I think about what happended to the Professor. I never saw him again and I don't think he ever went back to medicine. Some say he ended up teaching quietly in a boys' boarding-school, others that he killed himself one summer in a little seaside town. He still remains in many ways the most brilliant man I've ever met. The dark turning he took in his work was soon going to be taken by many far more evil people. Does that make him as bad as them? I still don't know . . .

We watch MANDRY *disappear away from us into the night.*

For many years I found myself hoping that one day I might meet him in the street. That I'll see that tall figure coming towards me again . . .

Shots of CLARA, *larking around in the moments after the clock has stopped striking; she is looking radiant and anarchic and happy.*

Clara and I . . . we never got married, she insisted on remaining my common-law wife. She is sitting across the room as I dictate this, rolling her eyes in disapproval. We worked together for many years in a quiet country practice. We have fought a lot, of course, during that time – (*Shot of* PAUL *and* CLARA *laughing together.*) – but that was only to be expected . . .

We see a shot of the whole group in their extraordinary costumes, seen across the water, with the sign welcoming the new century glowing above their heads.

Nothing in my life, though, has every quite equalled the strange feeling that I had that night, excited and worried and hopeful as we moved together into a new century.

The new century sign blinking out in the night air.

Credits.

Fade-out.